Andrea Tyler, Lihong Huang, Hana Jan (Eds.)
**What is Applied Cognitive Linguistics?**

# Applications of
# Cognitive Linguistics

Editors
Gitte Kristiansen
Francisco J. Ruiz de Mendoza Ibáñes

Honorary Editor
René Dirven

## Volume 38

# What is Applied Cognitive Linguistics?

Answers From Current SLA Research

Edited by
Andrea Tyler
Lihong Huang
Hana Jan

ISBN 978-3-11-068514-5
e-ISBN (PDF) 978-3-11-057218-6
e-ISBN (EPUB) 978-3-11-056989-6
ISSN 1861-4078

**Library of Congress Control Number: 2018938680**

**Bibliographic information published by the Deutsche Nationalbibliothek**
The Deutsche Nationalbibliothek lists this publication in the Deutsche Nationalbibliografie;
detailed bibliographic data are available on the Internet at http://dnb.dnb.de.

© 2019 Walter de Gruyter GmbH, Berlin/Boston
This volume is text- and page-identical with the hardback published in 2018.
Typesetting: RoyalStandard, Hong Kong
Printing and binding: CPI books GmbH, Leck
♾ Printed on acid-free paper
Printed in Germany

www.degruyter.com

# Acknowledgments

We express our deep appreciation to all the authors who contributed to this book, for trusting our vision of Applied Cognitive Linguistics and for sharing their work in this collection. We also thank our generous internal reviewers, who helped improve the final quality of the volume with their expertise: Diana Boxer (University of Florida), Seth Lindstromberg (Hilderstone College), Narges Mahpekar (Georgetown University), Lourdes Ortega (Georgetown University), Mari Tsujita (Dokkyo University), and Amir Zeldes (Georgetown University). Our desire to champion new avenues of SLA research and more effective L2 instruction, grounded in Cognitive Linguistics, began in a series of workshops and panels at AAAL and ICLC. Many of the authors included here participated in those workshops. In addition, we want to acknowledge other participants, whose passion, dedication and intellectual acumen nourished our work on Applied Cognitive Linguistics. They include Salvadore Attardo, Heine Behrens, Franks Boers, Teresa Cadierno, June Eyckmans, Nick Ellis, Jong Oh Eun, Phillip Hamrick, Alberto Hijazo-Gascón, Vu Ho, Iraide Ibarretxe-Antuñano, Diane Larsen-Freeman, Charles Mueller, Hong Thi Phuong Nguyen, Mathew O'Donnell, Lourdes Ortega, Ute Römer, Susan Strauss, Helen Stengers, Marjolijn Verspoor, Johannes Wagner, and Jhuhyoung Youn. Special recognition goes to Marjolijn Verspoor who was a pivotal co-organizer and participant. Carol Moder was a co-organizer and participant in several of these forums. Her intellectual contributions, including her careful reading of many of the chapters included here, have contributed substantially to this volume. Finally, we owe a debt of gratitude to our editors at Mouton De Gruyter. We are particularly grateful to Gitte Kristiansen, our series editor, who gave continual support and encouragement to bring this volume to completion. Thanks go to Sabina Dabrowski, Francisco Ruiz de Mendoza Ibáñes, Julie Miesse, and Birget Sievert for the care they put into this project. Knowing we had their intellectual and professional care made working on this book rewarding.

# Table of contents

Acknowledgments —— v
Dedication —— ix

Andrea Tyler and Lihong Huang
Introduction —— 1

## I  Categories and constructions in context

Michel Achard
Teaching usage and concepts: Toward a cognitive pedagogical grammar —— 37

Søren W. Eskildsen
L2 constructions and interactional competence: Subordination and coordination in English L2 learning —— 63

Stefanie Wulff, Stefan Th. Gries, and Nicholas Lester
Optional *that* in complementation by German and Spanish learners —— 99

Maarten Lemmens and Julien Perrez
French onions and Dutch trains: Typological perspectives on learners' descriptions of spatial scenes —— 121

## II  Teaching construal and viewpoint

Barbara Dancygier and Carol Lynn Moder
*Since it is everywhere*: Viewpoint in second language teaching —— 153

Natalia Dolgova Jacobsen
Using blending theory to teach the English conditionals —— 181

Benjamin J. White
Making sense of the definite article through a pedagogical schematic —— 203

## III  Polysemy

Elizabeth M. Kissling, Andrea Tyler, Lisa Warren, and Lauren Negrete
Reexamining *por* and *para* in the Spanish foreign language intermediate classroom: A usage-based, cognitive linguistic approach —— 229

Helen Zhao, Thomas Siu-ho Yau, Keru Li, and Noel Nga-yan Wong
**Polysemy and conceptual metaphors: A cognitive linguistics approach to vocabulary learning** —— 257

Marlene Johansson Falck
**Embodied experience and the teaching and learning of L2 prepositions: A case study of abstract *in* and *on*** —— 287

**Index** —— 305

*This book is dedicated to the many graduate students we have worked with over the years (as mentees and colleagues) whose enthusiasm, probing questions, and insights challenged and inspired us.*

Andrea Tyler and Lihong Huang
# Introduction

## What is Applied Cognitive Linguistics?: Answers from current SLA research

This is a particularly exciting time for second language (L2) research and pedagogy in which a rapidly expanding body of research, inspired by over 30 years of discoveries in cognitive science, psycholinguistics, first language learning and linguistic theory, has emerged. These discoveries have changed the way leading researchers in these fields think about the mind – how humans represent knowledge, how human experience with the physical/spatial/social world shapes the mind, how we learn (see special issues by Mahon and Hickok 2016; Rogers and Wolmetz 2016; Daems et al. 2015) – and how this relates to the nature of language and language learning. Moreover, the evidence indicates that all aspects of human cognition, including language, are affected by the same general cognitive properties. Indeed, the commitment to explaining language in all its complexity in terms of general cognitive processes (the cognitive commitment) is at the heart of Cognitive Linguistics (CL), arguably the most fully developed theory of language that has emerged from this explosion of innovative thinking and theorizing. The contributors to the current volume hold that CL, in concert with other select frameworks, such as associative learning theory and discourse analytic theories, provides a unified account of how language is configured and learned and has much to contribute to L2 research and pedagogy. Somewhat surprisingly, even though many of the foundational principles of CL are extensions of well-established findings from psychology, cognitive science, first language learning and discourse analysis which have been widely recognized, many SLA professionals (both SLA researchers and language teachers) remain unaware of, or confused about, just what CL (and Applied Cognitive Linguistics) is and the tremendous potential this approach offers for our understanding of L2 learning and pedagogy. The volume aims to address this gap by presenting theoretically-grounded, empirically-based studies which illustrate the application of key concepts of CL and demonstrate the efficacy of using the concepts in the classroom or in basic L2 research. The volume brings together a range of recent work in Applied Cognitive Linguistics

**Andrea Tyler** and **Lihong Huang,** Georgetown University

https://doi.org/10.1515/9783110572186-001

(ACL), i.e., CL-inspired work on L2 learning and teaching, and points to the exciting new frontiers it offers for L2 research and instruction.

Over the past two decades, many language professionals have become increasingly convinced that the aforementioned discoveries concerning human cognition support a usage-based approach to language generally (e.g., Barlow and Kemmer 2000; Tomasello 2003; Gries and Wulff 2005; Robinson and Ellis 2008; Bybee 2010; Ellis and Cadierno 2009; Tyler 2012; Behrens and Pfänder 2016; Ellis, Römer, and O'Donnell 2016; Tyler and Ortega 2016; De Knop and Gilquin 2016; Ortega, Tyler, Park, and Uno 2016). From its inception, CL has advocated a usage-based perspective. In addition to the cognitive commitment, a key part of this perspective is recognition that humans are highly social and hence that naturally occurring language is social in function and crucially situated in communicative interaction. Langacker talks about the communicative nature of language in terms of a speaker crafting the message in order to make mental contact with a listener. Hence, actual language use is culturally, socially, and contextually embedded, because all usage events are tied to individual speakers and listeners, who are members of particular speech communities. Many of the papers in this volume examine the importance of contextualized L2 learning. Eskildsen, for instance, examines the development of an L2 learner's use of bi-clausal constructions and argues grammatical development is inseparable from the development of the learner's emerging conversational-interactional strategies.

Mental Space and Blending Theory (MSBT) is CL's unique contribution to explaining many discourse phenomena (e.g., Fauconnier 1997; Fauconnier and Turner 1998, 2000, 2002; Dancygier and Sweetser 2005). MSBT was developed to address discourse phenomena while exploring the cognitive processes involved in dynamic, on-line conceptualization. Mental space building and conceptual blending are argued to involve a set of ubiquitous cognitive mechanisms reflected in non-linguistic contexts, such as the merger of the concept of an old fashion, physical desk with the technological innovation of the personal computer to create the new conceptualization of the computer's desktop, to many aspects of the visual arts, to complex numbers, as well as language. MSBT provides an expanded set of conceptual tools for reconceptualizing the nature of language, and hence, potentially provides additional tools for analyzing and presenting language to L2 learners. This is the framework adopted by Dancygier and Moder and Dolgova Jacobsen to explore conditionals and speaker perspective within a discourse context.

Recent work on the organization and development of cognition also highlights the importance of embodied experience (e.g., Bergen, 2012; Lakoff and

Johnson 1999; Langacker 1991; Spivey 2008; Barsalou 2016). Namely, basic human interactions with the physical world provide a foundation for human conceptual and cognitive representations, which are in turn reflected in language. One of the central ways embodied experience is reflected in language is in conceptual metaphor (e.g., Lakoff 1987; Grady 1997; Gibbs 2015), which is ubiquitous in all languages. For instance, our physical experience of heavy objects as physical burdens is foundational to the way we think and talk about difficult situations, as reflected in language such as *Worry about our parents is weighing us down* or *emotional burdens*. Consider another aspect of embodied meaning; our knowledge of the world is filtered through our perceptual apparatus. Much of our mental representation of events and activities involves spatial scenes. As one instance, we observe recurring types of scenes among entities, such as an active agent performing some act on an entity (the patient or undergoer). Such scenes are typically coded in the transitive construction, as represented in a sentence such as *Mary threw the ball*. Importantly, we have access to multiple construals or vantage points on the scenes we observe. These multiple construals are reflected in language in terms of varying sentence patterns or constructions, which put focus on varying elements in the scene. The link between shifts in construal and grammar is illustrated by the variation between an active construction, which places focus on the agent, and the passive construction, which places focus on the patient (undergoer). In this volume, the contributions in the second section are particularly concerned with construal and viewpoint. Adopting a MSBT perspective, Dancygier and Moder examine shifts in viewpoint and speaker stance signaled by *since*; Dolgova Jacobsen examines speaker stance reflected in the choice of tense in conditionals. MSBT applications to L2 teaching and learning are richly represented by these authors. Speaker stance and discourse context are also central to White's analysis of the English definite article.

CL's commitment to experientially grounded and embodied meaning (Langacker 1991; Lakoff and Johnson 1999) results in several notable consequences. One particularly important consequence is that since much of language reflects our visual experience with the world, much of meaning can be captured through visual representations of conceptual-linguistic meaning. Indeed a hallmark of CL theorizing involves carefully constructed diagrams (e.g., Langacker 1991; Tyler and Evans 2003; Dancygier and Sweetser 2005). For Applied Cognitive Linguists, grammar diagrams as mediational tools for L2 learning have become a staple, as illustrated here in Dolgova Jacobsen, Falck, Kissling et al., and White, among others. A second ramification is that syntax (and all aspects of language) is meaningful because it reflects our meaningful bodily experiences with the world.

In CL, the position that language and language learning are meaning based is central to the analysis of all linguistic units. The meaning-centric commitment has several, interacting ramifications. The core concept that language emerges through use (Tomasello 2003) holds that linguistic structure cannot be fully understood if isolated from the study of how language is employed to create meaning. Underscoring this perspective is the position (supported by copious, detailed observation [e.g., Tomasello 2003; Lieven 2016]) that a user's language emerges as a result of exposure to repeated, situated instances when the language user understands and/or produces language to convey particular meaning in a specific communicative situation (Barlow and Kemmer 2000). This entails that the language a child is exposed to is very much a surface-level phenomenon, driven not by innate language-specific settings but by the processing of meaning. For instance, the child is exposed to a particular syntactic pattern, such as a question, in the context of someone trying to elicit information. The question pattern conveys information about the speaker's stance and intent in issuing the utterance. After multiple exposures, the child forms a generalization (or category or schema) about the syntax of a question. Once this generalization or schema is formed, it simultaneously allows the speaker to more efficiently interpret new examples and to integrate them into the existing category. It also sanctions new productions by the speaker. Thus, the question schema (or construction) itself is meaningful and conveys information about the speaker's stance and intention; it is distinct from other constructions, such as a general transitive construction. Langacker (1991) talks about the connection between the meaning of a particular linguistic construction and indication of speaker stance in terms of construal. The notion of construal is multifaceted, reflecting multiple properties of being human. At the least, construal reflects embodied experience (e.g., human's ability to take multiple perspectives on a scene), the social nature of language (e.g., the use of language to make mental contact between a speaker and a listener) and general cognitive processing (e.g., category formation and the position that linguistic constructions are complex categories).

CL makes the further argument that making meaning or communicating is central to how language itself is configured. As we saw with the question formation example, a key aspect to this perspective is that meaning is not housed solely in lexical items. Language at all levels, from lexis to syntax to discourse, is gradually built up from smaller chunks to fully formed entrenched categories or constructions, that is, form-meaning mappings. The question construction is a classic example of form-meaning pairing at the syntactic level. Notably, categories are formed from bottom-up, contextualized, exemplar driven input. However, once generalizations or categories are created, new information is understood and stored via the established categories and thus subject to top-down processing. For Second Language Acquisition (SLA), the dual nature of natural language learning and processing suggests a role for both implicit and explicit instruction. Achard (this volume) makes a case for particular types of constructions being more amenable to explicit versus implicit instruction. For SLA professionals, the take away lessons are that language teaching should involve broader meaning making and be viewed through the lens of language constructions rather than rules (Larsen-Freeman 2015; Tyler 2012) and that CL can provide guidance on whether we teach a particular element of language using implicit or explicit pedagogical techniques or both. It frees us from the all-or-nothing debate over implicit versus explicit pedagogy, providing a theoretical foundation for flexible, meaning-based pedagogy. While the perspective of language as ultimately meaningful is central to communicative approaches to language teaching, such as task-based language teaching and content-based language teaching, ACL adds a focus on a theory of grammar that points to cognitive processing and language use as its foundation.

One of the most central discoveries from cognitive science which has informed current theorizing and research is that much of human learning involves creating generalizations across multiple, individual exemplars, in other words, creating categories. These cognitive categories are ever changing as new exemplars are encountered and integrated into the existing knowledge categories. Categories take at least two forms: 1) hierarchically organized schemas (e.g., Rumelhart 1981; Wilson and Anderson 1986), and 2) those demonstrating prototype effects in which members of the category are organized around central exemplars with members of the category interpreted as being more good or less good exemplars of the category (e.g., Rosch 1978). (Think of the category BIRD and the exemplars robin versus kiwi.) Moreover, human categories have fuzzy boundaries, allowing a particular exemplar to be part of multiple categories. In terms of processing, this has the result of providing multiple access routes for a single entity or set of related entities. Another way of thinking of this cognitive organization is that cognition is populated with a vast array of complex, interconnected categories, evidencing both schema and prototype effects. Stepping back, we can recognize several facets of categories – they emerge through exposure to specific, meaningful exemplars, the emergence is generally gradual being built up over multiple exposures, the exemplars almost always occur in (meaningful) context, and categories are organized internally as well as having interconnections across categories. This understanding of categories informs current understanding of general human cognition, including the central role categories play in language and all language learning. This last position straightforwardly acknowledges that the learner comes to the L2 learning situation with a fully formed set of L1 conceptual categories linked to linguistic forms. It breathes new life into cross-linguistic typological studies. Ellis and Cadierno (2009) argue learning an L2 largely means recategorizing many aspects of the world. This recategorization extends past word, phrase and sentence-level phenomena to include discourse organization and information structure (Lemmens and Perrez, this volume) and development of social interactional strategies (Eskildsen, this volume). Clearly, the L2 learner's L1 has many potential facilitative as well as inhibitive effects on learning the L2. The chapters in the first section emphasize four different attributes of categories and linguistic constructions and how they relate to L2 learning and teaching. The key perspective in these studies is understanding the complex, variable nature of categories, including the cultural-specific component of category/construction, the influence of L1 categories on the processing of learning L2 categories, and the expansion of our understanding of contextualized categories to include sentence and discourse level patterning.

The phenomenon of polysemy was one of the earliest and most powerful CL explorations of complex categories (e.g., Lakoff 1987; Taylor 2002; Nerlich et al. 2003; Tyler and Evans 2003). Linguistic polysemy involves a single, stable phonological form (forms can range from a morpheme to sentential templates) associated with multiple meanings. Prepositions are one of the most studied areas of polysemy. Take the English preposition *over*, which is associated with a minimum of 15 meanings ranging from a spatial sense in which a focus element is located higher than a background element (as in *The picture is over the mantel*) to covering (as in *The child put her hands over her eyes*) to completion (as in *Class is over*). CL researchers have persuasively demonstrated that the many meanings associated with the phonological form are not an arbitrary list, but rather a systematically extended set of meanings related to the central sense via regular, recurring principles (e.g. Tyler and Evans 2001, 2003; Nehrlich et al. 2003). (See Achard [this volume] for his analysis of the polysemous lexical construction, French *canard*.) The majority of words are polysemous, but the systematic motivations for extensions are often not readily apparent from dictionary-type definitions. This quality of language poses immense challenges for L2 learners and teachers. Traditionally, the many meanings associated with a single form are considered arbitrary. Being able to explain the meaningful systematicity of a word's polysemy network potentially lessens the learner's memory load and helps provide strategies for figuring out the meaning of new uses they encounter in native speaker discourse. The chapters in the third section raise a distinct set of issues involved in exploring the polysemy of language and L2 learning. Kissling et al. base their investigation of L2 learning of Spanish *por y para* on the Principled Polysemy Model (Tyler and Evans 2001, 2003) which focuses on a methodology for establishing a central sense and a systematic set of principles by which additional meanings are extended from the central sense. Key among these principles for meaning extension are embodied experience (especially as encapsulated in Grady's experiential correlation or primary metaphor), real-world knowledge of force dynamics, and pragmatic inferencing. The paper offers a rich illustration of using this model to create engaging pedagogical materials and effective instruction. Zhao et al. provide fresh insights into differential learning of polysemous items whose central meanings stem from different facets of embodied meaning. Specifically, they examine patterns of L2 learning of English verbs *keep* and *hold*, with a strong emphasis on the embodied consequences of the human experience of holding, which involves the hand grasping an object, and the force dynamics involved with *keeping*, which shifts the emphasis to more abstract knowledge of force dynamics (involving sustained constraint and equilibrium of forces). Finally, using a large-scale corpus analysis, Falck offers an analysis of English *in* and *on* which gives particular emphasis to embodied experience with objects in *in* versus *on* configurations and focuses on having learners better understand the underlying consequences of embodiment that support the extended senses. Together the three papers underscore the vitality of considering polysemy as involving systematic semantic extension resulting in complex categories, rather than an arbitrary phenomenon resulting in a list of homophones.

The remainder of the chapter offers an overview of the papers appearing in this volume. They are organized into three sections: I Categories and constructions in context; II Teaching construal and viewpoint; III Polysemy.

# I Categories and constructions in context

The four papers in this first section shine new light on the role of categories and constructions in L2 learning, with a special emphasis on discourse context. Achard provides a nuanced presentation of the theoretical construct "construction" in CL, along with a discussion of the implications of taking a CL-constructional approach for L2 learning and pedagogy. He points out that work in cognitive science, as well as linguistic theorizing (e.g., Langacker 1991; Goldberg 1995), argues that human cognition is largely structured by categories. These categories represent a full range of cognitive instantiations, from representations of fully articulated individual exemplars to highly general abstractions, or "templatic schemas that capture the commonalities that exist across specific examples" (Achard, this volume). Moreover, categories/constructions found in language also reflect schema and prototype structuring.

Achard ties the variability in category representation to implications for the L2 classroom and argues that adopting a CL-category model would be highly beneficial for two reasons. First, viewing grammar through the lens of different types of constructions or form-meaning pairings, broadens the scope of grammatical instruction, especially by recognizing constructions that share semantics but not distinctive morphosyntactic features. Second, because categories/constructions themselves vary in nature, this model affords pedagogical flexibility by making two, theoretically-grounded, complementary strategies of grammatical presentation available to instructors, namely "grammar as usage" and "grammar as concept". Further, this dual perspective on grammar supports use of both implicit and explicit teaching and learning strategies.

Achard illustrates the first point with two types of French impersonal constructions – the middle impersonal *se* construction and the indefinite impersonal *on* construction. Typically, these two types of constructions are not taught because they lack distinctive morphosyntactic features. That is, while they overlap semantically by indicating an impersonal perspective, they also "share morphology with the much larger middle and indefinite constructions" (Achard, this volume). Another way of thinking about this is that both the *se* construction and the *on* construction are polysemous, complex categories which include, but are not limited to, an impersonal reading. Furthermore, the two constructions overlap in certain uses of the impersonal. Offering a close analysis of sentences extracted from authentic written materials, Achard finds that the middle impersonal *se* construction and the indefinite impersonal *on* construction only occur when particular contexts are present. Specifically, the appropriate context for the middle impersonal *se* includes two situations: (1) The process conveyed by the predicate represents an integral part of the content coded by the subject. For example, *le saucisson d'Arles **se** fait avec de la viande de mulet* 'the sausage from Arles is made [makes itself] with mule meat'. (2) The process expressed by the predicate is available to any generalized conceptualizer as the predicate pertains to social norms or conventions. For instance, *Il n'est pas d'usage de présenter du vin: il ne **se** boit qu'aux repas et au cabaret*. 'It is not customary to serve wine: it is only drunk [drinks itself] during meals or in a bar'. Similarly, the appropriate environments for the indefinite *on* involve two kinds of conceptual configurations: (1) All humans in a community are presented as a homogenous mass with similar experience, e.g., ***on** allait entrer dans l'hiver* 'winter was coming [**one** was about to enter winter]'. (2) Individual conceptualizer's experience is treated "as representative of a typically human and hence a maximally general reaction" (Achard, this volume), e.g., *Pendant qu'elle déballait les tissus brodés, je m'approchai de la fenêtre; **on** apercevait, comme* *d'habitude, Notre-Dame et ses jardins* 'While she was unloading the embroidered fabrics, I walked to the window; as usual, **one** could see Notre Dame and its gardens'. The two French impersonal constructions are schematic in the sense that they both convey a certain degree of generality. The insight that context determines the semantic appropriateness for the French impersonals *se* and *on* suggests a bottom-up, inductive pedagogical approach of "language as usage". Achard claims that constructions of this kind are best taught through activities that are focused on the contexts where these constructions are natural and frequently repeated, as it teaches students to "make the kinds of conventionalized choices target language speakers make in particular situations" (Achard, this volume). Achard also points out that the implicit teaching and learning methodology of "language as usage" alone is not sufficient. For example, the French impersonals *se* and *on* have semantic overlap and divergence. They both can be used to articulate sentences like 'this is visible [to one] in almost every novel that is written today'. However, the *se* construction highlights or topicalizes the object of the predicate, whereas the *on* construction does not. Achard suggests that this distinction might be better taught through explicit instruction by treating *se* and *on* constructions as emphasizing two different concepts in terms of topicality. In sum, a full treatment of the two impersonal constructions is best addressed through both implicit and explicit instruction.

Some linguistic constructions/categories do not have a hierarchical organization, instead, they have a radial categorical structure exhibiting prototype effects. Achard provides a persuasive analysis of the many meanings of *canard* (originally 'duck'), ranging from: i) a discordant musical note; ii) some erroneous piece of information; iii) a newspaper; iv) a sugar cube dipped into coffee or liquor. He demonstrates that all meanings arise from human experience with and observations of the behavior of ducks. For instance, he argues that the discordant musical note meaning stems from the honking sounds made by ducks and the piece of sugar dunked in coffee meaning stems from the typical motion ducks engage in when "fishing" for food. When viewed from an embodied experience perspective, the wide range of meanings appear quite systematic and intuitive. However, they too are culturally constrained. Although speakers of many languages have a specific lexical item/construction for 'duck', only French has developed the particular range of meanings associated with the French category *canard* ('duck'). For instance, English has extended the quick, dunking motion made by the water fowl *duck* when searching for food to the verb *duck* which indicates a quick action of leaving or coming, as in *I'm going to duck out for a few minutes*. Speakers of French and English have both observed ducks making the same motion, but have extended the associated meanings in quite different ways. While the French have privileged the noise made by these birds through lexicalization, English has not. This illustrates the CL claim that every physical, spatial phenomenon is complex and can be experienced from multiple perspectives; languages/cultures do not typically lexicalize all possible embodied perspectives, but choose among them. Achard claims that the implicit, inductive pedagogical strategy is not particularly helpful in teaching this kind of language/cultural specific category. Instead, the strategy of "language as concept" is effective by explicitly pointing out the strands between the different senses which form a conceptually motivated category. In sum, Achard provides persuasive arguments for attending to the uses of grammar as they occur in context, understanding grammar and lexis as constructions/categories, and recognizing the usefulness of employing a flexible pedagogy which exploits both implicit and explicit interventions.

Eskildsen combines a construction-based approach with a turn-by-turn conversational analysis (CA) to investigate how situational requirements and conversational circumstances inform the learning of subordination and coordination in L2 English. He presents a longitudinal (the data spans four years) case study of one L1 Spanish speaker, Carlos. The data is drawn from an audio-visual corpus consisting of nearly 4,000 hours of recordings of American English L2 classroom interactions. Thus, the study provides a record of contextualized, naturally occurring, emergent language learning.

Contrary to the prevailing idea that coordination precedes subordination in development, Eskildsen finds that the emergence of coordination and subordination in the L2 does not follow a linear trajectory as both coordination (e.g., the *but*-construction) and subordination (e.g., the *because*-construction) emerge simultaneously from the beginning. Moreover, the study reveals exemplar-based learning and lexical specificity at the early phases in the development of coordination and subordination. For example, *and*, *but*, and *because* occur primarily in copula constructions at the early stage. Interestingly, while Carlos' use of *and*, *but*, and *because* expands from exemplar-based uses in specific constructions to more varied functions of bi-clausal constructions, other conjunctions, especially the less frequently used subordinating constructions, mainly stay at the highly exemplar-based level. This suggests that Carlos has not acquired a general rule for coordination and subordination but is creating much more narrow, item-based schemas.

Rejecting the position that learning subordination is solely bound to syntax or issues of complexity, Eskildsen claims that learning subordination and coordination in L2 English is socially anchored and closely tied to mastering an increasing variety of interactional functions, such as managing turn-taking, giving accounts, and expressing disagreement. For example, Carlos initially uses *and* and *but* coordination not as an item to conjoin sentences, but as an interactional device. Specifically, in earliest uses, *and* appears at turn-initial positions as a response to a previous utterance of somebody else to build or restore continuity in a conversation. Only later is *and* used to sequence chronological events and finally to combine sentences to form bi-clausal coordination. Eskildsen notes that this trajectory might be influenced by the input. The earlier classroom interactions are primarily teacher-fronted conversations in which students make responses to the teacher's turns. Later more of the activities involve student-fronted individual talks in which students are invited to produce longer stretches of discourse. With ample empirical evidence, this study richly illustrates Tomasello's position that abstract linguistic knowledge derives from specific usage events in specific situations. Thus, the study offers persuasive evidence for the position that language learning is driven by situated language use.

The chapter by Wulff, Gries and Lester represents an expanding paradigm which interweaves insights from a construction perspective on grammar with comparative corpus analysis guided by principles from cognitive psychology. The paradigm examines the distribution of comparable target language units in the language of native speakers of a target language, in the L2 learners' native languages, and then compares these L1 patterns to their distribution in the target language of L2 learners. The methodology adds a substantial cross-linguistic, typological dimension to the study of L2 construction learning. These fine-grained analyses, in turn, allow a fuller, more precise picture of the constructions in each language and subtle, insightful comparisons across languages. Wulff et al. use sophisticated corpus analyses, which take multiple variables into account, to investigate possible L1 transfer effects on the variable presence of optional *that* in the English produced by L1 German and L1 Spanish speakers. They are particularly interested in discovering under which discourse circumstances L2 speakers more closely approximate the usage patterns of native speakers and under which conditions learners deviate from native speakers.

The linguistic target under consideration, the presence or absence of optional *that*, occurred in sentences such as *I thought (that) Nick likes candy*; *The problem is (that) Nick doesn't like candy*; and, *I'm glad (that) Stefan likes candy*. Wulff et al. begin by documenting the patterns of optional complementation in L1 speech, e.g., complementation patterns in English, Spanish and German, and found that, on a continuum, English corpora showed the highest level of complementizer omission, followed by German, with Spanish rarely evidencing omission. They confirmed established findings that in English, the presence of *that* is determined by a range of identifiable processing factors, such as the amount of material that precedes the main clause and how likely a particular verb stem (lemma) will be followed by a complement clause (the surprisal factor). Next they examined corpora of L2 English produced by L1 German and L1 Spanish speakers. Under conditions with relatively low processing demands, the L2 learners showed patterns very like those of L1 English speakers, although at a more conservative rate of *that* omission (but higher than the rate observed in their L1s), suggesting that they were becoming attuned to the English patterns. However, more pronounced differences between native English speakers and learners appeared with certain construction-specific, more cognitively demanding uses of *that*. For instance, for L2 learners, omission of the complementizer is especially low with adjectval and object complements.

Wulff et al.'s documentation of sensitivity to "surprisal" in both L1 and L2 speakers constitutes a particularly unique contribution to the comparative corpus literature. It is a fact of language use that certain verbs are more likely to be followed by complement clauses than other verbs; thus the verb lemma is a reliable cue to the likelihood of an upcoming complement clause. When the verb lemma is highly informative about the presence of an upcoming clause juncture, rates of *that* decrease for both native speakers (NS) and non-native speakers (NNS). As the first word of the complement clause becomes more surprising (i.e., the surprisal factor is higher), both NS and NNS increase their complementizer use; the NNS just do this with a higher rate of *that*-use. The overall main effects support the interpretation that NS and NNS are subject to similar processing pressures and react to them in similar ways.

A few L1-specific differences also emerged: the Spanish learners produce significantly more *that* complementizers than their German peers, matching the differences found in the native German and native Spanish corpora. This reflects fine-grained, construction-specific L1 transfer effects.

Recognizing that the L2 learner starts the L2 learning process with a fully constructed language, replete with language specific categories and constraints on syntactic constructions, gives us fresh insights into cross-linguistic analysis and how the L1 might influence learning the target language. This study demonstrates that a CL (construction)-corpus based approach to crosslinguistic differences allows for fine grained, discourse-situated analyses of language specific aspects of constructions. Moreover, the findings point to the power of frequency and humans' pattern finding abilities. Patterns of *that*-omission, such as the likelihood that a particular verb will be followed by a *that* clause, are rarely taught and rarely occur in English grammars. Wulff et al. conclude "*that*-variation may be taken as a powerful example of how much learners can pick up by implicitly scrutinizing the distributional patterns of their input even though the random effects also showcase considerable individual variation" (Wulff et al., this volume).

A well-established cross-linguistic categorizing principle for motion events (Talmy 2000) sorts languages into two typologies, verb-framed languages (V-languages) and satellite-framed languages (S-languages). V-languages, such as French, are languages in which the direction of the movement tends to be encoded in the main verb and manner of motion is optionally expressed in an adjunct phrase. This organization contrasts with S-languages, such as Dutch, in which manner of motion tends to be encoded in the main verb and the direction of movement in a satellite. A corollary of the V-framed/S-framed typology is that S-languages tend to have many verbs that indicate nuances of manner, while V-languages rely on more general verbs. The general assumption has been that this typological difference results in asymmetric learning challenges for L2 speakers. More specifically, native speakers of a V-language, which has few manner verbs, have a heavier burden learning appropriate uses of the multiple manner verbs when learning an L2 S-language relative to native speakers of an S-language learning the more general verb categories of a V-language (e.g., Cadierno et al. 2016). Lemmens and Perrez extend Talmy's verb-centered typology from motion events to how L1 speakers and L2 learners of typologically different languages (French and Dutch) encode locative events. The evidence shows that L1 French speakers learning Dutch experience difficulty with Dutch locative constructions at the lexical level, such as switching from a few general or neutral verbs (e.g., *être* 'be') to multiple posture verbs (e.g., *staan* 'stand', *zitten* 'sit' and *liggen* 'lie') and learning the appropriate context in which a particular posture verb is used. Going beyond the word level, Lemmens and Perez expand their examination out to syntactic constructions and discourse structures and by doing so, generate further insights into how locative events are encoded by native speakers of French and Dutch and by L2 learners of the typologically different languages.

Using a series of picture description tasks, the elicitation data not only confirms the typological differences between Dutch and French in the expression of locative events on the lexical level, but also breaks new ground by offering evidence that the typological differences occur at the syntactic construction level. Specifically, the L1 Dutch speakers produced more presentational constructions and basic locative constructions, whereas the L1 French speakers produced more transitive constructions and embedded basic locative constructions. Thus, both group of learners face challenges learning how to articulate locative events in the target languages, only gradually moving towards target language norms.

By further expanding the investigation to the discourse level, Lemmens and Perez offer fresh insights into how native speakers of these two languages tend to organize and categorize locative scenes within larger contexts. First, the analysis reveals that the information structure in the two languages is not the same. In Dutch, in about half of the cases analyzed, the matrix clause introduces a Figure that subsequently serves as the Ground for the location of another Figure expressed in the following subordinate clause. For example, *Er is ook een bed waar kleren op liggen* 'there is a **bed** where on **clothes** are lying'. In French, in contrast, the matrix clause tends to introduce a Figure and the following subordinate clause provides supplementary locative information on that same Figure. For instance, *je vois aussi des t-shirts qui sont collés au mur du fond* 'I see also **tee-shirts that** are stuck onto the wall at the back'. Lemmens and Perrez metaphorically term these two types of information structuring patterns as a "train model" (Dutch) and an "onion model" (French). The effect at the discourse level is that the French speakers frequently use an accumulative pattern with the locative information expressed in the subordinate clause being optional and backgrounded. Lemmens and Perrez point out that this pattern is parallel to the organization of motion events in V-languages in which manner of motion is subordinate. While in Dutch, although there are two different locative events represented by two different Figures, "from a functional perspective one could regard these as building one single event" (Lemmens and Perrez, this volume), targeting the location of the Figure in the subordinate clause. This is similar to the expression of path in the motion event by the path satellite attached to the main verb in S-languages. Finally, Lemmens and Perrez show that learners' descriptions fall in an intermediate position between the native speakers of Dutch and French, suggesting that they have become increasingly aware of the varying ways the two languages categorize locative scenes. The key take away points here are understanding the language/cultural-specific component of category/construction, the influence of L1 categories on the process of learning L2 categories, and the expansion of contextualized categories to include discourse level patterning.

## II Teaching construal and viewpoint

The first four chapters all dealt to some extent with discourse level phenomena. This section offers additional, even more discourse focused perspectives on the speaker's contextualized, grammatical choices. In this section, the first two papers illustrate Mental Space and Blending Theory (MSBT) (Fauconnier 1997; Fauconnier and Turner 1996, 1998, 2002), one of the most robust, well-developed representations of discourse-level phenomena and meaning-construction within

CL. The third paper takes on English article usage, a well-established discourse-level phenomenon (e.g., Celce-Murcia and Larsen-Freeman 2015).

The section opens with Dancygier and Moder who offer a well-articulated overview of the key components of MSBT, especially as it applies to viewpoint within naturally occurring discourse. Their presentation makes clear how this subfield of CL offers additional, important tools that further our understanding of the nature of language and cognition. They follow their introduction to MSBT and viewpoint with an application of its usefulness for L2 instruction.

MSBT holds that humans spontaneously create "packets" of cognitive content (i.e., *mental spaces*) for the purposes of on-line conceptualization. The content of the mental space involves the speaker's conceptual representations of entities in the pertinent scenarios as the entities are perceived, imagined, remembered, or otherwise understood by the speaker. During online conceptualization, humans are able to maintain multiple mental spaces for the purposes of combining information from different domains of knowledge. Mental spaces populated with our knowledge about a particular concept are represented as *input spaces*; knowledge from each pertinent input space can be selectively projected to a new, *blended space*. The projected elements are re-assembled in the blended space to create a new unique structure, or *blend*. The theory "emphasizes the speaker's use of language to mentally guide the listener to a conceptualization of the situation similar to that of the speaker's" (Dancygier and Moder, this volume).

The chapters by both Dancygier and Moder and Dolgova Jacobsen present studies of L2 learning of English conditionals. Key to these analyses is that the two clauses involved in any conditional construction each represent a different mental space and that linguistic cues, such as *if* or *since*, provide prompts for creating particular types of input spaces and creating a blended space. Conditionals are treated as a complex of constructions, each with a particular schematic meaning. Changes in the form, such as various tense choices, indicate variation in interpretation and thus account for the many types of conditionals, such as hypothetical, counterfactual, and factual, etc. Markers, such as *if*, *when*, and *since*, are signals to establish a particular mental space configuration in which two mental spaces are in a conditional relationship. More specifically, the choice of *since* versus *if* relates to the speaker/writer's perspective on the reality of the information in the space. For example, in a sentence such as *Since you're going to the store today, will you pick up some milk?*, the speaker indicates through the choice of *since* that she believes the addressee is going to the store. This is in contrast to *If you go to the store, will you pick up some milk?* in which the choice of *if* indicates the speaker is neutral or uncertain about whether the proposition is true (Dancygier and Sweetser 2000). Verb forms help signal the mappings and projections of the elements in the two alternative mental spaces, which results in the ultimate interpretation of the construction. In both the examples, the use of the simple present tense in the first clause establishes a conceptual space in which the speaker's current beliefs serve as the base for the request found in the second clause.

The two chapters take the position that an isolated consideration of key words such as *if* or *since* or rules concerning tense harmony are insufficient for L2 learners to appropriately interpret and produce conditionals. Rather, they argue for an understanding of the larger pattern or construction, as it is situated within a discourse context. Full understanding "depends critically on matching the grammatical construction in which *since* or *if* occurs with the discourse context of use and the ongoing cognitive relations between the speaker and the hearer" (Dancygier and Moder, this volume). Dancygier and Moder further argue that full comprehension and the appropriate use of *if* and *since* clauses require that the learners develop an awareness of viewpoint.

Guided by MSBT and with the goal of integrating the theory into L2 pedagogy, Dancygier and Moder developed a study focusing on viewpoint through the lens of constructions using *since*. They note that, like many linguistic units, *since* is polysemous, thus adding to the complexity of learning appropriate use. The following illustrates the meanings and grammatical polysemy:

(1) a. **Since** I **want** to improve my English, study abroad **is** one of the best choices I can make.

b. I **have studied** English as a second language **since** I **was** seven.

Sentence (1a) illustrates the use of *since* in a conditional construction, much like the *Since you're going to the grocery store...* example discussed above, in which the writer's viewpoint is presented as assuming the proposition expressed in the clause is true (or positively aligning with the proposition). This signaling of speaker stance is termed epistemic viewpoint. In (1b), the *since* construction is quite different, highlighting the speaker's view of the temporal origin of an experience. A key point is that *since* participates in two quite different constructions, each expressing a viewpoint or construal, i.e., epistemic versus temporal viewpoint. The distinct uses are established by the interaction between the main and subordinate clauses, i.e., the entire construction, including the tense-aspect choices made in each.

The target of instruction was *since* constructions found in naturally occurring discourse segments from two large US corpora. After examining 1425 uses of *since*, Dancygier and Moder find that the use of the present perfect in temporal *since* constructions is overwhelming. In contrast, in the epistemic *since* constructions, the most frequent tense/aspect form is the simple present. Based on the findings and the identified difficulties in students' uses of *since*, Dancygier and Moder designed a series of usage-based classroom activities, including sentence sorting tasks, discourse-based construction identification tasks, group discussion of highlighted sentences in a full text, and follow-up writing tasks. The results and student evaluations show increases in students' awareness and understanding of the distinct constructions and the different viewpoints signaled by the constructions, including viewing variations from a discourse perspective. Importantly, this study suggests that implicit cognitive pedagogy may be an effective approach to instantiating key aspects of unfamiliar conceptual categories, such as viewpoint constructions.

Dolgova Jacobsen offers us a vibrant example of how complex CL theory can guide innovative, engaging L2 teaching and learning, effectively weaving together MSBT, analysis of authentic English discourse, and principles of Task Based Language Teaching (TBLT). Her chapter presents an introduction to key tenets of MSBT which informed her 6-week long, effects of instruction study of advanced English learners in a university-level academic writing program. She situates the usefulness of using CL through an emphasis on how constructions are chosen by a speaker in order to try to make mental contact with the listener. Incorporating the notion of cross-linguistic transfer effects, she notes that L2 speakers are likely to bring all sorts of different background knowledge to the usage event, including "varying perceptions of contextual factors" (Dolgova Jacobsen, this volume) and differing conceptualizations of types of experiences (Robinson and Ellis 2008; Cadierno and Robinson 2009). Thus, within any given communicative situation, L2 speakers may start off with a different set of construal patterns compared with L1 speakers. She argues that CL is particularly potent for teaching because it privileges the notions of construal and constructions as linguistic means for presenting speaker perspective over grammar rules. More specifically, CL provides powerful tools that allow teachers to "highlight the characteristics of the L1 construal and make the learner aware of the construal options, as well as potential differences between the L1 and L2 systems" (Dolgova Jacobsen, this volume). In other words, the notion of construal provides learners with a perspective that allows them to begin to understand the L1 speaker's perspective and motivation for using particular constructions in particular communicative circumstances. Moreover, the perspective provided by CL and MSBT presents the language in a more comprehensive and systematic manner, offering important advances over existing, widely used L2 materials and textbooks. Specifically, she argues for the benefits of representing grammar in terms of form-meaning mappings which can be made "relatively transparent for the learners" (Dolgova Jacobsen, this volume). With the emphasis on language use as usage events, authentic excerpts of language and authentic context take the fore. Additionally, she makes the case for use of visuals to effectively make grammar patterns and their use more accessible (Tyler and Evans 2003; De Knop and Dirven 2008), noting that visual support functions as a natural extension of the key notions of embodied experience, embodied meaning, and their connection with language.

Dolgova Jacobsen's study focuses on teaching English hypothetical conditionals, relying primarily on Dancygier and Sweeter's (2005) MSBT analysis. As discussed above (see summary of Dancygier and Moder), the basic MSBT claim is that various linguistic markers (e.g., *if, when, unless*, etc.) signal that the propositional content of the clause is intended as conditional and verb forms in the clauses contribute to setting up different configurations of mental spaces. Key to the tense choice is the speaker's construal or perspective on the situation being discussed. In a sentence like *If prices go up, I will sell my car*, the base space would be the understanding of the current assumed reality in which prices have not gone up yet. The *if*-clause (*if prices go up*) works as a space-builder, signaling that the speaker has created a new mental space that provides possible different realities and allowing the predictive function to emerge. Subsequently, the speaker is able to express their assessment of the degree of reality with linguistic means (e.g., verb forms).

Anyone who has studied or taught English conditionals is familiar with the difficulties that tense choices pose. CL provides accessible insights into this complex area by positing that tense choice signals the speaker's stance on the likelihood of the alternative state being realized. Implications arise from our embodied experience. Present tense is associated with the "here and now" and the speaker's potential to physically observe and intervene in the current situation. Past tense carries a distancing interpretation as it is associated with "there and then", situations removed from the speaker's ability to physically observe and intervene. Dolgova Jacobsen adds that tense choice also carries information about the speaker's sense whether the situation can change and the potential control that allows the speaker to influence the situation. Essentially, tense choices are grounded in the speaker's background knowledge and understanding of the communicative context.

Dolgova Jaccobsen was also interested in exploring the potential extra benefit of adding an MSBT approach to task supported instruction. Three groups of English learners in a university-level academic writing program took part in the study: cognitive + task-supported, task-supported with rule-oriented grammar explanation, and control with no conditional instruction. The cognitive group received three interventions, which emphasized language structures as conveying meaning (with special emphasis on compositionality and variation within larger form-meaning pairings), and the general functions of conditionals, i.e., signaling speakers' perceptions of reasons and potential outcomes. The concepts were addressed through both teacher-led PowerPoint discussions which included watching episodes from popular video, such as "Alice in Wonderland", and brainstorming answers to such questions as "What would have happened if Alice hadn't seen the rabbit?" Students were introduced to the link between tense choice and speaker stance and asked to analyze tense combinations in various contexts and discuss the speaker's probable motivation for the choices and the unique point of view being presented. A unique component to Dolgova Jacobsen's materials involved the focus on speakers' meaningful choices in regard to tense and accordingly, the usage-based reality that L1 speakers are not bound to the standard tense pairings found in traditional English grammars. Given the fact that conditionals are structured within specific usage contexts, the speaker's perspective and perception of the local context and the surrounding information affect the tense composition of either of the two clauses. Participants took a pre-test, a post-test and a delayed post-test. Three participants from each group also participated in retrospective interviews. The cognitive group outperformed the task-supported and the control groups on the post-test and the delayed post-test. Participants in the CL treatment group expressed enthusiasm for the module. Dolgova Jacobsen concludes that integrating CL principles into task supported materials and teaching can create an improved pedagogical treatment, one which both provides details of the systematic organization of conditionals and highlights the meaningful, discourse situated uses in accordance with the L1 construal patterns.

Drawing on Langacker's notion of "ground" and the communicative goal of speaker and listener making mental contact, along with Fillmore's notion of semantic/conceptual frames, White offers a CL account and pedagogical treatment of the English definite article. Since the concept of making mental contact is at the heart of White's analysis of the definite article, construal and signaling speaker stance play a major role in his presentation. The treatment steps away from formulating a list of rules, which cover the long, seemingly arbitrary list of surface uses of the definite article, and guides teachers (and eventually learners) to conceptualize L1 speaker use of the article at a more abstract, meaning-centric level.

Traditionally, definiteness has been treated as signaling either a referent's familiarity (e.g., Christophersen 1939) or its uniqueness (e.g., Russell 1905). In regards to use of the definite article, perhaps the most pervasive, standard explanation is that the referent is unique and familiar by previous mention in the discourse. But there are many exceptions. Inspired by the CL treatment of grammar as meaningful and conceptual (e.g., Fillmore 1982; Taylor 2002; Croft and Cruse 2004; Radden and Dirven 2007; Langacker 2008), White's analysis represents the choice of article as conveying important information about the speaker's stance or construal of the scene. Within White's analysis, the meaning of the definite article is understood to be that of abstract deixis. The use of *the* indicates the speaker is "mentally pointing at a conceptual entity (within her own mind) with the assumption that the hearer can locate a similar conceptual entity (within his own mind)" (White, this volume), i.e., that the speaker and hearer can make mental contact with similar conceptual entities.

The analysis is encapsulated in a schematic image or diagram, which White terms a conceptual tool, meant to capture the abstract meaning of the definite article. The schematic image represents various conceptual frames, each of which has been argued to be at play in course of language processing (both creating and interpreting discourse). Within an overarching discourse frame, White posits three subframes: the situation frame, which reflects the physical situation interlocutors find themselves in; the text frame, which reflects the immediate ongoing discourse and whose primary deictic function is anaphoric and cataphoric reference; and the concept frame, which reflects interlocutors' background knowledge, including cultural knowledge.

A central question for White is whether the analysis, supported by the schematic diagram, can help international ESL teachers develop deeper, more coherent understandings of how L1 speakers use the definite article to make meaning. To this end, White presents a small scale study in which 5 international MS TESOL students were introduced to the CL analysis in conjunction with the schematic diagram. By using the schematic to analyze multiple, contextualized examples, i.e., using the schematic diagram as a discourse analytic tool, the participants were guided toward a more coherent, conceptually based understanding of definite article usage. The treatment does not aim for prediction or production; rather applying the schematic to authentic discourse is intended to "prompt [...] learners to consider the construal process and how speakers use *the* to help shape their message" (White, this volume).

The treatment involved individually presenting the schematic to the international MA TESOL students, for 6 sessions, over a period of 6 weeks. The use of articles from the students' own writing and relevant, authentic journal article abstracts were analyzed. In the first session, the participants orally offered their explanations for why the author used various instances of the definite article. Their explanations reflected a long list of unrelated rules. The intervention involved 4 sessions in which the participants were introduced to the schematic diagram and the CL-construal analysis of the uses of the definite article. Again, the participants were asked to identify articles used in authentic discourse, but now they offered explanations for the choice using White's schematic diagram and CL explanations. As part of their use, the participants were asked to draw pictures which illustrated how the article was acting as a deictic signal within one of the three subframes.

The final session consisted of the participants providing explanations of the article usage in the same discourse excerpts used in the first session and then comparing the two explanations. The main finding was that the explanations changed substantially from Elicitation A to B. The key pattern was that the participants provided a more unified, meaning-based explanation in Elicitation B, rather than an unsystematic list of discrete rules. White interpreted this pattern as evidence that the participants, with the aid of the schematic diagram and guided discourse analysis, were able to begin to reconceptualize the varying uses of the definite article and see its use as meaningfully signaling speaker stance.

White concludes, the visual "provided by the schematic can be utilized by instructors to explain the abstract meanings of the definite article in a more concrete way than that typically found in textbooks. [...] Just as it may be used to concretize abstract explanations through imagery, the schematic may also be used as a tool to make intuitions explicit. That is, it can provide learners and teachers concepts with which to clarify and express their unarticulated insights regarding articles" (White, this volume).

## III Polysemy

Many linguistic units – from morphemes (e.g., English tense markers, see Tyler and Evans 2001) to syntactic patterns (Goldberg 1995) – have been shown, through CL-based analysis, to have multiple, related meanings. Using CL-based insights such as embodied meaning, conceptual metaphor and experiential correlation, CL analysts have demonstrated that these many meanings are systematically connected to a central meaning. Thus, polysemous linguistic units are considered to be complex categories constituting systematic polysemy networks. In L2 studies, the polysemy of words has garnered the most attention. Of all the polysemous word classes, prepositions have been most intensively and extensively studied. Within CL, prepositions are understood as most centrally representing spatial relationships between an element in focus (or the element being located) and an element in background (or the element providing locating information). One of the most influential analytical frameworks for analyzing prepositions is the Principled Polysemy Model (PPM) (Tyler and Evans 2001,

2003). The framework aims to provide a replicable method for determining the central (spatial) sense and a constrained set of principles for extending meanings from the central meaning. Tyler and Evans (2001, 2003) focused on English prepositions, but hypothesized that the model could be applied to other languages. The chapter by Kissling, Tyler, Warren and Negrete uses Curry's (2010) successful application of the PPM to the highly complex polysemy networks associated with the Spanish prepositions *por* and *para*.

Kissling et al. offer an innovative effects-of-instruction study of English-speaking college learners of Spanish, focusing on *por* and *para*. These prepositions are widely recognized as being particularly intractable. Both are highly polysemous and both are commonly translated as 'for', even though this simple translation masks many of the actual uses of each preposition. Although Spanish FL learners in the U.S. typically receive a traditional, intensive grammar lesson (usually one day per semester) contrasting *por* and *para* several times during their high school and university language studies, their use of these prepositions usually remains highly inaccurate. Indeed, one landmark study showed that university-level Spanish students only increased their accuracy rates on the two prepositions by 8% over a four year period (Pinto and Rex 2006) and that the learners tended to use only two or three of the 10+ meanings for each preposition.

Drawing on Curry's (2010) PPM analysis, Kissling et al. created teaching materials which assumed the multiple meanings of *por* and *para* consisted of a systematically, motivated polysemy network. For each preposition, the guiding assumption was that the extended meanings could be systematically related back to the central, spatial meaning. The PPM analysis not only provided precise, accessible representations of each of the meanings, which drew on embodied experience and metaphor, but also provided a theoretically grounded order for presentation of the various meanings. A second, usage-based innovation was to present the meanings of the two forms gradually, building learners' knowledge in a series of scaffolded treatments, throughout the course of an entire semester, instead of the standard one intensive lesson per semester. Moreover, *por* and *para* were treated as independent and explicitly not presented in comparison to one another. Overall, this presentation was in stark contrast to the standard treatment which presents the multiple meanings of the two prepositions as arbitrary lists of meanings in one concentrated lesson and often focuses on a comparison of the two. A third area of interest was in examining the efficacy of providing explicit CL explanations of the prepositions.

The participants (n = 36) were divided into two groups. One received explicit CL explanations for the meanings of the various uses and emphasis on the relations among the meanings; the other received instruction based on CL principles but lacking explicit mention of notions such as metaphor or the systematic relationships among the meanings. The participants were assessed with fill-in-the blank and multiple-choice pretests and posttests as well as surveys. The results provided strong evidence in support of the gradual, scaffolded approach; learners' gain scores increased substantially both for many individual senses of the prepositions as well as the aggregate scores, with large effect sizes. The progress learners made in one semester stands in dramatic contrast to the minimal gains reported in the literature by similar learners in instructed university-level Spanish FL programs. Adding explicit CL explanations of *por* and *para* did not appear to make a difference. However, an effect of the CL analysis cannot be dismissed because the sequence of presentation, which was the same for both groups and based on the organized polysemy networks, might have had the effect of raising the awareness of all learners as to the semantic connections among senses. Thus this chapter represents the first stage in the larger investigation, and this first study indicates that a PPM analysis of the multiple meanings of prepositions allows teachers to offer more coherent, meaningful, scaffolded instruction as opposed to telling the learners to simply memorize an arbitrary list of meanings.

Using a model of polysemy in general alignment with the model used by Kissling et al., Zhao and her colleagues carried out an effects-of-instruction study focusing on learning the multiple meanings of the English verbs *hold* and *keep*, thus providing evidence that the PPM is applicable to word classes beyond strictly spatial language. Previous research has established that L2 learners often confuse the use of these two verbs, primarily because they share certain meanings involving possession and control while also having some distinct senses (e.g., Csabi 2004). Zhao et al. largely adopted the CL-analysis of the polysemy network of the two verbs developed by Csabi. They argued that the central senses of *hold* and *keep* are distinct in precise ways which offer motivated reasons for why their networks have developed both distinct senses and overlapping senses. In general, the central sense for *hold* focuses on an image of human hands involved in a grasping or supporting action. *Hold* has developed a semantic element which indicates continuous, but bounded action, as in *The officers held the young man for several hours*. Since the central image is of human hands manipulating or supporting an object, the scene has a limited or bounded aspect. An embodied semantics analysis argues that our experience of the world informs us that the time we can grasp something in our hands is of limited duration because our muscles eventually tire. In contrast, the central sense of *keep* involves possession more generally, relying on a force dynamic analysis (Talmy 2000) which emphasizes an equilibrium between exertion of force to maintain a static situation and resistance to that force towards change or motion. The central scene evoked by *keep* is more abstract and unbounded, lending a stronger durative quality, allowing for an extension of continuous action, as in *She kept a diary under her pillow*. Thus, the study also offers insight into the interaction between learning the verbs' lexical semantics and appropriate use of aspectual morphology. Finally, the study extends Csabi (2004) and Berendi, Csabi and Kovesces (2008) by developing more sophisticated, corpus-based teaching materials.

The participants were 33 L1 Chinese speakers enrolled in Hong Kong middle school (12–13 years old) learning English. They were divided into an experimental group and a control group. The experimental group received a 45 minute intervention which presented the meanings of the two verbs using CL explanations for meaning extension such as embodied experience and force dynamics (e.g., Talmy 2000), as well as conceptual metaphor (e.g., Kovesces 2010). The experimental materials emphasized diagrams and dynamic visualizations which illustrated the systematic connections between the central senses and the extended meanings. The intervention was carried out by the regular classroom teachers. In addition to an orientation session, the teacher for the experimental group was provided a teaching script and PowerPoint slides. The control group received instruction based on the current EFL texts used in the schools which emphasize learning the dictionary meanings as an arbitrary list associated with each form. Both the experimental and the control groups took a pretest, posttest and delayed posttest which consisted of a sentence-level cloze test that required participants to fill in the blank with the verb lemma *hold* or *keep* and the appropriate morphological inflection.

Post intervention, for both *keep* and *hold*, the experimental group outperformed the control group. The effect was significant at the time of the delayed posttest. The experimental group showed a steady increase in accuracy for both verbs across the five-week period. The control group showed some increase at the point of the immediate posttest, followed by a sharp decline in accuracy at the time of the delayed posttest. In explaining the differences between the two groups, the researchers suggest that the experimental group gained an understanding of the relationships between the central senses and the extended senses which allowed them to distinguish between the uses of the two verbs and continue to extend those distinctions. In contrast, the control group appeared to lack any principled understanding of the relationships between the central senses and the extended meanings which resulted in the multiple meanings for *keep* and *hold* tending to be jumbled over time.

Moreover, although the target of instruction was the core semantics of the two verbs, answers were scored for both accuracy of the core semantics and grammatical accuracy in terms of supplying the appropriate aspectual morphology.

Even though grammatical accuracy was not a target of instruction, the experimental group (but not the control group) showed significant gains in this area. Several polysemous senses of *keep* and *hold* involve notions of continuity and duration either with or without temporal boundaries. CL-instruction highlighted these senses and visualized their aspectual properties. In other words, CL-instruction may have incidentally helped learners on the lexical aspect (Vendler, 1957) of *hold* and *keep*, perhaps heightening their sensitivity to the temporal cues (e.g., adverbial phrases such as *for several hours*) that suggested continuity with a temporal boundary. The authors hypothesize that deeper understanding of the differing semantics of the two verbs helped the participants make more accurate judgments on the grammatical morphemes required for the context.

Finally, the study offers important insights into cognitive constraints on frequency effects, whose importance in language learning is well established (see Ellis, Romer, and O'Donnell 2016 for a thorough summary). The pretest results showed that both groups were initially more accurate on items involving *keep*. In part this was likely due to higher frequency of *keep* in the participants' input. Given what appeared like more initial knowledge of *keep*, one might reasonably hypothesize that the participants would build on that foundation and show greater accuracy on meanings of *keep* on the posttests. However, the experimental group showed significantly greater gains on the uses of *hold*. The authors hypothesize that this gain points to the power of embodied semantics, especially the imageability of the central sense for *hold*. The central sense for *keep*, which involves force dynamics, is more abstract and less imageable.

The study demonstrates that younger learners and their teachers can successfully adopt a novel, CL approach to vocabulary learning which emphasizes embodied semantics, force dynamics, conceptual metaphor, and semantic networks, aided by schematic diagrams and other visuals. The authors argue that animation provided in the PowerPoint slide was particularly helpful, especially during the explanation of the underlying force dynamics for the semantic network of the word *keep*, since different force patterns can be effectively illustrated through the movement of the objects. Participating teachers noted that students benefited from the perspective that polysemous word senses are systemtically related and can be acquired as a coherent network. In other words, these seemingly technical concepts can be made accessible and useful for L2 learning. The authors conclude that "polysemous words are teachable and teachers need not see them as a problematic topic in the classroom" (Zhao et al., this volume).

Although analyzing the polysemy of spatial language through the lens of organized networks of meaning has proven useful both in analysis and L2 pedagogy, Falck offers an alternative treatment which de-emphasizes the ways the various senses relate to each other as a network and instead focuses on learners considering embodied experiences with entities in core spatial configurations. The foundation of the study is a corpus based analysis of non-spatial uses of English *in* and *on* and the phrases/terms with which they collocate (Falck 2014). This initial analysis revealed patterns of usage falling into subcategories that systematically relate to specific types of embodied experience (or in Falck's terms world-body knowledge). For instance, the corpus analysis revealed a set of *in* phrases which referred to the contents of the cognitive concepts, thus representing thoughts, opinions, speeches, etc., as containers. In contrast, *on* phrases did not refer to the contents of concepts, but rather the relationships between people's thoughts and the content topic. These uses of *on* seem to represent people conceptualizing their thoughts or words as following a trajectory from the speaker/conceptualizer to abstract concepts, as in *I'm focusing my attention on the problem*. Falck argues that the systematic uses reflect "general categorization processes (cf. Rosch 1978) in which certain types of abstract concepts (i.e. ones involving the contents of cognitive concepts such as thoughts, opinions, views, and segments of language [...]) are construed one way (i.e. as *in* relationships), and other types of concepts (i.e. ones discussing the direction of cognitive concepts such as these [...]) construed another way (i.e. as *on* relationships). Given our embodied understandings of the world, *in* constructions appear more apt in talk about some abstract relationships, and *on* constructions in talk about others" (Falck, this volume). For each of these subcategories, diagrams representing the underlying world-body experience were created; these diagrams provided both a clearer representation of the dynamics revealed in the linguistic analysis and potential teaching tools.

The goal of the present study was to explore the usefulness of presenting L2 learners the multiple meanings of the prepositions in terms of patterns being sanctioned by the underlying bodily experiences. The focus was on raising students' awareness of embodied motivations for abstract language patterns through languaging-type discussions (Swain 2006). Falck argues that playful, collaborative discussions about embodied motivations for the subcategories of prepositional uses provide a powerful starting point for creative, collaborative grammar instruction.

The chapter reports on two small-scale qualitative studies of L1 Swedish speakers, ages 12 and 13, learning English. The learning targets were 177 uses of *on* and *in* which represented 11 of the subcategories revealed by the corpus analysis. The method was basically an organizing exercise in which participants considered the 177 phrases, grouped the uses into smaller categories, and offered world-body explanations for their groupings. The intervention for each group lasted less than 2 hours.

As a first step, a subset of the target non-spatial uses of *in* and *on* were presented to the participants in a randomized order and they were asked to check the instances they were familiar with. Participants indicated they were familiar with some uses, generally high frequency phrases. All reported that "they had no mnemonic rules for remembering uses of the two prepositions, did not know why *in* or *on* was used in a particular context or the other" (Falck, this volume).

Next, the experimenter guided the learners through a discussion emphasizing how bodily experiences in interaction with the external world are crucial for describing abstract concepts and relationships, such as temporal relationships represented in terms of spatial relations, e.g., the future is in front. The experimenter then led a brief discussion of a few sample phrases representing the embodied meaning categories she had established in earlier analyses (Falck 2014), accompanied by diagrams. For instance, participants were presented with phrases such as *What's going on in your head?*, *Keep this in mind*, and *I have an uneasy feeling in my gut* and were asked to find patterns or commonalities among the phrases. Under guided discussion, the participants came to the conclusion that the language locates feelings in the body, while thoughts or memories are in the head. In both cases, the body and head were treated like containers. Next, this category of *in* instances was contrasted with a set of *on* instances, for instance, *shame on* somebody and *imposing on* someone. The experimenter noted these instances had to do with things that are difficult for someone. This was a starting point for talking about how our experiences of physical burdens are reflected in uses such as these. Discussion was accompanied by a diagram intended to illustrate cognitive burdens on people.

After this preliminary discussion, the participants were encouraged to puzzle out the underlying categories for the 177 uses of *on* and *in*. A key part of this discussion was learners suggesting commonalities of experience which justified their groupings. They discussed, gestured, and drew pictures to help sort their uses and support their groupings. The sessions were recorded and the participants' comments along with short surveys were used to determine learning. The results showed that the participants increased in their ability to categorize the uses in terms of embodied similarities. Their categories were very similar to those found through the researcher's corpus analysis. Falck notes that with each new category, the participants had more comments and became more creative in finding experiential explanations for the uses. For instance, "one learner made a drawing of a comet coming towards the ground to illustrate *a great impact on*, and several of them made drawings of [...] dashed lines from people's eyes onto some other object to illustrate *focus on*" (Falck, this volume). Falck further reports that the participants demonstrated enthusiasm for the method and expressed desire for more grammar teaching involving creative discovery of body-world knowledge. At the end of the sessions, 7 out of 9 participants rated themselves as having a clearer understanding of when to use *in* and *on*.

Thus, Falck's study presents us with a rich example of how embodied experience and embodied semantics can provide potent tools for learning difficult polysemous items. Further, the study offers an impressive example of languaging (Swain 2006) in which overt discussion of language which previously seemed arbitrary to these young learners can be revealed to be systematic and meaningful. For these learners, tackling the polysemy of English prepositions became a game rather than a mindless memorization task.

## Concluding remarks

We began this essay by noting that we are in a particularly exciting time for SLA research and L2 teaching. For the authors gathered here, the emergence of Cognitive Linguistics – a theory of language which rests upon and is aligned with fundamental discoveries about human cognition and its reflection in language – is an important contributor to this sense of excitement. Collectively the authors provide a compelling answer to the question, "What is Applied Cognitive Linguistics?", by illustrating how many of the key, distinctive principles of CL can successfully be applied to investigations of language, language learning, and language teaching. For instance, through use of corpora and naturally occurring language, all the contributions illustrate the fundamental position that language is usage-based and that the purpose of language use is to make meaning. Some (e.g., Achard, Eskildsen, Wulff et al., and Lemmens and Perez) mine this orientation through careful analysis of how and under which circumstances particular lexical and grammatical patterns are employed in discourse (both L1 and L2), with impressive results. For others (e.g., Dancygier and Moder, Dolgova Jacobsen, White, Kissling et al., Zhao et al., and Falck), the concept that all linguistic units are employed in particular contexts and for the purpose of making meaning provided the basis for new, more precise analyses of target lexical-grammatical phenomena, which, in turn, led to more effective pedagogical treatments. Their research provides a platform for reconceptualizing what in language is systematic and teachable, as opposed to arbitrary and only open to rote memorization. A second tenet endorsed by the authors is that all language units are meaningful. This tenet is well captured in the notion of constructions, recurring form-meaning pairings; the studies offer fresh insights into how constructionism plays out at the word, sentence, and discourse levels. A key contribution is how an emphasis on constructions, rather than, for instance, isolated words, allows for accurate, effective presentation of such complex grammatical patterns as conditionals. Finally, the research in this collection is particularly robust as it includes new analyses of several languages, such as Dutch, French, German, and Spanish, as well as English. Moreover, the L2 learners under investigation represent native speakers of Chinese, Dutch, English, French, German, Spanish, and Swedish, thus allowing for deepening of our understanding of cross-linguistics issues such as the nature of L1 transfer, as well as demonstrating the applicability of the CL paradigm to learners of various L1 backgrounds.

In sum, the contributions to this volume give us a rich array of applications of CL tenets to the investigation of complex lexical-grammatical forms, L2 learning trajectories, cross-linguistic typologies, and pedagogical treatments across several languages. The work offers a vigorous endorsement for SLA researchers and practitioners to infuse their endeavors with a CL perspective.

# References

Barlow, Michael & Suzanne Kemmer. 2000. *Usage-based models of language*. Stanford: CSLI.
Barsalou, Lawrence W. 2016. On staying grounded and avoiding Quixotic dead ends. *Psychonomic Bulletin & Review* 23(4). 1122–1142.
Behrens, Heine & Stefan Pfänder. 2016. *Experience counts: Frequency effects in language*. Berlin: Walter de Gruyter.
Beréndi, Márta, Szilvia Csábi & Zoltán Kövecses. 2008. Using conceptual metaphors and metonymies in vocabulary teaching. In Frank Boers & Seth Lindstromberg (eds.), *Cognitive linguistics approaches to teaching vocabulary and phraseology*, 65–99. Berlin: Mouton de Gruyter.
Bergen, Benjamin K. 2012. *Louder than words: The new science of how the mind makes meaning*. New York: Basic Books.
Boers, Frank. 2000. Metaphor awareness and vocabulary retention. *Applied Linguistics* 21. 553–571.
Boers, Frank & Murielle Demecheleer. 1998. A cognitive semantic approach to teaching prepositions. *ELT Journal* 52(3). 197–204.
Boers, Frank & Seth Lindstromberg (eds.). 2008. *Cognitive linguistic approaches to teaching vocabulary and phraseology*. Berlin & New York: Mouton de Gruyter.
Buescher, Kimberly & Susan Strauss. 2015. A cognitive linguistic analysis of French prepositions *à, dans*, and *en* and a sociocultural theoretical approach to teaching them. In Kyoko Masuda, Carlee Arnett & Angela Labarca (eds.), *Cognitive linguistics and sociocultural theory*, 155–181. Berlin: Mouton de Gruyter.
Bybee, Joan. 2008. Usage-based grammar and second language acquisition. In Peter Robinson & Nick C. Ellis (eds.), *Handbook of Cognitive Linguistics and Second Language Acquisition*, 216–236. New York & London: Routledge.
Bybee, Joan. 2010. *Language, usage and cognition*. New York: Cambridge University Press.
Cadierno, Teresa. 2008. Learning to talk about motion in a foreign language. In Peter Robinson & Nick C. Ellis (eds.), *Handbook of cognitive linguistics and second language acquisition*, 239–275. New York & London: Routledge.
Cadierno, Teresa, Iraide Ibarretxe-Antuñano & Alberto Hijazo-Gascón. 2016. Semantic categorization of placement verbs in L1 and L2 Danish and Spanish. *Language Learning* 66. 191–223.

Cadierno, Teresa & Peter Robinson. 2009. Language typology, task complexity and the development of L2 lexicalization patterns for describing motion events. *Annual Review of Cognitive Linguistics* 6. 245–277.
Cadierno, Teresa & Søren W. Eskildsen (eds.). 2015. *Usage-based perspectives on second language learning*. Berlin: Mouton de Gruyter.
Cadierno, Teresa & Søren W. Eskildsen. 2016. *Usage-based perspectives on second language learning*. Berlin & New York: Mouton de Gruyter.
Celce-Murcia, Marianna & Diane Larsen-Freeman. 2015. *The grammar book: An ESL/EFL teacher's course*, 3rd edn. Boston, MA: Heinle ELT.
Christophersen, Paul. 1939. *The articles: A study of their theory and use in English*. Copenhagen: Munksgaard.
Croft, William & D. Alan Cruse. 2004. *Cognitive linguistics*. Cambridge: Cambridge University Press.
Csabi, Szilvia. 2004. A cognitive linguistic view of polysemy in English and its implications for teaching. In Michel Achard & Susanne Niemeier (eds.), *Cognitive linguistics, second language acquisition, and foreign language teaching*, 233–256. Berlin: Mouton de Gruyter
Curry, Kaitlin. 2010. ¿Pero Para? ¿Por Qué? The application of the principled polysemy model to *por* and *para*. Washington, DC: Georgetown University MA thesis.
Daems, Jocelyne, Eline Zenner, Kris Heylen, Dirk Speelman & Hubert Cuyckens (eds.). 2015. *Change of paradigms – New paradoxes: Recontextualizing language and linguistics*. Berlin: Mouton de Gruyter.
Dancygier, Barbara & Eve Sweetser. 2000. Construction with *if*, *since*, and *because*: Causality, epistemic stance and clause order. In Elizabeth Couper-Kuhlen & Bernd Kortmann (eds.), *Cause-condition-concession-contrast: Cognitive and discourse perspectives*, 111–142. Berlin: Mouton de Gruyter.
Dancygier, Barbara & Eve Sweetser. 2005. *Mental spaces in grammar: Conditional constructions*. Cambridge: Cambridge University Press.
De Knop, Sabine & René Dirven. 2008. Motion and location events in German, French and English. In Sabine De Knop & Teun de Rycker (eds.), *Cognitive approaches to pedagogical grammar: A volume in honour of Rene Dirven*, 295–324. New York: Mouton de Gruyter.
De Knop, Sabine & Gaëtanelle Gilquin (eds.). 2016. *Applied construction grammar*. Berlin: Mouton de Gruyter.
Ellis, Nick C. & Teresa Cadierno. 2009. Constructing a second language – Introduction to the special section. *Annual Review of Cognitive Linguistics* 7(1). 111–139
Ellis, Nick C. & Stefanie Wulff. 2015. Second language acquisition. In Ewa Dabrowska & Dagmar Divjak (eds.), *Handbook of Cognitive Linguistics*, 409–431. Berlin & New York: Mouton de Gruyter.
Ellis, Nick C., Ute Römer & Matthew Brook O'Donnell. 2016. *Usage-based approaches to language acquisition and processing: Cognitive and corpus investigations of construction grammar*. Malden, MA: Wiley-Blackwell
Eskildsen, Søren W. & Johannes Wagner. 2015. Embodied L2 construction learning. *Language Learning* 65. 419–448.
Eskildsen, Søren W., Teresa Cadierno & Peiwen Li. 2015. On the development of motion constructions in four learners of L2 English. In Teresa Cadierno & Søren W. Eskildsen (eds.), *Usage-based perspectives on second language learning*, 207–232. Berlin: Mouton de Gruyter.
Fauconnier, Gilles. 1994 [1985]. *Mental spaces: Aspects of meaning construction in natural language*. Cambridge: Cambridge University Press.

Fauconnier, Gilles. 1997. *Mappings in thought and language*. Cambridge: Cambridge University Press.

Fauconnier, Gilles & Eve Sweetser (eds.). 1996. *Spaces, worlds, and grammar*. Chicago: University of Chicago Press.

Fauconnier, Gilles & Mark Turner. 1998. Conceptual integration networks. *Cognitive Science* 22 (1). 133–187.

Fauconnier, Gilles & Mark Turner. 2000. Compression and global insight. *Cognitive Linguistics* 11. 283–304.

Fauconnier, Gilles & Mark Turner. 2002. *The way we think: conceptual blending and the mind's hidden complexities*. New York: Basic books.

Fillmore, Charles J. 1982. Frame semantics. In Linguistics Society of Korea (eds.), *Linguistics in the morning calm. Selected papers from SICOL-1981*, 111–137. Seoul: Hanshin.

Fillmore, Charles. 1990. Epistemic stance and grammatical form in English conditional sentences. *CLS* 26. 137–162.

Gibbs, Raymond W., Jr. 2006a. *Embodiment and cognitive science*. Cambridge: Cambridge University Press.

Gibbs, Raymond W. 2015. Metaphor. In Ewa Dąbrowska & Dagmar Divjak (eds.), *Handbook of cognitive linguistics*, 167–189. Berlin: De Gruyter Mouton.

Goldberg, Adele. 1995. *Constructions: A construction grammar approach to argument structure*. Chicago: University of Chicago Press.

Grady, Joseph. 1997. *Foundations of meaning: Primary metaphors and primary scenes*. Berkeley, CA: University of California dissertation.

Grady, Joseph. 1999. A typology of motivation for conceptual metaphor: Correlation vs. resemblance. In Raymond W. Gibbs and Gerard J. Steen (eds.), *Metaphor in cognitive linguistics*, 79–100. Amsterdam: John Benjamins.

Gries, Stefan Th. & Stephanie Wulff. 2005. Do foreign language learners also have constructions? Evidence from priming, sorting, and corpora. *Annual Review of Cognitive Linguistics* 3. 182–200.

Johansson Falck, Marlene. 2014. Temporal prepositions explained: Cross-linguistic analysis of English and Swedish unit of time landmarks. *Cognitive Linguistic Studies* 1(2). 271–288.

Kovescses, Zoltan. 2010. *Metaphor: A practical intoruduction*. New York: Oxford University Press.

Lakoff, George. 1987. *Women, fire and dangerous things*. Chicago: The University of Chicago Press.

Lakoff, George & Mark Johnson. 1999. *Philosophy in the Flesh*. New York: Basic Books.

Lam, Yvonne. 2009. Applying Cognitive Linguistics to teaching Spanish prepositions *por* and *para*. *Language Awareness* 18(1). 2–18.

Langacker, Ronald. 1987. *Foundations of cognitive grammar*. Vol. 1. *Theoretical prerequisites*. Stanford: Stanford University Press.

Langacker, Ronald. 1991. *Foundations of cognitive grammar*. Vol. 2. *Descriptive application*. Stanford: Stanford University Press.

Langacker, Ronald. 2008. *Cognitive grammar: A basic introduction*. Oxford: Oxford University Press.

Larsen-Freeman, Dianne. 2015. Research into practice: Grammar learning and teaching. *Language Teaching* 48(2). 263–280. Cambridge University Press.

Lieven, Elena. 2016. Usage-based approaches to language development: Where do we go from here? *Language and Cognition* (special issue on Usage-based approaches to language and language learning) 8.

Lindstromberg, Seth. 2010. *English prepositions explained*. Amsterdam: John Benjamins.
Mahon, Bradford Z. & Gregory Hickok (eds.). 2016. Arguments about the nature of concepts: Symbols, embodiment, and beyond [Special Issue]. *Psychonomic Bulletin & Review* 23(4).
Negueruela, Eduardo & James Lantolf. 2006. Concept-based instruction and the acquisition of L2 Spanish. In Rafael Salaberry & Barbara Lafford (eds.), *The art of teaching Spanish: Second language acquisition from research to praxis*, 79–102. Washington DC: Georgetown University Press.
Nerlich, Brigitte, Zazie Todd & David D. Clarke (eds.). 2003. *Polysemy: Flexible patterns of meaning in mind and language*. Berlin & New York: Mouton de Gruyter.
Ortega, Lourdes, Andrea Tyler, Hae In Park & Mariko Uno (eds.). 2016. *The usage-based study of language learning and multilingualism*. Washington, DC: Georgetown University Press.
Pinto, Derrin & Scott Rex. 2006. The acquisition of the Spanish prepositions *por* and *para* in a classroom setting. *Hispania* 89(3). 611–622.
Radden, Günter & René Dirven. 2007. *Cognitive English grammar*. Amsterdam: John Benjamins Publishing.
Robinson, Peter & Nick C. Ellis. 2008. Introduction. In Peter Robinson & Nick C. Ellis (eds.), *Handbook of cognitive linguistics and second language acquisition*, 1–23. New York & London: Routledge.
Rogers, Timothy T. & Michael M. Wolmetz (eds.). 2016. Conceptual knowledge representation: A cross-section of current research [Special Issue]. *Cognitive Neuropsychology* 33(3–4).
Rosch, Eleanor H. 1978. Principles of categorization. In Eleanor H. Rosch & Barbara B. Lloyd (eds.), *Cognition and categorization*, 27–48. Hillsdale, NJ: Lawrence Erlbaum.
Rumelhart, David. 1981. *Understanding understanding*. La Jolla, CA: University of California. Center for human processing.
Rumelhart, David E. & James L. McClelland. 1982. An interactive activation model of context effects in letter perception: II. The contextual enhancement effect and some tests and extensions of the model. *Psychological Review* 89(1). 60–94.
Russell, Bertrand. 1905. On denoting. *Mind* 14(56). 479–493.
Sanz, Cristina. 2015. Personal communication. Professor of Spanish, Georgetown University.
Slobin, Dan I. 2004. The many ways to search for a frog: Linguistic typology and the expression of motion events. In Sven Strömqvist & Ludo Verhoeven (eds.), *Relating events in narrative: Typological and contextual perspectives*, 219–257. Mahwah, NJ: Lawrence Erlbaum Associates.
Spivey, Michael. 2008. *The continuity of mind*. New York: Oxford University Press.
Swain, Merrill. 2006. Languaging, agency, and collaboration in advanced second language learning. In Heidi Byrnes (eds.), *Advanced language learning: The contribution of Halliday and Vygotsky*, 95–108. London: Continuum.
Talmy, Leonard. 2000. *Towards a cognitive semantics*. Cambridge, MA: MIT Press.
Taylor, John R. 2002. *Cognitive grammar*. Oxford: Oxford University Press.
Tomasello, Michael. 2003. *Constructing a language: A usage-based theory of language acquisition*. Cambridge, Massachusetts: Harvard University Press.
Tyler, Andrea. 2012. *Applying cognitive linguistics to second language learning: Theoretical basics and empirical evidence*. London: Routledge.
Tyler, Andrea, Charles Mueller & Vu Ho. 2010a. Applying cognitive linguistics to learning the semantics of English *to*, *for*, and *at*: An experimental investigation. *Vigo International Journal of Applied Linguistics* 8. 181–206.

Tyler, Andrea, Charles Mueller & Vu Ho. 2010b. Applying cognitive linguistics to instructed L2 learning: The English modals. *AILA Review* 23. 30–49.

Tyler, Andrea and Lourdes Ortega. 2016. Usage-based approaches to language and language learning: An introduction to the special issue. *Language and Cognition* 8. 335–345 doi:10.1017/langcog.2016.15

Tyler, Andrea & Vyvyan Evans. 2001. Reconsidering prepositional polysemy networks: The case of *over*. *Language* 77(4). 724–765.

Tyler, Andrea & Vyvyan Evans. 2003. *The semantics of English prepositions: spatial scenes, cognition, and the experiential basis of meaning*. Cambridge: Cambridge University Press.

Wilson, Paul & Richard C. Anderson. 1986. What they don't know will hurt them: The role of prior knowledge in comprehension. In Judith Orasanu (eds.), *Reading comprehension: From research to practice*, 31–48. Hillsdale, NJ: Erlbaum.

# 1 Categories and constructions in context

Michel Achard
# Teaching usage and concepts: Toward a cognitive pedagogical grammar

## 1 Introduction

Despite a large amount of attention over the past forty years, the contribution of linguistic models to the teaching of grammar has been less than optimal. There are two main reasons for this unfortunate state of affairs. First, the opinions of linguists about matters of language teaching are easy to discount because they have notoriously failed to reach a consensus on the very nature of grammatical phenomena. Second, linguists have seldom made the effort to explicitly spell out the pedagogical ramifications of their theoretical positions, which makes it difficult for instructors to create appropriate activities in the classroom. This chapter argues that the adoption of the cognitive linguistics view of language in the second language classroom would be highly beneficial for two main reasons. First, the recognition of different types of "constructions" (Goldberg 1995, 2006; Langacker 1987, 1991, 2005) considerably broadens the scope of grammatical instruction. Second, the model affords remarkable pedagogical flexibility by making available to instructors two complementary strategies of grammatical presentation, namely "grammar as usage" and "grammar as concepts".

Given the lack of durable influence of linguistic models over second language instruction, it may appear presumptuous to imagine that cognitive linguistics stands a chance to succeed where many others have failed. There are, however, at least two main reasons to hope that the model will make a more positive and lasting impact. The first one is its own interdisciplinary nature that renders collaboration between neighboring fields necessary: "Because CL holds that the basic units of language representation are constructions–form-meaning mappings, conventionalized in the child L1 learner and adult L2 learner speech communities, and gradually entrenched as language knowledge in the child L1 or adult L2 learner's mind–work within this approach links and builds with that in a range of research areas in Cognitive Science" (Robinson and Ellis 2008: 4). This is particularly true in the case of second language pedagogy because the mechanisms that contribute to entrenchment are not opaque and immune to observation but part of general cognitive abilities that can be strengthened by

**Michel Achard,** Rice University

instruction. Consequently, the model's possible pedagogical applications are important for its own theoretical plausibility: "Although extensive pedagogical application remains a long-term goal, I regard its effectiveness in language teaching to be an important empirical test for the framework" (Langacker 2008: 66). Second, and perhaps most importantly, the learnability of the model has already been tested with a broad range of phenomena that include among others polysemy in general and the polysemy of prepositions in particular (e.g., Verspoor and Lowie 2003; Tyler 2012; Tyler and Evans 2004; Tyler, Mueller, and Ho 2010a, Buescher and Strauss 2015), metaphor and metonymy (e.g., Boers 2000; Beréndi, Csábi, and Kövecses 2008), and modality (Tyler, Mueller, and Ho 2010b). Space considerations do not permit an exhaustive presentation of the findings of these studies, but they clearly attest to the beneficial influence of cognitive linguistic principles for second language pedagogy.

The overall orientation of cognitive linguistics and its application to specific constructions clearly indicate that the model can make a general and lasting contribution to second language instruction, but it will not reach its full pedagogical potential until its explanatory power has been demonstrated and the consequences of its positions are clearly specified. The remaining sections use the example of French impersonals to illustrate the profound effect of the cognitive linguistics model for second language grammar teaching. First, it demonstrates how instructors can broaden the scope of grammatical instruction by recognizing two constructions that are not typically taught because they lack distinctive morphosyntactic features. Second, it shows how the two pedagogical strategies of teaching grammar as usage and teaching grammar as concepts combine to capture the complex nature of grammatical phenomena and gives students the ability of "reconceiving grammar" (Larsen Freeman 2015: 272–274) from a static set of arbitrary rules to a dynamic system that allows them to adjust their contributions to the specific demands of the interactional context.

This chapter is structured in the following manner. Section two briefly introduces the notion of constructions and illustrates how they can be identified in the absence of distinguishing morphosyntax. Section three presents the two complementary views of grammar as usage and grammar as concepts. Section four discusses the pedagogical implications of the linguistic analyses for the second language classroom. Section five concludes this chapter.

## 2 Constructions and their identification

The primary function of language is to allow speakers to symbolically represent the world around them, and to that effect, it provides them with "an open-ended set of linguistic signs or expressions, each of which associates a semantic representation of some kind to a phonological representation" (Langacker 1987: 11). The grammar of a language is thus best described as a vast inventory of form-meaning mappings or "constructions" (Goldberg 1995, 2006; Langacker 1987, 1991, 2005). Constructions vary greatly in their levels of generality and abstraction. Of particular interest to this chapter, grammatical constructions take the form of templatic schemas that capture the commonalities that exist across specific examples. For instance, expressions such as *great movie*, *long journey*, *small problem* and many others, are all sanctioned by the template [ADJ, N] which governs adjective placement in English. This grammatical template (also referred to as "rule" in a pedagogical context) therefore captures the generalities observable across a set of expressions, it fully reflects the structure of the expressions it schematizes, and can be used as template for the expression of novel conceptualizations. Importantly, cognitive linguistics holds that grammatical templates are also meaningful, even though their meaning is generally more abstract than that of the expressions that instantiate them.

The task of the second language instructor therefore consists in providing their students with a sufficiently large set of native constructions to express their rich and subtle conceptualizations. The ultimate goal is obviously for that set to resemble the native inventory as closely as possible, so that students' linguistic choices may mirror native selections in similar situations. Teaching the massive set of constructions that compose the target grammar involves two main difficulties that cognitive linguists can help mitigate. The first one consists in identifying the relevant constructions, the second involves the selection of the right strategy to introduce them. The remainder of this section is concerned with the identification of constructions not usually described in grammar manuals, the selection of a specific grammatical strategy to introduce different kinds of constructions is addressed in the next section.

## 2.1 Identifying two French impersonal constructions[1]

Constructions have been previously described as form-meaning pairings. The most identifiable among them therefore contain distinctive form. For instance, the subjunctive morphology in Romance languages sets that construction apart from all other verb inflections. These very general constructions generally provide the core of the grammatical curriculum in the second language classroom

---

[1] All the examples in the remainder of this chapter are from Achard (2015).

because the acquisition of their specific morphology represents an important pedagogical goal. Not all constructions, however, can be identified by their morphology alone. For instance, both French reflexive (*il s'est coupé* 'he cut himself') and middle (*le verre s'est cassé* 'the glass broke') constructions contain the pronoun *se* 'itself', and therefore need to be distinguished by additional criteria. Furthermore, a large number of constructions simply do not possess distinctive morphology since the patterns they constitute can only be identified by the frequent co-occurrence of their individual components.[2] One of cognitive linguistics earliest contributions to second language instruction concerned the systematic exploration of the meaning of syntactically distinct grammatical constructions. The remainder of this section introduces two examples from French to show that cognitive analyses also benefit second language instruction by identifying the constructions that are not morphologically distinct. This is particularly important because it considerably increases the students' target language resources and brings their production closer to native range.

### 2.1.1 Middle impersonals

The French structure illustrated in the examples in (1)–(3) meets the criteria of a construction introduced at the beginning of this section because its form, characterized specifically by the presence of the middle voice marker *se* 'itself', maps onto a distinctive meaning that emphasizes the highest possible level of generality of the event that the predicate codes. More specifically, this "middle impersonal" construction (Achard 2015 Chapter 7) describes events that predictably occur whenever the right conditions are met. They are not restricted to a specific time, place, or participants, but universally available to a "generalized conceptualizer" (Langacker 2009: 115) in the appropriate circumstances:[3]

(1) *Il note que le pain sans levain est cuit sur des plaques de tôle et ressemble à de la galette ou aux crêpes de carnaval, que **le saucisson d'Arles se fait avec de la viande de mulet**.*
'He notes that yeast-free bread is cooked on flat metal sheets and resembles biscuits or the pancakes of carnival time; that the sausage from Arles is made [makes itself] with mule meat'.
(Durry, M. J. *Gérard de Nerval et le mythe*: 82)

---

[2] This is especially true for collocations. These types of constructions will not be considered in this chapter.
[3] I have argued in previous work that "French impersonals represent a coherent natural class because they systematically code highly general and predictable events available to anyone in

(2)  *Elle secoua la tête: "j'ai trente-sept ans et je ne connais aucun métier. Je peux me faire chiffonnière; et encore! – **Ça s'apprend**, un métier; rien ne t'empêche d'apprendre."*

'She shook her head: "I am thirty seven years old and I have no skills. I could be a rag picker, if that! – A trade, you can always learn it; nothing prevents you from learning"'.
(Beauvoir, S. de. *Les mandarins*: 283)

(3)  *Le crime du roi est en même temps péché contre l'ordre suprême. **Un crime se commet**, puis **se pardonne**, **se punit** ou **s'oublie**. Mais le crime de royauté est permanent [...]*

'The king's crime is at the same time a sin against the supreme order of things. A crime is committed, then it is forgiven, punished or forgotten. But the crime of royalty is permanent [...]'
(Camus, A. *L'homme révolté*: 151)

It is important to note that the generality of meaning that constitutes the semantic trademark of middle impersonals is not representative of middles generally. Semantically, the middle marker *se* 'itself' merely emphasizes the hybrid (agent-patient) role of the subject, and the great majority of middles lack the degree of generality characteristic of middle impersonals. For instance, the predicate in (4) describes a specific event that occurred at a precise time and place between uniquely identifiable participants, and is thus too specific to be interpreted as a middle impersonal:

---

the appropriate circumstances, the occurrence of which cannot be imputed to a specific, well-delineated source" (Achard 2015: 15). Consequently, the impersonal class should include:

> any structure that describes events at the highest level of generalization and predictability, regardless of their morphological realization. As initial selection criteria, let us suggest that any structure should be considered impersonal provided that (1) it defocuses or backgrounds the agent of the predicate, and (2) its predicate describes a situation at a degree of stability and prediction that makes it available to a generalized conceptualizer, or in other words virtually anyone in the appropriate situation.
> (Achard 2015: 16–17)

According to this definition, in addition to the universally recognized *il* construction, the category should also include some demonstrative (*ça*) constructions as well as the middle (*se*) and indefinite (*on*) constructions presented in this chapter.

(4) *Hero, brusquement: Tu m'as compris! (Il serrait son verre dans sa main,* **le verre se casse**.*) Ils regardent le verre tous deux dans la main de Héro qui dit doucement. Excuse-moi, mon vieux. J'aime casser.*

'Hero, suddenly: You understood me! (He was holding his glass in his hand, the glass breaks [itself].) Both of them look at the glass in Hero's hand, and Hero says softly: Excuse me, Old Man. I like to break [things]'.[4]
(Anouilh, J. *La répétition: ou, l'amour puni*: 75)

Because middle impersonals share middle morphology with other middle constructions but are distinguished by their semantics of maximal level of generality, their precise identification requires further investigation. It is worth noting that French middle predicates become increasingly more general as the affected entity (the subject of the predicate) becomes more and more "responsible" (Van Oosten 1977) for the occurrence of the process the predicate describes. The notion of responsibility is illustrated in (5) where the agent of the writing process is obviously the author, but the very topic of his work strongly contributes to its success. In this sense, the book itself may be claimed to be responsible for the easy writing process:

(5) *Mais tu as eu une critique étonnante, dit Louis d'un ton encourageant; il sourit. "Il faut dire que tu es tombé sur un sujet en or; pour ça tu es verni; quand on tient un pareil sujet,* **le livre s'écrit** *tout seul."*

'But your reviews were surprising, Louis said in an encouraging tone; he smiles. "You have to admit you came across a golden topic; you were lucky that way; with a topic like that, the book writes itself"'.
(Beauvoir, S. de. *Les mandarins*: 249)

More generally, while the agent internal to the lexical semantic structure of middle predicates brings about the process that this predicate codes, it may be assisted, in crucial ways, by characteristics intrinsic to the affected entity. This responsibility of the affected entity neutralizes the impact of individual agents on the described process and thus favors the latter's predictability and generality. Importantly for the purposes of this chapter, middles exhibit this particular feature in two specific environments that therefore constitute two middle impersonal constructional islands (Achard 2015).

---

**4** In Achard (2015 chapter 7) human activities predicates in (1) are distinguished from the spontaneous predicates in (4). This chapter only considers human activities predicates.

In the first one illustrated in (1)–(3), the process expressed by the predicate is constitutive of the subject in the sense that it represents an integral part of the definition of the entity that the subject codes. In (1), mule meat is part of the recipe for the *saucisson d'Arles*, an ingredient without which the latter does not deserve its name. Similarly, an apprenticeship period is part of the definition of a trade in (2), and the narrative purpose of the passage in (3) precisely consists in providing the definition of a crime in order to emphasize the heinous nature of the crime of royalty. The way in which the verbal process is included in the subject's semantic definition constitutes the pragmatic feature that groups together this first middle impersonal construction.

In the second constructional island illustrated in (6)–(8), the occurrence of the predicate is also fully predictable because it is required by a set of social norms or conventions. In this configuration, the predicates pertain to the socially acceptable way of performing certain activities, and because social norming applies to everyone, the process that the predicate codes is universally available to a generalized conceptualizer.

(6) *Il n'est pas d'usage de présenter du vin:* **il ne se boit** *qu'aux repas et au cabaret.*

'It is not customary to serve wine: It is only drunk during meals or in a bar'.
(T'Serstevens, A. *L'itinéraire espagnol*: 77)

(7) **"L'apéritif se prend** *obligatoirement sur la terrasse du Continental, à même le trottoir", raconte Lucien Bodard dans l'Humiliation.*

'"Drinks before meals have to be taken on the Continental's patio, right on the sidewalk", Lucien Bodard tells us in the Humiliation'.
(*Le Monde*)

(8) *Dans les livres, les gens se font des déclarations d'amour, de haine, ils mettent leur cœur en phrases; dans la vie, jamais on ne prononce de paroles qui pèsent.* **Ce qui "se dit"** *est aussi réglé que* **ce qui "se fait"**.

'In books, people claim their love or hatred for each other, they pour their hearts in their words; in life, no one ever pronounces words with any weight. What "is said [says itself]" is as tightly regulated as what "is done [does itself]"'.
(Beauvoir, S. de. *Mémoires d'une jeune fille rangée*: 119)

The examples in (6) and (7) describe the social conventions that govern the actions of drinking wine and having a drink before lunch or dinner respectively.

The quotation marks around *se dire* and *se faire* in (8) represent the highly conventionalized character of these predicates that describe the strict social codes that govern people's words and actions. Their deontic character is obvious. The example in (8) does not describe what people do and say, but what is socially acceptable to say and do. The deontic character of the predicate provides the semantic specificity of the second middle impersonal construction.

### 2.1.2 Indefinite impersonals

The indefinite impersonal construction illustrated in (9) is very close in meaning to the middle impersonals introduced in the preceding section. The predicate also describes a maximally general process available to everyone in the appropriate circumstances. In (9), for instance, the difficulty of finding a place to camp is shared by everyone traveling through Spain.

(9) **On ne trouve pas toujours facilement, en Espagne, un endroit pour camper,** *à cause de l'absence de bois, et de la culture intensive.*
'One cannot always easily find a place to camp in Spain, because of the lack of forests, and extensive agriculture'.
(T'Serstevens, A. *L'itinéraire espagnol*: 16)

Here again, this high level of generality is not characteristic of *on* constructions in general because numerous instances are far too specific to be generally available and hence called impersonal. This is illustrated in (10) where the referent of *on* is clearly identified as the two conversationalists in the bar. These participants are solely responsible for their interaction, and the latter cannot be expected to occur outside the particular time and place of the meeting. The example in (11) shows that even when the pronoun's referent is unidentified, it can nonetheless be uniquely responsible for the process the predicate describes (the finding event). Consequently, *trouver* 'find' in (11) also describes a specific process that occurred at a precise time and space between well-delineated participants, one of which is simply left unidentified.[5]

---

[5] These constructions behave as functional passives. See Achard (2015 chapter 8) for discussion.

(10) *J'envoyai un mot au jeune Bresson que je retrouvai un soir vers six heures au Stryx;* **on parla de Jacques**, *qu'il admirait; mais le bar était désert et il n'arriva rien.*

'I sent a note to young Bresson whom I met one evening around 6 o'clock at the Stryx; we talked about Jack whom he admired; but the bar was empty and nothing happened'.
(Beauvoir, S. de. *Mémoires d'une jeune fille rangée*: 268)

(11) *Me parle d'un jeune homme qui n'a pas pu continuer la lutte et qui s'est tué en absorbant une grosse quantité de gardénal, trop grosse, semble-t-il, car la mort a été longue à venir.* **On a trouvé** *dans sa poche des lettres et un chapelet* [...]

'[He] talks to me about a young man who couldn't continue the fight and killed himself by taking a large quantity of gardenal, too large a dose it seems, because it took a long time for him to die. Some letters and a rosary were found in his pocket [...]'
(Green, J. *Journal*. T. 5. 1946–1950: 221)

Indefinites become impersonal when the referent of the pronoun *on* is inclusive of all the members of a given community. This occurs when the pronoun's referent is not only unidentified, but also cannot be held responsible for the occurrence of the process the predicate describes. This ultimately general construal of the pronoun's referent is achieved by two kinds of conceptual configurations that present some conceptualizer's position as representative of a group of unlimited size.[6] The first configuration, where *on*'s referent is presented as a homogenous mass inclusive of all humans, describes stable characteristics of a community that everyone experiences in a similar manner. The yearly cycle of seasons in (12) or our failed attempts to eliminate misfortune in (13) are described as conditions homogenously experienced by everyone and thus generally available.

---

[6] These two conceptual configurations ultimately result from the social nature of human cognition (Tomasello 1999, 2003). According to Tomasello, the cognitive breakthrough that enabled human culture to distinguish itself from that of other mammals and primates stems from the realization that conspecifics are sentient beings very similar to the self. Consequently, all sorts of analogical conclusions can be drawn concerning others on the basis of what each of us experiences for her/himself. Our own internal landscape therefore constitutes a legitimate guide to predict, and possibly influence, other people's reactions, aspirations, motivations, and fears. This shared conceptualization of the world inside and outside of us allows us to recognize shared circumstances and express them as universal experiences.

(12) *Pendant quelque temps, il s'arrêta de travailler et réfléchit. Il aurait peint sur le motif si la saison s'y était prêtée. Malheureusement,* **on allait entrer dans l'hiver,** *il était difficile de faire du paysage avant le printemps.*

'He stopped working and thought for a while. He would have painted on the motif if the season had been right. Unfortunately, winter was coming [one was about to enter winter], it was hard to paint landscapes before the spring'.
(Camus, A. *L'exil et le royaume*: 1646)

(13) *Oui,* **on sait ce que ça coûte la résignation,** *l'égoïsme: mais il y a longtemps qu'***on le sait,** *sans profit.* **On n'a jamais réussi à arrêter le malheur, on n'y réussira pas de si tôt,** *en tout cas pas de notre vivant.*

'Yes, we know [one knows] the price of resignation, selfishness: but we have [one has] known that for a long time, without any benefit. We have [one has] never succeeded in stopping misfortune, we [one] won't succeed anytime soon, at least not in our lifetime'.
(Beauvoir, S. de. *Les mandarins*: 205)

The second impersonal configuration treats individual experience as representative of a typically human and hence maximally general reaction. Voltaire obviously expresses his own opinion of Rousseau's work in (14), but his evaluation is all the more scathing as it is presented as the reaction that every human would inescapably experience upon reading the book. Similarly, the scene in (15) is viewed through the narrator's eyes, but it is presented as any observer placed in similar circumstances would invariably view it:

(14) *La lettre de Voltaire était légère, aimable et malicieuse à son habitude: "j'ai reçu, monsieur, votre nouveau livre contre le genre humain, je vous en remercie ... on n'a jamais tant employé d'esprit à vouloir nous rendre bêtes. Il prend envie de marcher à quatre pattes* **quand on lit votre ouvrage...*"*

'Voltaire's letter was customarily light, friendly and witty: "Sir, I have received your new book against humanity, I appreciate it ... no greater wit has ever been used making us look like animals. One feels like walking on all fours when one reads your work..."'
(Guéhenno, J. *Jean-Jacques*. T. 2: 112)

(15) *Pendant qu'elle déballait les tissus brodés, je m'approchai de la fenêtre;* **on apercevait, comme d'habitude, Notre-Dame et ses jardins**:
'While she was unloading the embroidered fabrics, I walked to the window; as usual, one could see Notre Dame and its gardens:'
(Beauvoir, S. de. *Les mandarins*: 493)

In this configuration, the generalization of experience is achieved by conjuring up a virtual referent for the sole purpose of illustrating the inescapability of the process the predicate describes. The statements in (14) and (15) have universal value because *on*'s referent does not have independent existence in reality, but represents every possible human reading Rousseau's book or experiencing the view of Notre Dame. They therefore differ from those presented in (12) and (13) in that they do not describe an observed stable characteristic representative of a community, but the natural, i.e., predictable, consequence of a given action. In other words, their generality is not achieved by the homogenization of the relevant referents into a mass-like entity, but by making one conceptualizer's experience representative for that of the entire community.

The middle and indefinite impersonals share important characteristics. Both represent well delineated sub-constructions that share morphology with the much larger middle and indefinite constructions and therefore need to be actively identified and taught. Before we can consider how they can be introduced in the second language classroom, however, the next section briefly introduces the kind of grammatical instruction that the adoption of the cognitive linguistics view of language entails.

# 3 Aspects of a cognitive pedagogical grammar

Language teachers can legitimately wonder about the best possible implementation of the cognitive linguistics model in the classroom because the different tenets that compose it naturally lead them into different directions. This section introduces two possible pedagogical orientations that focus on two different aspects the model naturally inspires. More precisely, the position that "grammar is usage" suggests an emergent, inductive, and implicit type of instruction, while the "grammar as concept" position promotes a deductive and explicit presentation of grammatical phenomena. These two strategies are not incompatible; they merely describe the multidimensional aspect of grammar as a socio-cognitive phenomenon. Their recognition and integration into "teaching construal" allows instructors to use different pedagogical strategies to focus on both aspects appropriately, and thus provide their students with the most comprehensive form of instruction.[7]

---

[7] The vocabulary used in the remainder of this chapter is borrowed from Langacker's Cognitive Grammar (henceforth CG; Langacker 1987, 1991, 2008) because it represents the most exhaustive model of grammatical description, but the ideas developed naturally extend to the entire cognitive linguistics movement.

The central tenet of CG is its usage-based orientation (see also Barlow and Kemmer 2000, Bybee 2001) in which usage shapes grammar. The most basic constructs of language are "usage events", namely instances of language use in which speakers make use of the symbolic tools language provides to structure their conceptualizations:

> It is not the linguistic system per se that constructs and understand novel expressions, but rather the language user, who marshals for this purpose the full panoply of available resources. In addition to linguistic units, these resources include such factors as memory, planning, problem solving ability, general knowledge, short- and long-term goals, as well as full apprehension of the physical, social, cultural, and linguistic context. An actual instance of language use, resulting in all these factors, constitutes what I will call a **usage event** (Langacker 2000: 9–10, emphasis in the original).

When trying to evaluate which pedagogical strategy best promotes grammatical knowledge, the very nature of usage events leads language instructors into two different directions depending on whether we focus on how generalizations (i.e. grammatical rules) emerge, or on the specific cognitive operations speakers perform when they select particular structures among all the possible candidates to express their conceptualization. This section focuses on these two crucial aspects of usage events in turn.

## 3.1 Grammar as usage

As was briefly mentioned in the previous sections, "usage events are the source of all linguistic units" (Langacker 2008: 220) because they provide the specific instances from which individual units arise and more abstract units emerge. More precisely, linguistic units are extracted from usage events by the processes of schematization and categorization. They are abstracted from the context of specific utterances, and "emerge via the progressive entrenchment of configurations that recur in a sufficient number of events to be established as cognitive routines" (Langacker 2008: 220). Importantly, since grammar emerges from usage, the frequency of specific linguistic forms, the collocations they favor, or their semantic prosody, to name just a few of the relevant criteria, fundamentally shape the way in which we mentally represent them. From the fully social and linguistic context of the specific usage events speakers hear and participate in, they gradually learn the set of conventionalized units that constitutes their linguistic system.

The emphasis on usage events provides the model with its "bottom up" orientation (Langacker 2000: 1). Linguistic patterns emerge as abstract schemas over actually occurring expressions. These schemas are not separate from their instantiations; they are immanent in them and merely represent another facet of speakers' grammatical knowledge. Importantly, the usage-based model is also "maximalist" (Langacker 2000: 1) because the speaker needs to learn both the generalized patterns and instantiations. Linguistic knowledge is therefore represented by a complex system of overlapping networks: "The vision that emerges is one of massive networks in which structures of varying degree of entrenchment, and representing different levels of abstraction, are linked together in relationships of categorization, composition, and symbolization" (Langacker 2000: 5). Importantly, linguistic knowledge incorporates the full range of these networks, from the most general to the particular: "Substantial importance is given to the actual use of the linguistic system and the speaker's knowledge of the full range of linguistic conventions, regardless of whether these conventions can be subsumed under more general statements" (Langacker 2000: 1).

**3.1.1 Teaching usage**

The recognition that grammatical patterns emerge out of usage has clear pedagogical implications. First, since no independent "language faculty" programs students to acquire grammatical structures in natural sequences (Krashen 1981), grammatical constructions need to be learned, and hence potentially taught. Furthermore, their instruction should not be fundamentally different from that of lexical items because grammatical patterns are also meaningful in and of themselves (Achard 2004). This is particularly important because teachers often reduce linguistic knowledge to structural knowledge separate from meaning and assume that actual language use naturally follows (Widdowson 1978: 49–60). Research within the usage-based tradition has shown that it is not the case. For example, I have argued elsewhere (Achard 2008) that the structural rules that French introductory textbooks propose in order to teach the distribution of definite and partitive articles do not reflect meaningful use in any satisfying manner, and therefore cannot help students develop the proper patterns of article use (in other words, the appropriate form-meaning mappings).

Second, since grammatical constructions generalize over specific instances, inductive instruction is likely to be particularly effective. Usage-based teaching helps learners recognize the constructions or patterns of form-meaning pairings by emphasizing the commonalities between their instances. Students are first exposed to a large number of instances, so that they can, in turn, understand the motivations for the specific groupings they have observed. Additionally, the fact that knowledge of a construction and its instantiations merely represents two alternative ways of accessing linguistic information (since schemas are immanent in their instances) makes it unlikely that students will find the metalinguistic vocabulary designed to describe grammatical constructions very helpful. In fact, taking a usage-based approach can help avoid the need to use this confusing jargon.

## 3.2 Grammatical constructions as concepts

The previous section focused on the emergence of grammatical constructions out of usage events. However, on the other hand, in order to perform usage events, speakers need to use constructions in specific ways. A complete understanding of the nature of grammar therefore also necessarily includes examining the way in which speakers use constructions to structure their conceptualizations.

The coding of a conceptualized scene with a linguistic expression is akin to categorization; the speaker's task consists in selecting from a range of alternatives the construction that best fits her conceptualization. If the target structures accord with the units regularly used by speakers of the target discourse community, they are fully sanctioned by the grammar. For instance, the description of the drinking vessel sitting on my desk as *mug* involves the selection of the unit 'mug' as the most appropriate to categorize the observed object. Since the target structure accords with one unit that exists in the language, it is fully sanctioned by the grammar. If no unit exists in the language to describe a conceptualization, speakers will select the closest conventionalized structure to partially sanction it. For example, if a group of children are playing soccer with a tin can, the decision to call that object *ball* emphasizes its relevance in the context of the game rather than its shape and everyday function. Novel creations extrapolate existing patterns to new instantiations. For instance, Langacker (1987: 72–73) points out that in the utterance *I don't like it, it's too apricoty*, the creation *apricoty* conforms to an existing schema extracted over many instances such as *nutty, salty, spicy*, etc. The expression *apricoty* recognizes the speaker's categorizing judgment that it is a well-formed expression coherent with a regular pattern.

All grammatical expressions regardless of their level of abstraction therefore serve a categorizing function. For instance, the decision to use an imperfect or preterit aspect in Spanish also represents a categorizing judgment of the internal structure of the conceptualized event. Because grammatical constructions allow the conventionalized structuration of specific aspects of the world, they can be considered linguistic concepts. Teaching a foreign language therefore essentially amounts to teaching a different conceptual system where students need to be introduced to the vast array of symbolic resources that the members of the target community use in their daily interactions.

### 3.2.1 Teaching concepts

The difficulties of teaching unfamiliar concepts are well known. The students' own semiotic system can interfere with the target system in unpredictable ways, and even when similar concepts exist in both languages, they often cover different semantic ranges. For example, French *canard* translates to English 'duck', but the lexical categories the terms evoke in their respective languages vary greatly. Both *canard* and 'duck' describe the animal and its meat, but in addition, in French *canard* possesses four other senses, namely i) a discordant musical note, ii) some erroneous piece of information, iii) a newspaper, iv) a sugar cube dipped into coffee or liquor sometimes given to children at the end of a meal. These same semantic extensions do not exist in English. Thus, despite the presence of 'duck' in their native system, English speakers need to learn the specific motivated extensions that constitute the French category.[8]

In terms of pedagogy, note that the kind of inductive exposition presented in the previous section is not particularly helpful because it is hard to see how prolonged exposure to numerous instances of the different senses would allow students to generalize the underlying system that motivates their common lexical label. Presenting each sense in isolation fares no better because it misses the point that the category is motivated by specific principles of meaning extension and those principles constitute an aspect of French grammar in their own rights. A more effective strategy of teaching the category as a conceptually motivated entity involves pointing out the strands between the different senses, or perhaps placing students in the position to identify them themselves. This entails teaching the multiple meanings of *canard* by pointing out that the category is bound together by our shared experiences interacting with ducks. By discussing the behaviors of these birds, students will notice that their sound motivates the 'discordant note' sense, and that the manner in which they dive for food constitutes the source of the 'sugar cube dipped in coffee or liquor' sense. The two final senses can be taught in the same manner. The 'discordant note' and 'erroneous piece of information' are connected by an analogy of dissonance, and 'erroneous piece of information' is related to 'newspaper' by metonymy.

---

[8] Note in Figure 1 that consistent with the family resemblances model (Wittgenstein 1953), not all senses are related to the central sense. Also note that the relation between the central cense (the animal) and its meat is an instance of categorization by schema because the meat is fully compatible with the animal's specifications. However, the other relations represent examples of categorization by prototype (indicated with a dashed arrow) because the targets of categorization are not fully compatible with the animal.

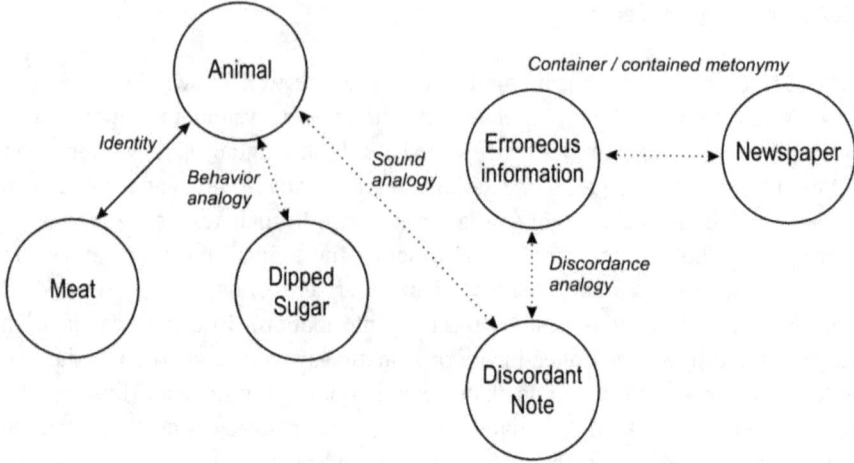

**Figure 1:** The *canard* 'duck' lexical category

Lexical categories are not usually difficult to teach because they are obviously meaningful and the expression of their semantic contribution directly draws on the students' knowledge of the world. Grammatical categories are more problematic because their semantic import is considerably more abstract and their motivation more difficult to precisely identify. The temptation is therefore great to strictly focus on their form, and teachers need to be reminded that learning new morphological forms is not sufficient for second language learners who need to understand the communicative intentions that motivate the use. More generally, "[s]econd language instruction is a matter of not only learning new forms but also internalizing new or reorganizing already existing concepts" (Negueruela and Lantolf 2006: 81) regardless of their level of complexity or abstraction. This is the case in the simple lexical example illustrated in Figure 1, but also for much more complex and abstract categories such as aspect selection in Spanish: "The key task for the learner is not so much to master the suffixes as to understand the meaning potential made available by the concept of aspect and to learn to manipulate this in accordance with particular communicative intentions" (Negueruela and Lantolf 2006: 82). In order to maximize students' ability to connect meaning and form, instructors are therefore encouraged to explicitly mention the conceptual range of specific grammatical morphemes: "Concept-based instruction supports explicit instruction in grammar to promote the learner's awareness and control over specific conceptual categories as they are linked to formal properties of language" (Negueruela and Lantolf 2006: 82).

The systematic investigation of the semantic import of grammatical constructions and the conditions that motivate the different senses of linguistic entities constitutes cognitive linguistics' strongest contribution to second language pedagogy. This is in particular the case in the domain of prepositional polysemy (Verspoor and Lowie 2003; Tyler 2012; Tyler and Evans 2004; Tyler, Mueller, and Ho 2010a, Buescher and Strauss 2015), and Tense Aspect Modality constructions (Tyler, Mueller, and Ho 2010b). The existing literature therefore clearly demonstrates the benefits of the cognitive linguistic assumptions and methods to teach well identified formal categories as concepts, but it is much more tacit about the model's usefulness to show students how grammatical patterns can be identified when they lack formal representation. The next sections argue that the identification of these patterns is best accomplished using the "grammar as usage" strategy, and that both "grammar as usage" and "grammar as concept" are needed for successful grammatical instruction.

## 3.3 Teaching construal: Complementary dimensions of grammatical instruction

It is important to bear in mind that a usage event is "an actual instance of language use, in all its complexity and specificity" (Langacker 2008: 220), and that this specificity crucially includes the social conditions of the utterance. The social dimension of language acquisition to the development of the linguistic system cannot be overstated. Tomasello (1999, 2003) successfully argued that the socio-pragmatic abilities of shared attention and imitative learning figure prominently among the factors that make linguistic development possible for children. For second language development, drawing on initial work by Vygotsky, Sociocultural theorists (Negueruela and Lantolf 2006) point to the importance of praxis, namely the space where instruction and development are drawn together "into an organic unity that arises in concrete practical activity" (Negueruela and Lantolf 2006: 80).

In the specific context of second language instruction, the classroom therefore becomes where the conditions that facilitate linguistic development have to be maximized: "the true test of a theory resides in its ability to promote development in the very sites where ordinary activity transpires, and this includes pedagogical activity in the school setting" (Negueruela and Lantolf 2006: 80). This clearly sets up the respective tasks of instructors and students since instruction is understood as "any directive which elicits new activity", and development as "the reorganization of consciousness through the activity" (Axel 1997: 131). Generally speaking, whatever topic is being taught, the goal of instructors is to guide the conceptual development of their students: "Schooled instruction is about developing control over theoretical concepts that are explicitly and coherently presented to learners as they are guided through a sequence of activities designed to prompt the necessary internalization of the relevant concepts" (Negueruela and Lantolf 2006: 80).

The preceding sections have shown that the new activity that the classroom context seeks to stimulate goes in two seemingly opposite directions. On the one hand, following the position that grammatical constructions arise as a matter of language use directs instructors toward an inductive and implicit instruction where students gradually infer rules as they have been exposed to a large number of instances. On the other hand, the recognition that grammatical categories are concepts that speakers use to categorize the world around them paints a different picture. Second language learners already possess a mature system in their own language, and perhaps the best way of stimulating the reorganization process by which they acquire the target system is to help them reason out the various steps that guide the selection of specific forms. In this view, effective grammatical instruction is therefore explicit, deductive, and often metalinguistic.

These opposite conclusions merely reflect the nature of language acquisition and the specificity of second language learners. Importantly, neither strategy used in isolation provides learners with all the help they need. "Grammar as usage" underestimates the difference between first and second language learning, the entrenched categories students bring to the L2 learning situations, as well as students' desire to understand the motivations of linguistic use. Consequently, even though implicit inductive grammatical instruction can effectively be incorporated in the classroom (Achard 2004), exclusive use of this strategy is likely to feel unsatisfactory to learners who also seek to understand the reasons why the target system is organized the way it is. Conversely, the exclusive use of "grammar as concept" is dangerous for two reasons. First, it may easily become overly bulky and intrusive if students focus their time and energy on explaining their choices to the detriment of language practice. If the instructor is not careful, other skills necessary to second language proficiency may be left out of the curriculum. Even with the greatest care, selecting the constructions that deserve specific grammatical focus is challenging, and the specificity of this type of grammatical instruction may reintroduce an unfortunate split between grammar and other classroom activities. Second, and perhaps most importantly, the "grammar as concept" strategy is most productive with constructions with distinctive morphosyntactic features because it capitalizes on the explicit connection between meaning and form. As the previous section showed, however, some categories cannot be recognized by their specific morphosyntax and need to be recognized in different ways.

It therefore seems clear that in order to provide their students with the kind of control over target categories they need for meaningful interactions, second language instructors need to incorporate both "grammar as usage" and "grammar as concept" in their pedagogical strategies. I have previously argued that successful grammatical instruction involves teaching construal, rather than structure (Achard 2008). The idea simply consists in teaching students to make the kinds of conventionalized choices target language speakers make in particular situations, but its ramifications are far reaching because it entails giving students control over as much as possible of the vast array of symbolic units available to the native speakers of the target language.[9] In order for their students to gain that control, instructors need to equally focus on the conditions in which linguistic rules emerge (grammar as usage), and the explicit mention of the meaning of these native concepts (grammar as concept). The next section illustrates this position with some pedagogical suggestions concerning the French middle and indefinite constructions presented in the previous section.

# 4 Teaching middle and indefinite French impersonals

We can now come back to the pedagogical challenges that the middle and indefinite impersonals pose. Note, first of all, that students highly benefit from being introduced to these constructions because they are extremely frequent in French, and their appropriate usage grants their users a high level of valued native-like colloquialism. Second, neither the "grammar as usage" nor the "grammar as concept" strategy alone is sufficient to properly present these constructions, so both approaches need to be combined for best results.

Neither middle nor indefinite impersonals can be taught as concepts (at least initially) because they are not formally distinct from their non-impersonal counterparts. Consequently, their specific form cannot predictably be used to access their meaning. These constructions are thus best approached as semantic islands of regularity and taught by placing students in positions where native speakers are more likely to use them, in order to allow the relevant constructions to naturally emerge. I have argued elsewhere that inductive grammatical

---

[9] It also involves providing students with a massively complex array of native-like conceptual tools that include "an elaborate **conceptual substrate**, including such matters as background knowledge and apprehension of the physical, social, and linguistic context" (Langacker 2008: 4, emphasis in original). This aspect of construal will not be discussed here.

activities should generally be narrower, more focused and repetitive than other communicative activities because the meaning of grammatical constructions is considerably more abstract than that of lexical items (Achard 2004: 184). The pedagogical challenge of the middle impersonals therefore consists in finding narrow contexts where these constructions are not only natural but also frequently repeated. A possible series of activities might involve the preparation of a travel guide to teach Americans about different aspects of French daily life in the form of short definitions of relevant cultural objects.[10] In the food section for instance, the term *café* 'coffee' will elicit definitions such as *le café se boit le matin et à la fin du déjeuner* 'coffee is drunk in the morning and at the end of lunch'. In this highly restrictive context, the repetition of utterances such as *la salade se mange à la fin du repas* 'salad is eaten at the end of the meal', or *le vin blanc se boit frais* 'white wine is drunk chilled' and many others will quickly allow students to make the relevant generalizations.[11]

Indefinite impersonals are also best presented inductively by allowing the students to make the appropriate generalizations. Perhaps the best introduction strategy consists in taking advantage of the specific syntactic context in which many instances of generalization by virtualization occur. Note that the examples in (14), (16), and (17) are formally constructed in a similar formal manner, namely a subordinate clause introduced by *si* 'if' or *quand* 'when' clause accompanied by a main clause with *on* as the subject of the predicate.

(16) *Pour tout esprit impartial, il est évident qu'un territoire qui est à la France depuis 1911 est français de droit pour l'éternité. C'est ce qui apparaît d'ailleurs encore plus clairement **si on se reporte à l'histoire du Maroc**.*

'For any objective mind, it is obvious that a place that has belonged to France since 1911 is rightfully French for all eternity. This appears ever more clearly if one considers the history of Morocco'.
(Weil, S. *Écrits historiques et politiques*: 58)

---

[10] The classroom activities designed for grammatical instruction should conform to the principles of Communicative Language Teaching (Savignon 2005). They can, for instance be presented as "tasks" (Long 1985, Ellis 2003). The Standards for Foreign Language Learning that define the pedagogical priorities put forward by ACTFL are available online at http://www.actfl.org/i4a/pages/index.cfm?pageid=3392. The translation of linguistic analyses into a pedagogical format that language teachers recognize and trust represents an important factor of the linguists' contribution to second language pedagogy. It is not, however, considered in this chapter.

[11] Note that at this stage of the presentation, the students do not need to distinguish between the two middle constructions since the activity elicits both constitutive and deontic middles. The instructor may choose to point out the difference between the two if she deems it relevant.

(17) *Je me méfie toujours des histoires que je n'ai pas contrôlées de visu;* **si l'on devait croire**, *par exemple, toutes celles que des écrivains aveugles ont racontées sur la Polynésie,* **on se ferait de ses archipels une idée complètement fausse**.

'I am always suspicious of stories I haven't checked for myself; if one were to believe, for example, all that blind authors have said about Polynesia, one would have a totally false idea of what these islands are like'.
(T'Serstevens, A. *L'itinéraire espagnol*: 248)

I suggest that this formal temporal or hypothetical context be used to show students that indefinite impersonals code situations that invariably occur when the conditions described in the subordinate clause are met. Instructors can easily design activities to illustrate the process of generalization by virtualization. For instance, they can ask a student to go to the window and describe what s/he sees: *Qu'est-ce-que tu vois quand tu vas à la fenêtre?* 'What can you see when you go to the window?' After several students have been asked the same question and provided the same response, the generalized construction can be introduced by a single recapitulative statement of the type: *Quand on va à la fenêtre on voit...* 'When you go to the window you can see...' When the structure is well understood and reproduced, students can extend virtualization of experience to the type of structures that do not share the same formal structure.

At this point of the pedagogical sequence, the middle and indefinite impersonal construction have been identified. Their independent introduction should also reveal their close semantic proximity illustrated in the examples in (18) and (19) [where (19) results from the manipulation of the content of (18)]:[12]

(18) *Le geste doit révéler ce qu'il y a au fond de l'âme; c'est son rôle; les phrases ne sont que de l'amplification. On voit cela dans presque tous les romans* **qui s'écrivent** *aujourd'hui.*

'Gestures must reveal the content of the soul; it's their role; sentences merely serve to amplify them. This is visible in almost every novel that is written today'.
(Green, J. *Journal*. T. 5. 1946-1950: 272)

---

12 The # sign indicates that the example is manufactured.

(19) #*Le geste doit révéler ce qu'il y a au fond de l'âme; c'est son rôle; les phrases ne sont que de l'amplification. On voit cela dans presque tous les romans **qu'on écrit** aujourd'hui.*

'Gestures must reveal the content of the soul; it's their role; sentences merely serve to amplify them. This is visible in almost every novel that is written today'.

The semantic distinction between (18) and (19) is subtle and needs to be explained. A second stage of instruction therefore consists in contrasting the two kinds of impersonals as two different constructions that capture slight meaning differences. The distinction between the two constructions presents some degree of systematicity, the choice of the middle construction generally being determined by the high level of topicality of the (logical) object of the predicate. Perhaps the best way to introduce this distinction to the students is to emphasize such pairs as *Comment dit-**on** 'brother' en français*? 'How do you say "brother" in French?' and *Et 'brother', comment ça **se** dit en français*? 'How about "brother", how do you say that in French?' where the indefinite or middle impersonal construction matches the level of topicality of 'brother'. At this stage of the presentation, the two constructions are best considered as different concepts, and their meaning (expressed in terms of topicality of the object of the predicate) systematically related to their form. Consistent with the "grammar as concept" strategy, students should be encouraged to evaluate the level of topicality of the object of the predicate in order to choose between the two kinds of impersonals.[13] This kind of activity is particularly important because it shows students that speaking a language is not only a matter of following strict rules, and that they possess a certain amount of control over their linguistic production.

# 5 Conclusion

This chapter presented a preliminary attempt at establishing durable collaboration between cognitive linguists and second language instructors to improve the teaching of grammar in the second language classroom. This collaboration is important because the adoption of the cognitive linguistics model of language would have far reaching consequences for students and instructors alike. First and foremost, it radically changes the scope of grammatical instruction. One of the tacit assumptions most instructors and second language manuals share is

---

[13] This type of activity is in the spirit of the verbalization charts found in sociocultural approaches to grammatical instruction (Negueruela and Lantolf 2006).

that the grammatical agenda for each level of instruction is well understood and rigidly set. In this popular view, the grammar of the target language is essentially composed of well-recognized, broad, morphologically distinct constructions that interact according to a rigid set of rules that students need to learn and follow. This chapter has shown that this view of grammar does not adequately represent native usage. By contrast, cognitive linguists view grammar as a very large number of form meaning pairs, recognize that most of these constructions are not morphologically distinct, and speakers select the most appropriate ones to structure their conceptualization. Importantly, the inventory of these constructions is not set but constantly evolving as language changes. It is therefore important for linguists to make their research available to second language instructors, so they can focus their teaching on the whole range of usage patterns that characterize native speech, including those that lack morphological distinction.[14] This approach to grammatical phenomena would not only considerably broaden the scope of instruction, but also foster a change of attitude toward grammar itself. By treating the target grammar as a set of symbolic resources that speakers select to fit their interactive needs, the cognitive linguistics model frees speakers from a rigid system of rules to highlight the amount of control they enjoy over their own linguistic production.

Second, the cognitive linguistics model affords the flexibility to treat constructions as concepts or usage patterns, which accommodates a wide range of pedagogical practices. The two strategies of "grammar as usage" and "grammar as concept" are not intended as rigid pedagogical guidelines that each benefit a specific kind of constructions. They are merely intended to emphasize the dual role of grammar as a set of emerging patterns and a collection of linguistic concepts. This dual role is present in any construction, and instructors therefore no longer need to wonder whether inductive or deductive instruction should be privileged, and concentrate on finding the best entry point into specific constructions depending on their semantic and syntactic context.

A great deal of work still remains to be done before a true cognitive pedagogical grammar can be proposed for a specific language. The different kinds of constructions to be taught in the classroom need to be described in a much more systematic fashion, and the grammatical activities to teach them need to be integrated in current pedagogical models of instruction, but the preliminary steps undertaken in this chapter show that the collaboration between cognitive linguists and second language instructors is not only possible but eminently desirable.

---

[14] Collocations have not been considered in this chapter for the sake of brevity, but they are certainly amenable to the same kind of analyses.

# References

Achard, Michel. 2004. Grammatical instruction in the natural approach: A cognitive grammar view. In Michel Achard & Susanne Niemeier (eds.), *Cognitive linguistics, second language acquisition, and foreign language teaching*, 167–194. Berlin: Mouton de Gruyter.

Achard, Michel. 2008. Teaching construal: Cognitive pedagogical grammar. In Peter Robinson & Nick Ellis (eds.), *Handbook of cognitive linguistics and second language acquisition*, 432–456. Mahwah, NJ: Lawrence Erlbaum Associates.

Achard, Michel. 2015. *Impersonals and other defocusing constructions in French*. Human cognitive processing series 50. Amsterdam & Philadelphia: John Benjamins.

Axel, Erik. 1997. One developmental line in European activity theories. In Michael Cole, Yrjö Engeström & Olga Vasquez (eds.), *Mind, culture, and activity: Seminal papers from the laboratory of comparative human cognition*, 128–146. Cambridge: Cambridge University Press.

Barlow, Michael & Suzanne Kemmer. 2000. *Usage-based models of language*. Stanford: CSLI.

Beréndi, Márta, Szilvia Csábi & Zoltán Kövecses. 2008. Using conceptual metaphors and metonymies in vocabulary teaching. In Frank Boers & Seth Lindstromberg (eds.), *Cognitive linguistic approaches to teaching vocabulary and phraseology*, 65–100. Berlin: Mouton de Gruyter.

Boers, Frank. 2000. Metaphor awareness and vocabulary retention. *Applied Linguistics* 21. 553–571.

Buescher, Kimberly & Susan Strauss. 2015. A cognitive linguistic analysis of French prepositions *à*, *dans*, and *en* and a sociocultural theoretical approach to teaching them. In Kyoko Masuda, Carlee Arnett & Angela Labarca (eds.), *Cognitive linguistics and sociocultural theory*, 155–181. Berlin: Mouton de Gruyter.

Bybee, Joan. 2001. *Phonology and language use*. Cambridge & New York: Cambridge University Press.

Ellis, Rod. 2003. *Task-based language learning and teaching*. Oxford: Oxford University Press.

Goldberg, Adele. 1995. *Constructions: A construction grammar approach to argument structure*. Chicago: University of Chicago Press.

Krashen, Steven. 1981. *Second language acquisition and second language learning*. Oxford: Pergamon Press.

Langacker, Ronald. 1987. *Foundations of cognitive grammar*. Vol. 1. *Theoretical prerequisites*. Stanford: Stanford University Press.

Langacker, Ronald. 1991. *Foundations of cognitive grammar*. Vol. 2. *Descriptive application*. Stanford: Stanford University Press.

Langacker, Ronald. 2000. A dynamic usage-based model. In Michael Barlow & Suzanne Kemmer (eds.), *Usage-based models of language*, 1–63. Stanford: CSLI.

Langacker, Ronald. 2005. Construction grammars: Cognitive, radical, and less so. In Francisco J. Ruiz de Mendoza Ibáñez & M. Sandra Peña Cevel (eds.), *Cognitive linguistics: Internal dynamics and interdisciplinary interaction*, 101–159. Berlin: Mouton de Gruyter.

Langacker, Ronald. 2008. *Cognitive grammar: A basic introduction*. Oxford: Oxford University Press.

Langacker, Ronald. 2009. *Investigations in cognitive grammar*. Berlin & New York: Mouton de Gruyter.

Larsen-Freeman, Dianne. 2015. Research into practice: Grammar learning and teaching. *Language Teaching* 48(2). 263–280. Cambridge University Press.

Long, Michael. 1985. A role for instruction in second language acquisition: Task-based language teaching. In Kenneth Hyltenstam & Manfred Pienemann (eds.), *Modelling and assessing second language acquisition*. Clevendon: Multilingual Matters.

Negueruela, Eduardo & James Lantolf. 2006. Concept-based instruction and the acquisition of L2 Spanish. In Rafael Salaberry & Barbara Lafford (eds.), *The art of teaching Spanish: Second language acquisition from research to praxis*, 79–102. Washington DC: Georgetown University Press.

Robinson, Peter & Nick Ellis. 2008. Introduction. In Peter Robinson & Nick Ellis (eds.), *Handbook of cognitive linguistics and second language acquisition*, 1–23. Mahwah, NJ: Lawrence Erlbaum Associates.

Savignon, Sandra. 2005. Communicative language teaching: Strategies and goals. In Eli Hinkel (ed.), *Handbook of research in second language teaching and learning*, 635–651. Mahwah, NJ & London: Lawrence Erlbaum Publishers.

Tomasello, Michael. 1999. *The cultural origins of human cognition*. Cambridge, Massachusetts: Harvard University Press.

Tomasello, Michael. 2003. *Constructing a language: A usage-based theory of language acquisition*. Cambridge, Massachusetts: Harvard University Press.

Tyler, Andrea. 2012. *Cognitive linguistics and second language learning. Theoretical basis and experimental evidence*. New York & London: Routledge.

Tyler, Andrea & Vyvyan Evans. 2004. Applying cognitive linguistics to pedagogical grammar: The case of *over*. In Michel Achard & Susanne Niemeier (eds.), *Cognitive linguistics, second language acquisition, and foreign language learning*, 257–280. Berlin: Mouton de Gruyter.

Tyler, Andrea, Charles Mueller & Vu Ho. 2010a. Applying cognitive linguistics to learning the semantics of English *to*, *for*, and *at*: An experimental investigation. *Vigo International Journal of Applied Linguistics* 8. 181–206.

Tyler, Andrea, Charles Mueller & Vu Ho. 2010b. Applying cognitive linguistics to instructed L2 learning: The English modals. *AILA Review* 23. 30–49.

Van Oosten, Jeanne. 1977. Subjects and agenthood in English. *Chicago Linguistic Society* 13. 451–471.

Verspoor, Marjolijn & Wander Lowie. 2003. Making sense of polysemous words. *Language Learning* 53. 547–586.

Widdowson, Henry G. 1978. *Teaching language as communication*. Oxford: Oxford University Press.

Wittgenstein, Ludwig. 1953. *Philosophical investigations*. Oxford: Basil Blackwell.

Søren W. Eskildsen
# L2 constructions and interactional competence: Subordination and coordination in English L2 learning

## 1 Introduction

Following Eskildsen (2012a), this chapter draws on the construction-based approach to language and language learning as espoused by usage-based linguistics (UBL) and micro-analytic principles from conversation analysis (CA) to investigate how situational requirements and conversational circumstances inform the learning of subordination and coordination in L2 English. The empirical point of departure is an audio-visual corpus consisting of nearly 4,000 hours of recordings of American English L2 classroom interaction. The data for my focal student Carlos, a Spanish-speaking student from Mexico, span almost four years from beginning to intermediate level. While Carlos makes use of both subordinate and coordinate constructions from early on, he seems to be operating initially on a very limited number of conjunctions (*and, or, because*), thus substantiating the idea of L2 learning as exemplar-based. Furthermore, the data reveal that use and learning of subordinate and coordinate constructions is characterized by turn-initial (e.g., *Because I no remember*) and turn-second conjunctions (e.g., *yes but my question is...*). This implies that the use and learning of such constructions is fundamentally woven into the developing interactional competence of L2 speakers over time in the sense that such usage is inherently dependent on the preceding turns of which they are an interactional continuation. The emergence of subordination and coordination in L2 English, then, is not exclusively, perhaps not even primarily, a matter of an individual speaker/learner going from simple to complex clause construction; it is also inextricably linked to mastering an increasing variety of interactional resources, such as monitoring on-going turns, managing turn-taking, giving accounts, and calibrating preference organization (Pekarek Doehler and Pochon-Berger 2015). This paves the way for refining the usage-based notion of construction as a form-meaning pairing in terms of an interactional resource for action.

**Søren W. Eskildsen**, University of Southern Denmark

https://doi.org/10.1515/9783110572186-003

# 2 Usage-based linguistics and language development

Usage-based linguistics (UBL) is a cover-term for a range of models within functional-cognitive linguistics and social-constructivist child language research (Ambridge and Lieven 2010; Barlow and Kemmer 2000; Cadierno and Eskildsen 2015; Ellis, O'Donnel, and Römer 2013; Eskildsen 2009; Hopper 1998; Langacker 1987; Tomasello 2003; Tummers, Heylen, and Geeraerts 2005). The core principle uniting these models is the fundamental importance ascribed to language use. Language development, phylogenetic and ontogenetic, is shaped by language use, and linguistic structure emerges in and from language use as pairings of form and meaning in usage events.

The idea that language learning is driven by language use and the experienced reality of language users is not new, nor is it uncontroversial. In the 60s, of course arguing against the recent cognitive revolution spurred on by Chomsky's famous critique of behaviorism, Dell Hymes proposed that language learning must always be situated in a wider frame of language use, and that what people are primarily learning is to connect utterances to their relevant contexts of use (Hymes 1962, 1972). As such, Hymes, the anthropologist, was interested in language as communicative action and not solely the patterns of language – linguistic structure, roughly speaking – employed in the communicative act. To Hymes, the crucial focal construct was "the speech event", arguably a forerunner of the usage event of UBL, where – according to usage-based models – learning begins. Thus, the usage-based movement, as it were, can be traced back to anthropological linguistics of the 60s.

In the 70s, psychologists had begun to take socially grounded theories of language learning seriously, and MacWhinney (1975) was among the first child language researchers to discuss child language acquisition as item-based and usage-based. He showed that children learned productive language on the basis of recurrent exemplars of the same constructions. Studying two Hungarian children learning their first language (L1), MacWhinney found that their early competence was based on a finite set of item-based patterns (translated into English, they include *more* + X, X + *too*, and *see* + X). These patterns are characterized by a recurring lexical item and an open slot for the insertion of semantically and structurally sanctioned items. In total, 42 such patterns accounted for 85–100% of a total of 11,077 utterances; one central finding was that children's developing grammars are much more concrete than previously thought. In recent longitudinal research the focus has been on investigating how a more creative linguistic inventory comes into being on the basis of concrete recurring linguistic material in use (e.g., Dabrowska and Lieven 2005; Lieven, Salomo, and Tomasello 2009; Tomasello 2003; Brandt et al. 2011). This research has found language learning to be concrete, exemplar-based, and rooted in usage, following a trajectory from specific recurring multi-word expressions to partially fixed, partially schematic utterance schemas to increasingly schematic constructions based on systematic commonalities among patterns. The commonalities, derived by the language user through social interaction, come to be represented in the mind, at the most advanced levels of learning, as schemas sanctioning the use, understanding and learning of novel expressions of the same kind.

A constructionist approach informed by the advances made in child language studies has been gaining rapid attention within SLA research. The ontological status of constructions as form-meaning pairings in L2 learning has been empirically supported (e.g., Bartning and Hammarberg 2007; Collins and Ellis 2009; Ellis 2015; Ellis and Ferreira-Junior 2009a, 2009b; Ellis, O'Donnel, and Römer 2013; Goldberg and Casenhiser 2008; Gries and Wulff 2005, 2009; Robinson and Ellis 2008; Waara 2004), and a growing body of research (Ellis and Ferreira-Junior 2009a; Eskildsen 2009, 2011, 2012a, 2014, 2015, 2017; Eskildsen and Cadierno 2007; Eskildsen, Cadierno, and Li 2015; Li, Eskildsen, and Cadierno 2014; Mellow 2006; Roehr-Brackin 2014; Theodórsdóttir and Eskildsen, 2015; Yuldashev, Fernandez, and Thorne 2013) is documenting and discussing L2 learning over time in terms of an exemplar-based process where the L2 user is constantly developing a repertoire of interrelated constructions on the basis of recurring exemplars.

# 3 Previous L2 research: Bi-clausality, formulaic language, and interactional competence

The present chapter expands on the body of longitudinal usage-based L2 research by exploring the specific ways in which a classroom learner of English constructs his bi-clausal inventory. Bi-clausality is a broad concept encompassing subordination and coordination, but in actual fact the empirical focus becomes narrow; there are not that many different instances in the data. In a usage-based perspective, working bottom-up, the specific instances constitute the starting point of the investigation; in this case, bi-clausality is the abstract linguistic category which the analyst may use to refer to the phenomenon. The same thing applied to Mellow (2006) who investigated the emergence of relative clauses in a 12-year-old Spanish speaking ESL learner, Ana. Although Mellow takes a different linguistic path into the analysis of his data, using HPSG, the data substantiated L2 learning as fundamentally item-based and following a trajectory of expansion based on lexical specificity; Ana started off with a small number of tokens and through pattern expansion moved towards grammaticalization. This has wide-reaching implications for our understanding of the learning of syntax: If L2 learning is truly item-based (and it seems to be), then the notion that L2 syntax is learned on the basis of a variety of rules, each to be applied instantaneously across constructions, should be abandoned (Eskildsen 2012a, 2014, 2017). Instead, the rules (or schemata, as UBL would have it) emerge on the basis of and are the result of numerous occasions of use of the same and similar constructions. L2 learners figure out these constructional similarities as they collect instances through use and experience (Ellis 2002). So when I refer to something as "bi-clausality" I do not mean to imply that this is what people are learning in the first instance, or accessing and producing via a generic syntactic competence. It is the recognizable category for analysts, but what people are learning are all the examples that constitute the category, in essence what makes the category possible in the first place. Over time, people may create categories or schemas as generalizations over the encountered exemplars, allowing for recognition of new patterns of the same kind.

Other research that has taken up subordination usually does so within a broader interest in examining complexity in L2 learning. In this tradition the learning of subordinate clauses is not in itself a focal point but is rather used as an indicator of complexity and hence L2 development in so-called CAF research (complexity, accuracy, fluency) (for a relatively recent overview, see Housen and Kuiken 2009). This is by no means uncontroversial, methodologically and epistemologically (cf. discussions in Norris and Ortega 2009; Ortega 2012; Pallotti 2015; Baten and Håkansson 2015), but space does not allow me to enter that discussion in detail, nor is it central to the present exploration. The points that I am interested in here are empirically driven and concern how bi-clausal resources, coordinated and subordinated, are learned through usage. The results may be read as either supporting or challenging the prevailing idea that coordination precedes subordination in development – explored in Bardovi-Harlig (1992) and reiterated in Norris and Ortega (2009), and held as one of the findings that add to the alleged robustness of Pienemann's Processability Theory (PT) (Pienemann et al. 1988) – but what will have the arrow pointing one way or the other will be the reader's epistemological considerations and, consequently, favoured operationalizations of phenomena. Usage-based approaches differ from PT, for example, in not distinguishing between "instances" and "rules""; the UBL view of language as form-meaning pairings learned on the basis of recurring exemplars is simply incompatible with making that principled distinction. This means that when a linguistic phenomenon is investigated in UBL it is done via lexically specific instances. In PT, although an emergence criterion was formulated already in Meisel et al. (1981), various researchers have operationalized this criterion differently, numerically (ranging from 1–5 examples) or qualitatively (verb type variation) (Baten and Håkansson 2015), in order for a structure to be considered as "having emerged". In doing so, PT researchers get rid of formulaic chunks that are thought to be rote-learned and thus not requiring the processing capacity that non-formulaic exemplars of the same structure do. It goes without saying that such differences in operationalization procedures have quite an impact on the results (as also noted in Glahn et al. 2001). Instead, by accepting that such chunks are part of the emergent linguistic inventory, and remain available as such over time as symbolic units to be deployed in communication (Langacker 1987), UBL insists that language learning consists of an interplay between linguistic patterns of a more or less formulaic / schematic nature in response to situational changes.

Central here is of course the discussion of stable and creative aspects of linguistic production, a discussion which has been undertaken before in SLA in terms of the antagonistic pair "formulaic expressions" and "creative grammar" (e.g., Myles et al. 1998, 1999; Nattinger and De Carrico 1992; Pawley and Syder 1983; Weinert 1995). Instead of compartmentalizing language into what is "formulaic" and what is "creative", UBL assumes that all linguistic units are fundamentally identical, psycholinguistically (e.g., Croft and Cruse 2004; Goldberg 2003). What is formulaic and what is not is, in UBL, a matter of degree of abstraction rather than a question of either-or. Empirical L2 research in this vein has accounted for the ways in which such chunks feed into the rest of the emergent L2 on the basis of type and token frequency (e.g., Bybee 2008; Ellis 2002; Eskildsen 2012b; Eskildsen and Cadierno 2007), the learner's ability to break down chunks and derive the schematic characteristics that allow for the insertion of new lexical material in the created slots and forms the backbone of schematization (Eskildsen 2009, 2014, 2017; for L1, see Lieven, Salomo, and Tomasello 2009), as well as the role of interactional context in the process (Eskildsen 2011, 2012a, 2015; Eskildsen, Cadierno, and Li 2015).

A final leg of research that the present chapter draws on is concerned with the development of interactional competence (Kramsch 1986). This research studies change across time in people's methods for accomplishing practices and actions in talk-in-interaction (Hellermann 2008, 2011; Markee 2008; Pekarek Doehler 2010; Kasper and Wagner 2011; Pekarek Doehler and Pochon-Berger 2015). In their recent state-of-the-art overview, Pekarek Doehler and Pochon-Berger (2015: 236) summarize this research as follows:

These [studies] typically focus on a distinct action or course of action (e.g. initiating repair, disagreeing with others, opening a story) and investigate how speakers' systematic procedures (including language use) for accomplishing that action or course of action change over time. Existing work has explored the development of practices for taking turns at talk (Cekaite 2007), for disengaging from classroom tasks (Hellermann 2008; Hellermann and Cole 2009), for disagreeing (Pekarek Doehler and Pochon-Berger 2011), for opening tasks (Hellermann 2007) and storytellings (Hellermann 2008; Pekarek Doehler and Pochon-Berger forthcoming) or for responding to such tellings (Ishida 2011), for repairing conversational troubles (Hellermann 2009, 2011; Farina, Pochon-Berger and Pekarek Doehler 2012), for formulating requests in interaction (Al-Gahatani and Roever 2013), for shifting conversational topics (Lee and Hellermann 2014) and more generally for managing participation (Achiba 2012; Nguyen 2011; Rine and Hall 2011; see also Pallotti 2001).

A related, more linguistically-semiotically oriented branch of research traces changes in the interactional use of particular linguistic items over time (Eskildsen 2011; Eskildsen and Wagner 2013; Hauser 2013; Ishida 2009; Kim 2009; Markee 2008; Masuda 2011; Theodórsdóttir and Eskildsen 2015), sometimes with special attention to how the linguistic items develop not only interactionally but also constructionally. The present study traces how particular instantiations of a subset of semiotic resources, subordinate and coordinate constructions, are put to use and learned over time. It will be shown that the learning of these constructions follows usage-based predictions about exemplar-based L2 learning and the locally lexical nature of grammar. Moreover, it will be shown that the learning of these constructions is closely linked with particular aspects of a developing interactional competence, in particular expressing disagreement, managing preference structure. As such, this chapter proposes a way forward for carrying out longitudinal research in the interface between L2 construction learning and L2 interactional competence.

# 4 Data

The data source for the present study is the Multimedia Adult English Learner Corpus (MAELC), which consists of audio-visual recordings of classroom interaction in an English as a Second Language (ESL) context. The classrooms, in which the recordings were made, were equipped with ceiling-mounted video cameras and microphones, and students wore wireless microphones on a rotational basis; the teacher always wore a microphone (Reder 2005; Reder, Harris, and Setzler 2003). This is a longitudinal study of Carlos (pseudonym), an adult Mexican-Spanish speaking male learner of English, who was judged to be a successful learner (by standardized assessments and progress through the language school program). The final database of the inquiry consists of transcripts from sessions in which Carlos is either wearing a microphone or sitting next to someone wearing a microphone. In addition, the sessions in which Carlos took part but was not assigned to wear a microphone were viewed for any interactions involving Carlos that might have been picked up by the generic microphones (cf. Eskildsen 2015, forthcoming).

**Table 1:** Overview of Carlos's time in class

| Recording period (RP) | Dates | Level |
|---|---|---|
| 1 | Sept. 27–Nov. 29, 2001 | A |
| 2 | January 7–March 15, 2002 | B |
| 3 | April 2–June 7, 2002 | B |
| 4 | Sept. 23, 2003–March 12, 2004 | D |
| 5 | Sept. 30, 2004–March 3, 2005 | D |

Note: *Level* refers to Portland Community College's program levels, spanning from beginner (A) to high intermediate (D) (Reder, 2005). Carlos was assigned to Level C at the end of Level B but did not attend class that term. When he returned he was placed in Level D.

# 5 Analysis

In this main section of the chapter, I trace the development of Carlos's resources for coordinating and subordinating utterances. Five general types are found with respect to the syntactic dependence on prior utterances, turn-placement of the conjunction[1], and degree of clausal integration (i.e., the extent to which the full bi-clausal construction is delivered as a fluent turn-at-talk):
- dependence on other's prior turn (DPTO), turn-initial placement
- dependence on other's prior turn (DPTO), turn-second placement
- no dependence on other's prior turn (NDPTO), turn-final placement
- no dependence on other's prior turn (NDPTO), delayed bi-clausal (DBS), turn-medial placement
- no dependence on other's prior turn (NDTPO), full bi-clausal integration (FBCI), turn-medial placement
- no dependence on other's prior turn (NDTPO), full bi-clausal integration FBCI), turn-initial placement

---

[1] Unless otherwise explicated, *conjunction* and *complementizer* are used interchangeably.

However, as will be shown, not all these types of constructions are instantiated by the same conjunctions. I next discuss the observed developmental trajectories and show their locally contextualized nature (Eskildsen 2009, 2012a).

## 5.1 Carlos's developmental trajectory and local affordances

Table 2 displays Carlos's bi-clausal resources in terms of types (coordination and subordination), subtypes (the five constructions mentioned above), examples, and times of occurrence. The most important overall observations are that both coordination and subordination are in use from the beginning, that some uses wax and wane in the data, that some constructions emerge later in development, and that not all conjunctions are in use for all coordinating and subordinating constructions, respectively.

In a usage-based and bottom-up exploration of Carlos's development of his bi-clausal inventory, the most fundamental empirical observation is that the majority of these constructions are represented throughout development, or go in and out of use over time, as displayed in the rightmost column with the header "Occurrence". This does not mean that they are all learned at the same time or that no developmental sequence can be ascertained; some constructions appear at odd times, some disappear from use, and some are learned late in development. Important for the present exploration, however, is the notion that the learning of the constructions investigated here is best thought of as an inherent, if not central, part of a developing interactional competence (e.g., Hall et al. 2011; Kramsch 1986; Pekarek Doehler and Pochon-Berger 2015). That is, Carlos uses coordination and subordination to carry out particular actions, and his ability to do so is rooted in interactional competence, e.g., monitoring on-going turns-at-talk, managing turn-taking, and managing preference organization, all to be explored below. Moreover, Carlos's use of coordination and subordination springs from an inherently social resource as much of it builds directly on interactional contingencies, such as other people's prior talk. These uses are occassioned and locally contingent which, in essence, is the empirical epitome of Tomasello's (2003) statement that no matter how abstract linguistic knowledge may ultimately become, it derives in the first instance from specific uses and occurrences in specific situations. In the following analyses I will show the pattern-based and locally contextualized developmental trajectories for Carlos's bi-clausal coordination and subordination structures. In the discussion of coordination I will also show how the construction learning relates to Carlos's developing interactional competence.

**Table 2:** Overview of bi-clausal resources

| Type | Subtype | Example | Occurrence (RPs) |
|---|---|---|---|
| Coordinate | DPTO, turn-initial *and* / *but* / *or* / *so* | And she go open | 1,2,4,5 |
| | | But the carpet is dirty | 1-5 |
| | | Or you can say | 1,3,5 |
| | | So right now I live with them | 4,5 |
| | DPTO, turn-second *and* / *but* / *so* | Yes and a lot of people… | 4 |
| | | Yes but my question is… | 1,2,4,5 |
| | | Yeah so sometimes I like listen music | 3,4,5 |
| | NDPTO, turn final *or* | You like to play music or | 4-5 |
| | NDPTO, DBC, turn-medial *and* / *but* / *or* / *so* | This one is Sandy (2) and this one is Burnside | 1-5 |
| | | I single (2) but if you want marry with me it's okay | 1-5 |
| | | How many daughters you have ( ) or how many children | 4 |
| | | … the middle of the group ( ) so ( ) somebody wants to sit… | 4,5 |
| | NDPTO, FBCI, turn-medial *and* / *but* / *or* / *so* | I work for two years and after that I come to take… | 4-5 |
| | | Is very easy but I don't know | 1-5 |
| | | You say is he or you say she | 1,2,4,5 |
| | | I have a headache so I can't come | 4,5 |
| Subordinate | DPTO, turn-initial *because, when, if* | Because like is the verb | 1-5 |
| | | When I have cold | 1,3,4 |
| | | If you can read | 1-2 |
| | DPTO, turn-second *because,* | No because sometimes I smoke | 1-5 |
| | NDPTO, DBC, turn-medial *because, when, after, than* | This no is correct (1.5) because the question is he | 1-5 |
| | | You give me the information ( ) when come back | 2-4 |
| | | I take the shower ( ) after I brush my teeth | 2 |
| | | The rent was a little cheaper ( ) than where I live before | 4 |
| | NDPTO, FBCI, turn-medial *because, how, if, when, what, Ø, why, where, who* | They can't answer because they're thinking | 1-5 |
| | | I don't know how dyou say | 1-5 |
| | | Let me see if it's correct | 1,3,4,5 |
| | | How do you say in English when I stay in the donkey | 1-5 |
| | | Ask it what it want | 1,4,5 |
| | | I think (Ø) it's that | 2,4,5 |
| | | I understand why you put emb | 1,4 |
| | | The name the restaurant where they have… | 4,5 |
| | | You know who is veronica castro | 1,2,4,5 |
| | NDPTO, FBCI, turn-initial *if[2], when,* | If you eat a lot you emb | 2-5 |
| | | When I listen the music my hands is everyways like that | 2-5 |

---

**2** The example *I single (2) but if you want marry with me it's okay* is counted as a turn-initial, fully integrated bi-clausal use of "if" that is not syntactically dependent on a previous turn by an interlocutor. Strictly speaking, it is not turn-initial, but the important thing in the case of this example is that it is an integrated bi-clausal construction introduced by a conditional *if*-clause.

### 5.1.1 Emergence of coordination

As may be inferred from Table 2, Carlos is developing resources to do bi-clausal coordination from early on, primarily on the basis of turn-initial and delayed bi-clausal uses of *and*, *but*, and *or*. Utterance-second uses of *but* are also frequent from early on. In recording period 1 (RP1), there are only two instances of bi-clausal constructions produced as fluent units, namely an *or*-construction (Extract 10) and a partially afforded *but*-construction (Extract 14). An overview of this is displayed in Table 3.

**Table 3:** Emergence of coordination, recording period 1 (RP1)

|     | Turn-initial | Turn-second | Turn-final | Delayed Bi-clausal | Bi-clausal |
| --- | --- | --- | --- | --- | --- |
| And | RP1: 27/9-2001 | RP4: 20/1-2004 |  | RP1: 5/11-2001 | RP4: 20/1-2004 |
| Or  | RP1: 1/11-2001 |  | RP4: 10/2-2004 | RP1: 27/9-2001 | RP1: 1/10-2001 |
| But | RP1: 1/11-2001 | RP1: 8/10-2001 |  | RP1: 8/11-2001 | RP1: 22/10-2001 |

Note: Dates marked in grey are not from RP1. Blurred fields are empty.

The gradual emergence of bi-clausal production, however, does not only spring from other bi-clausal productions. These uses are also preceded by bi-phrasal uses of the conjunctions *and* and *or*, e.g., *between me and Rosa*, and *friends or students*, i.e., uses where Carlos is not conjoining clauses but phrasal lexical items, predominantly nouns. The general tendency, then, is that bi-clausality as a resource does not come prepackaged to be learned as such but emerges slowly in interaction through use of bi-phrasal constructions and situated utterances that are predominantly contingent upon other utterances in situ, and develops alongside an emergent interactional competence. The next section is concerned with the emergence of these coordinating resources and the co-developing interactional competence. As the three main coordinating conjunctions *and*, *but*, and *or*[3] are used for different purposes interactionally and emerge in different constructions at slightly different points in time, the analysis will handle them separately, starting with *and*.

---

[3] *So* is also a coordinating conjunction that Carlos learns to use over time. It emerges in recording period 3 (RP3) and becomes gradually more widespread in recording period 4 (RP4). Its learning, however, is too complex to be dealt with in this chapter whose main purpose is to present an overview of coordination and subordination learning, and will only be mentioned in passing when relevant to the analyses of the interactions where Carlos is using other conjunctions.

There are 11 instances and two syntactic types of *and*-uses in RP1. Four of them are turn-initial and seven of them are delayed bi-clausal. An example of the former is represented in Extract 1, and an example of the latter is given in Extract 2. At first glance it might seem that both uses are turn-initial, but the two examples differ from each other in that in the first example Carlos is adding something to an on-going action by somebody else, whereas in the second he is continuing, or concluding, his own on-going action (listing a pair of things). The definition of "delayed bi-clausality", therefore, should not be understood as implying deficiency, e.g., in terms of processing capabilities; rather, the defining criterion is interactional: if Carlos is continuing or concluding a prior turn-at-talk by himself by means of a turn-initial *and*, it is understood as "delayed bi-clausality". Another point in support of not writing these instances off as poor processing skills is that Carlos, already in RP1, is producing "full bi-clausal structures" using *or* and *but*. In actual fact, these findings show that language is a social tool for action, and that learning of constructions for performing these actions is exemplar-based, a matter of a locally lexical grammar. More on this later; for now, we turn to the data to look at emergent *and*-constructions, starting with the first turn-initial (Extract 1) and the first delayed bi-clausal (Extract 2) *and*-uses in the data.

Extract 1. Turn-initial *and*: Adding to the teacher's on-going action, Sept. 27, 2001[4]

```
01   TEA:   you need to mo::ve oka:y okay .hh Martina could [you please come and=
02   CAR:                                                   [teacher
03   TEA:   =sit over here
04   CAR:   and this one [table is a same the:[::::
05   TEA:                [thank you
06   TEA:                                     [↑↑we:::ll just a minute...
```

In Extract 1, the teacher is reorganizing the classroom so as to not have students with the same L1 sitting next to each other. She is asking students to move to other places if they are sitting together with a student with whom they share the L1 (lines 1–3). The line of interest to us is line 4, where Carlos is pointing out an additional table where two students share the L1. To achieve his interactional purpose he deploys a turn-initial *and* linking his own turn to the on-going activity. As such, Carlos's "and" is not a traditional bi-clausal conjunction but a different although related tool that he uses to display being in contingency with the on-going interaction. Rather than conjoining his own utterances he is collaborating with the teacher to stitch together the fabric of this social interaction. Line 5 is the teacher's response to the students who have moved upon her

---

4 Transcription conventions are found at the end of the chapter.

request, and at line 6 she is orienting to Carlos's turn. The teacher is showing an early understanding of where Carlos is going; even though he has not yet completed his turn, she lets him and the rest of the class know that she is not quite done with the reorganization yet and will be getting to that table, too. This is clear in the interaction that follows (left out here due to space considerations).

The line of interest in the next extract (Extract 2) is line 17 where Carlos is continuing his own turn from line 15. However, before that point several moments have led up to this first production of a delayed bi-clausal construction. The students have been instructed to ask each other about their neighborhoods, and prior to Extract 2, Martina (MAR) has asked Carlos if there is a bus stop in his neighborhood. Carlos has responded in the affirmative and stated that there are two bus stops close to where he lives. This resulted in some comprehension trouble on Martina's part that they are still working on solving in the beginning of Extract 2. At line 1, Carlos is saying (again) that there are two bus stops, and at line 2 Martina, in overlap with Carlos, produces a change-of-state token (Heritage 1984) and repeats *two*, thus displaying understanding of the "two bus-stop scenario".

Extract 2. Delayed bi-clausal *and*: Adding to own on-going action, Nov. 5, 2001

```
01   CAR:   yes I [have two↓ I-]
02   MAR:         [a::h two:::  ]
03   MAR:   e[:h-]
04   CAR:   [and] I have- ye[s (.) I have ?two? ]
05   MAR:                   [a- e::h what number] deh
06   CAR:   [( )] the: one stop↑
07   MAR:   [mm ]
08   MAR:   and
09   CAR:   n:umber twelve↓
10   MAR:   mhm writes
11   CAR:   and the eh [o-
12   MAR:              [and↑
13   CAR:   and the other stop (.) number nineteen (.) and (.) number twenty
14   MAR:   m:hm:
15   CAR:   this one is eh the Petal
16          (1.6 - MAR is writing)
17   CAR:   and this the: (.) the Starlight
```

At line 4, it seems that Carlos was already beginning to move on with his talk about the bus stops or maybe something else in his neighborhood, as he begins his turn *and I have-*. However, he abandons this and instead confirms the information about the two bus stops, apparently orienting to Martina's change-of-state token as calling on confirmation. Again in overlap, Martina then asks *what number* (line 5) to which Carlos responds number 12 for the one stop (lines 6–9) and, using an *and*-continuer (lines 11, 13) number 19 and 20 for the other stop. In between, Martina gives acknowledgment tokens and writes down the answers (lines 10, 14). Carlos then, at lines 15–17, explains where the stops are (Petal and Starlight are pseudonyms for street names in Portland), again using *and* to bind his two turns together.

The difference between the uses in the two extracts, then, is that in Extract 1 Carlos is adding to somebody else's actions and in Extract 2 he is adding to, or continuing his own. In both cases, *and* works to enhance or restore continuity in the discourse (Turk 2004). It may therefore be viewed first and foremost as an interactional device rather than an item that conjoins sentences. This is especially evident in Extract 1 where the link created through *and* explicitly refers to somebody else's previous action (cf. also Schiffrin 1986). It will also be noted that from a sentence-grammatical perspective Carlos's clauses are incomplete with lacking copulas in three of the four clauses, but this does not impact the interactional achievement. *And* has still been employed successfully to achieve interactional continuity.

Four of the seven "delayed bi-clausal" uses in RP1 are similar to the two examples in Extract 2 (the other examples are ... ( ) *and the fire station is here*; ... ( ) *and the next block is the-*; ... ( ) *and Friday is after*), and three of the four turn-initial "and"-constructions are similar to the example in Extract 1 (the others being: *And the number five and six*; *And October too*). From a constructional perspective it will also be noted that these uses are recurring exemplars seeing as they are all copula constructions, "and THING (is) (X)"[5]. Whereas these seven uses share the feature of combining or putting things into order (concrete, as in *table* or more abstract as in *The Sandy*), the three remaining uses display an incipient learning of expressing sequencing of events instead. The two instances of delayed bi-clausal sequencing of events are co-constructed (Extracts 3 and 4), and the turn-initial "and"-construction is used to produce an addition to the teacher's previous turn (Extract 5).

In the next extract (Extract 3), the primary interest is in lines 6–7, where Carlos is continuing his turn, using *and*. The extract comes from a direction-giving exercise where the students have been asked to guide the teacher from place A to place B on a map in their course book. Prior to the extract the teacher has elicited constructions to be used, and at line 1 she acknowledges positively a student's candidate construction *go down*. At line 2, Carlos picks it up and gives a candidate response, continued at line 4, namely that the teacher needs

---

[5] Some of them lack the copula, hence it is in paranthesis.

to go down Sixteenth Avenue (line 4). In partial overlap the teacher gives the same street name (line 5). Carlos then continues the direction-giving by way of a linking *and* and the instruction to *turn left* (lines 6–7). The rising intonation patterns (lines 2, 4, 5) may be indicative of try-marking, which indicates uncertainty (Sacks and Schegloff 1979), or they may serve the event-sequencing nature of the interaction where rising intonation signals continuation (Heritage 2012). Carlos's turns seem to belong to the former, seeing as he leaves space for other people to respond; at lines 5–6, the lines of interest to us, the teacher confirms his candidate response by way of a partial repeat following which he continues.

Extract 3. Delayed bi-clausal *and* used for sequencing of events, Nov. 5, 2001

```
01   TEA:    go do:wn↑ uh[uh
02   CAR:               [you go down↑
03   THA:    °go down°
04   CAR:    [sixteen avenue↑]
05   TEA:    [sixtee::nth    ] avenu:e↑ (.) [a::]nd
06   CAR:                                   [and]
07   CAR:    a:nd turn- and turn (1.5) the: left
```

In Extract 4 below, the students are describing a cartoon strip, in itself of course a sequentially ordered series of events. In the cartoon a woman sees a wallet on the sidewalk and the teacher has asked the students what they think will happen next. Following some discussion of the most likely scenario, Carlos proposes that she will be tempted to keep the money (lines 1, 3, 6). The format of his turns is simplified: *she oh so much money and put in the bag*. The scenario is ultimately accepted by the teacher as possible (lines 7–8).

Extract 4. Delayed bi-clausal *and* used for sequencing of events, Nov. 8, 2001

```
01   CAR:    I don't know [bec- yu:h (.) but maybe   ] she:: ↑↑oh so much=
02   TEA:                 [okay okay we don't know oka-]
03   CAR:    =money ok[ay
04   MUL:             [hah [hah hah
05   TEA:                  [yes maybe sh-
06   CAR:                       [eh heh heh heh [.hh a:nd put in the bag
07   TEA:                                       [maybe she takes it and put it in her
08           pocket
```

In both the examples, classified as "delayed bi-clausal construction", Carlos is designing his turns in a particular way. The part before the *and* is designed so as to elicit response; in Extract 3 Carlos achieved this through try-marking intonation, and in Extract 4 by producing a laughable and ending his turn with an *okay* that invites a response. All this is yet another reason not to claim that the "delay" of the *and*-initiated turn is due to processing deficiency. Rather, the examples show that Carlos has the interactional competence to invite a response and then move on with the turn if prompted by the response. Importantly, he uses *and* to display the interconnnectedness of the turns he is producing.

Extract 5 comes from the same cartoon description exercise a few moments earlier than Extract 4. This is at the point in the story where the woman has just seen the wallet and the teacher asks what she might do next. That turns into a moment of teaching "pick it up". Line 1 in Extract 5 marks the teacher's closing down the teaching sequence by repeating the construction and asking *and then what?* Carlos offers *and she go op- open the* (line 2) which receives a positive acknowledgement and an embedded repair from the teacher, *opens it uhuh*, which Carlos picks up, *opens it* (lines 3–4).

Extract 5. Turn-initial *and* used to add to the teacher's previous turn, Nov. 8, 2001

```
01   TEA:   she's going to ←pick it up→ and then what↑
02   CAR:   eh eh and she go op- (.) open the:
03   TEA:   opens it uhuh
04   CAR:   opens it
```

Extract 5 is therefore an example of a continuation of a turn by somebody else, but common to Extracts 3–5 is that they show Carlos's early use of *and* as a resource to talk about a sequence of events, an important aspect of building storytellings[6]. The three uses also display a developmental move away from the reliance on the exemplar-based copula construction as discussed above. This early learning of how to put events in their right order can be seen as a forerunner of a more complex interactional competence in development. This, however, seems to be a long time in the making; the next recording period, RP2, sees a distribution of types and functions of *and*-uses that is similar to that in RP1. There are six uses in total, one of which is turn-initial and a list-contributing turn, and five of which are "delayed bi-clausal". Four of these are list-building turns, and the last one (Extract 6) is an "event sequencer", interestingly not unlike Extract 3 where Carlos first learned direction-giving in class (Li

---

**6** For research on storytelling in L2 learning, see e.g., Hellermann (2008) and Barraja-Rohan (2015).

2014). We will not go into an analysis of the interaction, suffice it to note that Carlos is here at line 3 continuing his turn from line 1 which was produced with rising intonation inviting a response, following a minimal response token from the teacher at line 2, by way of an *and*-construction.

Extract 6. Delayed bi-clausal *and* used for sequencing of events, Mar. 15, 2002

```
01   CAR:   you take the:: here number nine↑
02   TEA:   mhm
03   CAR:   and you go down in e:h
04   TEA:   tseh e⌈ightys-
05   CAR:        ⌊the Powell↑
06   TEA:   e- mhm
07   CAR:   cross the:h (.) seventy two
08   TEA:   mhm
```

Extract 7, from recording period 3 (RP3), shows the next step in the learning of event-sequencing. The students have been instructed to make activity plans for their weekend and then ask each other about these. At line 1, Carlos's partner in the task, Nguyen, asks him about his plans for Saturday. Following a request for specification (lines 2–3), Carlos begins telling about his plans. His talk is structured around a sequence of events: first when he gets up and the first thing he does, going to the gym (lines 4–5). Following a yawn from Nguyen and laughter from Carlos, Nguyen nods and Carlos continues with what he is going to do when he gets back (lines 6–9), using *and* to build continuity. The next sequence of events is a three-part list (I take the shower, eat the breakfast, and watch the TV) that only requires an *and* before the third part (lines 9–12). While this is not storytelling per se, it is clear that Carlos is using *and* in a systematic way to build continuity across turns and the events that he is relating, and the non-use in the three-part list is also indicative of this systematicity. He is learning when to use *and* and when not to; he is learning to control semiotic resources for the appropriate actions at the appropriate moments in time.

Extract 7. *and*-uses in next step in the learning of event-sequencing, May 17, 2002

```
01   NGU:   what- what are you going to do hm Saturday er morning
02   CAR:   the morning↑
03   NGU:   mhm
04   CAR:   mm I get up ah I get up up at ah six: six forty five in the morning↑ (.)
05          I'm going to the eh exercise↑
```

```
06   NGU:   yawns
07   CAR:   hh heh heh heh .hh
08   NGU:   nods head once
09   CAR:   and afte:r (.) tseh (1.0) I I back in my ho:me↑ (.) I take the
10          shower ↑ (.) tseh
11   NGU:   nods head once
12   CAR:   I:↓ (.) I eat the breakfast↑ (2.0) an:d tseh watch the TV→
13   NGU:   nods head once
```

In RP3 the distribution of *and*-uses is different from those seen in RPs 1 and 2. There are five uses in total and all of them are of the kind seen in extract 7, i.e., sequencing of events. The ones not shown here appear in a very similar task environment where the students ask each other about weekend plans. This shows that Carlos's developing interactional competence is locally situated in recurring situations and suggests that development is contingent upon the ways in which the environment occassions language use. The data from RPs 1 and 2 suggest a high degree of teacher-fronted activities in the classroom; much of what the students do, they do in response to teacher initiations. This changes as the students move through the levels assigned to them by Portland Community College; the more proficient they are assessed to be, the more the activities in the classroom come to rely on student-student dyads and, in some cases, group talks with invited English L1 speakers.

Recording periods 4 (RP4) and 5 (RP5) further attest to this. There are 19 uses of bi-clausal *and* in each of the two periods and these display a greater interactional variety, not only in Carlos's contributions but also in terms of activities in the classroom. The extracts below that showcase Carlos's developing story-telling skills (Extracts 8 and 9) come from sessions with L1 English conversation partners, students from Portland State University who earned credits for their own studies by participating in the ESL classes (see also Eskildsen and Theodórsdóttir 2017). In addition, Carlos adds to his interactional competence as he begins to use "yes and"-constructions to display agreement and continuity with what has been said and done (not shown due to space considerations).

In Extract 8, Nancy, the conversation guest, has asked Carlos how long he has been in the US and how long he has taken English classes. At lines 1–3, Carlos is explaining that when he first came to the US he worked for two years before taking classes. He is using an *after that*-construction that can be seen as a refined version of the one he used in the example in Extract 7 ("and after" without "that"). The sequence is closed as Nancy commends Carlos for his English (line 7).

Extract 8. Bi-clausal: Sequencing of events in story-telling, Jan 20, 2004

```
01  CAR:  because e:h when I com:e to here .hh (.) u:hm: (1.5) I work for (0.8) two
02        years and after that I come to e:h (1.2) I come to take the classes
03        be[cause e:h I need e:h speak English because I don't spoke anything
04  NAN:     [yeah
05  NAN:  mh heh heh
06  CAR:  so right now eh
07  NAN:  I think you're doing really well...
```

Extract 9, recorded 9 months after Extract 8, shows that Carlos is becoming a skillful story-teller. Again, the interaction involves a conversation guest who is asking Carlos what he would be for Halloween. He says he does not know and then begins telling a story of how he was a vampire two years ago (lines 1–6) and how they had a big party with many people. The story is interrupted by the guest who makes a joke that is partially inaudible (lines 7–8), but Carlos continues the story about how great it was, how they did many things, and how they danced (lines 8–11).

Extract 9. Bi-clausal: Structuring events in story-telling, Oct 14, 2004

```
01  GUE:  yeah what would you be↑
02  CAR:  I don't kno:w um this time I don't know because u:h (2.8) las:
03        last (1.1) two years ago (2.1) I were the:: the vampire
04  GUE:  o:h [vampire
05  CAR:      [so we have the big party and uh many many friends eh
06          [were the:-
07  GUE:    [( ) beautiful girls though [hehhehhehhehheh
08  CAR:                                [hehhehhehhehheh .hh an: (0.8) ehm
09        this was u:h really great because (0.3) eh we had the big party eh
10        did many many things an: we had the: .hh the music eh we danced
11        the: the song of the: (.) Michael Jackson↑
12  GUE:  a:h [yeah]...
```

The interesting element for the present purposes is Carlos's elaborate uses of *and*. The first time is at line 5, where he is connecting information about the big party and the many guests. Following the joke interruption, he picks up the story with a turn-initial *and* (line 8) that links his current turn back to his previous turn. The final part of the story concerns the music and the dancing, also linked by an *and* (line 10) that works to structure the sequence of events that Carlos is relating. This story is more complex than the one in Extract 8, where there was a clear sequencing of events (first he worked, then he came to take classes) that was straightforwardly structured by the *and after that*-construction. This does not work in the same manner here, where the sequencing of events is less chronological. This can also be seen in the use of "so" (line 5). This is another conjunction that is emerging which Carlos uses to structure his story-telling, in this case to continue the story in a way that is reminiscent of the *so*-usage described by Bolden (2009) as story-telling resumption in casual American conversations. Thus what the uses of "so" and "and" do here is structure the story that Carlos is telling into discernible parts for the recipient to make sense of. As such, the conjunctions contribute to Carlos's developing interactional competence.

To sum up the developmental trajectory of *and*-uses, it was noted that from a constructional perspective the starting point was exemplar-based, centered on copula constructions. Interactionally, Carlos moved from using *and* to add to previous actions by others or himself to organizing events into a chronological sequence and further on to using *and* to structure his storytelling. An additional use of *and* in *yes and*-constructions to express agreement and continuity at the same time was also noted as part of his developing interactional competence.

The next item under investigation is *or*. Carlos does not use *or* as frequently as *and*, and the developmental trajectories for the two items also differ. Where the learning of *and* could be seen as the marriage of constructional and interactional competence in that as Carlos was learning to organize the sequencing of events in tellings, he was also learning to combine clauses using *and*, it seems that for *or* he is capable from the beginning of expressing a choice between two options by using bi-clausal *or*. On his first day in class, there is an example of delayed bi-clausal production ("we are students (1.0) or we are teachers"), and two weeks later he produces his first bi-clausal construction using *or* (Extract 10).

Extract 10. Bi-clausal *or*, used to express a choice between two options, Oct 1, 2001

```
01   CAR:   teacher (.) eh one question u:h (.) like that is correct↑
02          or includedly I [need put eh] es
03   TEA:                   [it's::    ] plural right because there is
04          more than one so you need an es at the [end
05   CAR:                                          [es↑
06   TEA:   very good
```

In Extract 10 there is no pause between the two parts of the *or*-construction. This use of *or*, however, does not differ semantically or functionally from the first instance (not shown) where there was a pause between the two parts: Carlos is still expressing a question about a choice between two options. This is the way in which Carlos uses *or* in RPs 1–3. The learning that can be traced in the data regarding his use of *or* in subsequent RPs concerns a developing interactional competence. The uses become more varied, e.g., in lists with more than one alternative (Extract 11, line 13) or as part of a placeholder in longer turns at talk (Extract 11, lines 15–16) where the construction itself is the same, "X or Y", but where the Y does not represent a direct alternative to X as was the case in previous uses.

Extract 11. *or I don't know* – "*or*-construction" as placeholder, Jan. 27, 2004

```
06 CAR:  e:hm (2.9) I'm from mexico↑
07 UNI:  nods
08 CAR:  I've been here (0.9) for (1.2) four years↑
09 UNI:  nods
10 CAR:  so: (0.9) I come here for the: job because in: mexico it's it's
11       hard eh the work and the save money but in here is is good because
12       we have in here we have have opportunities for the work eh we have
13       ah (1.2) one job or two jobs or sometimes three jobs↑ in mexico no:
14       (.) no good ( ) a:h tseh so: in here is- in usa is my first time
15       (.) so I like- I like here so maybe: I no come back to mexico or I
16       don't know so maybe: (1.0) I don't know (1.2) bu:t I like here I
17       like to live here because here a::h the: American people is is is
18       friendly: is (.) is nice people is: no bad people is very friendly
19       an:d (2.4) ahm (.) tseh
20 NAN:  ↑↑that's good
```

Before moving on to *but*, one final thing about *or* deserves to be mentioned; a new feature of interactional competence is developing in RPs 4 and 5 as Carlos begins to use *or* at the end of turns to display uncertainty about the current topic and signal speaker transition relevance (Drake 2015) (Extract 12).

Extract 12. Turn-final *or*, used to express uncertainty and signal speaker change, Feb. 01, 2005

```
01 CAR:  they was talking about ho how was the accident or:
02 CAM:  uh yeah...
```

*But* is Carlos's most frequently used coordinating conjunction. He uses it initially in *yes but*-initiated turns to express a dispreferred response (cf. Schegloff 2007). The *yes* works to align with the on-going talk, and the *but*-part works to express a form of disagreement or disalignment as in this case (Extract 13) by way of a display of lack of epistemic access. Dispreferred response, it should be noted, is a sequential term from CA and has to do with what forms of actions typically follow other forms of action, e.g., invitation – acceptance, as the preferred response pattern. When speakers need to produce responses that deviate from the preferred patterns, they typically do so in a mitigated fashion. One such form of mitigation is the "pro forma agreement marker" (Schegloff 2007) before the expression of disalignment. Carlos's propensity for designing dispreferred turns in a mitigated fashion has been shown to be a marker of an advanced level of interactional competence (Pekarek Doehler and Pochon-Berger 2011, 2015), so the fact that he uses *but* in turn-second position rather than "full bi-clausal constructions" should not be seen as an interlanguage deficiency of any kind.

Prior to Extract 13, the teacher has pointed to a lock and asked the students if they know what it is. She gets no response and goes on to ask if they have one and use one at home. She still gets no response and then reformulates the question, using a negative (lines 1–3). Negative questions are used when something unexpected has happened and usually projects confirmation (Turk 1999). However, Carlos disaligns with the projection, initiating a dispreferred response, using a *yes but*-construction. It appears that the reason why he, for one, did not respond in the first instance was that he does not know the English word for lock. At the end of the sequence the teacher of course provides the word which yields a choral repetition by the students (lines 8–9). Before that, she commends Carlos for his way of saying that he does not know the word; there might be an embedded repair in her turn (line 6), or perhaps she does not hear Carlos's ungrammaticality.

Extract 13. *yes, but…* as dispreferred response, Oct. 22, 2001

```
01   TEA:   you don't have one↑ you don't use it↑
02          (0.5)
03   TEA:   no↑
04          (0.8)
05   CAR:   ye:s but eh I don't know how d'you say
06   TEA:   I don't know how to say↓ goo:d [okay it's goo:d I like that=
07   CAR:                                  [hh hh heh heh
08   TEA:   =okay it's a lock
09   MUL:   lock
```

Extract 13 represents Carlos's second production, chronologically, of a *yes but*-construction. His first bi-clausal use of *but*, also from Oct 22, 2001, 15 minutes before Extract 13, is of the same interactional type, i.e., a dispreferred response displaying lack of epistemic access (Extract 14). Here, holding a tape dispenser, the teacher has been asking the students if they know what it is. Getting no response she says it is called tape. She then comments that it's very easy and repeats that it's tape (line 1). Carlos and the teacher both repeat *very easy* (lines 2–3), and the teacher then remarks that all the vocabulary work they are doing is good for them, in overlap with which Carlos produces the *but*-construction (lines 3–5). As was the case in Extract 13, he is using it to disalign with the teacher's on-going actions, and in both cases he is employing a formal agreement marker (*yes / is very easy*) before uttering the disaligning *but*-part. Interestingly she goes on to account for why they are doing these vocabulary activities which implies that she is also orienting to Carlos's contribution as a dispreferred response in that she carries out interactional work to restore alignment (not included in transcript).

Extract 14. *is very easy, but...* as dispreferred response Oct 22, 2001

```
01   TEA:   it's very easy (.) it's a- it's ta⌈pe
02   CAR:                                     ⌊very ea:sy .hh
03   TEA:   it's very easy a lo:ts of vocabulary today it's ⌈good for you⌉
04   CAR:                                                   ⌊is very easy⌋ but I
05          I don't know.
```

Carlos's first use of *but* for a different purpose is an afforded and co-constructed bi-clausal construction used to express a contrast or a qualification (Extract 15). The students are practicing talking about their environment and the teacher has just reviewed the vocabulary items "clean" and "dirty" by establishing agreement with the students that the carpet in the classroom is dirty and eliciting the opposite of "dirty", namely "clean". She then asks the students if their classroom is clean or dirty (line 1). Carlos suggests that it is clean which the teacher accepts and writes on the board (lines 3–4). She then adds *but* as an invitation to the students to add a contrastive element to that statement – which is what Carlos eventually does after some embodied assistance by the teacher (lines 6–8). The teacher accepts and elicits a repetition from Carlos which she gets (lines 9–12).

Extract 15. *but* used to contrast statement, Nov 1, 2001

```
01   TEA:   is our classroom clean or dirty
02          (2.2)
03   CAR:   it's clean
04   TEA:   .hh our classroom is clean (7; teacher writes on board) ↑↑but (.) hh heh
05          heh heh heh .hh ↑↑but
```

```
06  CAR:  but
07  TEA:  stamps on the floor twice
08  CAR:  the: carpet is very dirty
09  TEA:  okay
10  CAR:  a[rh very dirty] a[h heh heh heh .hh  ]
11  TEA:  [thank you      ] [very dirty but the] carpet
12  CAR:  but the carpet is dirty
13  TEA:  okay...
```

It is interesting to note that in this teaching sequence, the teacher is focusing on the function of *but* that we know from grammar books and dictionaries: a coordinating conjunction used to connect two clauses where the second clause expresses a contrast to or a qualification of that which has been said in the first clause. Of course, this is not wrong; *but* does have that function. It is just not the most frequent function in spoken interaction (Biber et al. 2002). In fact, Carlos's use and learning of *but* in contexts such as Extracts 13 and 14 reflects quite well how *but* is most frequently used in talk.

The uses of *but* in RPs 1–3 are predominantly turn-initial (as in Extract 15) or turn-second (as in Extract 13). Bi-clausal uses are slowly becoming productive in RP1, as already indicated by the partially afforded use in Extract 14, and during RPs 4 and 5 they become roughly as frequent as turn-initial and turn-second uses. In RP1 there are two additional, somewhat hesitant bi-clausal uses, appearing a week after Extract 15. One of them is found at line 1 in Extract 4 above, and the other one is "*he take the bus because but- (+) but the wallet is the floor*"; in these two examples it seems that *but* is somehow eclipsed by *because* in on-going talk, perhaps because at this point in development, Carlos is more frequently using *because* than *but*. An interesting observation in itself, indicating that coordination does not necessarily precede subordination in L2 development, it also shows that *but* and *because* are closely related, an idea that will be further explored in the section on subordination below. The final thing to note about *but* is that from a constructional perspective, its uses are lexically specific. The first five occurrences are either *but I don't know* (2) or *but THING is X* (3). The latter construction, a copula construction, is similar to that observed in the initial uses of *and* suggesting that Carlos may be operating on some schema that sanctions both, *and/but THING (is) X*.

Summing up coordination before moving on to subordination, it will be noted that learning is socially anchored–Carlos initially uses *and-* and *but-* coordination to respond to a previous action by somebody else. He then gradually builds his inventory to use coordination to build on his own prior turns and eventually to build longer turns-at-talk, for instance in storytelling. Another thing that linked *and* and *but* in development was the shared lexical material in what might be a locally lexical grammar that applies to both these items. It will also be noted that there was a high degree of reliance on affordances (van Lier 2000), i.e., uses occasioned by the immediately surrounding interactional environment, especially concerning the initial *but*-uses.

For *or*, the picture was different. Although *or* is also used by Carlos to provide an alternative to something said by someone else, he was using *or* in bi-clausal turns from very early on. Learning could still be traced in terms of interactional competence, with varying uses of *or* in longer turns-at-talk, and with a late emergence of turn-final *or*, which is used to display uncertainty and signal upcoming speaker transition.

### 5.1.2 Emergence of subordination

This section gives an overview of the pattern-based development of Carlos's subordination and the conjunctions *how, who, what, where, when, if,* and *because*.[7] The inventory of conjunctions found indicates a high degree of lexical and functional specificity which is especially clear in the case of *how, who, what, where*. These four complementizers are used by Carlos in lexically specific subordinating environments predominantly following *I don't know*. The word *how* can be traced in development as follows:

> **RP1**: I don't know how do you say → **RP2**: I don't know how you write/use / I don't know how many years she has → **RP3**: check how you write → **RP4**: depend how you eat / I don't know how many population we have → **RP5**: I don't know how they understand / talking about how was the accident.

*Who, what*, and *where* occur in similar linguistic environments (You/I (don't) know who is X; I don't know what happened; I don't know where we going to put this one), but there are so few instantiations outside of these environments that it is difficult to say anything about developmental aspects. *Who* does not evolve at all, it seems; *what* occurs in *ask it what it want* in co-constructed talk about a ghost (!) (RP4) and in *I have here what mean the darkness* in talk about

---

7 Subordination without a conjoining particle ("Ø") is very lexically specific: I think it's X / I have X / i think the US celebrate fourth of july (RP4) → I think the opposite of the fauna is desert (RP5). There are no examples that do not begin with "I think". As such, this may be a prime example of just exactly how locally lexical grammar can get. *Why* as conjunction is found only twice in the data and is therefore left out here.

the word "darkness" (RP5); and *where* recurs a few times in other lexically specific environments, *where I/you live* and *where I'm from* as well as *where I put X* and *where they have X*.

*When* is used by Carlos in contexts that are different from the other WH-complementizers. There are only two uses in RP1, *hospital when you have accident* (item+*when*-construction) and *it's when you go the shopping* (*it's when*-construction). In RP2 there is another instance of the item+*when*-construction as well as some new uses. These are turn-initial *when* (three instances) where Carlos adds a temporal clause to something that is happening in the environment ("when you are very young" as a comment to a picture of a classmate, "when I have cold?" as a confirmation request to the teacher, and *when come back* as an addition to his own previous turn), *how do you say when*-constructions (two instances), as well as a turn-initial use of *when* in a bi-clausal construction (*when I listen the music, my hands is everyways like that*). These first nine instances in the first two RPs are quite specific: item/it's + *when*-construction; turn-initial *when*-construction; *how do you say when*-construction; and a turn-initial bi-clausal construction. In subsequent RPs, Carlos's use of *when* becomes more varied and much more frequent although he retains the preference for turn-initial uses to introduce temporal *when*-clauses.

*If* exhibits two developmental trajectories, one for the interrogative function, and one for the conditional function. The interrogative function emerges in RP1 as a display of understanding in a response to the teacher's turn *can I read* ("oh if you can reh yeah"). The next use is "do you know if people have one or two Ps?" and throughout Carlos's time in class he only uses interrogative *if* with the verbs "know", "ask" and "see". The local grammar of interrogative *if* is therefore lexically specific. The conditional *if* has a lexically specific starting point, too, as the first two occurrences are *if you want*-constructions. Then, following a session in which the students are practicing conditional *if*-use by way of asking each other hypothetical questions, Carlos's use of conditional *if* expands rapidly to other linguistic contexts. Classroom practices, it may be inferred, may assist the L2 speaker in expanding his/her linguistic repertoire and therefore, by implication, it may also be conducive to schematization processes (cf. Eskildsen 2015). As was the case with temporal *when*-clauses, however, Carlos keeps a preference for using *if* in turn-initial position to introduce conditional clauses.

*Because* is by far the most frequent subordinating conjunction used by Carlos, and his uses of *because* in RP1 have three predominant common denominators: they are lexically specific as they center on copula constructions (e.g., *because like is the verb*), and *because* is either utterance-initial (e.g., *because like is the verb*) or utterance-second (e.g., *no because sometimes I smoke*). As such, the lion's share of *because*-uses in RP1 (20/26, 77%) are responses to something that is going on in the environment, either a response to a *why*-question, or an account or explanation of something. It is important to recall the discussion of *but* in the section on coordination. It was mentioned there that *but* initially was somehow eclipsed by *because* in some instances, perhaps because at this point in development, Carlos was more frequently using *because* than *but*. It also indicates that in terms of schemata, Carlos may at this stage have been expanding his *but*-uses on the basis of existing and known *because*-uses. The schema suggested to underlie *and* and *but* may therefore be expanded to include *because*: *because/and/but THING (is) X*. This again has ramifications for the way we think about coordination and subordination as syntactic phenomena – and for how people seem to be learning them in L2 English.

For *because* there are also "delayed bi-clausal turns" where Carlos is explaining or accounting for a point he has made himself. Bi-clausal turns with no pauses also emerge slowly in RP1, and Extract 16 nicely illustrates the afforded nature of this learning. The extract comes from the same activity as Extract 15, but this time the teacher is asking the students if they think the streets of Portland are clean or dirty (line 1). This yields a response from Martina who says they are not dirty (line 2) and from an unidentified students who says they are not clean (line 6). Following a confirmation check from the teacher, Carlos then expresses agreement with this at line 8 and attempts an explanation, using a *no because*-construction. He runs out of words, however, and embarks on a word search using both Spanish and gestures. At this point it is uncertain where he is going with it.

Extract 16. Afforded nature of bi-clausal *because*, Nov. 1, 2001

```
01     TEA:    the streets of Portland (.) aro[und here
02     MAR:                                  [not very dirty
03             (1.0)
04     MAR:    eh heh h heh heh [heh heh heh .hh ] heh [heh heh .hh]
05     TEA:                     [what do you think]
06     UNI:                                            [not clean ]
07     TEA:    not clean↑
08     CAR:    [no because ] ah s[pn, gestures upwards because the: looks up,
                points
09             gestures upwards again
Lines omitted
```

```
12   TEA:   the streets are clean okay yes what points at carlos tell me
13          mirrors Carlos' gesture from before
14   CAR:   it's dirty because a::h gestures upwards again

15   TEA:   e:::h the rain↑
16   ABE:   the tre[e
17   CAR:         [( ) the the tree gestures something falling
18   TEA:   mirrors Carlos' gesture the trees- .hh o::::::h I see okay
```

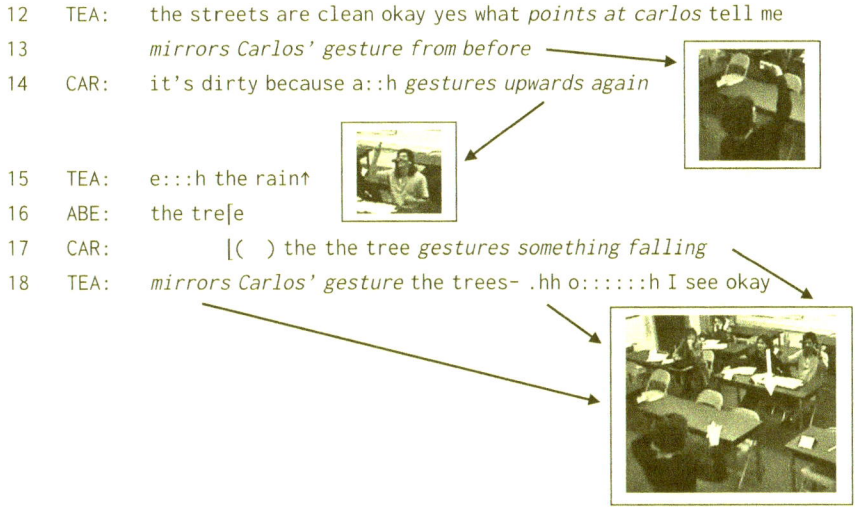

In the omitted lines other students chip in, and at line 12 the teacher repeats one of the contributions, *the streets are clean*, followed by an acknowledgment token, *okay*. She then specifically addresses Carlos verbally (*yes*, *what*, *tell me*), by pointing, and through a repetition of the gesture he made during his turn at lines 5–6. Carlos then restarts the turn *it's dirty because* – relevant because a repetition of *no because* would not have made sense here – and runs out of words in the same spot in the construction, looks up and gestures upwards (line 14). Following co-constructed work with Abelardo, a fellow student, and more gesturing (Carlos is miming something falling down, which the teacher also mirrors, cf. de Fornel's return gestures (de Fornel 1992; Eskildsen and Wagner 2013, 2015), the teacher produces an elaborate change-of-state token and expresses having understood (*o:::::h I see okay*; line 18). In the interaction that follows (not included here) it becomes clear that Carlos was referring to foliage from the trees making the streets dirty.

This situation is the first bi-clausal *because*-construction in Carlos's data and it seems to build on preliminary work drawing on a known construction (*no because* …, line 5). In the subsequent recording periods the bi-clausal *because*-constructions become more varied and more frequent, but the turn-initial and turn-second uses remain the most frequent ones.

# 6 Conclusion

Carlos's resources to express coordination and subordination develop at different points in time, but all of them are essentially traceable to his first period in the

ESL class. The tracing here has been done first for coordination and then for subordination, following the usage-based dictum of investigating lexically specific patterns. Hence the investigation was based on conjunctions and complementizers. The investigation revealed recurring patterns across coordination and subordination – for many of the constructions, Carlos makes use of turn-initial and turn-second uses of the coordinating and subordinating items as well as delayed bi-clausal and bi-clausal constructions. *But* and *because* are the only conjunctions that are used in all these kinds of constructions from the beginning, and therefore it seems safe to assume that these two are central to Carlos's learning of coordination and subordination. While there is a tendency for the bi-clausal constructions to emerge later in development than turn-initial and turn-second uses of items under investigation, it seems premature to write this development off as a matter of increased processing abilities only, because the delayed bi-clausal constructions in many instances are an interactional phenomenon, the pause in the construction serving a purpose in situ, and because such uses remain available for Carlos. It was argued that this developmental phenomenon might be explained by recourse also to the nature of the classroom interaction; in lower levels in this class, the interaction is centered on teacher-fronted activities, and thus most of what the students say works as responses to the teacher and/or the environment. Later practices in the class are more inviting for longer stretches of individual talk, such as storytelling.

It was also noted that there was a great deal of lexical specificity, especially at early phases in development. *And, but,* and *because* were all dominated by copula constructions, and seeing as these three conjunctions are among the earliest to emerge, it may be suggested that there is some form of experientially-deduced schema guiding the use of constructions based on these items. The instances shown in some of the interactions where Carlos seems to be mixing *but* and *because* lend further support to this hypothesis. Other conjunctions, especially the less frequently employed subordinate conjunctions, were highly exemplar-based throughout development and displayed little or no change over time. It is questionable if Carlos arrives at a schema for expressing coordination and subordination in general given the high degree of lexical specificity surrounding the uses of especially the interrogative clauses and the Ø-complementizer; however, it seems possible that he is operating on some form of representation that sanctions the uses of the more frequently employed conjunctions *and, but, or,* and *because* and that such a representation guides the learning of additional conjunctions such as *so*.

Finally it should be mentioned that the use and learning of these constructions is fundamentally woven into the developing interactional competence of L2 speakers over time in the sense that turn-initial conjunctions are inherently dependent on the preceding turns of which they are an interactional continuation, and in the sense that the constructions are learned as ways to achieve particular interactional purposes; development for both *and* and *but* was argued to be a matter of co-developing interactional and constructional resources. It was shown for *and*, *but*, and *because* that Carlos's learning of these was inextricably linked to his understanding of the on-going discourse, his turn-taking management skills, and his ability to produce relevant turns-at-talk as situated actions. It was also shown that Carlos was learning to perform a variety of such situated actions while learning the constructions. As such, the inventory of semiotic resources, form-meaning pairings, may be thought of as an inventory of semiotic resources for carrying out social actions. Langacker (1987) described language knowledge as an inventory of form-meaning pairing used for communicative purposes but, using insights from CA, we can qualify the notion of communicative purposes by proposing that these communicative purposes are actions occasioned by local circumstances of social interaction, such as responses to prior turns-at-talk (Schegloff 2007).

The emergence of subordination and coordination in L2 English, then, is not exclusively, perhaps not even primarily, a matter of going from simple to complex clause construction; rather, it is inextricably linked to mastering an increasing variety of interactional resources, such as monitoring on-going turns, managing turn-taking, and giving accounts. Thus, subordination and coordination are found in increasingly complex interactional environments over time as the learner's conjunction usage goes from initiating simple second pair parts to mitigating dispreferred responses and accounting for his own assessments and opinions. I will therefore argue that people's ways of carrying out social actions are the driving force for the learning of the inventory of semiotic resources as it is conceived in UBL and make a call for further research that builds on and advances a view of language as a tool for social action and investigates L2 learning as an inherently social rather than individual competence.

## Transcription conventions

| | |
|---|---|
| CAR:, TEA: | Participants |
| wei[rd wo]rd | Beginning and end of overlapping talk |
|    [yeah ] | |
| *Words in italics* | Embodied behaviour |
| (1.0) | Pause/gap in seconds and tenth of seconds |
| (.) | Micropause (< 0.2 seconds) |
| word= | |
| =word | Multi-line turn |

| | |
|---|---|
| wo_rd | Prosodic emphasis |
| wo:rd | Prolongation of preceding sound |
| ↑,↓,→ | Rising, falling, continuing intonation |
| ↑↑word | Shift to high pitch |
| °word° | Softer than surrounding talk |
| ←word→ | Slower than sorrounding talk |
| wo- | Cut-off (e.g., glottal stop) |
| ( ) | Non-audible speech |
| ?word? | Uncertain transcription |
| .hh | Hearable in-breath |
| hh | Out-breath |

# References

Achiba, Machiko. 2012. Development of interactional competence: Changes in participation over cooking sessions. *Pragmatics & Society* 3(1). 1–30.

Al-Gahatani, Saad & Carsten Roever. 2013. 'Hi doctor, give me handouts': Low-proficiency learners and requests. *ELT Journal* 67(4). 413–424.

Ambridge, Ben & Elena Lieven. 2011. *Child language acquisition: Contrasting theoretical approaches*. Cambridge: Cambridge University Press.

Bardovi-Harlig, Kathleen. 1992. A second look at T-unit analysis: Reconsidering the sentence. *TESOL Quarterly* 26. 390–5.

Barlow, Michael & Suzanne Kemmer (eds.). 2000. *Usage-based models of language*. Stanford: Center for the Study of Language and Information (CSLI).

Barraja-Rohan, Anne-Marie. 2015. "I told you": Storytelling development of a Japanese learning English as a second language. In Teresa Cadierno & Søren W. Eskildsen (eds.), *Usage-based perspectives on second language learning*, 271–304. Berlin: Mouton de Gruyter.

Bartning, Inge & Bjørn Hammarberg. 2007. The functions of a high-frequency collocation in native and learner discourse: The case of French *c'est* and Swedish *det är*. *International Review of Applied Linguistics* 45(1). 1–43.

Baten, Kristof & Gisela Håkansson. 2015. The development of subordinate clauses in German and Swedish as L2s–a theoretical and methodological comparison. *Studies in Second Language Acquisition* 37. 517–547.

Biber, Douglas, Susan Conrad & Geoffrey Leech. 2002. *Longman student grammar of spoken and written English*. Harlow: Longman.

Bolden, Galina B. 2009. Implementing incipient actions: The discourse marker 'so' in English conversation. *Journal of Pragmatics* 41. 974–998.

Brandt, Silke, Arie Verhagen, Eleven Lieven & Michael Tomasello. 2011. German children's productivity with simple transitive and complement-clause constructions: Testing the effects of frequency and variability. *Cognitive Linguistics* 22(2). 325–357.

Bybee, Joan. 2008. Usage-based grammar and second language acquisition. In Peter Robinson & Nick. C. Ellis (eds.), *Handbook of cognitive linguistics and second language acquisition*, 216–236. New York: Routledge.

Cadierno, Teresa & Søren. W. Eskildsen (eds.). 2015. *Usage-based perspectives on second language learning*. Berlin: Mouton de Gruyter.
Collins, Laura & Nick C. Ellis (eds.). 2009. Input and second language acquisition: The roles of frequency, form, and function. [special issue]. *The Modern Language Journal* 93(3).
Croft, William & D. Alan Cruse. 2004. *Cognitive linguistics*. Cambridge: Cambridge University Press.
Dabrowska, Ewa & Elena Lieven. 2005. Towards a lexically specific grammar of children's question constructions. *Cognitive Linguistics* 16(3). 437–474.
de Fornel, Michel. 1992. The return gesture: Some remarks on context, inference, and iconic gesture. In Peter Auer & Aldo Di Luzio (eds.), *The contextualization of language*, 159–176. Amsterdam: John Benjamins.
Drake, Veronika. 2015. Indexing uncertainty: The case of turn-final *or*. *Research on Language and Social Interaction* 48(3). 301–318.
Ellis, Nick C. 2002. Frequency effects in language processing–a review with implications for theories of implicit and explicit language acquisition. *Studies in Second Language Acquisition* 24(2). 143–188.
Ellis, Nick C. 2015. Cognitive and social aspects of learning from usage. In Teresa Cadierno & Søren W. Eskildsen (eds.), *Usage-based perspectives on second language learning*, 49–74. Berlin: Mouton de Gruyter.
Ellis, Nick C. & Fernando Ferreira-Junior. 2009a. Construction learning as a function of frequency, frequency distribution, and function. *The Modern Language Journal* 93(3). 370–385.
Ellis, Nick C. & Fernando Ferreira-Junior. 2009b. Constructions and their acquisition: Islands and the distinctiveness of their occupancy. *Annual Review of Cognitive Linguistics* 7. 187–220.
Ellis, Nick. C., Matthew B. O'Donnell & Ute Römer. 2013. Usage-based language: investigating the latent structures that underpin acquisition. *Language Learning* 63, Supplement 1. 25–51.
Eskildsen, Søren W. 2009. Constructing another language–usage-based linguistics in second language acquisition. *Applied Linguistics* 30(3). 335–357.
Eskildsen, Søren W. 2011. The L2 inventory in action: Conversation analysis and usage-based linguistics in SLA. In Gabriele Pallotti & Johannes Wagner (eds.), *L2 learning as social practice: Conversation-analytic perspectives*, 337–373. Honolulu, HI: University of Hawai'i, National Foreign Language Resource Center.
Eskildsen, Søren W. 2012a. Negation constructions at work. *Language Learning* 62(2). 335–372.
Eskildsen, Søren W. 2012b. Type and token frequency in SLA. In Peter Robinson (ed.), *The Routledge encyclopedia of second language acquisition*, 660–662. Routledge: London and New York.
Eskildsen, Søren W. 2014. What's new?: A usage-based classroom study of linguistic routines and creativity in L2 learning. *International Review of Applied Linguistics* 52(1). 1–30.
Eskildsen, Søren W. 2015. What counts as a developmental sequence? Exemplar-based L2 learning of English questions. In Jan Hulstijn, Rod Ellis & Søren W. Eskildsen (eds.), [special issue: Orders and sequences in L2 acquisition: 40 years on], *Language Learning*, 65(1), 33–62.
Eskildsen, Søren W. 2017. The emergence of creativity in L2 English–a usage-based case-study. In Nancy Bell (ed.), *Multiple perspectives on language play*, 281–316. Berlin: Mouton de Gruyter.

Eskildsen, Søren W. Forthcoming. *Usage-based L2 learning: The construction of linguistic and interactional resources in a L2*. New York: Routledge.

Eskildsen, Søren W. & Teresa Cadierno. 2007. Are recurring multi-word expressions really syntactic freezes? Second language acquisition from the perspective of usage-based linguistics. In Marja Nenonen & Sinikka Niemi (eds.), *Collocations and idioms 1: Papers from the first Nordic conference on syntactic freezes*, Joensuu, May 19-20, 2007 (Studies in Languages, University of Joensuu, Volum 41), 86-99. Joensuu: Joensuu University Press.

Eskildsen, Søren W., Teresa Cadierno & Peiwen Li 2015. On the development of motion constructions in four learners of L2 English. In Teresa Cadierno & Søren W. Eskildsen (eds.), *Usage-based perspectives on second language learning*, 207-232. Berlin: Mouton de Gruyter.

Eskildsen, Søren W. & Guðrun Theodórsdóttir. 2017. Constructing L2 learning spaces: Ways to achieve learning inside and outside the classroom. *Applied Linguistics* 38(2). 143-164.

Eskildsen, Søren W. & Johannes Wagner. 2013. Recurring and shared gestures in the L2 classroom: Resources for teaching and learning. *European Journal of Applied linguistics* 1(1). 139-161.

Eskildsen, Søren W. & Johannes Wagner. 2015. Emodied L2 construction learning. *Language Learning* 65(2). 419-448.

Farina, Clelia, Evelyne Pochon-Berger & Simona Pekarek Doehler. 2012. Le developpement de la competence d'interaction: une etude sur le travail lexical. *TRANEL (Travaux Neuchatelois de Linguistique)* 57. 101-119.

Glahn, Esther, Gisela Håkansson, Bjørn Hammarberg, Anne Holmen, Anne Hvenekilde & Karen Lund. 2001. Processability in Scandinavian second language acquisition. *Studies in Second Language Acquisition* 23. 389-416.

Goldberg, Adele 2003. Constructions: A new theoretical approach to language. *TRENDS in Cognitive Sciences* 7(5). 219-224.

Goldberg, Adele & Devin M. Casenhiser. 2008. Construction learning and second language acquisition. In Peter Robinson & Nick C. Ellis (eds.), *Handbook of cognitive linguistics and second language acquisition*, 197-215. New York: Routledge.

Gries, Stefan Th. & Stephanie Wulff. 2005. Do foreign language learners also have constructions? Evidence from priming, sorting, and corpora. *Annual Review of Cognitive Linguistics* 3. 182-200.

Gries, Stefan Th. & Stephanie Wulff. 2009. Psycholinguistic and corpus-linguistic evidence for L2 constructions. *Annual Review of Cognitive Linguistics* 7. 163-186.

Hall, Joan Kelly, John Hellermann & Simona Pekarek Doehler (eds.). 2011. *L2 interactional competence and development*. Clevedon: Multilingual Matters.

Hauser, Eric. 2013. Stability and change in one adult's second language English negation. *Language Learning* 63(3). 463-498.

Hellermann, John. 2007. The development of practices for action in classroom dyadic interaction: Focus on task openings. *The Modern Language Journal* 91(1). 83-96.

Hellermann, John. 2008. *Social actions for classroom language learning*. Clevedon: Multilingual Matters Ltd.

Hellermann, John. 2009. Practices for dispreferred responses using no by a learner of English. *International Review of Applied Linguistics* 47. 95-126.

Hellermann, John. 2011. Members' methods, members' competencies: Looking for evidence of language learning in longitudinal investigations of other-initiated repair. In Joan Kelly Hall, John Hellermann & Simona Pekarek Doehler (eds.), *L2 interactional competence and development*, 147-172. Clevedon: Multilingual Matters.

Hellermann, John & Elizabeth Cole. 2009. Practices for social interaction in the language learning classroom: Disengagements from dyadic task interaction. *Applied Linguistics* 30(2). 186–215.

Heritage, John. 1984. A change-of-state token and aspects of its sequential placement. In J. Maxwell Atkinson & John Heritage (eds.), *Structures of social action*, 299–345. Cambridge, UK: Cambridge University Press.

Heritage, John. 2012. Epistemics in action: Action formation and territories of knowledge. *Research on Language and Social Interaction* 45(1). 1–29.

Hopper, Paul J. 1998. Emergent grammar. In Michael Tomasello (ed.), *The new psychology of language*, volume 1, 155–175. Mahwah, NJ: Lawrence Erlbaum.

Housen, Alex & Folkert Kuiken. 2009. Complexity, accuracy, and fluency in second language acquisition. *Applied Linguistics* 30. 461–473.

Hymes, Dell. 1962. The ethnography of speaking. In Thomas Gladwin & William C. Sturtevant (eds.), *Anthropology and human behavior*, 13–53. Washington DC: Anthopology Society of Washington.

Hymes, Dell. 1972. Models of the interaction of language and social life. In John Gumperz & Dell Hymes (eds.), *Directions in sociolinguistics: The ethnography of communication*, 35–71. New York: Holt, Rhinehart & Winston.

Ishida, Midori 2009. Development of interactional competence: Changes in the use of *ne* in L2 Japanese during study abroad. In Hanh T. Nguyen & Gabriele Kasper (eds.), *Talk-in-interaction: Multilingual perspectives*, 351–386. Honolulu: University of Hawai'i.

Ishida, Midori. 2011. Engaging in another person's telling as a recipient in L2 Japanese: Development of interactional competence during one-year study abroad. In Gabriele Pallotti & Johannes Wagner (eds.), *L2 learning as social practice: Conversation-analytic perspectives*, 45–85. Manoa: University of Hawai'i at Manoa.

Kasper, Gabriele & Johannes Wagner. 2011. A conversation-analytic approach to second language acquisition. In Dwight Atkinson (ed.), *Alternative approaches to second language acquisition*, 117–142. New York: Taylor & Francis.

Kim, Younhee. 2009. Korean discourse markers in L2 Korean speakers' conversation: An acquisitional perspective. In Hanh T. Nguyen and Gabriele Kasper (eds.), *Talk-in-interaction: Multilingual perspectives*, 317–350. Honolulu: National Foreign Language Resource Center.

Kramsch, Claire. 1986. From language proficiency to interactional competence. *The Modern Language Journal* 70. 366–372.

Langacker, Ronald W. 1987. *Foundations of cognitive grammar*, volume 1. *Theoretical prerequisites*. Stanford: Stanford University Press.

Lee, Yo-An & John Hellermann. 2014. Tracing developmental change through conversation analysis: Cross-sectional and longitudinal analysis. *TESOL Quarterly* 48(4). 763–788.

Li, Peiwen. 2014. *On the development of second language learners' English motion constructions–a longitudinal usage-based classroom investigation*. University of Southern Denmark unpublished PhD dissertation.

Li, Peiwen, Søren W. Eskildsen & Teresa Cadierno. 2014. Tracing an L2 learner's motion constructions over time: A usage-based classroom investigation. *The Modern Language Journal* 98(2). 612–628.

Lieven, Elena. 2010. Input and first language acquisition: Evaluating the role of frequency. *Lingua* 120. 2546–2556.

Lieven, Elena, Dorothé Salomo & Michael Tomasello. 2009. Two-year-old children's production of multiword utterances: A usage-based analysis. *Cognitive Linguistics* 20(3). 481–508.

MacWhinney, Brian. 1975. Pragmatic patterns in child syntax. *Stanford papers and reports on child language development* 10. 153–165.
Markee, Numa. 2008. Toward a learning behavior tracking methodology for CA-for-SLA. *Applied Linguistics* 29. 404–427.
Masuda, Kyoko. 2011. Acquiring interactional competence in a study abroad context: Japanese language learners' use of the interactional particle ne. *The Modern Language Journal* 95(4). 519–540.
Meisel, Jürgen M., Harald Clahsen & Manfred Pienemann. 1981. On determining developmental stages in second language acquisition. *Studies in Second Language Acquisition* 3. 109–135.
Mellow, J. Dean. 2006. The emergence of second language syntax: A case study of the acquisition of relative clauses. *Applied Linguistics* 27(4). 645–670.
Myles, Florence, Janet Hooper & Rosamund Mitchell. 1998. Rote or rule? Exploring the role of formulaic language in classroom foreign language learning. *Language Learning* 48(3). 323–363.
Myles, Florence, Rosamund Mitchell & Janet Hooper. 1999. Interrogative chunks in French L2: A basis for creative construction? *Studies in Second Language Acquisition* 21(1). 49–80.
Nattinger, James R. & Jeanette S. DeCarrico. 1992. *Lexical phrases and language teaching*. Oxford: Oxford University Press.
Nguyen, Hahn T. 2011. A longitudinal microanalysis of a second language learner's participation. In Gabrielle Pallotti & Johannes Wagner (eds.), *L2 learning as social practice: Conversation-analytic perspectives*, 17–44. Honolulu: University of Hawai'i at Manoa.
Norris, John & Lourdes Ortega. 2009. Towards an organic approach to investigating CAF in instructed SLA: The case of complexity. *Applied Linguistics* 30. 555–578.
Ortega, Lourdes. 2012. Interlanguage complexity: A construct in search of theoretical renewal. In B. Kortmann & B. Szmrecsanyi (eds.), *Linguistic complexity: Second language acquisition, indigenization, contact*, 127–155. Berlin: Mouton de Gruyter.
Pallotti, Gabrielle. 2001. External appropriations as a strategy for participating in intercultural multi-party conversations. In Aldo Di Luzio, Susanne Gunthner & Franca Orletti (eds.), *Culture in communication: Analyses of intercultural situations*, 295–334. Amsterdam & Philadelphia: John Benjamins.
Pallotti, Gabrielle. 2015. A simple view of linguistic complexity. *Second Language Research* 31(1), 117–134.
Pawley, Andrew & Francis H. Syder. 1983. Two puzzles for linguistic theory. In Jack C. Richards & Richard W. Schmidt (eds.), *Language and communication*, 191–226. Harlow: Longman.
Pekarek Doehler, Simona. 2010. Conceptual changes and methodological challenges: On language, learning and documenting learning in conversation analytic SLA research. In Paul Seedhouse & Steve Walsh (eds.), *Conceptions of 'learning' in applied linguistics*, 105–127. New York: Palgrave Macmillan.
Pekarek Doehler, Simona & Evelyne Pochon-Berger. 2011. Developing 'methods' for interaction: Disagreement sequences in French L2. In Joan Kelly Hall, John Hellermann & Simona Pekarek Doehler (eds.), *L2 interactional competence and development*, 206–243. Bristol: Multilingual Matters.
Pekarek Doehler, Simona & Evelyne Pochon-Berger. 2015. The development of L2 interactional competence: Evidence from turn-taking organization, sequence organization, repair organization and preference organization. In Teresa Cadierno & Søren W. Eskildsen (eds.), *Usage-based perspectives on second language learning*, 233–268. Mouton de Gruyter.

Pekarek Doehler, Simona & Evelyne Pochon-Berger. Forthcoming. L2 interactional competence as increased ability for recipient design: A longitudinal study of storyopenings. *Applied Linguistics*.

Pienemann, Mandfred, Malcolm Johnston & Geoff Brindley. 1988. Constructing an acquisition-based procedure for second language assessment. *Studies in Second Language Acquisition* 10. 217–243.

Reder, Steve. 2005. The "Lab School". *Focus on Basics* 8(A). Available online: http://www.ncsall.net/fileadmin/resources/fob/2005/fob_8a.pdf.

Reder, Steve, Kathy A. Harris & Kristen Setzler. 2003. A multimedia adult learner corpus. *TESOL Quarterly* 37(3). 546–557.

Rine, Emily F. & Joan Kelly Hall. 2011. Becoming the teacher: Changing participant framework in international teaching assistant discourse. In Joan Kelly Hall, John Hellermann & Simona Pekarek Doehler (eds.), *L2 interactional competence and development*, 244–274. Bristol: Multilingual Matters.

Robinson, Peter & Nick C. Ellis (eds.), 2008. *Handbook of cognitive linguistics and second language acquisition*. New York: Routledge.

Roehr-Brackin, Karen. 2014. Explicit knowledge and processes from a usage-based perspective: The developmental trajectory of an instructed L2 learner. *Language Learning* 64. 771–808.

Sacks, Harvey & Emanuel A. Schegloff. 1979. Two preferences in the organization of reference to persons in conversation and their interaction. In George Psathas (ed.), *Everyday language: Studies in ethnomethodology*, 15–21. Irvington Press: New York, NY.

Schiffrin, Deborah. 1986. The functions of *and* in discourse. *Journal of Pragmatics* 10. 41–66.

Schegloff, Emanuel A. 2007. *Sequence organization in interaction: A primer in conversation analysis*, volume 1. Cambridge: Cambridge University Press.

Theodórsdóttir, Guðrun & Søren W. Eskildsen. 2015. Constructing another language on the fly: A longitudinal case study of L2 learning in the wild. Paper presented at *The Conference of the International Institute for Ethnomethodology and Conversation Analysis*, August 4–7, 2015, Kolding, Denmark.

Tomasello, Michael. 2003. *Constructing a language*. Cambridge: Cambridge University Press.

Tummers, Jose, Kris Heylen & Dirk Geeraerts. 2005. Usage-based approaches in cognitive linguistics: A technical state of the art. *Corpus Linguistics and Linguistic Theory* 1(2). 225–261.

Turk, Monica J. 1999. Negatively formulated questions in interaction. *Crossroads of Language, Interaction, and Culture* 1. 39–48.

Turk, Monica J. 2004. Using *and* in conversational interaction. *Research on Language and Social Interaction* 37(2). 319–350.

van Lier, Leo. 2000. From input to affordance: Social interactive learning from an ecological perspective. In James P. Lantolf (ed.), *Sociocultural theory and second language learning: Recent advances*, 245–259. Oxford: Oxford University Press.

Waara, René. 2004. Construal, convention, and constructions in L2 speech. In Michel Achard and Susanne Niemeier (eds.), *Cognitive linguistics, second language acquisition, and foreign language pedagogy, 51–75*. Berlin: Mouton de Gruyter.

Weinert, Regina. 1995. The role of formulaic language in second language acquisition: A review. *Applied Linguistics* 16(2). 180–205.

Yuldashev, Aziz, Julieta Fernandez & Steven L. Thorne. 2013. Second language learners' contiguous and discontiguous multi-word unit use over time. *The Modern Language Journal* 97(S1). 31–45.

Stefanie Wulff, Stefan Th. Gries and Nicholas Lester
# Optional *that* in complementation by German and Spanish learners

## 1 Introduction

This study examines the factors that govern the variable presence of the complementizer *that* in English object-, subject-, and adjectival complement constructions as in (1) to (3):[1]

(1) a. I thought that Nick likes candy.

   b. I thought Ø Nick likes candy.

(2) a. The problem is that Nick doesn't like candy.

   b. The problem is Ø Nick doesn't like candy.

(3) a. I'm glad that Stefan likes candy.

   b. I'm glad Ø Stefan likes candy.

The conditions under which native speakers (NS) decide to realize or drop the complementizer have been intensively studied (e.g., Jaeger 2010; Tagliamonte and Smith 2005; Thompson and Mulac 1991; Torres Cacoullos and Walker 2009), while few studies have investigated this phenomenon in non-native speakers (NNS) (e.g., Durham 2011; Wulff, Lester, and Martinez-Garcia 2014). In the present study, we therefore address the following research questions:
- What factors govern *that*-variation in intermediate-level German and Spanish L2 learners of English?
- How do these learners' preferences compare to those of native speakers? More specifically, under what conditions, how much, and why do learners deviate from native speaker behavior?

---

[1] The complementizer is optional in other constructions as well, including appositions, relative clauses of *it*-clefts, and with extraposed subjects; instances of these constructions, which are far less frequent than the three constructions examined here, were not considered in this study.

---

**Stefanie Wulff,** University of Florida
**Stefan Th. Gries** and **Nicholas Lester,** University of California, Santa Barbara

https://doi.org/10.1515/9783110572186-004

The paper is structured as follows. Section 2 provides a compact overview of the factors suggested to impact *that*-variation; specifically, Section 2.1 discusses *that*-variation in L1 English whereas Section 2.2 briefly describes the equivalents of *that*-variation in L1 German and L1 Spanish, the native language backgrounds of the L2-learners investigated here. Section 3 gives a brief summary of previous studies on *that*-variation in learner populations. In Section 4, we describe our data sample in detail, explain how the data were annotated for the different variables included in the study, introduce the statistical method employed, MuPDAR, and explain how this method was applied to our data. Section 5 summarizes the results, and Section 6 concludes by recapturing the main findings and their implications, in particular from the perspective of usage-based construction grammar.

## 2 Factors influencing *that*-variation

### 2.1 *That*-variation in native English

Over the last 25 years, *that*-variation has received a lot of attention. Space does not permit a detailed discussion of this body of research (see Wulff, Lester, and Martinez-Garcia 2014) so here we briefly summarize only those factors which have consistently emerged as relevant:

- *mode* (Biber 1999; Bryant 1962; Storms 1966): the complementizer is omitted more frequently in spoken than in written language; likewise, higher shares of zero-*that* are found in informal registers (both spoken and written).
- *structural complexity* (also referred to as *syntactic weight*; see Elsness 1984; Jaeger 2010; Kaltenböck 2006; Thompson and Mulac 1991; Torres Cacoullos and Walker 2009): syntactically light main and/or complement clause subjects as well as light complement clauses are correlated with zero-*that*, and these correlations are strongest with the structurally simple first person pronoun *I* in subject position in the matrix clause.
- *clause juncture* (Jaeger 2010; Kaltenböck 2006; Thompson and Mulac 1991; Torres Cacoullos and Walker 2009): chances of zero-*that* are highest when clause juncture is intact, i.e., when there is no intervening material anywhere. When material intervenes between the matrix clause subject and the verb, the matrix clause verb and the complementizer slot, or the complementizer slot and the ensuing complement clause, this raises the likelihood of *that* being realized. Some studies suggest that material preceding the matrix clause subject may also increase chances of *that* – while clause-initial material does not interrupt clause juncture, it adds to the overall complexity of the message.

- *properties of the matrix clause verb* (Dor 2005; Kaltenböck 2006; Rissanen 1991; Tagliamonte and Smith 2005): several studies point out that zero-*that* is especially likely with (typically highly frequent) matrix clause verbs that denote truth claim predicates (such as *think*, *know*, and *believe*). What is more, Wulff, Lester, and Martinez-Garcia (2014) found that beyond their absolute frequencies, some verbs are zero-favoring while others are *that*-favoring, as can be expressed in the association strength between a given verb and either construction, respectively.
- *surprisal* (Jaeger 2010; Levy 2008): matrix verb lemmas that are biased to occur in the complement clause construction carry enough information about the upcoming clause juncture to make the overt complementizer redundant. This informational boost is quantified using an information-theoretic measure known as surprisal, which Jaeger (2010) shows is positively correlated with rates of *that*-mentioning.
- *individual variation*: just like in many other (psycho)linguistic phenomena, there is individual variation among speakers.

In the next section, we provide a very brief overview of the equivalents of *that*-variation in German and Spanish.

## 2.2 *That*-variation in native German and Spanish

Regarding complementizer optionality, German is slightly less permissive than English: The complementizer *dass* is optional in subject and direct object complements, but obligatory in adjectival complements. German also differs from English in that the position of the verb in the complement clause is contingent on whether the complementizer is realized or not: When the complementizer is not realized, the verb follows the subject (which is the default word order for main clauses in German); when the complementizer is realized, the verb appears in clause-final position (which is the default word order for subordinate clauses in German). Examples (4) to (6) provide German translations of (1) to (3) respectively.

(4) a. *Ich   dachte,        dass   Nick   Suesses   mag.*
       I     think.3SG.PST  COMP   Nick   candy     like.3SG.PRS
       'I thought that Nick likes candy'

   b. *Ich   dachte,        Ø      Nick   mag           Suesses.*
       I     think.3SG.PST  COMP   Nick   like.3SG.PRS  candy
       'I thought Nick likes candy'

(5) a. *Das Problem ist,        dass   Nick  Suesses  nicht  mag.*
       the   problem  COP.3SG.PRS  COMP  Nick  candy    NEG   like.3SG.PRS
       'The problem is that Nick doesn't like candy'

   b. *Das Problem ist,        Ø     Nick  mag*
       the   problem  COP.3SG.PRS  COMP  Nick  like.3SG.PRS NEG
       *Suesses nicht.*
       candy    NEG
       'The problem is Nick doesn't like candy'

(6) a. *Ich bin        froh, dass  Stefan  Suesses  mag.*
       I    COP.1SG.PRS  glad  COMP  Stefan  candy    like.3SG.PRS
       'I'm glad that Stefan likes candy'

   b. *\*Ich bin        froh,  Ø    Stefan  mag         Suesses.*
       I    COP.1SG.PRS  glad  COMP  Stefan  like.3SG.PRS  candy
       'I'm glad Stefan likes candy'

Spanish, in turn, is even less permissive than German: the complementizer *que* is always obligatory. (7) to (9) are translations of (1) to (3), respectively.

(7) a. *Pensé         que   a   Nick  le       gustaban       los  dulces.*
       think.1SG.PST  COMP  to  Nick  CL.DAT.  like.3.PL.IMP  the  candies
       'I thought that Nick likes candy'

   b. *\*Pensé        Ø     a   Nick  le       gustaban       los  dulces.*
       think.1SG.PST  COMP  to  Nick  CL.DAT.  like.3.PL.IMP  the  candies
       'I thought Nick likes candy'

(8) a. *El  problema  es          que   a   Nick  no   le*
       the  problem   COP.3SG.PRS  COMP  to  Nick  NEG  CL.DAT.
       *gustan         los  dulces.*
       like.3.PL.IMP  the  candies
       'The problem is that Nick doesn't like candy'

   b. *\*El problema  es          Ø     a   Nick  no   le*
       the  problem   COP.3SG.PRS  COMP  to  Nick  NEG  CL.DAT.
       *gustan         los  dulces.*
       like.3.PL.IMP  the  candies
       'The problem is Nick doesn't like candy'

(9) a. *Me      alegra                 que  a  Stefan le*
       CL.DAT. makes-happy.3SG.PRS COMP to Stefan CL.DAT.
       *gustan       los  dulces.*
       like.3.PL.PRS the candies
       'I'm glad that Stefan likes candy'

   b. *\*Me     alegra                 Ø    a  Stefan le*
       CL.DAT. makes-happy.3SG.PRS COMP to Stefan CL.DAT.
       *gustan       los  dulces.*
       like.3.PL.PRS the candies
       'I'm glad Stefan likes candy'

Given these contrasts between English, German, and Spanish, we can assume that native-like use of *that*-variation should be overall easier to attain for German learners of English than Spanish learners, who should be most reluctant to omit the complementizer. Previous research in fact supports this hypothesis (Wulff 2016; Wulff, Lester and Martinez-Garcia 2014).

# 3 *That*-variation in L2 production

In contrast to the wealth of studies on native speakers, there are few studies to date that examine *that*-variation in L2 learners. One example is Durham (2011) on native speakers' and French, German, and Italian ESL learners' use of *that*-variation in emails. Durham reports that shares of zero-*that* hover around 35% overall; French and Italian learners are more likely to produce the complementizer than the German learners and native English speakers. Furthermore, Durham confirms that, as in native speakers, combinations of the first person pronoun *I* as the matrix clause subject and verbs like *think* and *hope* trigger the highest shares of zero-*that*. The German and Italian learners display sensitivity also to clause juncture constraints while the French learners do not.

Wulff, Lester and Martinez-Garcia (2014) examine what comprises the written part of the data sample of the present study (i.e., native English speakers, German L2 learners, and Spanish L2 learners). They include all of the factors listed in Section 4.2.1 (except for mode, surprisal, and individual variation) in a multi-factorial regression analysis. Their findings suggest intermediate-advanced level German and Spanish learners are quite attuned to native-like choices: they appear to be sensitive to the same factors as native speakers, and the directions of the effects for these factors are identical. That said, compared to the native speakers, both learner groups display a lower rate of zero-*that*. They also appear to be more impacted by processing-related factors such as structural complexity and clause juncture as opposed to lexical-semantic properties such as the choice of matrix clause verb.

Wulff (2016) expands Wulff, Lester, and Martinez-Garcia's (2014) study by adding spoken data to the sample. Her results are mainly in accord with the previous studies, and confirm that, like native speakers, second language learners (at least at an intermediate level of proficiency) are aware of the mode-dependent nature of *that*-variation.

In the present study, we are improving on Wulff's analysis in several important ways. First, the current analysis includes surprisal as a predictor. Second, the statistical analysis presented here is much more sophisticated than the binary logistic regression Wulff (2016) presents: firstly, we are using a two-step regression procedure that has been developed specifically for the analysis of differences between native and non-native language; secondly, the regressions we are using involve mixed-effects/multi-level models. This choice of model allows us to take complex hierarchical structures in the data into consideration, such as speaker- and verb-specific effects. We outline the specifics of this approach in Section 4.3.

# 4 Methods

## 4.1 Data

The data for this study were retrieved from different corpora. The NS data were obtained from the British component of the *International Corpus of English* (ICE-GB), a balanced, parsed, 1-million words corpus of British English, which comprises 60% written and 40% spoken data. Using the ICE-CUP software packet that accompanies the corpus, all instances of the three complement constructions that are contained in the corpus were retrieved.

The written NNS data were obtained from the German and the Spanish sub-corpora of the second version of the *International Corpus of Learner English* (G-ICLE and SP-ICLE; see Granger et al. 2009). ICLE comprises 3.7 million words of EFL writing from learners from 16 different L1 backgrounds. The spoken learner data came from the German and Spanish sub-corpora of the LINDSEI corpus (see Gilquin, De Cock, and Granger 2010). LINDSEI is a 1-million-word corpus of informal interviews with high intermediate-advanced proficiency EFL learners.

Unlike the ICE-GB, neither ICLE nor LINDSEI are syntactically parsed, so in order to retrieve hits from these corpora, the following procedure was adopted: A list of all verb lemmas attested in the ICE-GB across the three constructions was created and used to retrieve all sentences with these verb lemmas in G-ICLE, SP-ICLE, and LINDSEI. The resulting candidate list was then manually checked for true hits.

Table 1 provides a breakdown of the final data sample of 9,445 hits by L1 background, construction (ADJ vs. OBJ vs. SUB complementation), mode (spoken vs. written), and whether the complementizer was absent or present. Two things stand out immediately when we look at the learner populations: both German and Spanish learners use complementation constructions far less frequently in speaking than in writing (this is especially true for adjectival and subject complementation), which reverses the trend we observe in the native speaker data. Secondly, adjectival complementation is very infrequent in the Spanish learner data.

**Table 1:** Data sample of the present study

| L1 | Construction | Mode | *that* = absent | *that* = present | Total |
|---|---|---|---|---|---|
| English | ADJ | spoken | 107 | 57 | 164 |
| | | written | 41 | 35 | 76 |
| | OBJ | spoken | 2,446 | 1,235 | 3,681 |
| | | written | 528 | 651 | 1,179 |
| | SUB | spoken | 85 | 296 | 381 |
| | | written | 7 | 146 | 153 |
| | Total | | 3,214 | 2,420 | 5,634 |
| German | ADJ | spoken | 2 | 4 | 6 |
| | | written | 17 | 84 | 101 |
| | OBJ | spoken | 643 | 155 | 798 |
| | | written | 224 | 853 | 1,077 |
| | SUB | spoken | 12 | 21 | 33 |
| | | written | 9 | 213 | 222 |
| | Total | | 907 | 1330 | 2,237 |
| Spanish | ADJ | spoken | 0 | 2 | 2 |
| | | written | 0 | 3 | 3 |
| | OBJ | spoken | 437 | 173 | 610 |
| | | written | 176 | 682 | 858 |
| | SUB | spoken | 4 | 35 | 39 |
| | | written | 8 | 54 | 62 |
| | Total | | 625 | 949 | 1,574 |
| Total | | | 4,746 | 4,699 | 9,445 |

## 4.2 Variables and operationalizations

### 4.2.1 Frequently-used predictors

The 9,445 hits retrieved from the corpora were coded for the factors listed below. In order to understand how each factor was operationalized, let us consider the (fictional) example sentence in (10).

(10)   Seriously, I really hope very much that he likes this chocolate.

- **L1 background**: the native language of the speaker: English vs. German vs. Spanish;
- **Mode**: the sub-corpus from which an example came: spoken vs. written;
- **Complementizer**: complementizer presence: absent vs. present;
- **ComplementType**: the type of complement sentence: adjectival vs. object vs. subject;
- **LengthCIM**:[2] the length of any clause-initial material (before the matrix-clause subject) in number of characters;
- **LengthMatrixSubj**: the length of the matrix clause subject;
- **LengthComplementSubj**: the length of the complement clause subject;
- **LengthComplement**: the length of the complement clause;
- **LengthCCRemainder**: the length of any post-verbal material in the complement clause;
- **LengthMCSubjMCVerb**: the amount of material between the matrix clause subject and the matrix clause verb;
- **LengthMCVerbCC**: the amount of material between the matrix clause verb and the complement clause;
- **DeltaPWC/DeltaPCW**: the association of each verb attested in the data sample to *that* or zero-*that* was calculated and vice versa. The specific association measure employed here is a Delta-*P* association measure (using Stefan Th. Gries' *R*-script coll.analysis 3.2; Gries 2007), which involves two different scores: a Delta-$P_{WC}$ value (WC stands for 'word-to-construction') quantifies how predictive the verb is of the absence or presence of *that*, and a Delta-$P_{CW}$ value (CW stands for 'construction-to-word') indicates how predictive the absence or presence of *that* is for the verb in question (see Ellis 2006; Gries 2013). Delta-*P* values range between -1 when the first element strongly repels the second, via 0 (when there is no association), to 1 (when the first element strongly attracts the second).

---

[2] All length-related predictors were measured as the number of characters. While counting the number of syllables or words might seem more intuitive, for all intents and purposes, length counts in characters, words, phonemes, or syllables are so highly correlated (and, thus, come with no conceptual/interpretive disadvantages) that we opted for the ease of operationalizing length with automatically-countable character lengths.

Consider Table 2 for the annotation of (10):

**Table 2:** The annotation of example (10)

| | |
|---|---|
| Complementizer: present | ComplementType: object |
| LengthCIM: 9 ("Seriously") | LengthMatrixSubj: 1 ("I") |
| LengthComplementSubj: 2 ("he") | LengthComplement: 20 ("he likes this chocolate") |
| LengthCCRemainder: 13 ("this chocolate") | |
| LengthMCSubjMCVerb: 6 ("really") | LengthMCVerbCC: 8 ("very much") |
| Delta-$P_{CW}$ for *hope*: 0.1148 | Delta-$P_{WC}$ for *hope*: 0.167 |

As previously mentioned, we also included a predictor measuring the surprisal of the material spanning the clause juncture (i.e., the surprisal of moving from *much* to *Nick* in (10)). Given the relative scarcity of such applications in SLA research, we provide a more thorough discussion of this variable in Section 4.2.2. Finally, we added annotation to take into consideration speaker-specific and lexically-specific effects: each example was annotated for the corpus and the file it came from as well as for the verb form and the verb lemma of the main clause.

### 4.2.2 The information-theoretic notion of surprisal

*That*-variation has been shown to be affected by various probabilistic relationships between words (and larger units), both within and across the matrix and complement clauses. Jaeger (2010) showed that one particularly important relationship holds between the matrix verb lemma (uninflected stem, e.g., EAT for *eat, eats, eating, ...*) and the syntactic juncture between the matrix and complement clause. When the verb lemma was highly informative about the presence of an upcoming clause juncture, rates of *that* decreased. To measure the expectation of the clause juncture that is projected from the matrix verb lemma (in other words, the *redundancy* of the complementizer), Jaeger used an information-theoretic measure known as *surprisal* or *self-information*. Surprisal measures how uncertain one would be about observing some event – how 'surprising' that event would be – given a known probability distribution of related events. It is calculated by taking the negative binary log of the probability $p$ of a given event $x$ belonging to probability distribution $P$, as in (11).

(11)  $S(x: x \in P) = -\log_2 p(x)$

Because he was interested in the surprisal of the juncture given the matrix verb lemma, Jaeger (2010) substituted the conditional probability $p$ (juncture | matrix verb lemma) for the simple probability $p$. The generalized form of this substitution, which we shall henceforth refer to as *conditional surprisal* $S_c$, is

(12)  $S_c(y|x: y, x \in P) = -\log_2 p(y|x)$

In the present study, we replace Jaeger's (2010) conditional surprisal value with the bi-directional collostructional association measure Delta-P, and so measure directly the preferences of each matrix verb for the presence or absence of the complementizer (as opposed to the presence or absence of a complement *clause*). However, the notion of conditional surprisal can be applied at a finer resolution to explore local negotiations of informational load at the clause juncture. For instance, as Jaeger points out, the relative (un)expectedness of the first word following the clause juncture (i.e., the complement clause onset) may influence *that*-mentioning, such that more surprising onsets correlate with greater shares of *that*. Jaeger proposes that, ideally, the surprisal of the onset should be conditioned on the joint probability of the matrix verb occurring in a complement clause construction, that is, $S_c$(onset | verb, complement construction). However, this measure misses the fact that different verbs are differently associated with rates of the *that*-mentioning apart from their likelihood of occurring within the complement-clause construction (consider the logically possible case of a verb that only occurs in the complement-clause construction, but prefers *that*). Moreover, Jaeger's proposal overlooks the possible fluctuations in informational load that can be attributed directly to the words standing at either edge of the clause juncture (the left edge may contain a word other than the matrix verb). The relationships between these words may incrementally or instantaneously overturn (or reinforce) the expectations triggered by the matrix verb. Finally, by taking his measurements at the level of the matrix verb lemma, Jaeger increases the statistical reliability of his estimates, but glosses over the possibility that the different inflected forms of a verb will correlate with different patterns of use.

Therefore, we include among our predictors an additional estimate of conditional surprisal: We take the surprisal of the first word of the complement clause onset conditioned on the last word of the matrix clause prior to the clause juncture, regardless of whether the complementizer separates the words or not. For example, the sequence from (10) *hope (that) he* would be measured as $S_c(he|hope) = -\log_2 p(he|hope)$, which we operationalize based on data from the complete British National Corpus (World Edition). Thus, we measure how surprising the transition would be if no complementizer had been used, under the assumption that more surprising local transitions will correlate with higher shares of *that*. Importantly, despite the criticisms mentioned above, we do not intend that our measure should be seen as an alternative to the one employed by Jaeger (2010). Rather, we propose that our measure be seen to complement his at a finer granularity.

## 4.3 Statistical evaluation: MuPDAR

In order to tease apart how and why the NNS differ from the NS choices of *that*-complementation, we are using an approach called MuPDAR (Multifactorial Prediction and Deviation Analysis using Regressions), which was recently developed in Gries and Deshors (2014) and Gries and Adelman (2014). MuPDAR involves the following three steps:
- fit a regression $R_1$ that models the choices of speakers of the target language (here, English as operationalized by the ICE-GB) with regard to the phenomenon in question;
- apply the results of $R_1$ to the other speakers in the data (here, German and Spanish learners of English) to predict for each of their data points what the native speakers of the target language would have done in their situation;
- fit a regression $R_2$ that explores how the non-native speakers' choices differ from those of the speakers of the target/reference variety.

Crucially, in this study, both $R_1$ and $R_2$ are mixed-effects models that take into consideration the potential variability that is shared by all examples retrieved from one file and by all examples sharing the same verb (lemma), as will be detailed below; note that one can use any kind of classifier, not just regression.

After preparation of the data (logging several variables and factorizing others, see below), for $R_1$, we began with a regression model that predicted *that*-complementation patterns of the NNS on the basis of the following predictors, to which interactions were added as required by likelihood ratio tests: ComplementType, Mode, LengthCIM (factorized into three different levels given the highly skewed distribution of the data), LengthMatrixSubj (factorized into two levels), LengthMCSubjMCVerb (factorized into two levels), LengthMCVerbCC (factorized into two levels), both Delta-*P* values, and (the logged values of) LengthComplementSubj, LengthComplement, and LengthCCRemainder.[3]

---

**3** While factorizing numeric predictors is typically not recommended given the loss of information it incurs, we nonetheless opted for it here because initial exploratory analyses indicated potentially problematic distributional characteristics for several numeric predictors. For instance,

We then applied the final version of $R_1$ to the NNS data and added four columns to them: a column PredictionsNum (the predicted probabilities of a NS using *that* in the situation the NNS is in), PredictionsCat (the dichotomized decision following from PredictionsNum whether a NS would use *that* or not), Correct (whether the NNS made the nativelike choice or not), and, most importantly at present, a column called Deviation. Deviation contains a 0 if the NNS made the nativelike choice, and it contains 0.5-PredictionsNum if the NNS did not make the nativelike choice. That means, Deviation is >0 when the NNS used *that* while the NS wouldn't have, and Deviation is <0 when the NNS did not use *that* while the NS would have.

Finally, we developed a regression model $R_2$ that tries to predict Deviation, i.e. how nativelike the NNS choices were on the basis of the same predictors as in $R_1$, but also adding L1 as a predictor that could interact with all others. This last predictor, through interactions, allows us to determine which factors have L1-specific effects. We began with a model involving only main effects, then added interactions of those with L1, then interactions among all predictors (using LR-tests), testing for collinearity at each step and not admitting predictors that would raise variance inflation factors (*VIFs*) to ≥5.1. The final model of $R_2$ we adopted includes one predictor that was only marginally significant but interesting and was then explored and visualized, as outlined in the next section.

# 5 Results

## 5.1 Results of $R_1$ on the NS data

The result of the model selection process for $R_1$ were encouraging: $R_1$ featured a variety of highly significant predictors and arrived at a very good classification accuracy: 85.7% of the native speakers' *that* choices were classified correctly, which, according to exact binomial tests, is highly significantly better than either making the more frequent choice all the time (baseline$_1$: 68.5%) or making random choices proportional to the complementation frequencies (baseline$_2$: 56.8%); both *p*'s < $10^{-10}$. The *C*-value for this regression model is 0.91, thus

---

when <10% of all data points of LengthMCSubjMCVerb cover character lengths from 2 to 121, then estimating a regression slope for such a large but sparsely populated range of values is not going to yield reliable results, and a binary factorization of this predictor does not adversely affect the degrees of freedom. Also, note that factorization is a purely methodological choice – it does not reflect particular assumptions of ours regarding the cognitive mechanisms that go into selecting (to omit) a complementizer.

exceeding the typical threshold of 0.8, and the marginal and conditional $R^2$ are a reassuring 0.48 and 0.59. As for the random-effects structure of the model, we accounted for varying baselines of speakers to use/omit *that* (by including varying intercepts for files in the model) as well as varying preferences of verbs to use/omit *that* (by including varying intercepts for verb forms nested into lemmas in the model).

## 5.2 Applying $R_1$ to the NNS data

The application of the above regression model to the NNS data also yielded encouraging results: the NS regression model predicted 75.2% of the NNS choices correctly, which again highly significantly (both $p$'s < $10^{-100}$) exceeds both baselines (at 0.5, because the NNS chose to realize *that* nearly half of the time); the *C*-value for this prediction was 0.86.

## 5.3 Results of $R_2$ on the NNS data

Computing $R_2$, the model exploring to what degree NNS made nativelike choices, required a few tweaks: because of their high intercorrelations, the two Delta-*P* values as well as LengthCCRemainder and ComplementLength were each combined into a single variable (using principal component scores); the principal component for the Delta-*P*s, however, did not survive the model selection process. As above, we included a simple random-effects structure for files and verbs (forms nested into lemmas). $R_2$ returned a variety of significant predictors,

**Table 3:** Summary results of $R_2$

| Fixed effects predictor | Likelihood ratio test | *p* |
|---|---|---|
| LengthCIM | 40.103 ($df$ = 2) | <0.0001 |
| Surprisal | 10.434 ($df$ = 1) | 0.0012 |
| ComplementType : LengthComplementSubject | 23.902 ($df$ = 2) | <0.0001 |
| Mode : LengthComplementSubject | 18.792 ($df$ = 1) | <0.0001 |
| Mode : LengthMatrixSubj | 19.7 ($df$ = 2) | <0.0001 |
| ComplementLength/LengthCCRemainder : LengthMatrixSubj | 7.531 ($df$ = 2) | 0.0232 |
| L1 : LengthMCSubjMcVerb | 8.282 | 0.004 |
| L1 : LengthComplementSubject | 2.896 | 0.0089 ms |

both main effects and interactions (some pointing to L1-specific effects of the learners, some applying to both learner groups). The overall model $R^2$-values are less high than those of $R_1$: marginal and conditional $R^2$ are 0.13 and 0.3 respectively. Table 3 gives a brief overview of the highest-level predictors in the final model of $R_2$.

For reasons of space, we can unfortunately not discuss all effects in much detail; here, we will leave out the predictors involving the matrix subject. In our discussion, we will first turn to the main effects (Section 5.3.1), then we will turn to interactions, first those that apply to both learner groups (Section 5.3.2), then the ones that reveal differences between the German and Spanish learners (Section 5.3.3).

### 5.3.1 Main effects in $R_2$

Figure 1 shows the main effect of LengthCIM on Deviation: The more material precedes the main clause, the more the NNS make nativelike choices. What are the NS choices? The more material precedes the main clause, the more the NS use *that*, from 29.5% (for none) over 43.6% (for some) to 59.4% (for much). Our results show that the NNS exhibit the same tendency, but with higher proportions of *that*-use throughout: 44.6% over 67.5% to 77.4%. One possible explanation for this pattern is that, as the amount of material before the main clauses grows, both NS and NNS benefit more from inserting *that* as a structural marker between main clause and complement clause.

Figure 2 shows that, as the first word of the complement clause becomes more surprising given the last word of the main clause, NNS make significantly more nativelike choices. Both NS and NNS increase their complementizer use with higher rates of surprisal, and as before, the NNS just do this with a higher overall baseline of *that*-use. This difference reflects the fact that even what is expected by NS remains rather unexpected to NNS, a likely consequence of their lesser experience with naturalistic English use. Nevertheless, under conditions of high uncertainty, both groups appear to use *that* to smooth spikes in informational load (as reported for NS by Jaeger 2010).

In sum, both overall main effects are compatible with the interpretation that NS and NNS are subject to similar processing pressures and react to them in similar ways even though NNS have a much higher baseline of *that*-use.

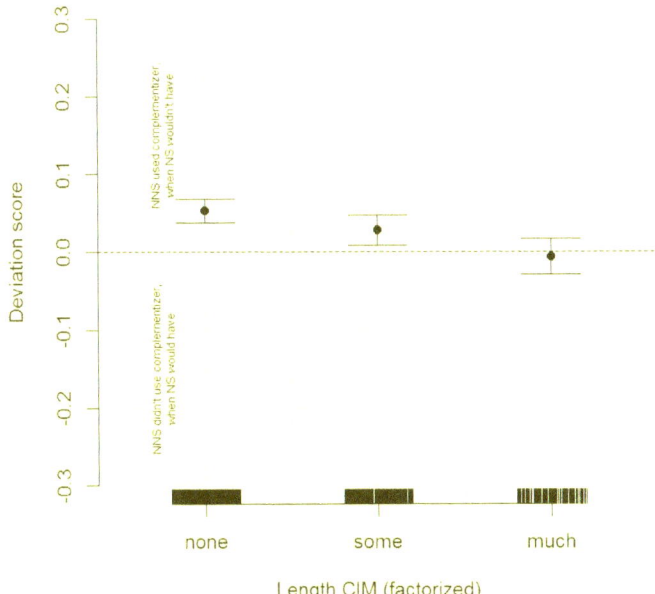

**Figure 1:** The effect of LengthCIM in $R_2$

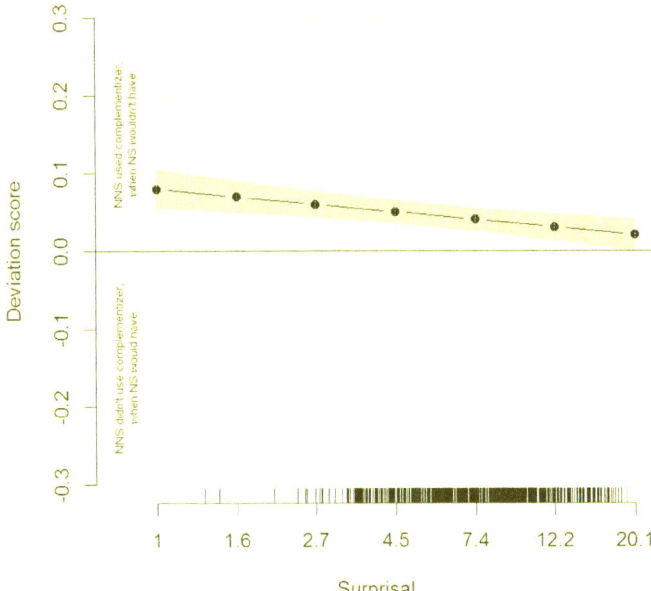

**Figure 2:** The effect of surprisal in $R_2$

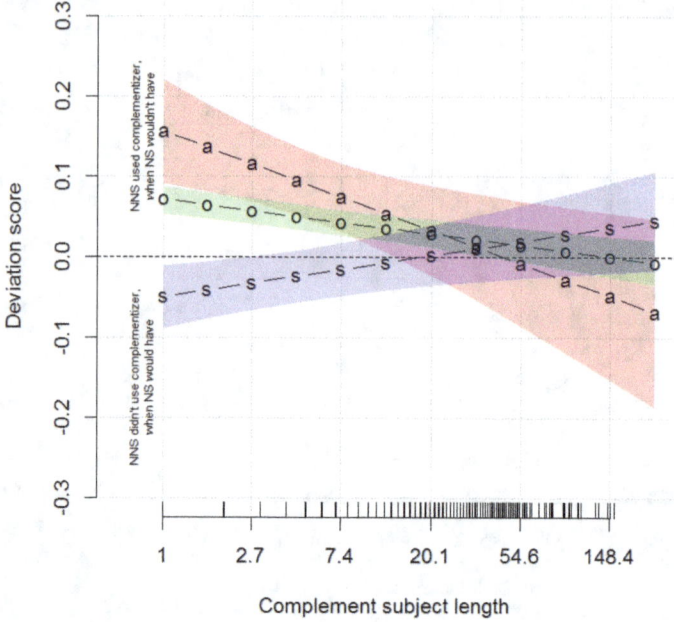

**Figure 3:** The effect of ComplementType : LengthComplementSubj in $R_2$

### 5.3.2 Interactions in $R_2$ that do not involve L1

Figure 3 shows the interaction ComplementType : LengthComplementSubj; the former predictor is represented by three regression lines with the initial letters of the complement types, the latter is represented on the *x*-axis. While the sample size in particular for ComplementType: Adjective is very small, as reflected in the wider confidence band, the corresponding effect in the NS data is that, with increasing length of the subject of the complement clause, speakers use *that* more. The NNS exhibit a similar trend: As the length of the subject of the complement clause increases, they also use *that* more, just like the NS. However, when the subjects of the complement clauses are short, the NNS overuse *that* in adjectival and object complement clauses and are fairly close to NS all the time in subject complement clauses. It is very plausible that this is due to transfer: In Spanish, the complementizer is obligatory in object and adjectival complement clauses, and in German, it is obligatory in adjectival complement clauses. The fact that both NNS L1s require the complementizer in at least one complement construction suggests that functionally specific transfer could be responsible for the overuse of *that* by our sample of NNS.

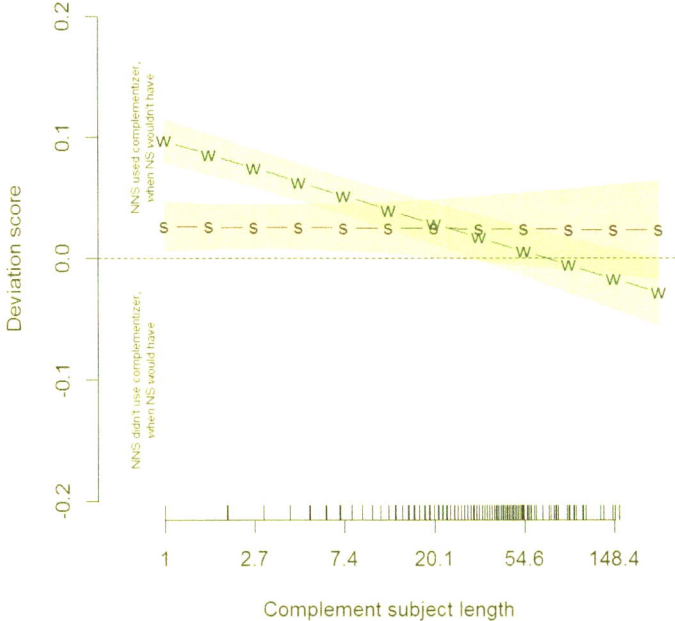

**Figure 4:** The effect of Mode : LengthComplementSubj in $R_2$

Figure 4 reflects a clear-cut effect. NS use *that* more in writing and less in speaking while the NNS are fairly close to the NS in speaking but still overuse the complementizer regardless of the length of the complement subject. In writing, on the other hand, the NNS are more nativelike with longer subjects, but overuse *that* with short subjects (in particular *I*).

Both effects show that the length of the complement clause subject is important for all speaker groups and that the learners 'get' the overall preference; however, due to transfer from complementizer use in their L1s and exaggerating the difference between modes, intermediate learners still need to fine-tune their preferences.

### 5.3.3 Interactions in $R_2$ that involve L1

Let us finally turn to two interactions that reveal differences between German and Spanish learners. Figure 5 shows how the two learner groups (represented with separate regression lines) react differently to the length of the subject of the complement clause. As discussed above, all speakers – NS and NNS – are

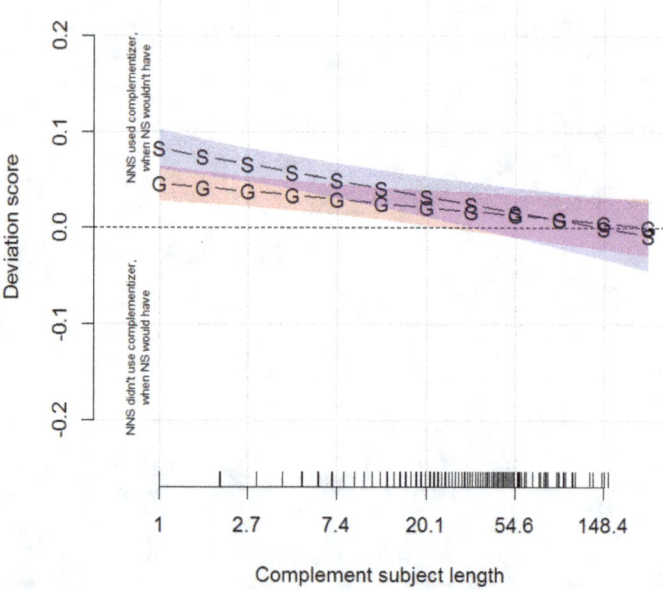

**Figure 5:** The effect of L1 : LengthComplementSubj in $R_2$

more likely to use *that* with longer complement clause subjects. However, the Germans are marginally significantly more similar to the NS with short complement subjects than the Spanish learners, who with short subject overuse *that* more than the Germans.

Finally, Figure 6 shows that, if there is material intervening between the subject and the verb of the main clause, then both German and Spanish speakers behave nativelike and use *that*, but when there is none, then both learner groups overuse *that*, and the Spanish speakers particularly much.

In sum, the German learners produce more nativelike rates of *that*-mentioning than the Spanish learners when it comes to the length effects studied in this section.

Space only permits a brief comment regarding the random-effects structure of the final model of $R_2$. The largest amount of the variance of the random effects by far was accounted for by the file names, i.e. our proxy for different speakers, namely 12.5%. The second most useful random effect was the verb forms (nested into the verb lemmas), which accounted for an additional 3.5%; verb lemmas contributed an additional 3.1%. While these numbers may not seem high, they point to the need for including such effects for more accurate results than

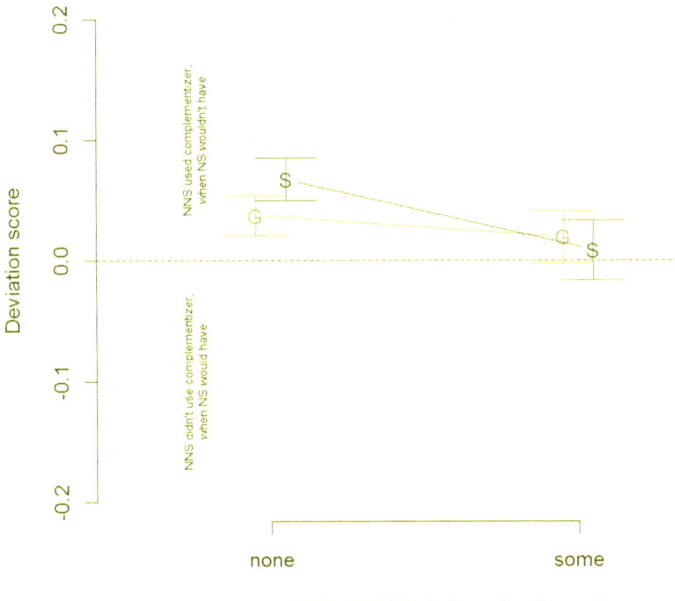

**Figure 6:** The effect of L1 : LengthMCSubjMCVerb in $R_2$

are usually provided in SLA research, and it needs to be borne in mind that our random-effects structure was restricted to varying intercepts only (given data sparsity) – more complex structures might well explain (much) more variability.

# 6 Discussion

The results of the MuPDAR analysis suggest that the intermediate-advanced German and Spanish learners are quite well aligned with NS norms overall. Minor (yet significant) differences were identified in the second regression: both learner groups employ comparatively higher shares of *that* as the processing demands increase, be it in the form of more material occurring at the onset of the clause or with longer complement subjects. More pronounced differences between NS and learners become visible when we consider construction-specific uses of *that* – learners overuse the complementizer in adjectival and object constructions – and register-specific uses of *that*: both learner groups overuse the complementizer especially in writing when the main clause subject is *I*. Finally, a few L1-specific differences emerge: the Spanish learners overuse the complementizer more frequently than their German peers do in contexts with short complement clause subjects and when clause juncture is interrupted.

These findings suggest that the intermediate-advanced learners examined here rely on the same basic mechanisms governing *that*-variation as native speakers, but at the same time display a comparatively more conservative behavior than the native speakers: learners produce the complementizerless utterances only in what we may call "ideal contexts" associated with low shares of *that* also in NS use, namely in speaking, with short subject and complement clause subjects, and with little or no increased processing costs imposed by optional additional and/or intervening material. When the context is less than ideal, the learners – and the Spanish learners more so than their German peers, arguably reflecting transfer from the L1 – resort to the "safe" strategy of realizing the complementizer as this choice is never, strictly speaking, ungrammatical, if only, at times, non-idiomatic.

Generally speaking, the learner behavior is not fundamentally different from NS behavior; rather, the thresholds for producing the complementizer are significantly lower compared to NS speakers, and they are reactive to the factors mentioned above. This stands in accord with usage-based models of L2 learning such as N. Ellis' Associative-Cognitive CREED model (Ellis and Wulff 2015) or Goldberg's (2006) usage-based Construction Grammar, to name but two examples; these models share the assumption that L2 learning is best characterized as the gradual approximation towards native-like representations. As one reviewer pointed out, questions regarding which specific mechanisms underlie the factors included here – cognitive load, learning as a result of usage, transfer effects, and/or instructional effects –, and how exactly each these mechanisms operate in the individual learner – even something as seemingly straightforward as cognitive load can be manifested on different levels of linguistic analysis and can interact with general intelligence, working memory, age, etc. – are beyond the scope of the present analysis, and possibly beyond a purely corpus-based approach. In the following, we can only speculate about the relationship between these factors and the cognitive mechanisms they potentially tap into.

Firstly, it is with regard to processing-related factors such as clause complexity and juncture that we see learners in need to further improve their alignments to the target norm. This reminds us of psycholinguistic accounts such as that of Kroll and her colleagues, who argue in favor of a tight link between bilingualism and cognitive cost: according to Kroll and Dussias (2013), speaking a second language entails a higher cognitive load because the speaker constantly has to juggle between the two (or more) languages (Kroll and Dussias 2013). From that perspective, it makes sense that our learners display lower tolerance thresholds for factors that themselves are directly related to cognitive cost, such as complexity or clause juncture: compared to native speakers, the learners have fewer cognitive resources to allot in the first place. As a result, they produce the complementizer more frequently.

In addition, we found that NS and NNS both responded in the expected fashion to spikes in uncertainty (based on Jaeger 2010) as captured by the conditional surprisal of the first word of the complement clause given the last word of the matrix clause. Both groups were more likely to produce *that* at high-uncertainty transitions. However, NNS also tended to overproduce *that* at lower surprisal junctures, suggesting again a conservative strategy. This effect, like that discussed above, is amenable to explanation in terms of cognitive cost, with NNS experiencing greater difficulty with transitions that are otherwise unproblematic for native speakers, but converging on native performance when the transitions reach a certain threshold of uncertainty.

As far as the implications of the present study for language teaching are concerned, one may conclude that overall, *that*-variation does not constitute an insurmountable challenge to learners: in spite of the fact that proper complementizer use is hardly if ever a topic of explicit classroom instruction, the intermediate-advanced learners investigated here seem to be well on their way to nearly native-like behavior. *That*-variation may be taken as a powerful example of how much learners can pick up by implicitly scrutinizing the distributional patterns of their input even though the random effects also showcase considerable individual variation. That said, the results, of course, point to room for improvement. For one, instruction could focus more on complementizer variability by comparing the L1 with the L2; especially the Spanish learners may benefit from their attention being directed at the optionality of *that* in adjectival and object complements in particular. Similarly, increasing awareness for mode-dependent differences may be useful for both learner groups examined here.

# References

Biber, Douglas. 1999. A register perspective on grammar and discourse: variability in the form and use of English complement clauses. *Discourse Studies* 1. 131–50.
Bryant, Margaret M. 1962. *Current American usage*. New York: Funk & Wagnalls.
Dor, Daniel. 2005. Toward a semantic account of *that*-deletion in English. *Linguistics* 43(2). 345–382.
Durham, Mercedes. 2011. I think (that) something's missing: Complementizer deletion in non-native emails. *Studies in Second Language Learning and Teaching* 1(3). 421–445.
Ellis, Nick C. 2006. Language acquisition as rational contingency learning. *Applied Linguistics* 27. 1–24.

Ellis, Nick C. & Stefanie Wulff. 2015. Usage-based approaches in second language acquisition. In Bill VanPatten & Jessica Williams (eds.), *Theories in second language acquisition: An introduction*, 75–93. London & New York: Routledge.

Elsness, Johan. 1984. *That* or zero? A look at the choice of objective clause connective in a corpus of American English. *English Studies* 65. 519–533.

Gilquin, Gaëtanelle, Sylvie de Cock & Sylviane Granger. 2010. *Louvain International Database of Spoken English Interlanguage*. Louvain-la-Neuve: Presses universitaires de Louvain.

Goldberg, Adele E. 2006. *Constructions at work: The nature of generalization in language*. Oxford: Oxford University Press.

Granger, Sylviane, Estelle Dagneaux, Fanny Meunier & Magali Paquot. 2009. *International Corpus of Learner English v2*. Louvain-la-Neuve: Presses Universitaires de Louvain.

Gries, Stefan Th. 2007. *Coll.analysis 3.2*. A program for *R* for Windows.

Gries, Stefan Th. 2013. 50-something years of work on collocations: What is or should be next ... *International Journal of Corpus Linguistics* 18(1). 137–165.

Gries, Stefan Th. & Allison S. Adelman. 2014. Subject realization in Japanese conversation by native and non-native speakers: Exemplifying a new paradigm for learner corpus research. In Jesús Romero-Trillo (eds.), *Yearbook of corpus linguistics and pragmatics 2014: New empirical and theoretical paradigms*, 35–54. Cham: Springer.

Gries, Stefan Th. & Sandra C. Deshors. 2014. Using regressions to explore deviations between corpus data and a standard/target: Two suggestions. *Corpora* 9(1). 109–136.

Jaeger, T. Florian. 2010. Redundancy and reduction: Speakers manage syntactic information density. *Cognitive Psychology* 61. 23–62.

Kaltenböck, Gunther. 2006. '... *That* is the question': Complementizer omission in extraposed *that*-clauses. *English Language and Linguistics* 10(2). 371–96.

Kroll, Judith F. & Paola E. Dussias. 2013. The comprehension of words and sentences in two languages. In Tej K. Bhatia & William C. Ritchie (eds.), *The handbook of bilingualism and multilingualism*, 216–243. Malden, MA: Wiley-Blackwell Publishers.

Levy, Roger. 2008. Expectation-based syntactic comprehension. *Cognition* 106(3). 1126–1177.

Rissanen, Matti. 1991. On the history of *that*/zero as object clause links in English. In Karin Aijmer & Bengt Altenberg (eds.), *English corpus linguistics*, 272–289. London: Longman.

Storms, G. 1966. *That*-clauses in Modern English. *English Studies* 47. 249–70.

Tagliamonte, Sali A. & Jennifer Smith. 2005. *No momentary fancy!* The *zero* 'complementizer' in English dialects. *English Language and Linguistics* 9(2). 289–309.

Thompson, Sandra A. & Anthony Mulac. 1991. The discourse conditions for the use of the complementizer that in conversational English. *Journal of Pragmatics* 15. 237–51.

Torres Cacoullos, Rena & James A. Walker. 2009. On the persistence of grammar in discourse formulas: A variationist study of *that*. *Linguistics* 47. 1–43.

Wulff, Stefanie. 2016. A friendly conspiracy of input, L1, and processing demands: *that*-variation in German and Spanish learner language. In Andrea Tyler, Lourdes Ortega, Hae In Park, & Mariko Uno (eds.), *The usage-based study of language learning and multilingualism*. Georgetown: Georgetown University Press.

Wulff, Stefanie, Nicholas A. Lester & Maria M. Martinez-Garcia. 2014. *That*-variation in German and Spanish L2 English. *Language and Cognition* 6. 271–299.

Maarten Lemmens and Julien Perrez
# French onions and Dutch trains: Typological perspectives on learners' descriptions of spatial scenes[1]

## 1 Scope and issues

Space is a universal cognitive domain whose linguistic realization shows a great deal of variation across different languages, as has been pointed out by numerous typological studies (see, for instance, Ameka and Levinson 2007; Levinson 2003; Talmy 2000).[2] One of the most influential taxonomies accounting for this variation is Talmy's typological distinction between verb-framed languages and satellite-framed languages. Verb-framed languages (from now on V-languages), like French, are languages in which the direction of the movement is encoded in the main verb and manner of motion is optionally expressed in an adjunct. Satellite-framed (from now on S-languages), like Dutch, are languages in which manner of motion is encoded in the main verb and the direction of movement in a satellite.

These typological differences between V- and S-languages have been confirmed (but also nuanced) by cross-linguistic studies focusing on the encoding of motion and locative events (see among others Gullberg 2009; Hellerstedt 2013; Hickmann 2007; Hickmann and Hendricks 2006; Lemmens and Slobin 2008; Özçalışkan and Slobin 2003), but also by studies analysing the co-verbal gestures produced when talking about space (see among others Brown and Chen 2013; Gullberg 2009; Kendon 2004; Kita 2009; Kita and Özyürek 2003; Tutton 2013). At the same time, it has become clear that these two types of languages should be considered as two extremes on a continuum rather than as sharp dichotomies (see Berthele 2004; Berthele, Whelpton, Naess, and Duijff 2015; Kopecka 2006; Slobin 2004).

---
[1] This research was supported by the Fonds Spéciaux de la Recherche, Grant C-13/100 awarded to Julien Perrez and by the ANR-DFG grant "Lexis and gesture in L2 expressions of static spatial relations" awarded to Maarten Lemmens.
[2] The authors would like to thank the anonymous reviewer(s) and Hae In Park for their constructive comments on an earlier version of this paper. All remaining inaccuracies are the authors' responsibility.

**Maarten Lemmens,** Université de Lille 3
**Julien Perrez,** Université de Liège

https://doi.org/10.1515/9783110572186-005

Applied to the domain of static location, the typological differences between V- and S-languages result in a tendency of the latter to specify the manner of location, by using a specific posture verb, like the Dutch verbs *staan* 'stand', *zitten* 'sit' and *liggen* 'lie', whereas the former tend to use a single dummy verbs like French *être* 'be' or *se trouver* 'find oneself' to encode the spatial orientation of entities in space, often leaving the manner of location unexpressed (see among others Hickmann 2007; Hickmann and Hendricks 2006; Lemmens and Slobin 2008). This quasi-automatic use of posture verbs to locate entities in space is not without impact on their frequency and their extensive and complex semantic networks, allowing them to express a whole range of metaphorical meanings going beyond the simple postural or locational, for instance to locate abstract entities in concrete space or concrete entities in abstract space (see Lemmens 2002 and Lemmens and Perrez 2010 for a detailed description of the semantic networks of the Dutch posture verbs).[3]

From the perspective of foreign language learning, these typological differences are a source of learning problems, especially in the case of native speakers of V-languages who learn S-languages (Ellis 1994; Gullberg 2009; Kellerman 1995). More particularly, going from a V-language to a S-language means that learners have to readjust semantic categories acquired in the L1; more specifically, they need to go from a single large semantic category in the L1 to several specific categories in the L2 (see Gullberg 2009; Ijaz 1986; Narasimhan and Gullberg 2011), which represent pedagogical challenges (see, for instance, De Knop and Perrez 2014). These learning difficulties have been reported for native speakers of V-languages learning S-languages, moving from a less complex system to a more complex system, but some studies have pointed out that also moving from a L1 S-language to a L2 V-language leads to learning problems (see, for instance, Cadierno 2004; Cadierno et al. 2016). More specifically, Cadernio et al (2016) show that intermediate Danish learners of Spanish tend to overgeneralize the use of the generic verb *poner* 'put' for configurations where more specific placement verbs such as *dejar* 'leave [in a place]' or *meter* 'put in' would be more idiomatic. They suggest that "when the two languages vary with respect to the number of semantic categories [...], the process of L2 meaning reconstruction becomes difficult irrespective of the nature of the transition that has to be made" (Cadierno et al. 2016: 214).

For French-speaking learners of Dutch, going from a L1 V-language to a L2 S-language, the semantic reconstruction process means they have to (i) get used

---

[3] Note that in this respect English stands out in the group of Germanic languages (all S-framed) by not using the posture verbs *sit*, *lie* and *stand* as often as do its Germanic peers (see Lemmens 2014) for some discussion.

to using a posture verb instead of general verb such as *être* 'be' commonly used in French in locative sentences, (ii) understand in which context a given posture verb is to be used, and (iii) deal with the metaphorical extensions of these posture verbs.

These alleged difficulties have been confirmed by cross-sectional studies, looking at various typologically different languages, focusing on the encoding of motion events (see, for instance, Cadierno 2004, 2008; Hendriks and Hickmann 2011; Hijazo-Gascon 2015), dynamic location events (see Gullberg 2009; Alferink and Gullberg 2014; Narasimhan and Gullberg 2011), and static location events (Lemmens and Perrez 2010; Lemmens and Perrez 2012). The study by Lemmens and Perrez (2010) concentrated on the use of the Dutch posture verbs *staan* 'stand', *zitten* 'sit' and *liggen* 'lie' by French-speaking learners in spontaneous written productions (learner corpus analysis). When compared to native usage, the learners tend (i) to underuse posture verbs in their target language ("posture verb underuse"), (ii) to select erroneous posture verbs to encode the location of given entities ("posture verb confusion"), and (iii) to use posture verbs in contexts where such verbs do not apply ("posture verb overuse"). As stressed by Lemmens and Perrez, these different characteristics of the learner use of postures verbs suggest their use is influenced by negative transfer from their mother tongue ("posture verb underuse" and "posture verb confusion") but also by patterns typical of a developing learner interlanguage ("posture verb overuse"). A more specific analysis of the contexts in which posture verbs were used further reveals that the learners tend to use the posture verbs in their basic postural and locational domains, whereas the natives more frequently used them in abstract metaphorical extensions.

In a follow-up cross-sectional experiment, based on an oral picture description task in which the subjects were to describe the location of entities on various pictures taken from a children's book, Lemmens and Perrez (2012) observed similar tendencies, namely (i) that French-speaking learners of Dutch, when compared to native speakers of Dutch, significantly overused neutral verbs and underused posture verbs in their spatial encodings, (ii) that about 30% of the erroneous uses of posture verbs were instances of posture verb confusion, and (iii) that some learners tended to overgeneralize the posture verbs in some contexts. Interestingly, when assessing the evolution of the use of posture verbs at various stages of foreign language development, Lemmens and Perrez (2012) observed that the use of posture verbs by French-speaking learners remains problematic even at a high level of foreign language proficiency. More specifically, although the most proficient learners appear to show a more native-like behaviour, in that their use of posture verbs significantly increases and their use of neutral verbs significantly decreases, they concurrently appear to produce a higher percentage of erroneous uses of these verbs.

Building on these two studies, the study reported on in this contribution further zooms in on how speakers of Dutch and French encode locative events on a more general level, by moving away from the (typical) exclusively verb-centred approach to a more global perspective by analysing the syntactic constructions used to encode locative events and the role they play in the overall discourse strategy in Dutch and French. The research questions underlying our study are thus the following. Are there any differences in the constructions used by learners of Dutch when giving spatial descriptions and, if so, what are these differences and how do they interact with lexical differences (cf. Lemmens and Perrez 2012)? Are they due to interference of their mother tongue (French) or to some other strategy (like overgeneralization or avoidance)?

This article is structured as follows. The following section (Section 2) sketches the methodological underpinnings of our study, presenting the data, the elicitation task, the participants, and the coding method. Section 3 presents the results and is structured around the discussion of constructional patterns on the one hand and discourse patterns on the other. The results are more specifically tackled from the perspective of the contrasting differences between French and Dutch and of developmental patterns of French-speaking learners of Dutch. Section 4 concludes the article.

## 2 Data and method

### 2.1 Task

The data on which this research is based are part of a larger data set for different languages (including English, Dutch, and French) and the procedure that has been used to collect these data has been described extensively in previous papers (see, for instance, Lemmens and Slobin 2008; Lemmens and Perrez 2012). In a nutshell, the data are free picture descriptions of five pictures from two wordless children's books.[4] Each picture depicts a different kind of environment: (1) a clothing shop for kids, (2) a shoe store, (3) a bedroom where a family is getting dressed for a party, (4) a street market, and (5) a butcher's shop; each

---

4 The two books are (1) Capdevila, R. 1984. *La festa* [The party]. SA Editorial. Dutch edition by Casterman 1996. ISBN 90-303-0658-0 (used for P1, P2, & P3) and (2) Ribas, T. P. Casademunt & R. Capdevila 1984. *Les botigues* [The shops]. SA Editorial. Dutch edition by Casterman ISBN 90-303-0653-X (used for P4 & P5).

picture thus has a typical array of objects, respectively clothes (P1), shoes and shoeboxes (P2), furniture and clothes (P3), vegetables (P4; at three vegetable stands), and meat and delicacies (P5). However, they also show people interacting with objects, such as a shop assistant carrying shoe boxes, a market woman holding up a bunch of carrots, a woman folding clothes on a counter, people trying on shoes, a man tying his tie in front of the mirror, or a butcher slicing meat or laying it on a dish.

The subjects were asked to describe each picture, one after the other, on the basis of a lead-question, targeting particular entities, e.g., for picture 1 (a clothing shop for kids) the lead-question was *Can you tell me where the clothes are in this shop and what type of clothes they are?* The resulting descriptions are monologic, told to the experimenter, situated in front of them. The subjects were presented one picture at a time, in a random order for different participants to avoid any order effect. The subjects were seated on a chair without armrests. Before starting the description, they could hold the picture for a while to study it and then were asked to place it on a stand placed slightly to the right of them (at about 1m distance) and start their description. The productions were videotaped and transcribed verbatim. Afterwards the data were annotated in ELAN (see below).

## 2.2 Participants

In total 46 participants took part to the elicitation study that we report on in this paper, 12 native speakers of (Belgian) Dutch (3 male and 9 female students from the University of Leuven, Belgium), 12 native speakers of French (7 male and 5 female students from the university of Lille, France), and 22 French-speaking learners of Dutch (18 female and 4 male students from the University Saint-Louis Brussels, Belgium). These learners are all undergraduate students majoring in Dutch and one other Germanic language (English or German in this case). Prior to the experiment, they all took a foreign language proficiency test, set at a B2-level of the Common European Framework of Reference. The test was developed at the Institute of Modern Languages (ILT) of the Katholieke Universiteit Leuven (University of Leuven) in collaboration with other institutions.[5] The test, composed of 80 items, aims at measuring the grammatical and lexical knowledge of the students as well as their reading and listening proficiency. The learners

---

[5] Many thanks to our colleagues of the Dutch department at the Leuven Language Institute at the KU Leuven (ILT) for generously granting us the privilege to use this test for our experiment. More information on this test can be found at http://www.itna.be/.

were divided into three proficiency groups based on a gap of 3 points which occurred between the MIN and MAX scores (53–56 for groups 1 and 2, and 64–67 for groups 2 and 3). An ANOVA test ($F_{(2,19)} = 121.58$, $p < 0.001$) confirms the significance of this division.

Both the learners and the native speakers have learned English as a foreign language at school; some may also have studied other languages. This has not been controlled for in this experiment but the influence of notably English on the learners' performance can be assumed to be minimal given that the preferred English verb for coding location events, *be*, is no facilitating factor in the semantic recategorization involved in the acquisition of Dutch posture verbs. Furthermore, the exposure to English (in mass media, films, etc.) is fairly limited in the southern French-speaking part of Belgium, most audiovisual cultural products being dubbed.

## 2.3 Coding

Our basic units of analysis are locative clauses. In our approach, a locative clause is broadly defined as any clause containing locative information, be it a locative verb (such as posture or placement verbs, e.g., *staan* 'stand' in example [1]) or a locative adjunct (adverbs like *there* or *here*, prepositional phrases like *on the bed* or *next to the counter*, or particles, such as in example [2]), or a combination of these two (example [1] is in fact such a combination).

(1) *De meeste schoenen staan in de etalage* (OPD-DU-01)[6]
    'most of the shoes stand in the display'[7]

(2) *Vous avez trois boîtes à chaussure sur une chaise au fond* (OPD-FR-02)
    'you have three shoeboxes on a chair behind'

While this may be straightforward at first sight, delineating what counts as a locative clause is more complex than it seems, due to embedding of different locative clauses. Consider the following example:

---

6 Examples with a reference like this are taken from our corpus of oral picture descriptions (OPD), the labels DU, FR and Du2F refer respectively to native speakers of Dutch, natives speakers of French and French-speaking learners of Dutch. The first digit (01, in this case) identifies the speaker and the second digit (only for the learners) refers to his/her level of proficiency, ranging from 1 (lowest) to *3* (highest).

7 While they are not glosses, the English translations are fairly literal (and thus possibly non-idiomatic), to capture the semantics of the original.

(3)  *tussen de twee [...] nachttafels is er een bed waarop [...] twee hemden en een broek liggen* (OPD-Du2F-12-2)

'between the two [...] bedside tables, there is a bed on which [...] two shirts and one pair of trousers lie'

From a strictly syntactic point of view, there are two separate locative clauses presenting two different locative events: the main clause (*tussen de twee nachttafels is er een bed* 'between the two [...] bedside tables, there is a bed') locates bed which functions as the Ground for the location of the clothes, presented in the following relative clause (*waarop twee hemden en een broek liggen* 'on which two shirts and a pair of trousers lie'). On a functional level, however, this can be regarded as one single locative event, as the speaker is targeting the location of the clothes, where the main locative clause is merely an auxiliary event to locate the Ground (the bed). In other words, while on the level of the main clause, the bed is a figure located within the room (Ground), it functions as a secondary Figure in the larger locative event the speaker is targeting, i.e., the location of the clothes which thus can be considered the primary Figure.

As we are interested in the expression of the location of entities, we have considered clauses as separate locative clauses whenever they locate two different figures; in the case of the example above, we have thus annotated the two clauses separately. At a higher level, these clauses will be taken together as a larger discourse unit. As detailed below, such complex clauses do reveal interesting strategies of information packaging, which turn out to be different in Dutch and in French.

Each locative clause has subsequently been annotated according to various parameters, including identification of the Figure (the entity located), of the Ground, the verb (lemma form), the (semantic) verb type, the construction type, and the verb satellites. This method makes it possible to analyse the encoding of location events from a combined lexical and constructional perspective.

The verb types have been characterized via the following categories:

– POSTURE verbs: *zitten* / *être assis* 'sit', *liggen* / *être couché* 'lie', *staan* / *être debout* 'stand', and *hangen* / *être suspendu* 'hang'[8]

---

[8] As specified earlier, French disfavours the use of posture verbs which cannot be used to refer to the location of inanimate entities; however, they do exist and can be used to refer to the posture of human (or human-like) beings. Strikingly, however, these verbs tend not to be used even in those contexts and French speakers will, unless there are reasons to the contrary, resort to using *être* 'be', leaving the posture unspecified (which can usually be pragmatically inferred).

- NEUTRAL verbs: verbs that are semantically quite empty, often existential or dummy verbs, e.g., *zijn* 'be', *zich bevinden* lit. 'REFLEXIVE find' = 'be found'; *être* 'be', *il y a* 'there is/are'
- DISPOSITIONAL verbs: these are (locative) verbs which provide some more precise information about how the entity is located in space. These can be attachment verbs, such as *coller, attacher* 'attach', arrangement verbs, such as *éparpiller* 'scatter', *verspreid* 'spread out', or configuration verbs, such as *drapé* 'draped'.
- PERCEPTION verbs, e.g., *zien/voir* 'see', as in *On voit des vêtements sur le lit* 'One sees some clothes on the bed'
- POSSESSION verbs, e.g., *De mevrouw heeft kleren over haar arm* 'The woman has some clothes over her arm'
- OTHER: any other verb that is used in what is considered a locative clause, e.g., *de papa knoopt zijn das voor de spiegel* 'the dad ties (= 'is tying') his tie in front of the mirror'
- ELLIPSIS: no verb, e.g., *er hangt vlees aan haken rechts en Ø worsten links* 'there hangs meat on hooks to the right and Ø sausages on the left'

The construction types in the data have been characterized as: basic locative constructions, presentational constructions, identificational constructions, transitive constructions, progressive constructions, non-locative constructions, and complex constructions (combinations of the previous ones). Each construction type is briefly presented below.

Basic locative constructions (BLC), a concept introduced by Wilkins (1998, 1999), are constructions of the form <Figure> + <predicate> + <relator> (mostly a preposition) + <Ground>, as illustrated in the earlier example (1) (reproduced here for convenience) which has the canonical word order (Figure precedes the Ground) and (4) which has a topicalized Ground.[9]

(1) *De meeste schoenen staan in de etalage* (OPD-DU-01)
    'most of the shoes stand in the display'

(4) *Naast het bed staan twee nachtkastjes* (OPD-DU-01)
    'next to the bed stand two night tables'

Presentational constructions (PRES) are constructions in which a figure is introduced by presentational markers such as *er* in Dutch or *il y a* in French, the equivalent of English presentational *there* constructions.

---

[9] Such word order changes are typically motivated by discourse constraints, i.e. when the Ground (the bed in this example) has been introduced previously and is thus old information. For the coding of the type of construction, abstraction has been made of these word order variations and both have been coded as basic locative constructions (BLC).

(5) *Er ligt een bloes in de badkamer* (OPD-DU-03)
'there lies a blouse in the bathroom'

(6) *et il y a donc une dame à la caisse* (OPD-FR-04)
'and there is thus a woman at the desk'

Identificational constructions (ID) are typically introduced by cleft-markers to identify a given figure.

(7) *les premiers clients que je vois, c'est une dame et une petite fille à la caisse* (OPD-FR-06)
'the first clients that I see, it is a lady and a little girl at the desk'

Transitive constructions (TRANS) include various constructions with transitive verbs (as opposed to intransitive location verbs or copula-like existential verbs); they come in various subtypes (usually because of the type of verb that is used) such as perception constructions (see [8]), possessive constructions (including viewer-based possession clauses such as in [9] as well as character-based possession clauses, such as in [10]) or causative constructions (see example [11]).

(8) *en in de slaapkamer ziet ge een stapelbed* (OPD-DU-06)
'and in the bedroom you see bunk beds'

(9) *à droite de ces chaussettes, on a des tee-shirts avec différents motifs* (OPD-FR-09)
'to the right of these socks, one has tee-shirts with different patterns'

(10) *en ze heeft ook nog kisten onder haar tafel, allez één kist en een mand* (OPD-DU-08)
'and she has also boxes under her table, I mean one box and a basket'

(11) *de verkoper legt ook worsten in een weegschaal* (OPD-DU-10)
'the shop assistant is also laying sausages in the scales'

A special category had to be created for progressive constructions (PROG) which in Dutch can either be built with *aan het V zijn* 'be at the V' (the verb 'be' followed by a nominalized infinitive expressing the ongoing activity) or, more relevant to the current study, with a (grammaticalized) posture verb followed by an infinitive, as illustrated in example (12). Although such constructions are primarily used to refer to the ongoing or durative aspect of an event, and not so much to locate entities in space, the fact that they are structured around one of the three basic posture verbs *staan* 'stand', *liggen* 'lie' or *zitten* 'sit' does, to some extent, add some manner of location information to the event.[10]

(12)     *en iemand die in de etalage staat te kijken* (OPD-DU-04).
        'and someone who in the display stands to look (= is looking into the display window)'

Non-locative constructions (NON-LOC) are constructions where there is no locative complement (a prepositional phrase, a locative adverb, etc., see example [13]). Although such constructions are not locative in nature (but more existential or purely presentational), they were still included and annotated because they can be used to introduce some information that can be used in a subsequent locative clause (between square brackets), such as in example (14).

(13)     *en dan zijn er ook winkeltjes [die eerder kledij verkopen]* (OPD-DU-02)
        'and then there are also shops [that rather sell clothes]'

(14)     *Er is ook een bed [waar kleren op liggen]* (OPD-DU-01)
        'there is a bed [where clothes (on) are lying on]'

Another context in which a clause was marked as NON-LOC is when a clear locative verb (such as a posture verb) was used without any locative complement, as in the example below:

(15)     *Dus [...] vlees hangt* (OPD-Du2F-20-2)
        'so [...] meat is hanging'

(16)     *Een andere vrouw die staat* (OPD- Du2F-19-2)
        'another woman who is standing'

---

**10** Interestingly, the Dutch posture verbs in such progressive constructions have undergone a grammaticalization process, such that the locative meaning of the verb in such constructions does not always correspond to the basic human posture prototypically denoted by the verb when used in isolation. At the same time, they do retain a certain locative character, as argued in Lemmens (2005, 2015, 2017).

Example (15) is considered a locative clause in our data set following the criterion that there is a posture verb, but the absence of a locative phrase is quite marked (though not impossible). Example (16) is a pure postural clause which says something about the posture of the (human) Figure, but it is only indirectly locative (she necessarily stands somewhere). The mark-up NON-LOC allows us to distinguish these from clauses where there is an overt locative complement (e.g., 'there lie clothes on the bed', 'people stand near the counter'). As it turns out, this will be relevant for the analysis of learner data (overusing the NON-LOC pattern) and for complex constructions, discussed below.

In addition to these categories, there are also complex constructions in which one type of construction is embedded in another construction. This is more specifically the case with basic locative constructions (BLC), which can be introduced by a presentational construction (17) or a perception (transitive) construction (18).

(17) [*en daarnaast zijn er ook schoenen* [*die zich voor de zetel bevinden*] ] (OPD-DU-02).

'[and next to it are there also shoes [that find themselves in front of the sofa] ]'

(18) [*je vois aussi des t-shirts* [*qui sont collés au mur du fond*] ] (OPD-FR-04)

'[I see also tee-shirts [that are stuck onto the wall at the back] ]'

Because such complex constructions are a specific way of construing a spatial event where the first construction is used to introduce the Figure and the subsequent locative construction (the second clause) specifies its location, these embedded basic locative constructions have been regarded as a separate category, coded as X+BLC, where the X represents the type of matrix construction, e.g. PRES+BLC for example (17) and PERC+BLC for example (18).

In such complex cases, the main clause can either have a locative complement, e.g., *daarnaast* 'next to it' in example (17), or not, as in (18), with a perception verb.

Elliptical constructions have also been marked as such; while it may sometimes be possible to reconstruct the construction type, this may not always be so and it is therefore deemed relevant to be able to exclude these.

Finally, the category OTHER unites constructions of various types that are less relevant to (pure) locative events, like intransitive or transitive constructions (active or passive) with verbs such as *verkopen* 'sell', *passen* 'try on', etc.

# 3 Results and analysis

## 3.1 Overview of the data set

The learners produced on average 33.8 locative clauses per interview. Although there is a slight, but non-significant ($F_{(2,19)}$ = 0.207, p = 0.815) increase of the average number of locative clauses across the levels of proficiency (level 1: 41.8; level 2: 39.1; level 3: 44.0), the high level of individual variation in the learners' production of locative clauses is quite striking, both within and between proficiency groups. For instance, the most prolific learner (FLP1) produced 70 locative clauses, whereas the least prolific one (FLP2) only produced 22 locative clauses. The same observation goes for the native speakers: the most prolific one produced 115 locative clauses, whereas the least prolific one only produced 41 clauses (which equals the mean production score of the learners). The high level of individual variation in the production of locative clauses is illustrated by Figure 1, which suggests that the native speakers on average produce more locative clauses per interview than the learners (means for each group: FLP1: 41.87; FLP2: 39.14; FLP3: 44.00; Natives: 75.66). A one-way ANOVA confirms that this difference is significant ($F_{(3,30)}$ = 10.502, p < 0.0001). Further post-hoc tests

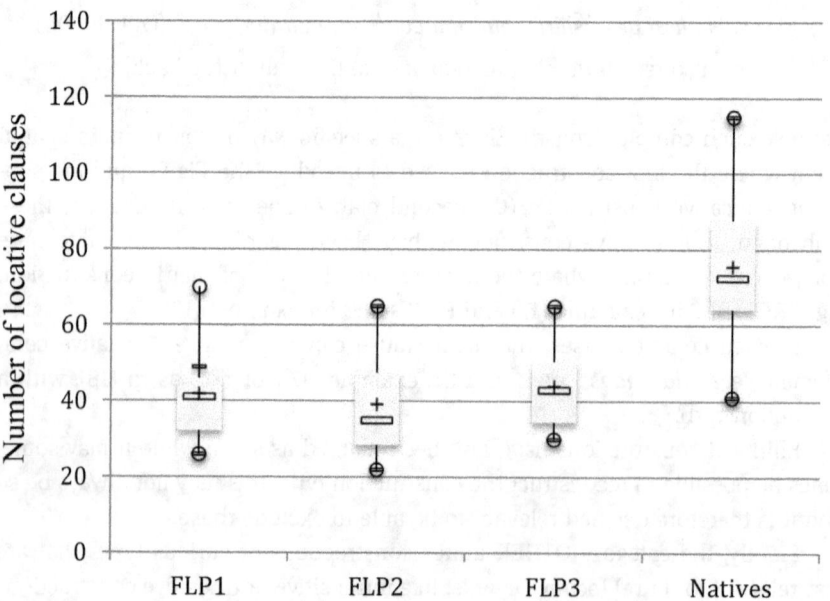

**Figure 1:** Production of locative clauses across the proficiency levels (Dutch; from Lemmens and Perrez 2012)

(Bonferroni) indicate, on the one hand, that the native speakers significantly produce more locative clauses than the learners of the three proficiency groups (Natives vs. FLP1: p < 0.002; Natives vs. FLP2: p < 0.001; Natives vs. FLP3: p < 0.001) and, on the other hand, that are no differences between the learners of the different proficiency ($F_{(2,19)}$ = .092, p = .912; p = 1.000 for all inter-group comparisons). These results suggest that the overall production of locative clauses by the learners is not dependent on their level of proficiency in the target language.

## 3.2 Lexical patterns

The aim of the present article is to complement the typical exclusively lexical focus of comparative studies with a constructional perspective, i.e., to evaluate the role that particular constructions play on the choice of lexical items (in both native and learner data). As extensively discussed in Lemmens and Perrez (2012), there are relevant lexical differences. Figure 2 nicely summarizes these: at all three levels, the learners still follow the tendency of their native language (French) of using a neutral verb in locative contexts; there is a decrease over the three levels (49.5% – 44.9% – 38.2%), but Level 3 speakers still use these verbs almost twice as often as the native Dutch speakers (38.2% vs. 20.2%). However, this decrease is not paralleled with a comparable increase of posture verbs (only 5% increase). Once again, at all three levels, the learners underuse the posture verbs compared to the native speakers, confirming the overall underuse of these verbs in their descriptions ($\chi^2$ = 12.735; df = 3; p < 0.005).

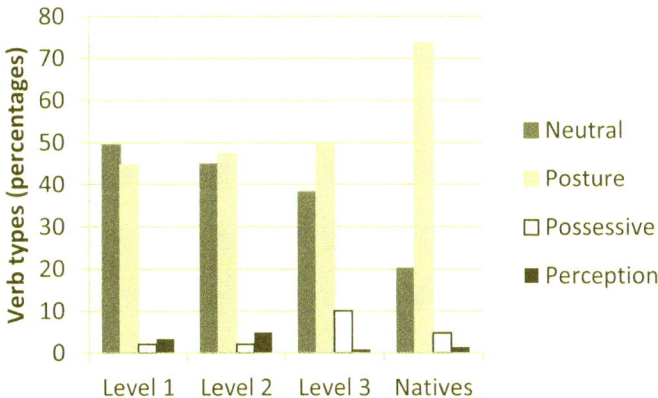

**Figure 2:** Overall distribution of verb types for learners and native speakers (Dutch; from Perrez and Lemmens 2012)

## 3.3 Constructional patterns

The analysis presented in Lemmens and Perrez (2012) focused on the lexical choices made by native and non-native speakers, with a particular attention to the degree of idiomaticity (qualitatively and quantitatively) in the learners' use of posture verbs. One of the surprising results in the analysis is that the native Dutch speakers still had a fairly high use of the neutral verb *zijn* 'be' (about 20% versus 73% posture verbs); intuitively, most speakers of Dutch would regard the use of *zijn* in a locative clause, such as for example, *De kleren zijn op het bed* 'the clothes are on the bed' or *Er zijn kleren op het bed* 'there are clothes on the bed' as (highly) unidiomatic or even incorrect. However, when the perspective is widened to include construction types, the high percentage of *zijn* 'be' can be explained, as will be shown in this section.

Table 1 summarizes the overall frequencies of the various constructions for the three language data sets, represented visually in Figure 3 for the relevant construction types. As far as the native speakers are concerned, the following tendencies can be observed. Firstly, the L1 speakers of Dutch appear to produce more presentational and basic locative constructions than the native speakers of French (respectively 26% vs. 24% and 32% vs. 22%). The French speakers, in turn, are more inclined to produce more transitive constructions on the one hand (respectively 11% vs. 4%) and more embedded basic locative constructions on the other (12% vs. 3%, see Section 2.3 Coding). Concerning the former, a more fine-grained analysis, given in Figure 4, shows that the high proportion of transitive constructions can be attributed to a more frequent usage of perception constructions.

**Table 1:** Frequencies of the construction types in the productions of native speakers of French, native speakers of Dutch and French-speaking learners of Dutch

| CX Type | French L1 | | Dutch L2 | | Dutch L1 | |
| --- | --- | --- | --- | --- | --- | --- |
|  | N | % | N | % | N | % |
| NON-LOC | 65 | 13.4 | 126 | 12.98 | 77 | 8.71 |
| ID | 2 | 0.41 | 4 | 0.41 | 9 | 1.02 |
| TRANS | 57 | 11.75 | 59 | 6.08 | 40 | 4.52 |
| PRES | 114 | 23.51 | 342 | 35.22 | 232 | 26.24 |
| BLC | 111 | 22.89 | 290 | 29.87 | 289 | 32.69 |
| X+BLC | 60 | 12.37 | 61 | 6.28 | 31 | 3.51 |
| PROG | 0 | 0.00 | 0 | 0.00 | 42 | 4.75 |
| ELLIPSIS | 72 | 14.85 | 84 | 8.65 | 136 | 15.38 |
| OTHER | 4 | 0.82 | 5 | 0.51 | 28 | 3.17 |
| TOTAL | 485 | 100 | 971 | 100 | 884 | 100 |

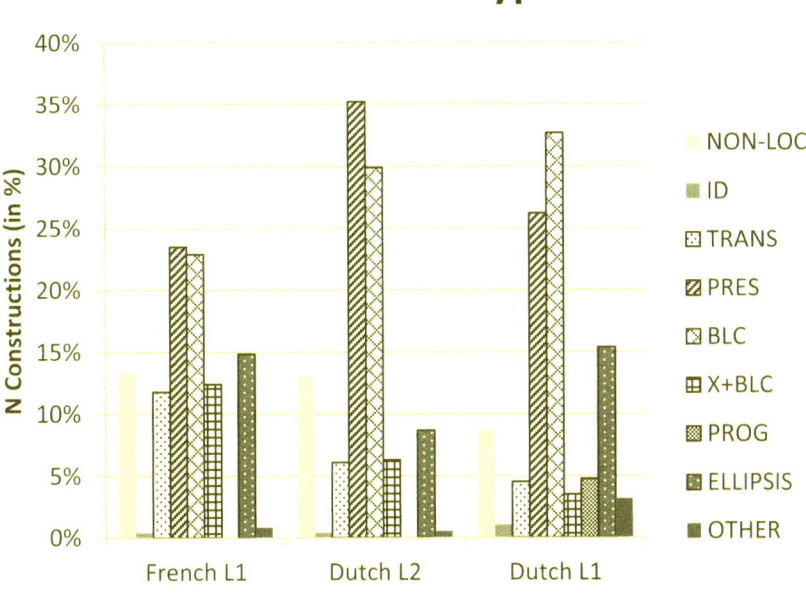

**Figure 3:** Construction types in the three language data sets

Turning to the learner data, one can summarize the main developmental tendencies over the different proficiency levels as follows. The number of presentational sentences decreases over the three levels and the number of BLCs increases. Similarly, the non-locative constructions go down over the different levels as does the frequency of X+BLC, both coming closer to the native speaker frequencies. Also the frequency of elliptical constructions increases over the three levels towards those of the native speakers. However, two of these evolutions are not linear: the FLP2 group has a strikingly higher percentage of BLCs than both FLP1 and FLP3; conversely, it has a strikingly lower percentage of non-locatives compared to the other groups. We will return to this below, after a more detailed discussion of these evolutions.

The learners occupy an intermediate position between the native speakers of French and the native speakers of Dutch as far as the use of transitive and basic locative constructions are concerned. This observation emphasizes the developmental processes they undergo when going from constructions that appear to be typical of their mother tongue to constructions that are more typical of their target language.

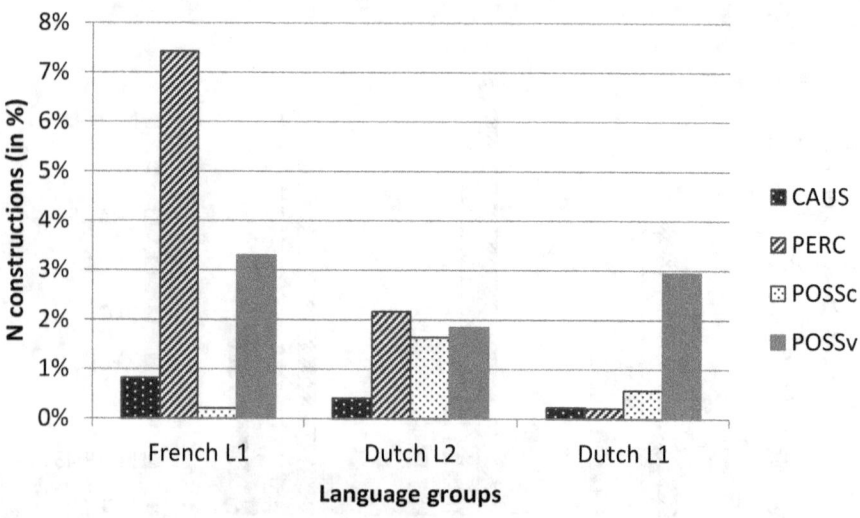

**Figure 4:** Transitive constructions in the three language data sets

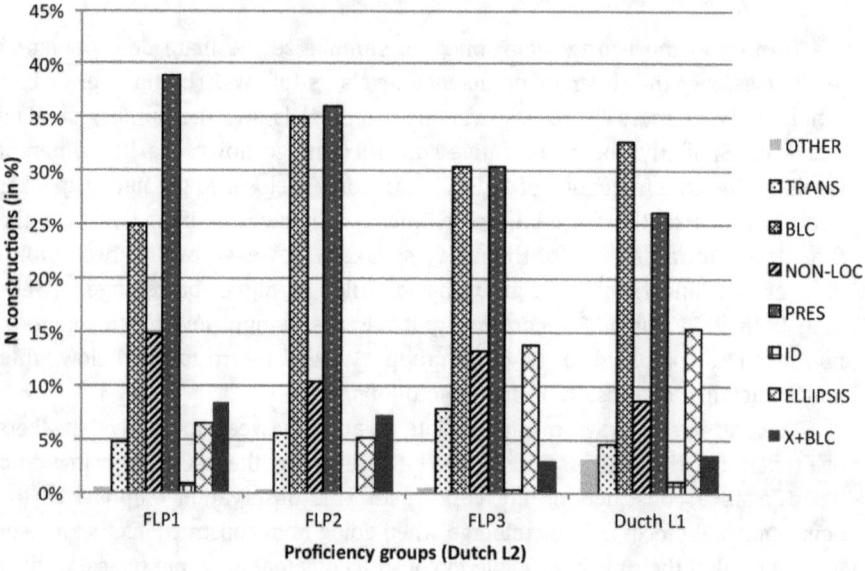

**Figure 5:** Construction types across the Dutch L2 proficiency levels

Interestingly, the French-speaking learners of Dutch show a peak in their use of presentational constructions, which – despite a clear improvement as the level of proficiency increases (FLP1: 38.92% > FLP2: 36.11% > FLP3: 30.51%) – remain overrepresented in their locative descriptions, in comparison to both the native speakers of French (23%) and the native speakers of Dutch (26%). This peak could be explained by the learners' tendency of using the presentational construction as equivalent of the French *il y a*-construction ('there is/are'-construction in English) as a kind of prefab construction that is repeatedly applied to produce locative descriptions. Since this tendency does not appear to be typical of native-like usage in French, it could more globally be regarded as being part of a developmental compensatory strategy consisting in the repeated use of an "all-purpose or catch-all" construction (cf. Dörnyei 1995) in such descriptive contexts. It is, after all, also quite frequent in the descriptions by the native Dutch speakers (PRES being the second most frequent construction). This strategy can be illustrated by the following longer passage in which this learner almost invariably begins each new utterance with this *er is/er zijn*-construction (for the sake of clarity, these have also been highlighted in the gloss).

(19)  *Dus we zijn in een schoenenwinkel. Er zijn veel schoenen. Er zijn schoenendozen in het voorhand van de winkel euh naast het sofa euh links van de prent. Er zijn ook dozen euh in de handen van de winkelier euh in het midden van de prent. Er zijn ook dozen naast het glas?* [...] *Er zijn ook dozen euh voor het sofa rechts van de prent en ook voor het sofa links van de prent. Euh er zijn dozen euh ... ja, het is alles voor de dozen, denk ik. Ah, nee nee! Er zijn ook dozen op de stoel naast de kassa euh en er zijn schoenen boven de twee grote sofa's. Er zijn ook schoenen voor de klant die probeert te dragen, die probeert de schoenen te dragen. En er zijn veel schoenen in het euh in de etalage.* (OPD-Du2F-02-01)

'So we are in a shoe shop. There are many shoes. There are shoeboxes in the front of the shop err next to the sofa err left of the picture. There are also boxes err in the hands of the shopkeeper err in the middle of the picture. There are also boxes next to the glass? [...] There are also boxes err in front of the sofa right of the picture and also in front of the sofa left of the picture. Err there are boxes err ... yes, that's it for the boxes, I think. Ah, no no! There are also boxes on the chair next to the counter err and there are shoes above the two large sofas. There are also shoes in front of the customer who tries to wear who tries to wear the shoes. And there are many shoes in the err in the display window'.

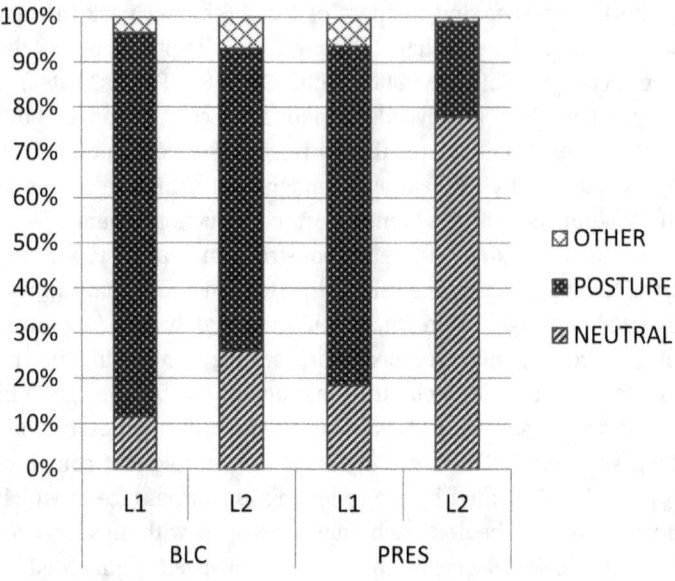

**Figure 6:** Verb types in presentational and BLC constructions in Dutch L1 and L2 data

Technically speaking, this construction is a correct construction in Dutch, but two elements make it stand out as unidiomatic. Firstly, the presentational construction in this excerpt (illustrative of the learner data in general) almost invariably occurs in a syntactically simplex clause ('there is X LOC', with LOC being the location where X is) while the native data shows a different pattern (see below). Secondly, the accumulation of such (identical) constructions in such a short text span suggests this learner is relying on one of the few constructions s/he knows to encode locative information, which results in a low level of constructional variation. Besides, the overall production shows, because of this repetition, a low level of target language idiomaticity, which seems to go hand in hand with a lower level of foreign language proficiency.

This example moreover suggests that French-speaking learners of Dutch tend to use neutral verbs (mostly *zijn* 'be') in their presentational constructions. This tendency is confirmed by a more specific analysis of the verb types used by the learners and the natives when producing presentational and basic locative constructions (see Figure 6). This analysis confirms that the learners are strongly inclined to use neutral verbs in presentational constructions (77% of the cases) whereas the natives show the reverse tendency of using a higher proportion of posture verbs (*zitten* 'sit', *liggen* 'lie', *staan* 'stand') in such constructions; 75% of the presentational constructions are thus of the form 'there lie/sit/stand X'. The

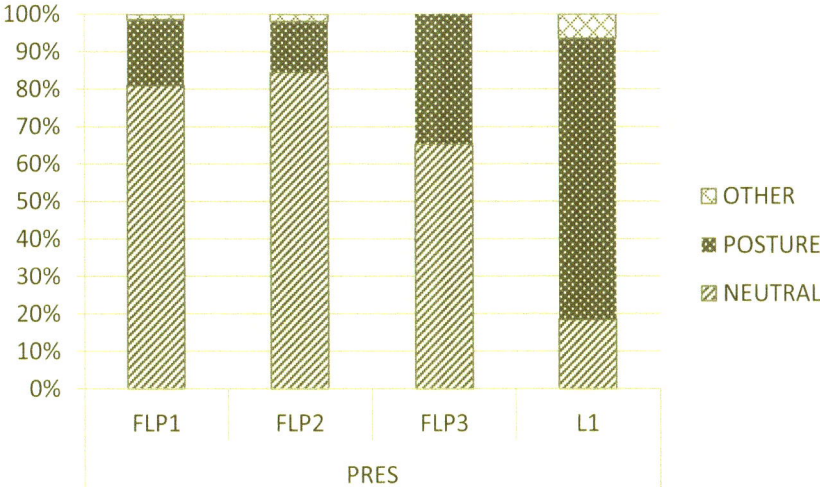

**Figure 7:** Verb types in presentational constructions across different levels of foreign language proficiency

use of posture verbs in presentational constructions remains fairly limited in the productions of the learners, suggesting that such constructions, specific to Dutch, only appear at an advanced stage of language development. This suggestion is partly confirmed by Figure 7 which shows an increase of the use of posture verbs in presentational constructions over the different proficiency levels (FLP1: 17%, FLP2: 13%, FLP 3: 34%), suggesting that such constructions typically appear at a later stage of foreign language development, even though this specific structure remains underrepresented in the productions of the learners with the highest level of proficiency in comparison to the natives. More generally, these results tend to confirm the observations made in Lemmens and Perrez (2012) according to which the learners with the highest level of proficiency tend to come closer to native-like patterns when encoding locative information.

When turning to basic locative constructions (Figure 8), our data indicate a strong decrease of neutral verbs in the production of the learners (26% of the cases) which goes hand in hand with a higher proportion of posture verbs (67% of the cases). When producing basic locative constructions, the learners thus seem to prefer posture verbs. This observation applies at all levels of foreign language proficiency, but it is more outspoken for the intermediate and most advanced learners.

These two figures reveal the mixed nature of the second level group (FLP2): they do have a higher frequency of posture verbs in the BLC than the FLP1

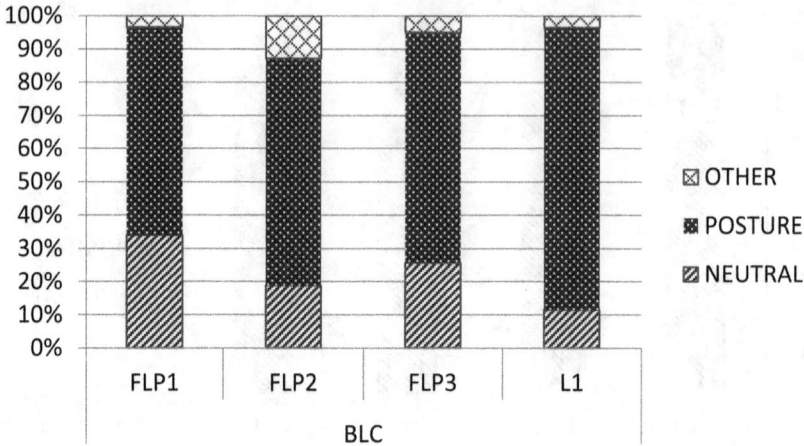

**Figure 8:** Verb types in basic locative constructions across different levels of foreign language proficiency

group, but at the same time a higher frequency of neutral verbs in the presentational construction than the lower level which goes counter to what could be expected. This suggests that this group is indeed struggling to reconcile lexical and constructional features of the target language. This provides an explanation for the non-linear (and opposite) developments for BLC and PRES in Figure 5 above.

When further considering the interaction between the construction types and the verb types used by the learners in their description of locative events, another interesting tendency emerges, viz. the learners' non-idiomatic use of posture verbs without any other specific locative element, as in the following two examples (coded as NON-LOC).

(20)   *Dus euh vlees hangt* (OPD-Du2F-20-02)[11]

   'so euh meat hangs'

(21)   *Er is een vrouw die in de winkel werkt en die staat euh debout*
   (OPD-Du2F-19-02)

   'there is a woman who in the shop works and she stands euh debout'[12]

---

[11] In this sentence, the learner also omits the (neuter) definite article (*het*) required in front of the noun *vlees* 'meat'; this has the same effect as the omission of the definite article in English (generic reading instead of a definite one). As this error is not relevant to the current discussion, we will ignore this.

[12] The learner is mixing up the French construction *être debout* lit. 'be upright' (= 'stand') and the Dutch posture verb, leading to *staan debout*.

Although such non-locative constructions with a posture verb are quantitatively fairly limited (see Table 2), they occur with comparable frequency in the productions of both the L1 speakers of French and the L2 learners of Dutch (around 2% in both cases). In such examples, the posture verb is used in isolation, not so much to express the location of an entity but rather to specify the posture of an entity. Such examples illustrate that some learners have picked up the explicit focus on the postural information typical of Dutch, which can be regarded as a sign of their growing awareness of the importance of Dutch posture verbs in Dutch spatial descriptions. Strikingly though, such non-locative constructions with a posture verb are quite unidiomatic in the kind of locative descriptions that the learners produce. A locative description with a posture verbs generally requires the specification of a ground; the more idiomatic counterpart to example (20) would have been *Het vlees hangt aan een haak* 'the meat hangs on a hook', that of example (21), *Er staat een vrouw in de winkel (te werken)* 'there stands a woman in a shop (to work)'. Uses of posture verbs without a Ground, as the learners do here, are purely postural, whereas what is needed here is a locative use of the posture verb (even if it still expresses the posture or orientation of the Figure). In other words, in Dutch *De man staat* 'The man stands' and *De man staat voor het huis* 'The man stands in front of the house' do not express the same thing, even if in both cases the man is necessarily in a standing position. The former is exclusively postural, the latter is postural and locative.[13] In French, such descriptions of posture are more idiomatic, especially when added in a subclause:

(22) a. *en bas, à droite, il y a trois filles qui essayent des chaussures*,

'below, on the right hand side, there are three girls who are trying on shoes',

b. *dont deux qui sont assises.* (OPD-FR-05)

'two of whom are sitting'.

In other words, while such "non-locative" uses of posture verbs could be indicative of the learners' increased awareness of the postural logic in Dutch, it cannot be excluded that this is a simple transfer from their native language (French).

Table 2: Non-locative constructions with a posture verb in the three language data sets

| CX Type | French L1 | | Dutch L2 | | Dutch L1 | |
|---|---|---|---|---|---|---|
| | N | % | N | % | N | % |
| NON-LOC with posture verb | 12 | 2.47 | 23 | 2.37 | 2 | 0.23 |

---

[13] Such exclusively postural uses are often used in a contrastive context, e.g., 'the bottles do not lie, they stand' or when the (postural) properties of the entity are at issue.

Summing up the findings for the learner data, these observations point at different developmental stages in the interlanguage of the learners with respect to the encoding of locative events. The first stage is characterized by a frequent use of presentational constructions with neutral verbs, as part of a compensatory strategy resulting in the use of the *er is/zijn*-construction as a prefab construction. In the second stage, the learners tend to produce basic locative constructions with neutral verbs, a pattern that is present in French as well. In the third stage, characterized by an increase in proficiency and a growing awareness of the importance of posture verbs in Dutch to encode not only postural information but also locative information, the learners use posture verbs in BLCs. In the fourth stage they tend to produce presentational constructions with posture verbs. Although these different stages are partly confirmed by our data, their validity should be verified by further experimental research.

## 3.4 From syntax to discourse: French onions and Dutch trains

As in any text, the constructions do not appear in isolation in the elicited descriptions produced by the informants, but in a given discourse with a particular focus and information flow. Due to the limitations of our coding schedule, a full-blown discursive analysis is currently not possible, but our data have allowed us to uncover some pertinent differences between Dutch and French at discourse level, pertaining to the way in which locative information is provided. In a nutshell, the difference is that between an onion-type structuring of information (French; see Figure 10 below) versus that of a train-structure (Dutch; see Figure 11 below).

This difference is revealed in our data through the basic locative constructions embedded in a main clause (coded as X+BLC, see above). These embedded constructions are instances of complex clauses in which more locative information about an entity that has been introduced in the first part of the matrix clause is given in a subclause as, for instance, in examples (15), (17) and (18) already mentioned above and repeated here for convenience, and example (23).

(15)   *Er is ook een bed waar kleren op liggen* (OPD-DU-01)
       'there is a bed where on clothes are lying'

(17)   [*en daarnaast zijn er ook schoenen* [*die zich voor de zetel bevinden*] ]
       (OPD-DU-02).
       '[and next to it are there also shoes
       [that find themselves in front of the sofa] ]'

(18) [*je vois aussi des tee-shirts [qui sont collés au mur du fond]* ]
(OPD-FR-04)

'[I see also tee-shirts [that are stuck onto the wall at the back] ]'

(23) *On peut y apercevoir un tabouret sur lequel il y a une robe orange*
(OPD-FR-04)

'we can see there a stool where on there is an orange dress'

The information structure in these examples is not the same. In examples (15) and (23), the matrix clause introduces a Figure ('bed' and 'stool', respectively) which subsequently serves as the Ground for the location of another Figure ('clothes' and 'dress', respectively). In examples (17) and (18), in contrast, the matrix clause introduces a Figure ('shoes' and 'tee-shirts', respectively) and the following subclause provides supplementary (locative) information on that same Figure. Recall that in our coding scheme the former are considered as two separate locative clauses, whereas in the second, they are not.

As illustrated by Figure 9, when independent and embedded BLCs are taken together, their frequencies in French and Dutch are comparable (respectively 35% and 36%). However, when considering both construction types separately, embedded BLCs are more frequent in French than in Dutch: 12% of the overall constructions in the L1-French corpus and 3.5% in the L1-Dutch corpus. The learners situate themselves perfectly in the middle (6%).

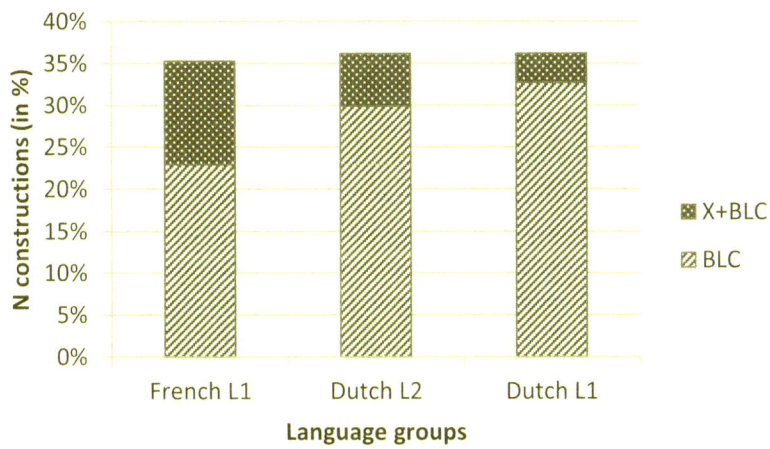

**Figure 9:** Independent vs. embedded BLCs in the three data sets

These findings suggest two important differences between French and Dutch with respect to information structuring. Firstly, the data indicates that in French BLCs are more often presented in a subordinate clause in comparison to Dutch. This suggests that the locative information is often backgrounded, much like manner of motion is subordinate in the case of motion events (see Slobin 2003, among others). Secondly, this points at different ways of structuring locative information in French and Dutch, in particular with respect to Figure and Ground relations. In French, native speakers have the tendency to introduce an entity (Figure) and then provide supplementary locative information on that same entity, such as in example (18). This explains the higher percentage of embedded basic locative constructions in the L1 French corpus, as the French speakers typically use such an accumulative pattern. While such patterning is clearly possible in Dutch (see example [17]), it is not very common (only 3.5%); the typical information structuring pattern in Dutch, illustrated by example (15), is to locate an entity which subsequently serves as the Ground for the location of another entity expressed in the following subclause.

Metaphorically, the difference can be characterized in terms of an onion-model (French) versus a train-model (Dutch). Consider the following examples, representing the contrast.

(24)  *vous avez un premier client qui est assis sur un fauteuil vert* (OPD-FR-02)
'you have a first customer who is seated on a green sofa'

(25)  *tussen de twee [...] nachttafels is er een bed waarop [...] twee hemden en een broek liggen* (OPD-Du2F-12-2)
'between the two [...] bedside tables, there is a bed on which [...] two shirts and one pair of trousers lie'

The French pattern is that of a layered onion: the centre is the Figure ('customer'), to which an additional layer of information is added ('sitting on sofa'); the Dutch pattern is that of a chain of information, much like wagons in a train, where different entities play different roles: Figure$_1$ ('bed') becomes the Ground for Figure$_2$ ('clothes'). Schematically, these information structure models can be represented as in Figures 10 and 11.

As indicated by the event labels, in the French example, we are dealing with the same locative event in both clauses (location of the customers), whereas in the Dutch example, we are dealing with two different locative events, even if, as we mentioned earlier, from a functional perspective one could regard these as building one single event, targeting the location of the clothes. In such a perspective, the first locative event (location of the bed) is auxiliary to the second (the location of the clothes).

**Figure 10:** The French onion model

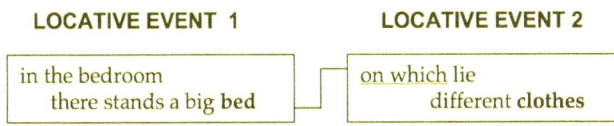

**Figure 11:** The Dutch train model

These different tendencies are confirmed if we look at the Figure-Ground relationships within subordinate clauses, presented in Figure 12 below.

The tendency for French is clear: in 91% of the cases the following sub-clause gives further information on the entity (either the Figure or the Ground) already introduced the Matrix clause (cf. +BLC above). The tendency for Dutch is more mixed: in about 40% of the cases, more information is given on a Figure or Ground and in about 40% there is a Figure-Ground reversal, i.e., the Figure in the matrix clause becomes the Ground to locate a new Figure (two different locative events). Strikingly again, the learners straddle the middle.

The above results clearly point to differences between Dutch and French with respect to both the weighing of information (backgrounded in a subordinate clause or not) and the structuring of information (onion-type layering vs. train-like chaining). However, some caution is in order. First of all, the tendencies represented in Figure 12 only concern subordination; in the current analysis, we have not (yet) included coordinated patterns. Secondly, we have not considered non-clausally expressed locative information, such as in the following examples (relevant parts have been highlighted).

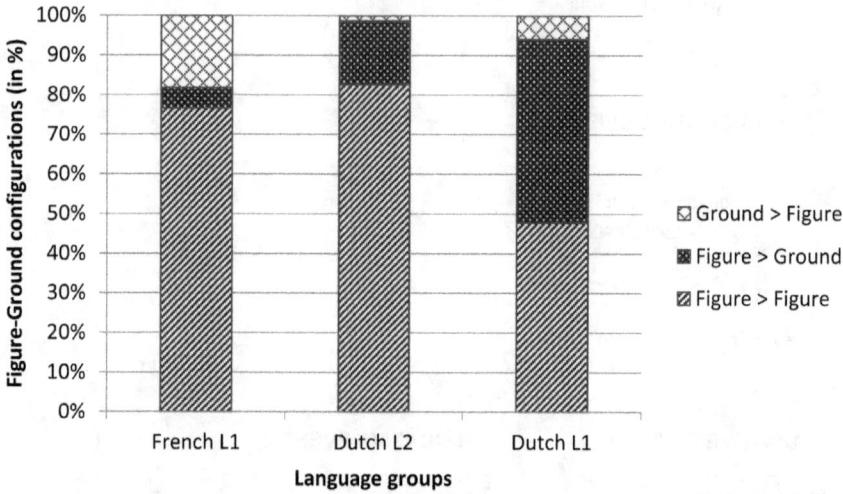

**Figure 12:** Figure-Ground relationships in complex sentences

(26) *In de slaapkamer staat een stoel* **met jas erover** (OPD-DU-09)
 'In the sleeping room stands a chair **with a jacket there on**'

(27) *A gauche de cette entrée, il y a une chaise* **avec une veste turquoise dessus** (OPD-FR-04)
 'On the left hand side of this entrance, there is a chair **with a turquoise jacket on**'

In these non-clausal encodings of location, there is also a Figure-Ground reversal where the first Figure that is introduced clausally serves as the Ground for the prepositional complement phrase. Even for these prepositionally encoded locative events, things are more complicated than they seem, since the prepositional phrase can be with or without an explicit locative element. The examples above both have such a locative expression, but in a sentence like *Er is een vrouw met een roze jurk* 'there is a woman with a pink dress' there is no such locative element in the prepositional phrase.

In sum, while the above discursive perspective on the data confirms the locative nature of Dutch that has been established by the lexical and constructional patterns, some more careful research on the different strategies of information structuring is needed.

## 4 General Discussion

The elicitation study reported on in this paper confirms the typological differences between Dutch and French in the expression of location. Overall, the data confirm the Talmian typology, in that Dutch typically expresses the manner of location via posture verbs and French is essentially "manner-poor", much like in the expression of motion events. As confirmed by our data, French-speaking learners of Dutch struggle with the abundant use of the posture verbs in Dutch, even if there is an improvement for the higher levels of proficiency. At the lowest proficiency level, learners clearly overuse neutral verbs, a cross-over from French, but they do use them more often (but not necessarily correctly) as they get more proficient. The lexical difficulty French learners face is thus that of the one-to-many mapping that Viberg (1985, 1998) and Gullberg (2009) talk about: instead of one general verb (*être* 'be'), they have to use three verbs (*liggen* 'lie', *zitten* 'sit' and *staan* 'stand') that each come with their own semantic specifications and constraints (see also Cadierno *et al.* 2016).

An important complement that was offered via our study is that these typological difficulties go beyond the verb, but also concern the construction type which interacts in intricate ways with the verbs that are used. Also here, a similar progression was observed in the type of constructions that the learners use: low-proficient speakers overuse the presentational construction with a neutral verb (*er zijn* 'there is/are') as a formulaic all-round prefab. In the two higher levels of proficiency, one notices a significant increase of locative constructions (BLCs) as well as presentational constructions with posture verbs.

Looking at the complex clauses in our data has further generated insights into how locative information is either foregrounded or backgrounded and how the information is structured. Also in this area, the data confirm the high locative nature of the Dutch descriptions, which present the location of entities in a more autonomous fashion than do the French descriptions; Dutch speakers chain individual locative events (in about half of the cases with a Figure-Ground reversal), whereas French speakers talk about one entity and give complementary information on this entity (which often is not locative information at all). Also here, the learners nicely straddle the middle between the two and develop an intermediate language system by combining the different locative features of French and Dutch.

In other words, our data show that learners become increasingly aware of the overall locative nature of Dutch in the context at hand (picture descriptions targeted at the location of entities), as reflected in lexis, grammar, and information structure. The challenge for French learners is not just restricted (as the previous studies by Viberg and Gullberg may have led one to believe), to figuring out the correct one-to-many lexical mappings but learning how to "locativize" their descriptions, not just through the use of the correct lexical items, but also via the constructions (notably, the use of the BLC) and the way in which they present the locative information in the discourse (not independent of the constructions, as has been shown). Currently, we are also investigating how non-verbal gestures complement the information that is verbally expressed. Also here, differences in learner and native speaker productions point at different degrees of locativization of their narrations. It would also be interesting to reverse the perspective and see to what extent Dutch speakers learning French succeed in "de-locativizing" their descriptions of such scenes. This is a study planned for the future.

# References

Alferink, Inge & Marianne Gullberg. 2014. French-Dutch bilinguals do not maintain obligatory semantic distinctions: Evidence from placement verbs. *Bilingualism: Language and Cognition* 17. 22–37.

Ameka, Felix K. & Stephen C. Levinson. 2007. The typology and semantics of locative predicates: posturals, positionals, and other beasts. *Linguistics* 45. 847–871.

Berthele, Raphaël. 2004. The typology of motion and posture verbs: A variationist account. In Bernd Kortmann (eds.), *Dialectology meets typology. Dialect grammar from a cross-linguistic perspective*, 93–126. Berlin & New York.

Berthele, Raphaël, Matthew Whelpton, Åshild Naess & Pieter Duijff. 2015. Static spatial descriptions in five Germanic languages. *Language Sciences* 49. 82–101.

Brown, Amanda & Jidong Chen. 2013. Construal of manner in speech and gesture in Mandarin, English, and Japanese. *Cognitive Linguistics* 24. 605–631.

Cadierno, Teresa. 2004. Expressing motion events in a second language: A cognitive typological perspective. In Michel Achard & Suzanne Niemeier (eds), *Cognitive linguistics, second language acquisition and foreign language pedagogy*, 13–49. Berlin: Mouton de Gruyter.

Cadierno, Teresa. 2008. Learning to talk about motion in a foreign language. In Peter Robinson & Nick C. Ellis (eds), *Handbook of cognitive linguistics and second language acquisition*. 239–275. New York & London: Routledge.

Cadierno, Teresa, Iraide Ibarretxe-Antuñano & Alberto Hijazo-Gascón. 2016. Semantic categorization of placement verbs in L1 and L2 Danish and Spanish. *Language Learning* 66. 191–223.

De Knop, Sabine & Julien Perrez. 2014. Conceptual metaphors as a tool for the efficient teaching of Dutch and German posture verbs. *Review of Cognitive Linguistics* 12. 1–29.

Dörnyei, Zoltán. 1995. On the teachability of communication strategies. *TESOL Quaterly* 29. 55–85.

Ellis, Nick C. 1994. Implicit and explicit language learning–An overview. In Nick C. Ellis (eds.), *Implicit and explicit learning of languages*, 1–31. London: Academic Press.

Gullberg, Marianne. 2009. Reconstructing verb meaning in a second language: How English speakers of L2 Dutch talk and gesture about placement. *Annual Review of Cognitive Linguistics* 7. 221–244.

Hellerstedt, Maria. 2013. *L'utilisation et l'acquisition des verbes de position en suédois L1 et L2*. Paris, France : Université Paris-Sorbonne doctoral dissertation. Available at: http://www.e-sorbonne.fr/sites/www.e-sorbonne.fr/files/theses/hellerstedt_maria_2013_these.pdf

Hendriks, Henriëtte & Maya Hickmann. 2011. The expression of caused motion events in Chinese and in English: Some typological issues. *Linguistics* 49. 1041–1076.

Hickmann, Maya. 2007. Static and dynamic location in French: Developmental and cross-linguistic perspectives. In Michel Aurnague, Maya Hickmann & Laure Vieu (eds), *The categorization of spatial entities in language and cognition*, 205–231. Amsterdam & Philadelphia: John Benjamins.

Hickmann, Maya & Henriëtte Hendriks. 2006. Static and dynamic location in French and in English. *First Language* 26. 103–135.

Hijazo-Gascón, Alberto. 2015. Acquisition of motion events in L2 Spanish by German, French and Italian speakers. *The Language Learning Journal* 43. 1–26.

Ijaz, Helene I. 1986. Linguistic and cognitive determinants of lexical acquisition in a second language. *Language Learning* 36. 401–451.

Kellerman, Eric. 1995. Crosslinguistic influence: Transfer to nowhere? *Annual Review of Applied Linguistics* 15. 125–150.

Kendon, Adam. 2004. *Gesture: Visible action as utterance*. Cambridge: Cambridge University Press.

Kita, Sotaro. 2009. Cross-cultural variation of speech-accompanying gesture: A review. *Language and Cognitive Processes* 24. 145–167.

Kita, Sotaro & Asli Ozyürek. 2003. What does cross-linguistic variation in semantic coordination of speech and gesture reveal?: Evidence for an interface representation of spatial thinking and speaking. *Journal of Memory and Language* 48. 16–32.

Kopecka, Anetta. 2006. The semantic structure of motion verbs in French. In Maya Hickmann & Stéphane Robert (eds.), *Space in languages: Linguistic systems and cognitive categories*, 83–101. Amsterdam & Philadelphia: John Benjamins.

Lemmens, Maarten. 2002. The semantic network of Dutch posture verbs. In John Newman (ed.), *The linguistics of sitting, standing and lying*, 103–139. Amsterdam & Philadelphia: John Benjamins.

Lemmens, Maarten. 2005. Aspectual posture verb constructions in Dutch. *Journal of Germanic Linguistics* 17. 183–217.

Lemmens, Maarten. 2014. Une grammaticalisation ratée? Une étude diachronique de stand en anglais. *Anglophonia* 18. http://anglophonia.revues.org/327; DOI: 10.4000/anglophonia.327.

Lemmens, Maarten. 2015. *Zit je te denken of ben je aan het piekeren?* Persistentie in het synchrone gebruik van de PREP- en POS-progressiefconstructies in het Nederlands [Persistence in the synchronic use of PREP- and POS progressives in Dutch]. *Nederlandse Taalkunde* 20. 5–36.

Lemmens, Maarten. 2017. A Tale of two progressives. In Anastasia Makarova, Stephen M. Dickey, and Dagmar S. Divjak (eds.) *Thoughts on language: Studies in cognitive linguistics in honor of Laura A. Janda*, 175–194. Bloomington, IN: Slavica Publishers.

Lemmens, Maarten & Julien Perrez. 2010. On the use of posture verbs by French-speaking learners of Dutch: A corpus-based study. *Cognitive Linguistics* 21. 315–347.

Lemmens, Maarten & Julien Perrez. 2012. A quantitative analysis of the use of posture verbs by Fench-speaking learners of Dutch. *Cognitextes* 8. http://cognitextes.revues.org/609 (last accessed on 12 October, 2016).

Lemmens, Maarten & Dan I. Slobin. 2008. Positie- en bewegingswerkwoorden in het Nederlands, het Engels en het Frans [Posture and movement verbs in Dutch, English and French]. In Philippe Hiligsmann, Mélanie Baelen, Anne Lore Leloup & Laurent Rasier (eds.), *Verslagen en mededelingen van de Koninklijke Academie voor Nederlandse Taal- en Letterkunde* 118, 17–32.

Levinson, Stephen C. 2003. *Space in language and cognition: Explorations in cognitive diversity.* Cambridge: Cambridge University Press.

Narasimhan, Bhuvana & Marianne Gullberg. 2011. The role of input frequency and semantic transparency in the acquisition of verb meaning: Evidence from placement verbs in Tamil and Dutch. *Journal of Child Language* 38. 504–532.

Özçalışkan, Şeyda & Dan I. Slobin. 2003. Codability effects on the expression of manner of motion in Turkish and English. In Sumru A. Özsoy, Didar Akar, Mine Nakipoglu-Demiralp, Eser Erguvanli-Taylan & Ayhan Aksu-Koç (eds.), *Studies in Turkish linguistics*, 259–270. Istanbul: Boğaziçi University Press.

Slobin, Dan I. 2003. Language and thought online: Cognitive consequences of linguistic relativity. In Dedre Gentner & Susan Goldin-Meadow (eds.), *Language in mind : Advances in the study of language and thought*, 157–192. Cambridge, MA: MIT Press.

Slobin, Dan I. 2004. The many ways to search for a frog: Linguistic typology and the expression of motion events. In Sven Strömqvist & Ludo Verhoeven (eds.), *Relating events in narrative: Typological and contextual perspectives*, 219–257. Mahwah, NJ: Lawrence Erlbaum Associates.

Talmy, Leonard. 2000. *Towards a cognitive semantics.* Cambridge, MA: MIT Press.

Tutton, Mark. 2013. A new approach to analysing locative expressions. *Language and Cognition* 5. 25–60.

Viberg, Åke. 1985. Lexikal andraspråksinlärning. Hur polsk-, spansk- och finskspråkiga lär in svenskans placeraverb [Lexical second language acquisition. How Polish, Spanish and Finnish speakers acquire the Swedish placement verbs]. *SUM-rapport* 2. 5–92.

Viberg, Åke. 1998. Crosslinguistic perspectives on lexical acquisition: The case of language-specific semantic differentiation. In Kirsten Haastrup & Åke Viberg (eds.), *Perspectives on lexical acquisition in a second language*, 175-208. Lund: Lund University Press.

Wilkins, David P. 1998. The semantic extension of basic locative constructions cross-linguistically. In Sotaro Kita & Laura Walsh Dickey (eds.), *Max Planck Institute for Psycholinguistics: Annual report*, 55–61.

Wilkins, David P. 1999. The verbal component in basic locative constructions. In Veerle Van Geenhoven & Natasha Warner (eds.), *Max Planck Institute for Psycholinguistics: Annual report*, 61–71.

II **Teaching construal and viewpoint**

Barbara Dancygier and Carol Lynn Moder
# *Since it is everywhere*: Viewpoint in second language teaching

## 1 Introduction

Cognitive linguistics has alerted linguists, whether working in a theoretical or applied context, to the role concepts and cognition play in the grammatical choices speakers make. Much work has gone into understanding the conceptual structures underlying lexical forms, but also into larger constructions such as phrases or sentence patterns, to elaborate on the connections between syntax and meaning. Throughout this work much had to be said about spatial configurations, as well as about categories, in particular the category of viewpoint or speaker stance. A particularly important theoretical framework for understanding viewpoint phenomena, especially at the discourse-level, involves cognitive or mental spaces, which are conceptualizations of situations involving bundles of information brought together (or activated) on the fly while creating ongoing communication.

Before we go into a fuller discussion of viewpoint and mental spaces, let's consider an example adapted from an online blog giving advice about whether or not a young woman interested in music should go to college.

(1) a. **Since** she doesn't want to go to college because she wants to pursue music, she should take a year off to start her path in music.

b. **If** she doesn't want to go to college because she wants to pursue music, she should take a year off to start her path in music.

In second language grammar such examples have traditionally been dealt with as isolated sentences. The differences between them, if considered at all, would be described largely in terms of differences inherent in the semantics of the words *since* and *if*, but such a treatment would be unlikely to lead a learner to the deeper distinctions inherent in the natural use of these two words. Specifically, isolated consideration of the words overlooks that they occur within larger meaningful patterns or constructions which contribute to the contextualized

**Barbara Dancygier,** University of British Columbia
**Carol Lynn Moder,** Oklahoma State University

https://doi.org/10.1515/9783110572186-006

interpretation. Control of deeper meaning-based choices depends critically on matching the grammatical construction in which *since* or *if* occurs with the discourse context of use and the ongoing cognitive relations between the speaker and the hearer. In this chapter, we argue that in order to fully comprehend and master the alternatives that such sentences present, a speaker or writer must develop an awareness of viewpoint. The theory we rely on to develop this argument involves the notion of mental or conceptual spaces, which emphasizes the speaker's use of language to mentally guide the listener to a conceptualization of the situation similar to that of the speaker.

From a cognitive usage-based perspective, the choice of *since* or *if* in (1) relates to the blogger/writer's perspective on the reality of the information in the first clause. The choice of *since* in (1a) indicates that the blogger/writer has chosen to take a positive stance towards the proposition – that is, the writer positions himself as believing or having evidence that the young woman does not want to go to college for the reason stated. The use of *since* cues the reader to that stance. On the other hand, the choice of *if* in sentence (1b), indicates a neutral or negative stance – that is, the writer positions himself as neutral, uncertain, or doubtful about whether the proposition is true (Dancygier and Sweetser 2000). In both sentences, the use of the simple present tense in the first clause establishes a conceptual space in which the young woman's current beliefs or desires serve as the base for the advice provided in the second clause. With the use of *since*, the writer signals that only one belief/desire space is active and the belief asserted is presented as being accepted as true by the writer; it further signals that the belief is cognitively active for the reader who originally raised the issue in the blog posting. In contrast, with the use of *if*, the writer suggests two alternative possibilities or alternative scenarios. In one, the young woman does not want to go to college; in the alternative scenario, which is not explicitly stated, she does want to go to college. The writer thus marks his uncertainty about the desires or beliefs of the young woman. Again, present tense plays a role in the interpretation, indicating the writer believes the articulated proposition. (Note the sense of a weaker belief in the young woman's desire to pursue music if the proposition is articulated with the past tense, "If she **didn't** want to go to college because she **wanted** to pursue music, she should take a year off to start her path in music".) The use of the modal *should* in the second clause, provides an indicator that what follows is the writer's advice, but this advice must be viewed against the background of the cognitive scenario or mental space presented by the *if* or *since* clauses. In conjunction with the *since* clause, the writer is understood as offering relatively strong advice; in conjunction with the *if* clause, the writer is understood to be providing more tentative advice.

In this example, we have seen how a writer uses *since* and *if* to signal stance or viewpoint on a proposition. The category of viewpoint has recently been used more and more often to explain increasingly rich areas of language phenomena. While initially associated with visual perspective taking, the concept is now understood much more broadly, to include temporal viewpoint, epistemic stance, and other kinds of alignments. As this work progresses, researchers find ever more material to discuss in terms of viewpoint phenomena. The analyses have begun to interact in interesting ways with more basic concepts of space, time, and stance[1]. In this chapter, we explore why viewpoint (or stance) needs to be included in pedagogical representations of grammatical phenomena, and how it helps bring together various important issues that SLA researchers are attempting to solve.

## 2 Viewpoint and grammatical choices

First of all, how can we now define viewpoint? Possibly the simplest definition would present it as a conceptual alignment, prompted by linguistic expressions (and/or embodied behavior). In (1), the writer's choice of *since* conceptually aligns him with the proposition that the young woman does not want to go to college. As we see in this example, viewpoint does not require a physical, concrete context; on the contrary, it is a concept which is quite useful in explaining grammatical choices in the expression of abstract thought as well. In what follows, we will look at some examples of connections between viewpoint and grammatical form, but also focus on some aspects of a well-established teaching area – English conditional constructions – to illustrate the way in which viewpoint underlies primary aspects of the constructions' use.

Any analysis of viewpoint needs to start with the concept of the deictic center. The consideration of deictic phenomena often begins with the speaker and hearer dyad (e.g., "I" and "you"), engaged in interaction at a given place (e.g., "here") and a given time (e.g., "now"). However, if we consider further consequences of this basic interactional set-up, we will notice that it is also rich in viewpoint and the interlocutors need to understand much about the environment of the conversation. For example, the speaker knows that her spatial location gives different possibilities for vision, action, etc., than the location of the hearer. The deictic center thus relies strongly on visual viewpoint,

---

**1** Some recent ideas on the subject of conceptual viewpoint can be found in the articles in Dancygier and Sweetser (2012) (especially Sweetser [2012] introduction); also Sweetser (2013).

and builds on spatial and temporal landmarks, so that it is typically clear what expressions such as *now, here*, or *over there* mean in the context. However, the uses of deictic categories do not end with the here-and-now; these concrete alignments can be extended to abstract alignments. For example, even in a simple exchange, the speaker saying *I like it here* might be referring to the current pleasant location (a park, or a nice café), but she can also use the expression to comment on the good working conditions her current job offers, which are not necessarily displayed in the immediate context. Switching from *here* to *there* often opens other viewpoint possibilities, where *there* is not a location but a situation (as in *Let's not go there*, when the speaker wants to prevent discussion of slippery topics). The deictic center thus offers the basics of here-and-now interaction, but these basics can be coopted to express viewpoint on situations outside of the here-and-now.

These kinds of uses yield themselves easily to analysis in terms of mental spaces theory[2]. Mental spaces are conceptualizations of situations, which include space, time, and participants, as well as other information. Crucially, mental spaces do not have to refer to concrete, real situations, but often involve future or fictional situations, as when we talk about predicted results or desires. In (1), both versions rely on some specific mental spaces, represented by clauses. There are two "desire" spaces representing the emotional attitudes of the young person referred to (wanting to go to college, wanting to study music), as well as an "advice" space, profiling a suggested future action of taking a year off. Each of these spaces has a participant, a temporal location, an action of the participants, and the viewpoint on that action – either "her" wish or the writer/blogger's suggestion. Mental spaces are thus rich conceptual structures which often come in the scope of viewpoint markers such as the modal *should* or the verb *want* (indeed, English uses a whole range of stance verbs, such as *think, doubt, know, hope, wish*, to establish mental spaces).

Conceptually, we often align ourselves with mental spaces (rather than simply locations) to mark viewpoint on an issue. For example, Rubba (1996) talks about interviewees using *here* to refer to a rather distant neighborhood, to mark alignment with the ethnic and cultural values of that neighborhood. Even though the neighborhood is spatially distant, what is presented linguistically through the deictic element, *here*, is the entire spectrum of ideas about the neighborhood.

---

[2] Basic accounts of mental spaces can be found in Fauconnier ([1985] 1994), Fauconnier (1997), Fauconnier and Sweetser (1996).

## 3 Viewpoint and constructions

Thus far, we have looked at simple word choices which signal viewpoint, but constructions as wholes are also often viewpoint markers. These are form-meaning pairings occurring at the phrase, clause or multiclausal levels. Indeed, full interpretation of a construction can even tie to the discourse level. One such example is the family of constructions called conditionals, such as those in (1) above, which rely on mental spaces and viewpoint in crucial ways. They can profile situations that are distant in time or unreal and they allow the speaker to reason within these contexts and predict potential events from there, while also marking the participants' perceptions of likelihood of or attitudes towards the proposition. These complex meanings are expressed through a rich constellation of markers of time, stance, and other viewpoint categories. More will be said about these aspects of conditionals below, and in the paper by Dolgova Jacobsen (this volume). In what follows we will look at viewpoint aspects of constructions profiling mental spaces, to show the complexity and viewpoint-driven nature of conditionals in more specific terms. We will consider the possibility for constructions as wholes to be expressions of viewpoint, and we will look at the viewpoint-related meanings of verb forms and modals – two crucial grammatical aspects of what is typically said about conditionals in a classroom context.

Conditionals rely on viewpoint in many ways, but are primarily constructions displaying various kinds of reasoning – predictive, inferential, etc. It is important to also note, however, that some forms and constructions in fact specialize in profiling viewpoints. For example, the construction represented by *One person's trash is another person's treasure* is specifically comparing viewpoints and attitude (cf. Dancygier 2009). The object of evaluation is not mentioned, the actual participants aligned with these viewpoints are also not mentioned, but the comparison is made between viewing the object as useless and viewing it as desirable. Importantly, the overall viewpoint potential of the construction is built through three independent aspects of its formal set-up. The genitive form *person's* is one of them. (Note that variations on this construction include *One man's trash is another man's treasure*, *Someone's trash is someone else's treasure*.) The example is not talking about a person physically possessing a piece of trash or another person physically possessing a treasure, but rather about people possessing opinions or perspectives and ultimately viewing a single object through these differing perspectives. The construction mentions two compared viewpoints by mentioning two people (*one person's* and *another person's*) and through the predicative construction *X is Y*; the lexical expression of those viewpoints is made clear through the stance-rich or evaluative expressions *trash* and *treasure*. While this particular construction makes the viewpoint role of the genitive very clear, it is also seen in (1), where the possessive pronoun *her* in *her path in music* points to the kinds of experiences that will follow the person's decision to devote her life to music – so we are linking viewpoint to possessives again but in a conditional construction. Even in this brief overview, we see that aspects of viewpoint are profiled at all levels of grammatical structure (e.g., genitive morphology, deictic function words, constructional forms). Later in the chapter, we will briefly discuss other viewpointed constructions.

## 4 Spatial and temporal viewpoint: Understanding verb forms

We suggested above that there are three types of viewpoint that are perhaps most pervasively present in grammatical choices our students face: spatial, temporal, and stance-related (i.e., strength of speaker's commitment to the proposition or epistemic). The most basic category, at least in terms of human experience, is the spatial one: looking at an object from *below* or from *above*, seeing things up *close* or from a *distance*, understanding that the phone on my *right* is on the *left* from the perspective of someone sitting *across* the table, etc. There are many such expressions that learners have to grasp as lexical items, to some degree using their experience in the first language to match translational equivalents. But also, they will rely on the context to understand the spatial configuration in which these expressions might be used. They will need to include the knowledge of different viewpoint positions of different interlocutors, to understand that individual spatial viewpoints vary: the cup of tea *close* to me maybe very *distant* from you, so you wouldn't be able to reach it.

Additionally, much has also been said about the fact that spatial construals are the source for a range of expressions of time, and in fact time is hardly ever talked about in its own terms. There are two pervasive phenomena here.

The most commonly discussed one is choice of lexical expressions, motivated by conceptual metaphor.[3] If a speaker talks about *approaching the end of term* or notes that *the end of term is approaching*, the image used is that of a timeline, extending spatially from the past into the future. The present moment is the

---

[3] The literature on time metaphors is very broad. For basic concepts, consult Lakoff and Johnson (1980, 1999), and Dancygier and Sweetser (2014).

position the speaker occupies there (it is also somewhere before the event of "end of term"), and there are two possible motion trajectories: either the event is moving towards the speaker, who remains stationary, or the speaker is moving towards the stationary event. Many temporal expressions, such as *getting there*, *going forward*, *putting something behind*, etc., rely on this spatial configuration.

Using grammatical temporal marking to indicate perspective is less studied but also highly frequent. Can temporal marking be directly described in terms of spatial concepts? Not in actual linguistic choices, but some explanatory insights into how native speakers of English use temporal marking can build on spatial viewpoint phenomena. Let us consider the interaction between tense and aspect in English.

Teaching materials often describe English perfect aspect in terms of anteriority – talking about an event which took place at an unspecified time before another event. Drawing on a spatial image of events in time as occurring along a spatial continuum, the expressions which combine Present Tense and Perfect Aspect, such as *I **have** seen the movie already*, assume that the event of movie-going is located (we are using the word deliberately) before the present moment, the time of speech; by the same token, *I **had** seen the movie before you mentioned it* locates the event before another past event – of the movie being mentioned. *I will have seen the movie before you come back* moves the whole relation into the future. In each of these cases, we can think of a location (present, past, or future) from which the event in question is seen as preceding it, even if it is not itself located on a specific point on the timeline. In a sense, we are assuming that the speaker, who moves through the "time-landscape" looking forward, stops for a moment and looks back – to see the "movie-going" in the past region of space. This is a clear example of spatial viewpoint used to profile temporal viewpoint.

But we have another issue here. The Present plus Perfect uses the Present Tense to mark something close to the moment of speech – which becomes a viewpoint from which the past or the future can be observed.[4] However, the Past plus Perfect requires that the speaker, who remains physically in the "now" position, aligns herself mentally with "then" and takes that distant point to be the viewpoint. It looks as though the verb form system in English relies on viewpoint phenomena in an important way – the basic concepts of present, past and future can be seen as viewpoint (actual or distant) that the speaker uses to relate other events to these viewpointed locations. Importantly, aligning oneself with such a spatial construal brings in other conceptual consequences – the

---

4 For a more elaborate mental spaces analysis of viewpoint in temporal expressions see Cutrer (1994) and Fauconnier (1997).

speaker is relying on spatial viewpoint as epistemic viewpoint (such as "I can look back at the past behind me, see the event, and so I know about it and it affects my epistemic stance now").

We can add that in English the simple present tense is not used to describe an event occurring in the actual present or the moment of speaking (unlike in many languages of the world). Specifically, when talking on the phone, we cannot answer the question *What are you doing?* by saying *I talk to you*. It has to be *I'm talking to you*, with progressive aspect added. If the simple present tense does not describe the present (what is happening at the moment of speaking), what does it describe? We saw above that it serves as a kind of "viewpoint marker" in the case of the Perfect, and it is possible to describe it as a viewpoint marker when it helps to construe an action as ongoing (the Progressive does that) right "now" (or "then", if the tense is Past). And when it is used for imperfective meanings (*I talk on the phone every evening*), it provides a viewpoint from which a certain extended "time-zone" can be viewed as surrounding the Present moment. This is of course just one way of explaining the use of tense and aspect, but it has the advantage of linking grammar with the lexical choices, which clearly depend on the viewpointed conceptualization of time as space and thus providing a consistent, unified analysis.

We can take this analogy further. It is commonly observed that Past Tense may signal a number of functions independent of time. It can indicate politeness (**Were** *you going to eat this cookie?*) or unreal meanings or irrealis (*I wish I* **were** *a blonde!*). A whole range of such meanings is often referred to as "distanced" – to account for the fact that in spite of referring to situations occurring in the future or present, the situations are described using past tense morphology to mark unlikelihood, politeness, impossibility, etc. (cf. Fleischman 1989). If we go back to our viewpointed timeline metaphor, it makes sense – the speaker is relying on the viewpoint which makes the events described less proximal, less accessible, less visible, or less likely to affect the speaker or the hearer now. Metaphorical spatial distance is realized linguistically as temporal distance to express social or epistemic (expressing commitment to reality status of the proposition) distance; importantly, the viewpoint phenomenon is still of the same nature.

## 5 Epistemic viewpoint: Modals and beyond

We mentioned above the possibility for various forms, especially verb morphology, to express epistemic viewpoint.[5] Verb forms are, however, only one among many areas of expressions of epistemic viewpoint.

---

5 For a basic introduction to issues of stance, especially in conditionals, see Fillmore (1990).

The area which is probably best described and most efficiently taught is the use of modal verbs. They express the speaker's attitude towards events, in terms of logical prediction and speaker surety (epistemic concepts) and force of speech acts (deontic concepts) such as commands, suggestions, advice, etc. To make things more subtle, modal verbs often also have past forms, and use them in ways outlined above – for politeness and other kinds of distancing or signaling lessening of the force of the speaker's utterance. Modal verbs and their present and past forms play crucial roles in conditionals, where, along with tense morphology, they participate in expressing the speaker's stance on the likelihood of the future events occurring or the past events being factual. The result is that conditionals are often taught with strong emphasis on the combinations of verb forms, even though the reasons for those choices are not always clearly explained. Much has been said about counterfactual and distanced meanings of conditionals (Dancygier 1998; Dancygier and Sweetser 2005), and the issue will be elaborated in this paper and the one by Dolgova Jacobsen (this volume).

The fact that the choices of modal verbs and tense in conditionals are so important to meaning also calls for comparisons with other languages. English signals negative epistemic stance through past tense, while many languages rely on subjunctive mood morphology for the same purpose, which makes the rich meaning potential of the Past Tense in English all the more important. What is often less noticeable is the range of differences between the conjunction *if* and conditional conjunctions in other languages. One important difference seems to be that English distinguishes clearly between *when* (which profiles a positive epistemic stance, i.e., signals that speaker's surety of the proposition) and *if* (which profiles neutral and negative stance, i.e., signals lessened speaker surety). In contrast, many Slavic languages use a different combination of grammatical forms to indicate speaker surety or epistemic stance. Slavic speakers can attach subjunctive mood endings, which typically appear on the verb, to the conjunction, and, at the same time, temporal conjunctions (equivalents of *when*) are used with conditional meaning. As a result, for example in Polish, stance is essentially either negative or not – the distinction between neutral and positive is hard to make, and the negative stance is off-loaded onto the mood marker *-by* as it appears on the conjunction. Not all Slavic languages follow this pattern; in Serbian, negative stance requires an independent conjunction.[6] Conjunctions themselves are thus a rich source of viewpoint information and the strong reliance on the conjunction and verb forms in English is a cross-linguistic variation which needs to be explained in these terms.

There are also other important expressions of stance – for example, English uses a whole range of stance verbs, such as *think, doubt, know, hope, wish*, etc.

---

6 For an overall view of conditionals in Polish and Serbian see Dancygier and Trnavac (2007).

Some require verb form adjustment (like *wish*), while others do not, but there are also other issues, the most important of which is negation. We often assume that negative expressions are clear and straightforward and no explanation is really required, since we can expect negation to be present everywhere. It is not always so. Mental spaces theory has shown that negation is always used for a reason, typically to reject or question a positive claim present in the background, or to draw the hearer's attention to deficiencies. So when a speaker says *I don't want to go* or *We don't have any salt!*, the statements rely on an easily available suggestion or situation. The use of negation is thus often also an expression of viewpoint (lack of desire, need for action). It becomes more complicated when negation is combined with stance verbs. It is common for linguists to claim that expressions such as *I don't think X* simply move negation from the position where it would negate a situation, to the position where it negates the epistemic stance – so that in effect the meaning is *I think not X*. As recent studies show, however, that is not the whole story. Negation can be talked about as being another stance expression (and the examples above support that), sometimes used metalinguistically (as in *I am not tired, I'm exhausted!*) and sometimes to reject another speaker's stance (as in *I don't **think** you lost my keys, I know it!* in which the *think* is stressed).

We also have to note that negation, as a stance expression, interacts differently with different stance verbs (cf. Dancygier 2012). While *I don't think so* is perfectly natural, *I don't hope so* is not – we would definitely prefer *I hope not*. *I don't wish* is also confusing, because the clause in the scope of *wish* inherits the negative stance, marked by the verb forms (as in *I wish I could contribute*, where the speaker is marking the desire, primarily via the verb *wish*, but also needs to use the Past Tense in the clause in the scope of *wish* – *I could*, rather than *I can*). The issue of negation and stance verbs can also be seen in the sentences in (1). The *since* and *if* clauses use the negation (*she doesn't want to go to college*) in a specific sense – marking a lack of desire as a stance, or the viewpoint, taken by the person referred to. Looking at these facts jointly, as viewpoint phenomena, offers explanations of seemingly irregular behavior of very common verbs.

The interaction between stance expressions – which is the problem of multiple viewpoints in one utterance – is a complex issue. The examples above already show how complex the resulting meaning can be. But such interactions are an important element of how grammar is in fact used, and the bigger the number and scope of stance expressions, the harder the explanations are. For example, inserting the *I don't think so* expression into a conditional clause yields interesting results. In a sentence such as *If you don't think so, who will?*, the *if*-clause is echoic, very close to the positive stance (even though it is in the scope of *if*). But it would be hard to use it with negative stance – *If you hadn't thought so, I would have acted different*ly suggests that the hearer actually did "think so", so the negation is part of the counterfactual meaning, not of the expression *I don't think so*. Too much stance in one construction? Probably. But there are also conditional constructions which use negation in a rather specific way, as in *If it weren't for you, I would have never got the job*. As the conjunction and the verb forms make clear, the stance is consistently negative, counterfactual. But the construction *If not for X* itself is a trigger of negative stance, so the negation is specific to this construction, while also playing the role in the conditional as a whole.

These kinds of examples are not currently part of any second language curriculum – they are complex, and rely on skills which take a while to acquire. But they do enter the linguistic experience of learners, and are occasionally brought into the classroom context by puzzled students with a good ear for natural discourse. Designing lessons around such issues is hard too. But the recognition of multiplicity of viewpoints may help incorporate such examples into the teacher's and the learner's thinking. At the same time, approaching such expressions in constructional terms allows one to talk about an expression as having its peculiar meaning as a whole. The construction-plus-viewpoint approach offers a way to address meanings of individual lexical and grammatical forms, while also looking at how they contribute to more complex expressions.

# 6 Viewpoint in second language teaching

In what follows we will illustrate how the concept of viewpoint might be integrated into second language teaching, focusing on constructions using *since* to code temporal and epistemic viewpoint (Dancygier and Sweetser 2000, 2012). The context for the illustration is a second language ESL writing class at an American university. We constructed the activities within contemporary approaches to the teaching of grammar in second language contexts, consistent with an emergentist, dynamic systems view of second language acquisition (Ellis and Larsen-Freeman 2006; Ellis 2008; Larsen-Freeman and Cameron 2008). Our goal was to promote noticing and raised consciousness of viewpoint constructions through input structuring in usage-based discourse activities. This approach entailed a focus on item-specific discourse-based meanings of the *since* constructions (Thompson 1985; Ford 1993; Diessel 2005; Moder 2010), and the variation of individual discourse experience (Larsen-Freeman 2006; Eskildsen 2008; Verspoor, Lowie, and Van Dijk 2008).

Our process for adapting viewpoint concepts to the SLA context included analysis of discourse data from genre-based concordances, development of usage-based instructional materials, and consideration of factors influencing the effectiveness of pedagogical activities for advanced second language learners.

## 6.1 *Since* constructions

A complication for second language students who seek to interpret usage in context is the polysemy of key lexical items and their differing roles in different grammatical constructions. The problem is illustrated with the examples from student compositions in (2).

(2)  a.  I **have studied** English as a second language **since** I **was** seven
   b.  **Since** I **want** to improve my English, study abroad **is** one of the best choices I can make

In (2a), we find *since* in a construction which highlights the speaker's view of the temporal origin of an experience that is of current relevance. It is of note that the expression of this temporal perspective makes use of the elements of the present perfect discussed above. In this construction, the writer's use of the present perfect in the main clause (*I have studied English*) establishes the writer's perspective that the event which began in the past continues to have a direct impact on and relevance in the ongoing discourse. It serves as an epistemic ground for a viewpoint experience that the writer will elaborate in the discourse. In the subordinate clause, *since* introduces the specific point of origin of the experience. The *since* clause in (2a) uses the past tense, indicating that the writer presents the original event as one precise starting point in the past. The construction thus projects a viewpointed timeline in which the single point of origin forms the starting point for the experience or understanding that grounds the current viewpoint of the writer.

In (2b), we find an example of *since* in an epistemic construction in which the author's evidence is presented and that aligns the writer with the proposition expressed in the clause. The writer's desire to improve her English is presented as a premise that she views as true, a viewpoint reinforced by the use of the present tense. (Recall our previous discussion on the multiple meanings of tense and the use of the present tense to signal speaker surety or sense of realis.) The proposition in this clause provides the epistemic basis for her assertion in the main clause that study abroad was the best choice.

What is of note in these examples is that the lexical item *since* participates in two different constructions expressing distinct points of view. The meaning differences in these uses of *since* are discerned through the distinctive tense/aspect forms common to each construction and spread across both clauses. To elaborate this point, consider the clause *since she cleaned the bathroom*. In isolation, the clause could either be temporal or epistemic – the combination of *since* and past tense could occur in either type of construction. We need to see the full construction in order to disambiguate it. This is illustrated in (3).

(3) a. Since she cleaned the bathroom, you should take out the garbage.

   b. It has happened since she cleaned the bathroom.

Here, the temporal and epistemic uses of *since* are made distinct by considering the interaction between the two clauses, i.e., the entire construction. A key point is that the interpretation of the *since* clause is dependent on the information in the main clause. In (3a), the *since* clause appears first, indicating that the information it contains is presented as accessible to the hearer. This clause is followed by a clause using the modal *should*, which indicates that the *since* clause is presented as the epistemic ground for the proposal that the hearer should take out the garbage. In (3b), the *since* clause is preceded by an event clause in the present perfect, indicating a temporal use. The event in the *since* clause is the point of reference for what has happened. It is the grammatical coding of the entire structure of both clauses in combination with the semantic content of those clauses that establishes how the writer is using *since* to present a particular viewpoint.

The examples above uncover some of the primary difficulties in the learning of constructions with *since*. The students have to recognize the fact that the sentence-final adverbial clauses may be used very differently from the sentence-initial ones. They also need to understand how the concept of the timeline and temporal viewpoint is reflected in verb form choices in different clauses of the same construction, so that the grammar of the verb is not only an issue of appropriate representation of time, but also of sequence of events and of temporal viewpoint. Finally, the type of reasoning represented by the construction (and especially the types of viewpoints it represents) complicate matters further. In understanding the use of *since*, learners have to understand a number of viewpoint phenomena and their representation at many levels of grammar.

## 6.2 *Since* constructions in academic English

To develop a fuller cognitive usage-based understanding of the forms and functions related to temporal and epistemic *since* constructions for the target group of students, it is useful to consider more closely the ways that these constructions are typically realized in academic English. To do so, we examined the use of *since* in two American English corpora, the Michigan Corpus of Academic Spoken English (MICASE) and the academic samples from the Corpus of Contemporary American English (COCA). MICASE provides a broad view of the ways the constructions are used in both more and less formal spoken academic contexts. For this study, we looked at all examples of *since* produced by native speakers of American English, a total of 425 uses in 118 speech events. The academic section of COCA provided formal written uses, mostly from published academic research articles. Since COCA is a large corpus, we selected a random sample of 1000 examples of *since* as the basis for extended examination. From the examination of these uses, some key features of these constructions were identified.

In these corpora, epistemic uses were more frequent than temporal uses. The difference was large in the spoken MICASE corpus; only 23 % of the uses of *since* were temporal, compared to 73% epistemic uses. In the sample from the written COCA Academic corpus, the distribution was more even: 52% epistemic compared to 48% temporal uses. We will look first at the features of the temporal *since* construction and then consider the epistemic construction.

### 6.2.1 Temporal *since*

Reflecting their coding of a specific point of origin, the temporal uses of *since* occur most frequently, not in full clauses, but in nominal expressions that code a point in time. For example, expressions like *since 1997* or *since the inception of the program* were much more common than full clauses, like *since the picture was taken*. Table 1 shows the variations in the forms following *since* occurring in the 114 temporal uses in MICASE and in the 468 temporal examples from COCA academic. In both corpora, temporal *since* is typically followed, not by a clause, but by a noun phrase that denotes a particular point in time, often a specific date or year. In addition, the specific phrase *since then* is quite frequent in its own right. The high frequency of these forms suggest that such uses could easily serve as models for acquiring the temporal *since* construction. The use of a full finite clause following *since* is much less frequent at 22% of temporal uses in MICASE and only 10% in the COCA academic sample.

Table 1 also shows the use of *since* as an adverb in clause final position, as in *have guided decision-making ever **since***, and also as an adverb in present perfect verb forms, as in *has **since** been lifted*. These adverb uses are presented as part of the distributional information here, but will not be the focus of this analysis.

**Table 1:** Temporal uses of *since* form variation

| | Example | MICASE 114 uses | COCA Academic 468 uses |
|---|---|---|---|
| *Since* [year/date] [time phrase] [other noun phrase] | *Since 1973* *Since the beginning* *Since the civil rights era* *Since his 1993 talk* | 57% | 81% |
| *Since then* | *A million times since then* *Since then, the drug control system* [...] | 9.5% | 6% |
| *Since* [clause] | *Since I was in graduate school* *Since the project began* | 22% | 10% |
| *(ever) since.* *has since V* | *have guided decision making ever since.* *has since disappeared* | 11.5% | 6% |

What can the corpora tell us about other specific features of the construction in which temporal *since* occurs? If we consider the tense/aspect coding, we find that the use of the present perfect in temporal *since* constructions is overwhelming. The widespread use of the present perfect occurs even in the spoken Academic corpus. In MICASE, the present perfect occurs in 76% of verbs in the main clause (*It's **been** 15 years since I read these books*). In 20% of the uses, the main clause verb is in the simple present tense, but the *since* clause appears in the present perfect (*It's so long since I**'ve looked** at it*). Thus, in 96% of the uses in MICASE, at least one of the clauses is in the present perfect. In the COCA Academic sample, the main clause occurs with a present perfect in 73% of the examples with a finite verb. Other perfect forms, like the present perfect progressive and the past perfect, also occur, but with much lower frequency. If we add these to the present perfect instances, we find that perfect aspect occurs in the main clause in 91% of the temporal examples.

When temporal *since* does occur in a full finite clause, the verb in that clause is most typically in the past tense: 74% in MICASE and 94% in COCA Academic. The examples in (4) illustrate the typical tense/aspect forms for this construction.

(4) Tense/aspect in temporal *since* constructions
    a. ***Since** then*, *meetings **have happened** periodically in both countries.*
    b. ***Since** 1987, however, the economic situation **has improved**.*
    c. ***Since** we **started**, we **have identified** a total of 140 buildings.*
    d. *The world **has moved** further ahead **since** the Queen **died**.*

**Table 2:** Typical form of temporal and epistemic *since* constructions

|  | Typical form | Tense aspect correlates | |
|---|---|---|---|
|  |  | *Since* clause | Main clause |
| Temporal *since* | *Since 1987, the economic situation **has improved**.* | Nonfinite clause most frequent | **Present Perfect** Most frequent |
|  | *Since we **started**, we have identified […]* | In full clause, **past tense** most frequent |  |
| Epistemic *since* | *Since intranets **are** a solid and uniform standard, setup and protocols **are** simplified […]* | **Present tense** 58% Most frequent: speaker aligns with general truth of the statement | **Present tense** 46% Most common: speaker aligns with content |
|  | *Development of these systems **may be** difficult since one **has** to keep track […]* |  | **Present modals** 18% Writer limits alignment with consequence, conclusion |
|  | *Since **most** of the customers **were** transient, they never **complained*** | **Past tense** 20% Speaker presents ground as restricted to a particular context | **Past tense** 27% More writer distance from generality of the content |

This survey of the form-meaning pairings in temporal *since* clauses highlights the critical ways in which tense/aspect relates to the viewpoint coded in the construction.

#### 6.2.2 Epistemic *since*

In the epistemic *since* construction, by far the most frequent tense/aspect form for the verb in the *since* clause is the simple present, accounting for 58% of epistemic *since* clause verbs in MICASE and 67% in COCA Academic. The simple past tense follows at 20% in MICASE and 23% in COCA Academic. The use of the simple present tense is consistent with the status of the *since* clause as evidence; writers often present information that is the basis for an action or belief as generally true and the simple present tense fulfills this viewpoint function in English. We see such uses in (5a) and (5b). Some frequent collocates of *since* in these clauses are *most* (as illustrated in [5c]), *all, few, many*, and *only*, words which also denote general statements of fact or belief. In (5c), we see the use of the past tense in the *since* clause. This use designates a belief or fact that is restricted to a particular period or set of circumstances. In this example, the discussion concerns a specific case study.

(5) Epistemic *since* constructions
   a. **Since** *variation* **is** *undesirable, just* **ignore** *it.*
   b. *Touch* **is** *an intersensory process,* **since all** *the receptors and cerebral areas* **cooperate** *in such a way as to converge to create tactile perception.*
   c. *Occasionally, the food spoiled and customers got food poisoning, but* **since most** *of the customers* **were** *transient, moving through town, they never really* **complained**.

This overview of epistemic uses of *since* shows that there are clear distinctions in the two *since* constructions. These are summarized in Table 2.

## 6.3 Teaching application

Using the information from the corpus study, we designed classroom activities to raise student awareness about the two *since* constructions and their form and meaning correlates. It is important to note that these activities were conducted by a researcher, not the regular classroom teacher, and took place over only three days in a 14-week term. As such, they demonstrate the effect of very limited classroom application of the principles we have discussed.

### 6.3.1 Participants

Participants in the study were 34 students enrolled in the second of two first year composition courses required of all undergraduate students. Students had a variety of majors and language backgrounds. Prior to arrival in the U.S., they reported studying English from 1 to 10+ years. They had been in the U.S. from 1 month to 3+ years.

In order to target the instruction more closely to student needs, we examined samples of student writing from journal entries and essay assignments. Before the activities, students' use of *since* in these writings ranged from 0 to 20 uses per student. There were a total of 108 uses by 27 students. Of these, 27/108 uses or 25% were temporal and 81/108 or 75% were causal. Twelve of the students used both epistemic and temporal *since*, nine used only epistemic forms, six used only temporal, and seven used no *since* constructions in the writing samples.

**Table 3:** Student uses of temporal *since* prior to instruction, total uses = 27

| | Example | Token ∫ | % temporal uses | Main clause present perfect | | *Since* clause past | |
|---|---|---|---|---|---|---|---|
| *Since* [year/date] [time phrase] [other noun phrase] | since 1960 since the beginning since high school | 3 | 11% | 1/3 | 33% | – | |
| *Since then* | | 12 | 44% | 5/12 | 42% | – | |
| *Since* [clause] | since she was a small girl. since they are learning since young age | 12 | 45% | 4/12 | 33% | 10/12 | 83% |
| TOTAL | | 27 | | 10/27 | 37% | | |

For the temporal uses, students used a large proportion of *since* constructions with full clauses. In the *since* clauses, they predominantly used the past form, though two students used the simple present. In the main clause, however, the students used the present perfect only 37% of the time – which suggests that the difficulty in distinguishing temporal viewpoint from temporal allocation of events and mental states is a major source of difficulty. In (6) below we see specific student temporal uses.

(6) Student temporal uses
   a. Amy **has** always **been** a lucky person since she **was** a small girl.
   b. Since I **was** ten years old my goal **was** [...]
   c. American students **have been exposed** to these policies since they **are** in high school
   d. I **learn** English since I **was** in primary school
   e. This warriors **practice** every day since they **are** little children

With respect to the epistemic uses, students varied widely in their awareness of the way the tense/aspect correlates and the positioning of the clauses related to the accessibility of information to the reader. We also found evidence that for some students the interaction of the two constructions might be causing confusion.

On the basis of the student uses, we determined that one focus would be on raising student awareness of the temporal and causal (or epistemic) uses as distinct constructions. In other words, one focus would be on the difference in viewpoint offered by the two constructions. A second focus would be on raising student awareness of the present perfect in temporal since constructions and the viewpoint perspective that it imposes. We included a third set of activities designed to bring epistemic viewpoint to the fore by contrasting *since* with *if* in particular discourse contexts. Given that some students were already using target forms effectively, we posited that a Language Experience Approach (Swain and Lapkin 1998), in which students worked in groups to analyze specific examples could be productive.

### 6.3.2 Activities

Sorting Task: To promote awareness of the two constructions as distinct, we adopted a sorting task. Students were divided into groups of three or four and asked to sort a set of 10 to 12 sentences into as many groups as they thought appropriate and then to discuss the reasons that they grouped the items as they did. The specific sentences were selected to reflect the variation found in the academic corpora. Note that (7a) illustrates the temporal viewpoint construction while (7b) and (7c) illustrate the epistemic.

(7) Sample sorting sentences
   a. *In international tests in math and science, U.S. 8th graders in* **have shown** *little improvement* **since** *the tests* **were last given** *in 1995.*
   b. **Since** *everybody's work* **was grounded** *in the family it* **wasn't** *so surprising, that women's work was also.*
   c. **Since I'm** *a woman in a traditionally male field, I* **end up** *being an advocate for women.*

In the following class period, the researcher led a full class discussion of the choices each group made and then presented an overview of the information relevant to each construction. This explanation highlighted the different viewpoints signals by the two constructions. See Appendix A for the *since* constructions handout.

Discourse Task: In groups of two or three, students read a text in which both *since* constructions occurred. They identified temporal and epistemic uses of *since* and then explained the use of the tense/aspect in each construction based on the context.

Epistemic Viewpoint *Since* and *If*: Students read a full text, focusing on highlighted sentences. They then discussed selected sentences. They were asked to indicate when *since* and *if* could be used and what meaning difference each would represent in this context. The activity used the blog text discussed at the beginning of this chapter. As a follow up activity, students considered the responses to the blogs. See Appendix B. They were then asked to write a response of their own.

### 6.3.3 Effects of instruction

Before and after the activities, students were asked to write five sentences using *since*. These sentences were scored for grammatical accuracy and semantic appropriateness. Comparison of the pre-activity and post-activity sentences, indicated that 15 students improved, 6 received the same score, and 11 received a lower score. These results suggest that even very limited activities which expose students to usage-based examples, can result in increases in students' awareness of the form and function features of viewpoint constructions. For those who scored lower on the post-test sentences, there was some evidence that the activities had disrupted their grammatical systems; students who had not used the present perfect for time clauses in the pre-test were attempting it in the post-test, but not always successfully. In the context of a dynamic systems approach to SLA, such disruptions would have the potential to lead to future acquisition, if the students have further exposure to these constructions in context. Furthermore, all students appeared to have a better understanding of the two types of constructions, as evidenced by their use of both types of sentences in the post-test. A week following the last activity, students wrote a journal entry reflecting on the activities. Some excerpts from these journals appear in (8).

(8) Student evaluations of the activities
I am more aware of their uses than I was before, but I think I have to practice more often to learn more about them. (noticing differences in temporal versus epistemic viewpoints, need for more input)

Before the speaker came, I thought that they have the same uses and there is nothing different between them. (form discrimination and recognizing viewpoint differences)

> [I]t made me realize that diverse uses of [since and if], and how could a slight editing in a sentence change the meaning of the sentence. Moreover, it helped me know that using each one of them changes the voice and the statement tone, which is important when we communicate (function, epistemic stance or viewpoint)
>
> After the class, I feel like I am able to explain the difference to someone who is having difficulties (explicit awareness)

As these comments suggest, students generally reported that the activities helped them to notice the forms, to understand the distinct constructions and their differences in signaling distinct viewpoint, to tie formal variations to discourse functions, and/or to increase their explicit awareness of the constructions. The comments also indicated that the brief activities reported here might be more effective with further practice.

# 7 Conclusions

One of the concerns that teachers in second language contexts have about the incorporation of new and unfamiliar conceptual categories is that their introduction might be excessively time-consuming. The selection of the materials and the focus of the activities reported here were designed to instantiate key aspects of viewpoint constructions. However, the materials purposely refrained from the explicit introduction of unfamiliar terminology, relying on language that the participants themselves formulated in the sentence sorting task. This decision was made to allow the activities to fit more comfortably into existing classes that had not been designed to follow cognitive linguistic principles. The effectiveness of these activities for the majority of the participants suggests that the design and use of such implicitly cognitive materials might be a viable approach in many second language classes.

The selected examples we discussed above show that various lower level viewpoint expressions (the genitive, tense/aspect, modals, epistemic verbs, etc.) participate in complex viewpoint configurations represented by constructions. In particular, we have focused our attention on *since* and *if* constructions. However, there are many other aspects of grammar that involve viewpoint. We noted above that the concepts of proximity and distance affect English speakers' use of tense. These concepts, as they are represented in grammar, are not limited to verb forms (see Dancygier and Vandelanotte 2009). One of the harder issues to explain to a learner is the use of demonstratives *this/that, these/those*. Many languages have demonstratives and they are invariably extremely complex (to mention just one recent study, on Polish, by Rybarczyk 2015). The actual use of these function words in English is beyond the scope of this article, but it is important to note that the opposition between proximity and distance – the central, spatial meaning of demonstratives – is extended to many epistemic, social, emotional, and discourse uses. In each case, however, the more proximal concept represents the speaker as aligning herself with the concept at hand, and each distal use presents the speaker as cautious about such an alignment. Spatial, temporal, epistemic, and other viewpoints are related into a network of concepts presenting a stance the speaker is taking.

Considering viewpoint phenomena also prepares students better to process new and emerging constructional forms. As we discussed previously, *One person's X is another person's Y* contrasts viewpoints in a general way, in an almost proverbial tone, but there are other constructions which achieve similar effects to profile specific viewpoint contrasts, some of which are so popular that they have earned the name of a "snowclone" – a ubiquitous pattern applied to new situations all the time. One such viewpoint construction is the *X is the new Y* construction. When a person says that *60 is the new 40*, what is crucially being said is that there is now a new viewpoint on what counts as being senior. It used to be the case that a person aged 60 was considered quite close to being a senior, while now 60 is viewed the way the age of 40 used to be viewed. The construction is indeed extremely popular (viewpoints seem to be changing fast in today's world) and examples are easy to find: *Water is the new oil, Green is the new black* (to describe fashion), *Green is the new red* (in terms of political stances), etc. Students are most likely seeing many examples of the construction in colloquial usage, but instruction on these types of constructions is not a common occurrence – partly because they emerge too quickly to be included in teaching materials. But preparing both instructors and students to notice viewpoint phenomena in constructions may be an effective way of increasing learners' awareness and use of newly emergent forms. The form of the *X is the new Y construction* is very simple, and the meaning is not very complex, but requires a recognition of contrasted viewpoints. Getting a grasp of the viewpoint nature of the meaning may help learners develop more confidence in exploring new forms of contemporary discourse.

Given the prevalence of viewpoint constructions and the usefulness of the concept in understanding a variety of grammatical constructions, we believe it would be worthwhile for those designing new materials to consider a more explicit introduction of concepts like viewpoint, stance, and alignment. See Dolgova Jacobsen (this volume) for such an approach to the teaching of conditionals.

SLA has traditionally focused on constructions (without using the technical terms), but the methodology can now be enriched by correlating similar phenomena across various constructions. For example, past tense marks similar viewpointed construals in reported speech, in conditionals, and in the use of *wish*, but the connections are often not made. It might help to let the learners see how multiple viewpoints are the norm, not the exception.

It is often difficult to clearly draw the boundary between grammar and usage in a second language class, but the common expectation is that teaching grammar well will explain all relevant usage. If this is to work, we need to incorporate strategic issues such as viewpoint into the conversation. Not because it will solve problems, one at a time, but because it will build broader ground for coherent explanations across various phenomena.

# References

Cutrer, Michelle. 1994. *Time and tense in narratives and everyday language.* San Diego: University of California Ph.D. dissertation.

Dancygier, Barbara. 1998. *Conditionals and prediction: Time, knowledge, and causation in conditional constructions.* Cambridge: Cambridge University Press.

Dancygier, Barbara. 2009. Genitives and proper names in constructional blends. In Vyvyan Evans & Stephanie Pourcel (eds.), *New directions in cognitive linguistics*, 161–18. Amsterdam & Philadelphia: John Benjamins.

Dancygier, Barbara. 2012. Negation, stance verbs, and subjectivity. In Barbara Dancygier & Eve Sweetser (eds.), *Viewpoint in language: A multimodal perspective*, 69–93. Cambridge: Cambridge University Press.

Dancygier, Barbara & Eve Sweetser. 2000. Constructions with *if*, *since*, and *because*: Causality, epistemic stance and clause order. In Elizabeth Couper-Kuhlen & Bernd Kortmann (eds.), *Cause-condition-concession-contrast: Cognitive and discourse perspectives.* Berlin: Mouton de Gruyter.

Dancygier, Barbara & Eve Sweetser. 2005. *Mental spaces in grammar: Conditional constructions.* Cambridge: Cambridge University Press.

Dancygier, Barbara & Eve Sweetser (eds.). 2012. *Viewpoint in language: A multimodal perspective.* Cambridge: Cambridge University Press.

Dancygier, Barbara & Eve Sweetser (eds.). 2014. *Figurative language.* Cambridge: Cambridge University Press.

Dancygier, Barbara & Radoslava Trnavac. 2007. Conjunctions, verb forms, and epistemic stance in Polish and Serbian predictive conditionals. In Dagmar Divjak & Agata Kochańska (eds.), *Cognitive paths into the Slavic domain*, 181–120. Berlin: Mouton de Gruyter.

Dancygier, Barbara & Lieven Vandelanotte. 2009. Judging distances: Mental spaces, distance, and viewpoint in literary discourse. In Geert Brône & Joeren Vandaele (eds.), *Cognitive poetics: goals, gains, and gaps*, 319–370. Berlin: Mouton de Gruyter.

Diessel, Holger. 2005. Iconicity of sequence: A corpus-based analysis of the positioning of temporal adverbial clauses in English. *Cognitive Linguistics* 1. 465–490.

Ellis, Nick C. 2008. Usage-based and form-focused SLA: The implicit and explicit learning of constructions. In Andrea Tyler, Yiyoung Kim & Mari Takada (eds.), *Language in the context of use: Discourse and cognitive approaches to language*, 93–120. Berlin: Mouton de Gruyter.

Ellis, Nick C. & Diane Larsen-Freeman. 2006. Language emergence: Implications for applied linguistics. *Applied Linguistics* 27. 558–589.

Eskildsen, Søren. 2008. Constructing another language – Usage-based linguistics in second language acquisition. *Applied Linguistics* 30. 335–357.

Fauconnier, Gilles. 1994 [1985]. *Mental spaces: Aspects of meaning construction in natural language*. Cambridge: Cambridge University Press.

Fauconnier, Gilles. 1997. *Mappings in thought and language*. Cambridge: Cambridge University Press.

Fauconnier, Gilles & Eve Sweetser (eds.). 1996. *Spaces, worlds, and grammar*. Chicago: University of Chicago Press.

Fillmore, Charles. 1990. Epistemic stance and grammatical form in English conditional sentences. *CLS* 26. 137–162.

Fleischman, Suzanne. 1989. Temporal distance: a basic linguistic metaphor. *Studies in Language* 13(1). 1–50.

Ford, Cecilia. 1993. *Grammar and interaction: Adverbial clauses in American English conversations*. Cambridge: Cambridge University Press.

Lakoff, George & Mark Johnson. 1980. *Metaphors we live by*. Chicago: University of Chicago Press.

Lakoff, George & Mark Johnson. 1999. *Philosophy in the flesh: The embodied mind and its challenge to Western thought*. New York: Basic Books.

Larsen-Freeman, Diane. 2006. The emergence of complexity, fluency, and accuracy in the oral and written production of five Chinese learners of English. *Applied Linguistics* 27. 590–619.

Larsen-Freeman, Diane & Lynne Cameron. 2008. *Complex systems and applied linguistics*. Oxford: Oxford University Press.

Moder, Carol Lynn. 2010. Form, meaning, and construction: American English *like NP*. In Fey Parrill, Vera Tobin & Mark Turner (eds.), *Meaning, form, and body*, 203–221. Stanford: CSLI.

Rubba, Jo. 1996. Alternate grounds in the interpretation of deictic expressions. In Gilles Fauconnier & Eve Sweetser (eds.), *Spaces, worlds, and grammar*, 227–261. Chicago: University of Chicago Press.

Rybarczyk, Magdalena. 2015. *Demonstratives and possessives with attitude*. Amsterdam & Philadelphia: John Benjamins.

Swain, Merrrill & Sharon Lapkin. 1998. Interaction and second language learning: Two adolescent French immersion students working together. *Modern Language Journal* 82. 320–337.

Sweetser, Eve. 2012. Introduction: viewpoint and perspective in language and gesture, from the ground up. In Barbara Dancygier & Eve Sweetser (eds.), *Viewpoint in language: A multimodal perspective*, 1–22. Cambridge: Cambridge University Press.

Sweetser, Eve. 2013. Creativity across modalities in viewpoint-construction. In Mike Brokent, Barbara Dancygier & Jennifer Hinnell (eds.), *Language and the creative mind*, 239–254. CSLI Publications.

Thompson, Sandra A. 1985. Grammar and written discourse. Initial and final purpose clauses in English. In Talmy Givon (eds.), *Quantified studies in discourse* (Special issue of *Text* 5), 55–84.

Verspoor, Marjolijn, Wander Lowie & Marijn Van Dijk. 2008. Variability in second language development from a dynamic systems perspective. *Modern Language Journal* 92. 214–231.

# Appendix A

*Since* Post sorting explanation Handout Excerpt

***Since* introduces constructions with TWO main meanings:**
**Reason & Time**

**Reason uses: Most common use in academic English**
**Introducing a clause that states a reason or explanation**
   [Clause], *since* [reason]
1. The present investigation represents an important contribution, **since** it **provides** empirical evidence of the types of cognitive processes activated through feedback.
   *Since* [reason], clause
2. **Since** I'm a woman in a traditionally male field, I end up being an advocate for women.
3. **Since** everybody's work **was grounded** in the family it wasn't so surprising, that women's work was also.

**In Reason Uses: Tense/aspect of the verbs in the clauses will vary according to the context**. The most common tenses are:
   – **present**
      – for statement situated in the present, or generally true statements with which the writer agrees
   – **past**
      – for statements situated in the past or statements from which the writer distances him or herself.

**Position of Reason clauses:**
   *Since* [reason], clause is the most common order in academic English.

   This order requires that the information in the *since* clause has already been introduced in the previous text or is familiar to the reader.

**Time uses**

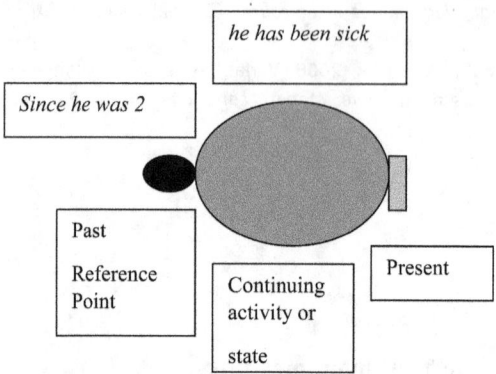

**Since + noun phrase**

**A.** *Since* [noun phrase which describes a past reference point] [clause with verb of continuing state or duration in PERFECT]

4. **Since** the early 1990s, the phenomenon of globalization **has been attracting** the attention of researchers, whose specializations are diverse both in nature and application.

**B.** [clause with verb of continuing state or duration in PERFECT] *since* [noun phrase which describes a past reference point]

5. Scientists **have been working** on this project **since** January.

**Since + clause**

**C.** [clause with verb in perfect] *since* [clause which describes a past reference point]

6. In international tests in math and science, U.S. 8th graders in **have shown** little improvement since **the tests were last given in 1995.**

**In Time uses: Main clause MUST have a verb in the PERFECT**
*Since* clause most commonly has a verb in the past tense.

# Appendix B

*Since* and *if* Follow-up Activity

*Since* vs. *if*?

Consider the alternative choices in the following excerpts from the responses to Mission2Win:

1) *I think it's okay to be a little naive and make stupid decisions when you're young.*

**a.** ***If that's not okay, then no one really has a childhood.***

**Or**

**b.** ***Since that's not okay, then no one really has a childhood.***

What is the difference in the meaning here between *since* and *if*?

Which form would you choose in this context and why?

2) ***If she doesn't want to go to college because she wants to pursue music, she should take a year off to start her path in music.***

**Or**

***Since she doesn't want to go to college because she wants to pursue music, she should take a year off to start her path in music.***

What is the difference in the meaning here between *since* and *if*?

Which form would you choose in this context and why?

3) *People should do what they love, but they should also accept the consequences of doing what they love. She will almost definitely need another job outside of music to support herself as a musician; is she willing to do that? Is she willing to consider attending college in the future? To explore other careers?*

***If she doesn't want to go to college, she's not ready for college.***

**Or**

***Since she doesn't want to go to college, she's not ready for college.***

What is the difference in the meaning here between *since* and *if*?

Which form would you choose in this context and why?

Now write a short response to Mission2Win, using both *since* and *if*.

Natalia Dolgova Jacobsen
# Using blending theory to teach the English conditionals

## 1 Introduction

Cognitive linguistic (CL) theory emphasizes the usage-based nature of language and inherent connections between form and meaning. In the last decade, usage-based approaches to language acquisition and instruction have gained greater recognition by the researchers in the field (Tyler 2010). Additionally, CL theory can serve as a coherent and relevant linguistic theory in second language teaching and learning materials, which could in turn help ensure the stability of teaching practices (de Knop and Dirven 2008; Tyler 2008, 2012).

A number of recent studies have explored applications of cognitive linguistics to second language instruction of various target forms; however, many of them (with few notable exceptions) did not follow methodological guidelines accepted in empirical instructed second language acquisition (SLA) research, nor did they utilize current pedagogical methods. Furthermore, conceptual blending has received comparatively less attention in applied CL research than other areas of cognitive linguistics (e.g., cognitive grammar and metaphor theory). Accordingly, the present study aimed to address these gaps by applying the CL analysis of the English conditionals to L2 instruction through the use of explicit task-supported language teaching.

This chapter begins with a summary of related literature. Furthermore, because of the noted dearth of studies on L2 applications of conceptual blending in particular, this article specifically aims to demonstrate in greater detail how conceptual blending was adapted to teaching materials in the present instructional context. The chapter concludes with reporting the study's results and discussing future research directions.

## 2 Literature review

### 2.1 Speaker construal in relation to L2 learning and teaching

In the process of linguistic *construal* (Langacker 2000), the speaker attempts to shape the message in a certain way, by choosing among linguistic constructions, in order to guide the listener to a similar conceptualization. For instance, the

**Natalia Dolgova Jacobsen**, George Washington University

https://doi.org/10.1515/9783110572186-007

same event can be conveyed with varying level of details, emphasizing various aspects of a scene or event, using different types of vocabulary (e.g., standard/neutral vs. emotionally loaded), or different grammatical forms and constructions. In addition to set linguistic conventions within each language, construal can also refer to the speaker's perspective and choice of linguistic items.

More specifically, conventionalized "chunks" of language are being combined together in response to a concrete *usage event*. When the speaker is trying to make mental contact with the listener, s/he is attempting to guide the listener to a conceptualization that is roughly similar to their own by shaping their message using the most (locally) appropriate linguistic means. Langacker characterizes a usage event as an "instance of language use as initiated by a language user who is in command of not only the linguistic expression but also other factors such as memory, planning, problem-solving ability, and general knowledge of the world, as well as a full apprehension of the physical, social, cultural, and linguistic context" (Langacker 2000: 9). In order to match a given usage event with corresponding and appropriate linguistic means of expression, the speaker needs to engage his/her background knowledge, as well as understanding of the local context and anticipation of possible consequences of his/her choices to convey a particular perspective. L1 speakers share the background knowledge conventionally encoded in the common language, and such shared background allows them to focus on selecting situationally appropriate linguistic means, instead of considering the full array of conventionalized forms or chunks.

L2 learners, on the other hand, do not have the same degree of access to linguistic conventions, as L1 speakers of that language do. L2 speakers also carry different background knowledge and possibly varying perceptions of contextual factors, as opposed to those of L1 speakers, during any given usage event. Language learning represents a complicated process that involves the full scope of cognition including remembering past experience, categorizing various types of experience, establishing patterns from linguistic stimuli, etc. (Cadierno and Robinson 2009; Robinson and Ellis 2008). Thus, when faced with a given communicative situation, L2 speakers are likely to be starting off with a different set of construal conventions than L1 speakers.

In situations where varying and often conflicting L1 and L2 construal patterns are involved, it is possible to use CL tools to highlight the characteristics of the L1 construal and make the learner aware of the construal options, as well as of potential differences between the L1 and L2 systems.

## 2.2 L2 language teaching and cognitive linguistics

In addition to language-inherent conflicting construal options, the other crucial L1/L2 distinction is that their corresponding learning experiences are drastically different from each other. In L1 acquisition context, learners are exposed to naturally occurring instances of language, where form co-occurs with live meaning-making. However, L2 learners do not usually have access to the same types of authentic language learning conditions as L1 learners. Classroom instruction frequently lacks direct contextual settings, and language forms are not typically reinforced through naturally occurring usage.

Furthermore, the vast range of existing L2 materials and textbooks do not uncover the systematicity present in language organization and portray many linguistic characteristics as largely arbitrary, often offering imprecise rules, which lead L2 learners to false generalizations. More generally, the field of L2 teaching has lacked a strong theoretical linguistic framework, which could work as a supportive pillar ensuring the stability of teaching practices across various aspects of language (de Knop and Dirven 2008; Tyler 2008, 2012).

To counter this situation, the underlying conceptual characteristics of cognitive linguistics make it a good candidate for the role of providing a comprehensive theory supporting successful L2 instruction (Tyler and Evans 2004; Achard and Niemeier 2004; Tyler 2012). Some of the clear benefits of using CL approaches in the classroom include:
- CL tools and terms can make form-meaning mappings relatively transparent for the learners;
- Grammar can be taught within the context of its authentic usage;
- Learners can access and utilize the conceptual tools for seeing the perspective of a native speaker.

That said, adapting CL principles to classroom needs can be difficult because, according to Meunier (2008), most learners today "still express a need for short and easy-to-understand explanations and rules of grammar" (Meunier 2008: 103). This pattern may be connected with the fact that decontextualized rules continue to constitute a bulk of teaching practices all over the world, and learners are most used to those psychologically. The challenge faced by proponents of usage-based instruction is to introduce learners to cognitive approaches to grammar in a controlled manner, targeting their level of comfort with the instructional practices and increased levels of L2 comprehension and production at the same time.

Visual support has been identified as one of the most effective tools for making CL analyses more accessible to learners, especially in regard to complex language structures. Notably, visual cues have been successfully used by de Knop and Dirven (2008) for teaching case marking and by Tyler and Evans (2003) for explaining the complex system of English prepositions. It has been found that visual support functions as a natural extension of the key notions of embodied experience, embodied meaning, and their connection with language.

Another approach to incorporating CL principles into instruction was centered around combining and contextualizing instruction of form and its use: for example, Niemeier and Reif (2008) approached teaching the English tense and aspect system by providing the semantic concepts for learners before (or simultaneously with) the introduction of morphosyntactic forms in order to help them better grasp the form-meaning connection.

Key lessons from prior applied CL research were adapted to the present context of L2 instruction of English conditionals. In the next section, I will highlight main aspects of the category and of the relevant CL theory.

## 2.3 English conditionals and blending theory

Even for language theorists, conditionals represent a particularly complex aspect of English: despite a great deal of multi-faceted research on the subject, linguists do not agree on the unified meaning or on a comprehensive classification of conditionals (Taylor 1997). Furthermore, a number of factors contribute to the difficulty of conditionals for L2 learners (Celce-Murcia and Larsen-Freeman 1999). First, because conditionals are a syntactic structure consisting of two clauses, the presence of subordination makes the structure harder to understand and acquire. Secondly, L2 textbooks provide a particularly limiting view of conditionals, largely relying on presentation of form, while ignoring aspects of meaning. Furthermore, textbooks often present knowledge in the shape of rules rather than general patterns that occur in natural language data.

Due to space constraints[1], I will refer only to the traditional classification of conditionals, as captured by Taylor (1997: 301–302) and provided in Table 1 below.

The seeming clarity of this classification does not apply to data in extended contexts. For instance, if we look at the following two sentences, keeping in mind the information provided in parentheses:

(1)  *If he said that (and we heard him say it!), he's a liar.*

(2)  *If he said that, he'd be a liar.*
     (Taylor 1997: 302)

– we will notice that the same *if*-clause in (1) and (2) can be interpreted as either factual or hypothetical, depending on the context and what is inferred outside of linguistic forms within the sentence.

---

[1] For a more in-depth analysis and discussion of how conditionals are presented in existing linguistic theories, classifications, and ESL/EFL textbooks, see Jacobsen (2012).

**Table 1:** Classification of conditional forms

| Type | Example | Meaning and typical form |
| --- | --- | --- |
| Factual | *If prices go up, I sell my car.* | Content of the *if*-clause is presumed to be real and true. |
| | | Form: present tense in the *if*-clause and present/future tense in the main clause |
| Hypothetical | *If prices went up, I would sell my car.* | Content of the *if*-clause is regarded as a possibility. |
| | | Form: past tense in the *if*-clause and a modal such as *would* (or similar form) plus a base verb form in the main clause |
| Counterfactual | *If prices had gone up, I would have sold my car.* | Content of the *if*-clause is regarded as not possible or contrary to the fact/current state of the world. |
| | | Form: past perfect in the *if*-clause and a *would* (or another modal) combined with the perfect form of the verb in the main clause |

Note: Examples come from Werth (1997: 243–245).

The following two sentences reveal another complicating aspect of conditional sentence types:

(3) *If he had seen your photograph before, then of course he was able to recognize you.*

(implies "he had seen your photograph before")

(4) *If he had seen your photograph before, he might have been able to recognize you.*

(implies "he had not seen your photograph before")
(Taylor 1997: 302)

The exact same *if*-clause in (3) and (4) can be interpreted as either factual or counterfactual, depending on what is known about the referent of "he". Accordingly, the degree of a certain event's likelihood can essentially move freely along the hypotheticality spectrum between the polar ends of complete certainty (factuality) and counterfactuality. The exact interpretation of the degree of hypotheticality conveyed by each conditional sentence seems to be directly dependent on the context and on the information that lies outside the realm of linguistic coding. It is clear that, to be able to use the tense combinations correctly, L2 learners need to be made aware of speaker linguistic tools and intentionality behind them. In this connection, CL theory and, in particular, work by Dancygier and Sweetser (2005) have the potential of being highly informative for L2 instructional purposes.

Specifically, the variety of meanings associated with conditional phrases can be explained succinctly through the use of Mental Space and Blending Theory (Fauconnier 1994; Fauconnier and Turner 1998, 2000, 2002). Mental Space theory is a theory of cognitive semantics centered around the idea of spontaneously created bundles (i.e. spaces) of mental content, which demonstrate the speaker's conceptual representations of entities in language or any given semantic scenarios as perceived, imagined, remembered, or otherwise understood by the speaker. More specifically, Fauconnier and Turner (1998) argue that blending occurs when the "structure from two mental spaces is projected to a third space, the 'blend'" (Fauconnier and Turner 1998: 143). The two original spaces providing material for the blend are called *input spaces*, and they have a common schematic structure that is represented as a *generic space*. Generic space maps onto input spaces, defining context and providing assumed knowledge that unites both spaces. Input spaces can be blends themselves, and by merging, they create yet another blend or emergent structure. Because the same scenario or meaning can be represented in multiple ways, mental spaces are used to partition incoming information about elements in the referential representation.

In the context of conditionals, Dancygier and Sweetser's (2005) claim that conditional *if*-clauses establish mental space structures and analyze how such a set-up happens through various markers (e.g., *if, when, unless*, etc.) and verb forms that contribute to different configurations of mental spaces.

For a more specific example, let us consider the analysis and schematic conventions proposed by Dancygier and Sweetser (2005) and apply them to the example of a factual conditional used earlier in the typologies – *If prices go up, I will sell my car*. In this case, the base, or the generic, space would be the understanding of the current assumed reality, i.e. the one in which prices have not gone up yet. The *if*-clause (*if prices go up*) works as a key space-builder, creating a new mental space that provides a view into a different kind of reality. The set-up of the mental space within the *if*-clause allows for the predictive function to emerge in this sentence: *if* functions as a mental space builder and allows the speaker to assume a number of possible outcomes that may subsequently follow from the *if*-clause. One such outcome is captured in the main clause (*I will sell my car*), which functions as an extension of the *if*-clause, or the space the emergence of which is made possible only through the introduction of the condition in the *if*-clause. The speaker is able to choose linguistic means in accordance with the kind of possible reality(-ies) that s/he deems most likely to occur. The following diagram represents the whole mental space set-up and interaction between the possible reality outcomes:

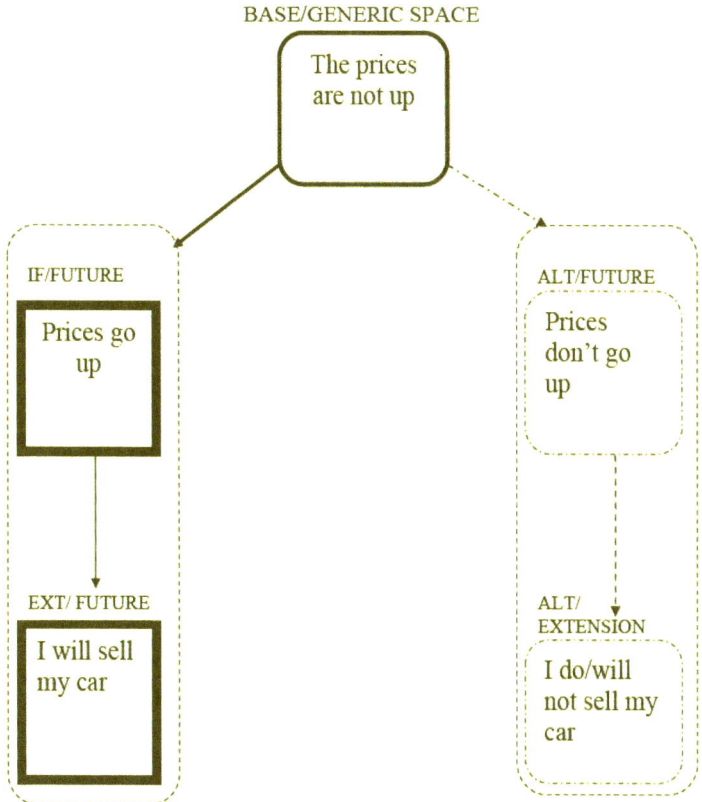

**Figure 1:** Mental space set-up of the conditional construction *"If prices go up, I will sell my car"*.

The base space in which prices have not gone up gives rise to two possible interpretations, or blends, each consisting of two inputs: the blend in which the prices will go up and the blend in which prices will not go up. The structure on the left represents a most likely succession from the base space: i.e., that the prices will go up. Solid bold lines in the two input spaces within the left blend represent the fact that the speaker will most likely choose this scenario as the most probable one and will accordingly choose corresponding grammatical constructions to express the ideas and support the anticipated mental space set-up. The *if*-clause refers to the future and leads to the extension that will also take place in the future: hence, the use of appropriately sequenced tense markers. The correlation between the two input spaces works as a unifying element for the overall conditional blend, where the emergence of the second space (the extension) becomes possible, only when the first space – the *if*-clause – is created. Essentially, the presence of a "more likely to happen" space and an alternative space are going to be constant elements of conditional phrases; and the exact relationship between them – or the degree of probability of each blend – will be determined based on a given speaker's choices and will be further grounded in a given communicative context.

In sum, a speaker construes the input spaces and produces a conditional blend depending on the information available to him/her at the moment of speaking, as well as depending on the stance s/he takes in regard to the situation in question.

Verb tenses function as a key element guiding the felicitous formation of conditionals, as they reflect specific construal options. Due to space constraints, only the standard tense combinations in conditionals are discussed in the next section; beyond that, Dancygier and Sweetser (2005) outline a full range of conditional mental space configurations, in which linguistic rules work in conjunction with the pragmatic communicative context and the speaker's stance.

## 2.4 Elements from blending theory used for instructional materials

Being a crucial element in conditionals, tenses occupy the center of instructional focus. The phenomenon of using "backwards" tenses when expressing a temporal correlation is called *backshifting* (Dancygier 1998; Dancygier and Sweetser 2005); it is used across all levels of conditional sentences depending on the assumptions held by the speaker and/or the composition of the generic space. Backshifting implies going back one tense category when expressing different hypothetical scenarios. Below are specific examples of different sentence types to demonstrate the details:

1) Factual conditional sentence: *If Hiro takes the card, then the data will be transferred to his computer* (Dancygier and Sweetser 2005: 32–33). Even though the event in the main clause has not taken place yet and is referring to the future, English does not code those types of situations with future tense. Instead, it is standard to use present tense to refer to the future in the *if*-clause and the future tense in the main clause.

2) Hypothetical conditional sentence: *If you got me a cup of coffee, I would be very grateful* (Dancygier and Sweetser 2005: 60). The *if*-clause technically refers to the present, but it uses past tense to create additional distance (and consequently to reduce the degree of pressure of the present moment

and its pragmatic needs onto the actions of the interlocutor). The main clause includes *would*, that was historically treated as the past tense of *will*; *would* here also fulfills the general backshifting/distancing function. This construction of past tenses in both of the clauses stems from the implied base space (the speaker's background knowledge) that the speaker's interlocutor ("you") has not had a chance to get a cup of coffee for the speaker yet and there is no reason to believe s/he will do so. Accordingly, the speaker's general assumption, also referred to as the *epistemic stance* in CL terminology, is negative, and the past tense is utilized here to capture this negative stance when referring to what is technically happening in the present, rather than in the past.

Dancygier and Sweetser use the term *negative* for this type of epistemic stance to highlight that the underlying condition is very unlikely to be true. The hypothetical scenario is established and developed in order to draw appropriate conclusions about an analogous situation in the reality space, and using past tense here is intended to highlight the lack of immediate control from the present. A similar situation applies to the construction of the counterfactual version of this sentence *If you had gotten me a cup of coffee, I would have been very grateful.*

In contrast, in sentences like *If prices go up, I will sell my car*, both clauses refer to the future, and the if-clause shifts back into the present, since the use of present tense implies that the situation can still change and that the speaker can execute some degree of control over it. Accordingly, in sentences with combinations of present and future tense, the epistemic stance of the speaker is *positive*.

Tenses and their interactions with the base space, or speaker's knowledge, are one of the key ways of representing speaker's perspective, which can convey a complex combination of emotional, epistemic, temporal, interpersonal, and spatial viewpoints manifested in mental-space structure. In addition to tense-related mental space building, perspective can be expressed through choices of personal pronouns (*she* as opposed to *you*), spatial characteristics (e.g., *here* rather than *there*), and through explicit references to participant roles in speech interactions (Dancygier and Sweetser 2005: 68).

To sum up, linguistic elements that are used to build conditional constructions are grounded in meaningful patterns that stem from the speaker's background knowledge and reasoning processes. If made pedagogically accessible, the basics of this analysis could be highly beneficial for L2 learners. The goal of this study was to utilize and to incorporate appropriate insights from the analysis from Dancygier and Sweetser (2005) into second language classroom materials. I argue that using CL principles to capture key aspects of conditional constructions and applying that information to pedagogical task design would be an important improvement over the existing treatments. Implementing a usage-based account of conditionals and highlighting the details of their conceptualization would ideally help learners see the native-like viewpoint of conditional usage.

## 3 Overview of the study

As determined by content analysis of learner data (for full description of the process, see Jacobsen 2012), hypothetical conditionals appear to be the construction causing learners most problems. The general direction of the study was concerned with testing the efficacy of different pedagogical approaches for the instruction of English hypothetical conditionals in the context of the graduate EAP (English for Academic Purposes) program at a large East Coast university.

Procedure: The study design consisted of a pre-test, post-test and a delayed post-test, administered over the course of six weeks total. Three groups (N = 57) took part in the study: cognitive, task-supported, and control. Task-supported language teaching was chosen because of its conceptual compatibility with the underlying principles of cognitive linguistics (both areas of research targeting complementary usage-based aspects of language), as well as its experimentally established superiority as a language teaching methodology. Three students from each treatment group also participated in retrospective interviews where they shared their comments regarding the instructional treatment.

Research questions: The research questions were concerned with exploring the efficacy of different types of instruction (cognitive and task-supported as opposed to task-supported-only) for the acquisition of English conditional phrases, as measured by a post-test and a delayed-post-test.

Cognitive group: Participants of the cognitive group (N = 18) received instructional treatment informed by the CL analysis of conditionals by Dancygier and Sweetser (2005) and completed six pedagogic tasks. They also had access to a supplementary piece called "the cognitive chart". One of the key adjustments was extensive use of relevant visuals and video. Also, all terminology was replaced with simple "layman" terms; for instance, the idea of a base space was conveyed through discussing the speaker's background knowledge. Since the participants of the cognitive group received both the cognitive explanation and the pedagogic tasks, they could potentially benefit from either or both interventions.

Task-supported group: Participants of the task-supported group (N = 19) received instructional treatment informed by traditional analysis/classification of conditionals (cf. Celce-Murcia and Larsen-Freeman 1999) and completed the same six pedagogic tasks as the cognitive group. The term "task-supported" refers to a version of task-based language teaching (TBLT), where tasks are not the only element of the curriculum – rather, they play a supplementary role. Because this group was not taught the cognitive account of conditionals, they did not have access to the cognitive chart either. The value of including this group was to determine whether pedagogic tasks combined with the traditional explanation of conditionals (i.e. without the cognitive account) could promote acquisition on their own.

Control group: Participants of the control group (N = 20) did not receive any explicit instruction of conditionals and only completed the three tests.

# 4 Materials design: Making blending theory accessible to L2 learners

A number of adjustments were made in order to make the CL insights appear meaningful to advanced English learners (due to the focus of this chapter, only the cognitive materials will be discussed in full detail).

## 4.1 Cognitive PowerPoint presentations

The cognitive treatment consisted of three PowerPoint (PPT) presentations, each structured as teacher-led discussion activities, and accompanied by pedagogic tasks. The first PPT was dedicated to expanding metalinguistic knowledge of the subjects and exposing them to usage-based view of language, which involved a brief characterization of such concepts from blending theory, as the generic space (referred to as speaker's background knowledge) and input spaces (referred to as scenarios).

The first cognitive presentation focused on expanding subjects' metalinguistic knowledge and exposing them to the meaning-centered reality of language. The concept of language compositionality was introduced through the metaphor of a puzzle: language structures work in combination with each other and produce a composite meaning. Next, general functions of conditionals – prediction and establishing cause-and-effect relations – were discussed. Then, students watched an episode from the movie "Alice in Wonderland" and brainstormed answers to the question "What would have happened if Alice hadn't seen the rabbit?" This activity's objective was to make students think about conditionals in terms of the familiar movie reality and to enable them to refer to concrete terms when thinking about conditional functions.

The next portion of the teacher-led presentation focused on highlighting the compound structure of a typical conditional clause. After discussing the students' previous knowledge of conditionals, the instructor raised the question of speaker reality and how conditional sentences can be used to signal speakers' perceptions of reasons and outcomes. Students were given additional pictures and asked to speculate about the outcomes of actions presented in the pictures. The purpose was to get students to think about the basic tenets of CL's view of language and to reinforce the understanding that language resources provide speakers with opportunities to code outcomes in precise ways.

In the second part of the presentation, students were given multiple conditional phrases with different tense configurations; each was analyzed more closely following the "adapted" blending scheme, where the base space of each phrase was referred to as background knowledge. Students were led to discuss possible scenarios coded in conditionals first with the teacher's guidance and next on their own in small groups. Finally, having been taken through the conceptual process of on-line building of conditionals, students were provided with a detailed description of the cognitive chart. A more detailed overview of the first presentation is available in Jacobsen 2012 and 2015.

In the second PPT, students were given a chance to analyze tense combinations in various contexts and to see how those created a unique point of view depending on the speaker's assumptions. Then subjects were asked to consider implications of human motion and activity as captured by a photograph as opposed to video. This debriefing served as a segue towards discussing the conceptual organization of English tenses: while past tense signifies actions that are remote and static, cannot be accessed through real-life senses, and lie outside of human control, the present tense captures actions that are relevant to "here and now", can be accessed through real-life senses, and potentially lie within the area of our control. The idea of control was discussed in terms of outcomes: the outcomes of actions from the past can no longer be affected, while the outcomes of actions from the present can still be affected.

Following the initial discussion of implications of tenses, subjects were taken through a range of non-conditional examples that highlighted how our use of present tense assumes at least partial presence of individual control and in contrast, how past tense signifies remoteness, distance, and lack of control (e.g., *I wish the students liked phonetics. Suppose your house burned down. Do you have insurance?* etc.). When discussing examples, students were asked to contemplate possible reasons for grammatical arrangements in each structure. The phenomenon of backshifting and specific tense configurations were discussed in locally relevant and usage-based terms.

The remaining portion of this presentation focused on how tenses can be combined within the conditional framework. Standard pairings of specific forms to be used in each clause were highlighted by discussing how the implications of different tense choices eventually affect the construction of conditional meaning. For instance, students were shown multiple slides with sentences similar to the following and asked which form was more standard:
– *If Amy takes the card, then the data will be transferred to his computer.*
– *If Amy will take the card, then the data will be transferred to his computer.*

Even though the textbooks usually capture the "prescribed" tense patterns associated with hypothetical and counterfactual conditionals, these tense patterns are not grammatically absolute, but instead are predominant in standard usage. It was stressed to the students that speakers have choices depending on what they are trying to say, and accordingly, may or may not have to resort to standard tense pairings. The discussion of standardized versus non-standardized tenses revolved around specific examples (taken from materials provided in the Corpus of Contemporary American English), so that subjects could see how the meanings of tenses were configured in actual usage contexts.

At the end, the subjects watched an excerpt from the movie "Avatar", in which the character is taken into an alternate reality and has to follow a life pattern that is completely different from what is considered normal in his world. This excerpt was used in order to illustrate the process of accessing a zone of control and how the perception of the zone of control may depend on the speaker in question. Upon viewing this excerpt, subjects discussed the following questions paying specific attention to the appropriate tenses:
– How would we as viewers treat the reality represented in the movie: is it in our zone of control, outside of zone of control, or twice removed from zone of control?
– What tense would we likely use to talk about this reality?

This was done to help students understand that tenses in conditionals are bound to capture what each speaker views as possible or impossible given the perceived limitations of their own life reality.

The third instructional PPT aimed at showing how conditionals are shaped within specific usage contexts and how surrounding information might affect the tense composition of either of the two clauses. The presentation started with drawing the students' attention to the idea of physical viewpoint and how different points of view can be captured by visual means: e.g., looking through a constrained vs. unlimited perspective.

The idea of grounding one's perspective in environmental characteristics was then articulated in connection with language. Linguistic perspective and perception of local context can be expressed through time reference (as discussed on the previous day of instructional treatment), through personal reference (i.e., how the speaker aligns him/herself with the environment), and through reference to spatial locations. In conditional sentences, whenever the speaker aligns him/herself with certain limitations of the context, the zone of control is referenced indirectly, which calls for preference for present tense usage. Alternately, whenever the speaker aligns him/herself apart from context limitations, his/her perspective gives away the assumption that s/he does not view him/herself as being inside the zone of control; hence, past tense combinations would be more appropriate in such contexts, e.g.:

– *The truth is, there are many reasons why people find themselves single. Sometimes, **it's** their own attitudes. But many other times, the timing just **isn't** right, their careers **are** too demanding, or they **need** to focus elsewhere. As a black woman who **has been** in a committed relationship for five years, nothing **is** more obvious to me than how random circumstance **plays** a major role in many happy relationships. If I **hadn't** missed a concert, I **wouldn't know** my boyfriend; if one of my friends **hadn't gone** to Mali with the Peace Corps, she **would have never been** on the same continent as her now-husband; if another friend **hadn't missed** her original train and **hadn't been wearing** a sweatshirt from her alma mater, she **would have never met** the man she would marry.*

Following this discussion of implications behind different types of speaker perspectives, subjects were taken through a variety of examples (first teacher-facilitated, then done in pairs/small groups), in which differences in individual perception were shown through specific linguistic means. Some of the examples featured multiple speakers and characters, which is why it was important for students to determine whose perspective was being expressed by each sentence and how subjective choices of possibilities were reflected through tense choices in corresponding conditional sentences, e.g.:

– *Had I been him, I would have thrown me out, but he said no, sure he'd talk, he'd be happy to, if I didn't mind.*

Last but not least, students were encouraged to keep in mind the limitations of a concrete discourse context and think about how tense choices might fit with such limitations.

## 4.2 Cognitive chart

In addition to the cognitive PowerPoint, the participants in the cognitive group received a *cognitive chart* (provided in Appendix A) that they could use both during the teacher-facilitated instruction and during the pedagogic tasks that they completed in class. The idea behind creating this supplementary piece for the cognitive group was to try to mirror/follow cognitive processes that should be taking place when conditional sentences are being created. The cognitive chart directs the learners' attention to different aspects of conditional forms that need to be taken into account when determining felicitous tense choices. Subjects in the cognitive group were allowed to use the chart when completing pedagogic tasks to facilitate their conditional reasoning processes. That said, even though all cognitive group participants were encouraged to use the chart, whether or not they actually used it during instructional time was not monitored directly. While this was a supplementary resource made available to everyone, no conclusions can be drawn about its distinct use and/or effectiveness.

## 4.3 Pedagogical summary

At the end of instructional treatment, the goal was to have the subjects at least partially internalize the following tenets of compositionality behind English conditionals:
- The speaker's background knowledge and local context knowledge determine which verb forms we use;
- Speakers have choices as far as verb forms are concerned;
- Hypothetical, counterfactual and factual *if*-constructions all reflect differing degrees of reality projected by the speaker;
- Tenses signal degrees of distance from the events and the degrees of reality perceived by the speaker (speaker perspective);
- Time markers such as adverbs add context knowledge and information and may influence how events are viewed in the long run by both the speaker and listener.

The next section will revert the focus back to the study at large, addressing the effectiveness of the treatment.

# 5 Results

The statistical analyses demonstrated that both conditions of instruction – cognitive and task-supported – were effective for producing L2 development of the target form. Both the cognitive and task-supported groups outperformed the control group on the immediate and delayed posttests. Furthermore, the cognitive group participants obtained greater production and overall test score gains between the pre-test and the post-test, than the participants of both the task-supported and the control groups did, which suggests that the combination of the cognitive and task-supported instruction proved to be more effective in the context of this specific study than the task-supported instruction alone.

The differences between the subjects' mean scores on all three tests were statistically significant for each group pairing (repeated measures ANOVA: $p < 0.001$ for all pairings, i.e. cognitive vs. task-supported, task-supported vs. control, cognitive vs. control; for full overview of quantitative results, please see Dolgova Jacobsen 2016).

As it can be seen in Table 2 below, a $t$-test comparison indicated that the differences between the cognitive and task-supported groups were significant (p = .004).

**Table 2:** $T$-test on overall gains scores: Cognitive and task-supported groups

| t | df | Sig. (2-tailed) | Mean difference |
|---|----|-----------------|-----------------|
| 3.13 | 33 | 0.004 | 5.55 |

Figure 2 provides a visual representation of overall test performance across three groups over time.

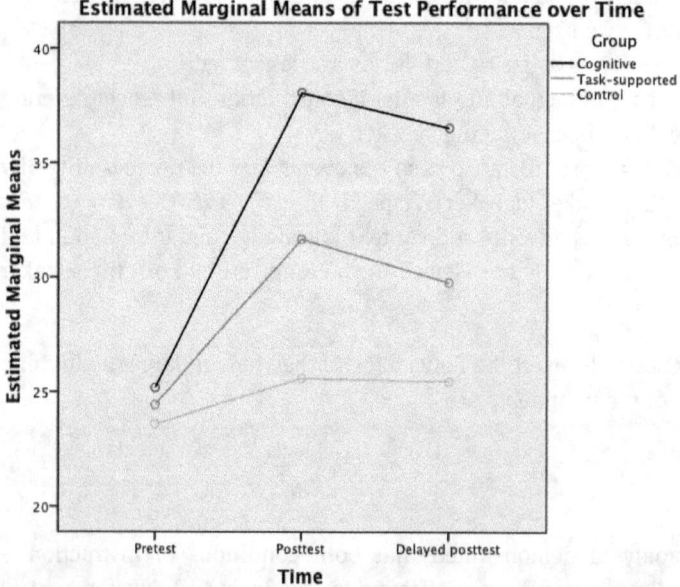

**Figure 2:** Means of test performance over time

Finally, retrospective interviews with select subjects from each treatment group demonstrated that CL task-supported instructional treatment elicited a generally more positive response among subjects than the traditional task-supported treatment alone. That said, tasks were perceived to be a favorable pedagogic format regardless of the accompanying theoretical contents. If drawing a comparison among task features, tasks that offered a rich context for completion and that called for active production and group work were considered most salient for the practice of the target feature and therefore most engaging in the pedagogical sense. The full account of this study's qualitative findings can be found in Jacobsen (2015) and is thus omitted here.

# 6 Lessons learned and directions for future research

The goal of this study was to address the majority of shortcomings of traditional approaches to instruction of the English conditionals. In particular, this chapter aimed to explain in full detail how tenets of conceptual blending were adapted to L2 materials and made accessible to learners.

First of all, unlike the traditional approaches, the CL treatment of conditionals allowed for representing their grammatical meaning as a connected system, emphasizing that syntactic structures are meaningful in their own right. The CL treatment conveyed to learners that the composition of the conditional subordinate organization is inherently affected by tense patterns and/or modal verb usage within each of the clauses, as well as by local discourse information. Secondly, the study provided multiple contexts for learners to experience the target structure usage, exposing them to input imitating authentic usage patterns. In other words, the study proved that it was possible to treat conditionals as symbolic units with their own meanings and to be able to break down the symbolic meaning of the whole phrase into teachable chunks (tense, combination of clauses, etc.).

In contexts where L2 learners are not getting a sufficient exposure to L1 input, it is particularly important to complement instruction with examples from and/or references to naturally occurring L1 discourse. As Tyler (2012) suggests: "carefully chosen authentic discourse should be a foundational component of L2 materials" (Tyler 2012: 85). Materials utilized in this study were informed by authentic discourse as captured through L1 corpora resources, and learners were asked to engage in analysis of such discourse on multiple occasions throughout the instructional treatment. There is no doubt that elements of visual support available through the CL treatment contributed to its eventual success in promoting

L2 development and production of English conditionals. This finding supports prior research that suggested positive effects associated with the use of visuals for CL instruction (Boers et al. 2008; de Knop and Dirven 2008; Tyler 2012).

More generally, this experiment has validated the use of a number of underlying CL assumptions relevant for second language instruction. Insights from cognitive linguistics and, in particular, cognitive grammar, can bring out the knowledge about grammatical features as meaningful "packages" accessible to language learners (Achard 1997). In situations where L1 and L2 construal patterns may be in conflict with each other, i.e. whenever learners may be experiencing difficulty construing or grasping certain aspects of target language structure(-s), CL tools can be used to highlight the specifics of the target construal and make the problematic structure(-s) more analyzable and transparent for the learner.

Considering the challenge of making theory comprehensible to learners, this study demonstrated that CL theory can be successfully transferred into instructional materials without disturbing learner expectations too much (however, a learning curve of some degree is inevitable) and making it a worthwhile and valuable enterprise overall. The methodological organization of this study and the statistically significant findings supporting the use of cognitive linguistics in L2 instructional contexts partially addressed the gap in applied CL research, where many previous studies were not sufficiently rigorous methodologically (Achard 2004; Boers and Demecheleer 1998; Chen and Oller 2008; Csabi 2004; etc.) and/or had a largely qualitative focus (Dirven 2001; Lindstromberg 1996; Meunier 2008; Niemeier and Reif 2008; etc.). This research supported the implications of some recent studies (Tyler, Mueller, and Ho 2010, 2011; Tyler 2012) suggesting that the efficacy of implementing cognitive linguistics into instruction can be tested within the ramifications of a controlled research design, which would hopefully allow to treat any conclusions regarding the use of cognitive linguistics in L2 contexts as more generalizable and replicable than before. A recommendation that can be made based on the outcome of the present study is that uses of cognitive linguistics in L2 instructional contexts should be explored further using standard methodology from the larger fields of SLA and applied linguistics (Mackey and Gass 2015).

# References

Achard, Michel. 1997. A cognitive grammar view of second language acquisition. *Journal of Intensive English* 11. 157–177.
Achard, Michel. 2004. Grammatical instruction in the natural approach: A cognitive grammar view. In Michel Achard & Susanne Niemeier (eds.), *Cognitive linguistics, second language acquisition, and foreign language teaching*, 165–194. Berlin: Mouton de Gruyter.
Achard, Michel & Susanne Niemeier (eds.). 2004. *Cognitive linguistics, second language acquisition, and foreign language teaching*. Berlin: Mouton de Gruyter.
Boers, Frank & Murielle Demecheleer. 1998. A cognitive semantic approach to teaching prepositions. *ELT Journal* 52(3). 197–204.
Boers, Frank, Seth Lindstromberg, Jeannette Littlemore, Helene Stengers & June Eyckmans. 2008. Variables in the mnemonic effectiveness of pictorial elucidation. In Frank Boers & Seth Lindstromberg (eds.), *Cognitive linguistic approaches to teaching vocabulary and phraseology*, 65–100. Berlin: Mouton de Gruyter.
Cadierno, Teresa & Peter Robinson. 2009. Language typology, task complexity and the development of L2 lexicalization patterns for describing motion events. *Annual Review of Cognitive Linguistics* 6. 245–277.
Celce-Murcia, Marianne & Diane Larsen-Freeman. 1999. *The grammar book: An ESL/EFL teacher's course*. Boston, MA: Heinle & Heinle.
Chen, Liang & John W. Oller. 2008. The use of passives and alternatives in English. In Sabine de Knop & Teun de Rycker (eds.), *Cognitive approaches to pedagogical grammar: A volume in honour of Rene Dirven*, 385–416. New York: Mouton de Gruyter.
Csabi, Szilvia. 2004. A cognitive linguistic view of polysemy in English and its implications for teaching. In Michel Achard & Susanne Niemeier (eds.), *Cognitive linguistics, second language acquisition, and foreign language teaching*, 233–256. Berlin, Germany: Mouton de Gruyter.
Dancygier, Barbara. 1998. *Conditionals and prediction*. Cambridge, UK: Cambridge University Press.
Dancygier, Barbara & Eve Sweetser. 2005. *Mental spaces in grammar: Conditional constructions*. Cambridge, UK: Cambridge University Press.
de Knop, Sabine & René Dirven. 2008. Motion and location events in German, French and English. In Sabine de Knop & Teun de Rycker (eds.), *Cognitive approaches to pedagogical grammar: A volume in honour of Rene Dirven*, 295–324. New York: Mouton de Gruyter.
Dirven, René. 2001. English phrasal verbs: theory and didactic application. In Martin Putz, Susanne Niemeier & René Dirven (eds.), *Applied cognitive linguistics II: Language pedagogy*, 3–28. Berlin: Mouton de Gruyter.
Dolgova Jacobsen, Natalia. 2016. T*he best of both worlds: Combining cognitive linguistics and pedagogic tasks to teach English conditionals. Applied Linguistics.* doi:10.1093/applin/amw030
Fauconnier, Gilles. 1994. *Mental spaces: Aspects of meaning construction in natural language*. Cambridge: Cambridge University Press.
Fauconnier, Gilles & Mark Turner. 1998. Conceptual integration networks. *Cognitive Science* 22 (1). 133–187.
Fauconnier, Gilles & Mark Turner. 2000. Compression and global insight. *Cognitive Linguistics* 11. 283–304.

Fauconnier, Gilles & Mark Turner. 2002. *The way we think: Conceptual blending and the mind's hidden complexities*. New York: Basic books.

Jacobsen, Natalia Dolgova. 2012. *Applying cognitive linguistics and task-supported language teaching to instruction of English conditional phrases*. Washington DC: Georgetown University unpublished dissertation.

Jacobsen, Natalia. 2015. A cognitive linguistic (CL) analysis of English conditionals in English for Academic Purposes (EAP) instruction: Implications from Sociocultural Theory (SCT). In Kyoko Masuda, Carlee Arnett & Angela Labarca (eds.), *Cognitive linguistics and sociocultural theory in second and foreign language teaching*, 103–125. Berlin: Mouton de Gruyter.

Langacker, Ronald. 2000. A dynamic usage-based model. In Michael Barlow & Suzanne Kemmer (eds.), *Usage-based models of language*, 1–63. Stanford: CSLI Publications.

Lindstromberg, Seth. 1996. Prepositions: meaning and method. *ELT Journal* 50(3). 225–236.

Mackey, Alison & Susan Gass. 2015. *Second language research: Methodology and design*, 2nd edn. New York: Routledge

Meunier, Fanny. 2008. Corpora, cognition and pedagogical grammars. In Sabine de Knop & Teun de Rycker (eds.), *Cognitive approaches to pedagogical grammar: A volume in honour of Rene Dirven*, 91–120. New York: Mouton de Gruyter.

Niemeier, Susanne & Monika Reif. 2008. Applying cognitive grammar to tense-aspect teaching. In Sabine de Knop & Teun de Rycker (eds.), *Cognitive approaches to pedagogical grammar: A volume in honour of Rene Dirven*, 325–356. New York: Mouton de Gruyter.

Robinson, Peter & Nick Ellis (eds.). 2008. *Handbook of cognitive linguistics and second language acquisition*. New York: Routledge.

Taylor, John. 1997. Conditionals and polarity. In Angeliki Athanasiadou & René Dirven (eds.), *On conditionals again*, 289–306. Amsterdam: John Benjamins.

Taylor, John. 2003. *Cognitive grammar*. Oxford: Oxford University Press.

Tyler, Andrea. 2008. Cognitive linguistics and second language instruction. In Peter Robinson & Nick Ellis (eds.), *Handbook of cognitive linguistics and second language acquisition*, 456–488. Mahwah, NJ: Lawrence Erlbaum.

Tyler, Andrea. 2010. Usage-based approaches to language and their applications to second language learning. *Annual Review of Applied Linguistics* 30. 270–291.

Tyler, Andrea. 2012. *Cognitive linguistics and second language learning: Theoretical basics and experimental evidence*. New York: Routledge

Tyler, Andrea & Vyvyan Evans. 2003. *The semantics of English prepositions*. Cambridge: Cambridge University Press.

Tyler, Andrea & Vyvyan Evans. 2004. Applying cognitive linguistics to pedagogical grammar: The case of *over*. In Michel Achard & Susanne Niemeier (eds.), *Cognitive linguistics, second language acquisition, and foreign language teaching*, 257–280. Berlin: Mouton de Gruyter.

Tyler, Andrea, Charles Mueller & Vu Ho. 2010. Applying cognitive linguistics to instructed L2 learning: The English modals. *AILA Review* 23. 30–49.

Tyler, Andrea, Charles Mueller & Vu Ho. 2011. Applying cognitive linguistics to learning the semantics of English *to*, *for*, and *at*: An experimental investigation. *Vigo International Journal of Applied Linguistics* 8. 181–205.

Werth, Paul. 1997. Conditionality as cognitive distance. In Angeliki Athanasiadou & René Dirven (eds.), *On conditionals again*, 243–272. Amsterdam: John Benjamins.

# Appendix A
## Cognitive Chart

**Cognitive treatment group flowchart**

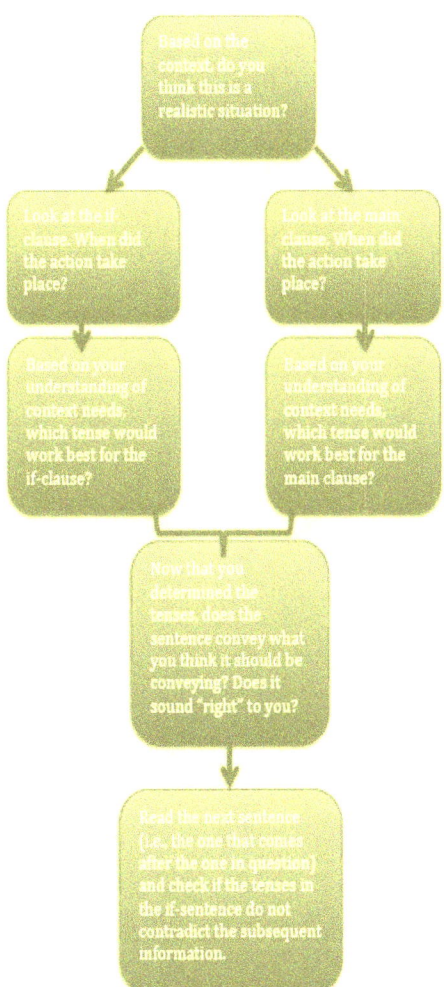

Benjamin J. White
# Making sense of the definite article through a pedagogical schematic

## 1 Introduction

A notoriously difficult area of grammar for learners of English as a second or foreign language (ESL/EFL) is the article system. This is well known by most ESL/EFL teachers and well attested in the second language acquisition literature (e.g., Bitchener, Young, and Cameron 2005; García Mayo and Hawkins 2009; Gass and Selinker 2008; Liu and Gleason 2002). Given that many languages do not possess articles and that there is variation in usage across languages that do (Larsen-Freeman and Celce-Murcia 2015), it is not surprising that ESL/EFL learners are prone to make article errors. Traditional textbooks offer a variety of rules for article use without much attention to how those rules are conceptually motivated or how they relate to one another (White 2010). Moreover, no coherent, comprehensive description of the English article system exists in the linguistics literature. As such, it is unsurprising that both learners and teachers often lack a clear understanding of articles.

This chapter presents a pedagogical schematic that learners (and teachers) may use in their efforts to make sense of the definite article. This schematic, or conceptual tool, is a simple image or diagram meant to reflect the abstract meaning of the definite article. By applying the schematic to multiple examples, learners are guided toward a more systematic understanding of definite article usage. This approach is inspired by the cognitive linguistics (CL) treatment of grammar as meaningful and conceptual (e.g., Croft and Cruse 2004; Langacker 2008; Radden and Dirven 2007; Taylor 2002). Toward exploring the potential of this tool, a small scale study is reported on in which five international MA TESOL students were trained on the schematic. Much of the content in this chapter is taken directly from the author's dissertation (White 2010).

### 1.1 Existing pedagogical approaches

As implied by the term *definite article*, the notion of definiteness is central to semantic analyses of *the*. Traditionally, definiteness has been treated by linguists

---

**Benjamin J. White,** Saint Michael's College

https://doi.org/10.1515/9783110572186-008

and philosophers as dependent on either uniqueness (e.g., Russell 1905) or familiarity (e.g., Christophersen 1939) of a referent. ESL/EFL textbooks tend to define definiteness as requiring the speaker and hearer to share knowledge of a specific thing. A learner will soon realize that this definition is unable to account for a variety of uses of *the*. For instance, in the context of two friends vacationing in a new city, no knowledge of a specific store is required for one friend to say to the other, "We should go to *the grocery store*". In a second example, one friend says to another, "Let me tell you about *the time I got lost in Paris*". Although the speaker has knowledge about a specific time, the hearer presumably does not.

Perhaps because there are so many uses of the definite article that seemingly fall outside the scope of a speaker and hearer sharing knowledge of a specific thing, it is not uncommon to find many different rules of thumb for uses of *the*. For instance, Cole (2000), a workbook for learners to practice English articles, presents 50 rules and 14 explicit exceptions for article use. Of these rules and exceptions, 32 are instructions on when to use the definite article. The rules range from "Use *the* when the noun has already been mentioned" (p. 112) to "Use *the* with the superlative degree" (p. 113), from "Use *the* when generalizing about an entire class of animals" (p. 113) to "Use *the* when the noun is made definite by a prepositional phrase" (p. 112).

While such rules of thumb may help learners interpret nativelike article use in various contexts, these rules tend to fix learners' attention on the surface of language rather than guide them toward a conceptual understanding of what the definite article actually does. Furthermore, Tyler (2012: 12) warns that when "systematicity between (...) multiple functions remains unexplored," the learner is left "with the impression that the various uses are arbitrary and with the learning strategy of rote memorization." While she was writing about English modals, the same description is apt for the definite article.

## 2 Pedagogical schematic

The goal of developing the pedagogical schematic is to provide learners a tool with which to examine the meaning of the definite article in context. The schematic is not meant to explain the cognitive processes involved in a speaker producing noun phrases (NPs) with *the* or a hearer interpreting them. It is, however, informed by certain cognitive operations that have been proposed in accounts of cognitive grammar. The schematic also does not predict uses of *the*. A quick glance at the multitude of rules and exceptions in Cole (2000) should make it apparent that article prediction is an incredibly challenging task. This is in large part because, as will be shown below, choice of article conveys important information about the speaker's stance or construal of the scene. Thus, the use of the definite article involves issues well beyond grammatical correctness. Instead of prediction, the schematic prompts learners to consider the construal process and how speakers use *the* to help shape their message.

The cognitive operation of grounding (see Langacker 2008, Chapter 9) is fundamental to the meaning of the definite article. The term ground is defined by Taylor (2002: 346) as the speech event, which includes "the participants in the event, its time and place, the situational context, previous discourse, shared knowledge of the speech-act participants, and such like." With respect to grounding in the nominal domain, a bare noun signals a type, while a NP signals an instance of the type. Grounding through a determiner connects the instance to the ground, that is, to the speaker and hearer. The definite article is said to highlight, or in CL terms profile, an entity (or instance) against other instances of that type. It is used when the speaker assumes the hearer can uniquely identify the entity. Taylor presents the following diagram, where T refers to type, I to instance, S to speaker, H to hearer, and G to ground.

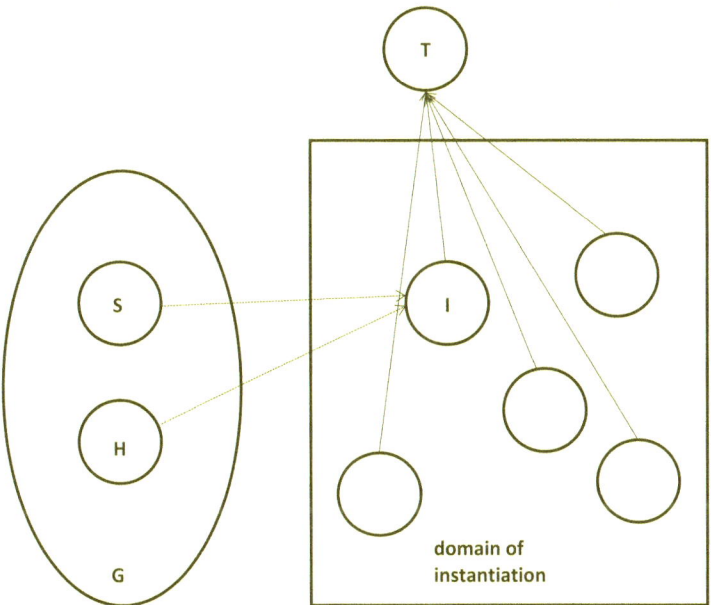

**Figure 1:** Representation of a grounded nominal (Taylor 2002: 349, Fig. 18.3)

The speaker and hearer are able to single out the entity from within the domain of instantiation, in which other instances of the type are present. Langacker

(2002: 122) notes that the definite article signals that both the speaker and hearer have made "mental contact" with the entity.

The pedagogical schematic in Figure 2 seeks to convey through visual means the abstract meaning of the definite article. It does this through a schematic image or diagram that is quite different from Taylor's above.

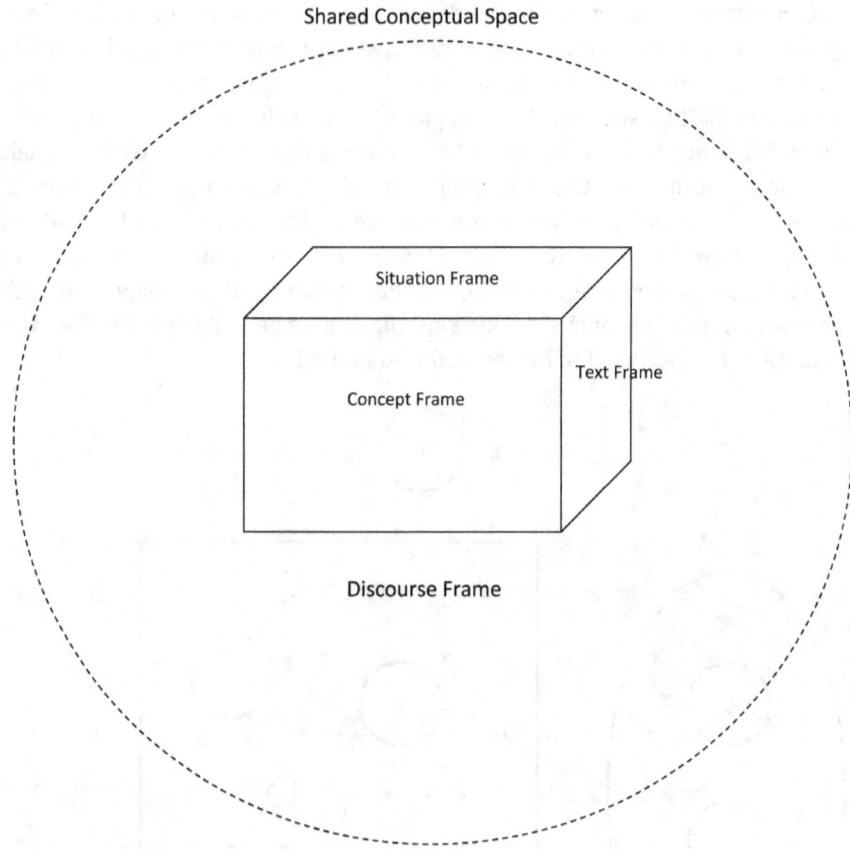

**Figure 2:** Pedagogical schematic for the definite article

The term *shared conceptual space* is meant to highlight for learners the importance of shared knowledge and joint attention between the speaker and hearer. Perhaps, the biggest departure from Taylor's diagram is in the representation of the domain against which an entity is singled out. Rather than an extremely abstract domain of instantiation with many instances of one type, the pedagogical schematic utilizes a domain called the *discourse frame*.

## 2.1 Discourse frame and use of *the*

The aim is to encourage learners to make connections between (1) use of *the* in the discourse and (2) the ground, specifically the shared knowledge of the speaker and hearer. Within the schematic, the meaning of the definite article is understood to be that of abstract deixis. The speaker is mentally pointing at a conceptual entity (within her own mind) with the assumption that the hearer can locate a similar conceptual entity (within his own mind), i.e. that the speaker and hearer can make mental contact with similar conceptual entities. Such abstract deixis is consistent with the origins of the definite article, which is derived from the demonstrative *that* (Halliday and Matthiessen 2004). The discourse frame provides a space for learners to consider from what exactly an entity is being singled out. This space is particularly important for examples of *the* where it is not immediately obvious that the speaker and hearer share knowledge of a particular referent, as was the case above with *the grocery store* and *the time I got lost in Paris*. Three sub-frames provide distinct spaces or frames within which to make mental contact with conceptual entities. Each sub-frame is detailed below.

### 2.1.1 Situation frame

The situation frame is relevant to that aspect of ground that is the immediate physical-spatial situation in which the speaker and hearer find themselves. This frame may be populated with mental representations of the things the speaker and hearer can identify through their five senses. Imagine two passengers in a taxicab as it travels down a gravel road. Each may reasonably assume that the other can uniquely identify the driver, the steering wheel, the meter, the windows of the car, the seats of the car, the sound of gravel crunching under the car's tires, the vibration within the seats as the car bounces along the road, etc. The passengers could introduce any of these entities into their conversation by using the definite article. Figure 3 attempts to represent what the situation frame might include should one of the passengers introduce the phrase *the steering wheel*. The index finger reflects that the mental representation of the steering wheel is being singled out from among representations of other entities (e.g., the driver, the meter, the seats, the doors, etc.).

Notice that plural entities in the situation frame are represented as groups of like entities. The phrase *the seats* signals that the group of entities to which this phrase refers can be singled out from other circled entities in the frame. Representation of the situation frame for *the seats* could include the very same

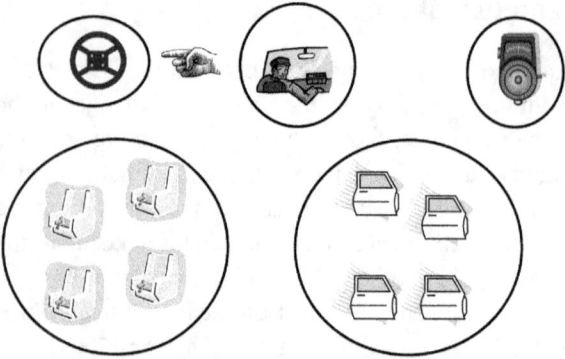

**Figure 3:** Possible situation frame for the steering wheel

contents as those in Figure 3. The difference, of course, would be that the index finger points at the seats rather than at the steering wheel. If a passenger said *the seat*, without any particular seat having been previously specified, this phrase would likely be infelicitous because the hearer could not be expected to uniquely identify the entity from other entities in the immediate situation. There is not enough information for the hearer to make mental contact with the entity that the speaker has in mind. Mention of *the seat next to the driver*, however, would be felicitous because the hearer would now be expected to single out the appropriate entity. The situation frame for this more descriptive NP would necessarily be different. Rather than one circle with uniform seats, one would expect different seats (e.g., a driver's seat, a back seat, a seat next to the driver), each within its own circle.

### 2.1.2 Concept frame

The contents of the concept frame do not come directly from the immediate physical-spatial situation; rather, they come from a speaker and hearer's mental schemata. Schemata have been referred to by other names such as frames (Fillmore 1982; Tannen 1993), scenarios (Brown and Yule 1983), and image schemas (Johnson 1987; Lakoff 1987). They are conventionalized knowledge structures that include expectations about regular interactions, social practices, and cultural institutions. Bednarek (2005: 695) suggests "an interaction between [schema] instigating words and expressions (which guide the application of a certain [schema] to a given piece of discourse), the [schemata] existing in a hearer's mind, and the creation of coherence".

The concept frame allows for the consideration of such an interaction when interpreting definite article use. To illustrate, consider the following utterance.

(1) I attended an interesting class this morning. *The teacher* was quite amusing.

It may be presumed, given the topic of what is being reported, that a *class* schema is active in the speaker's mind. Within this schema are many expectations about classes such as that there are multiple students in a class and one teacher, that a class typically takes place in a classroom with certain expected objects (like seats for the students, a teacher's desk, a blackboard, chalk, etc.), and that the teacher and students engage in a wide range of activities. Mention of the first sentence in (1) can be said to activate the same or a similar schema in the hearer's mind. Abstract deixis with respect to the NP in the second sentence is now possible, as the conceptual entity of *the teacher* is singled out from other conceptual entities associated with a class. The figure below provides a partial representation of what the concept frame for *the teacher* above might contain.

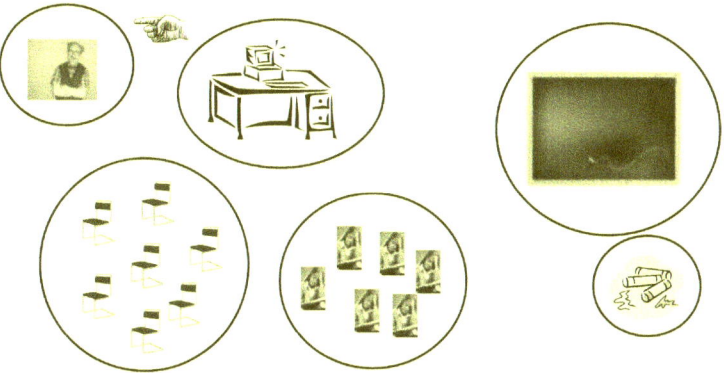

**Figure 4:** Possible concept frame for the teacher

A concept frame may also be related to the immediate situation in which interlocutors find themselves. For instance, in the example of two passengers sitting in a taxicab above, it is reasonable to assume that a taxi schema is active in both the speaker's and hearer's mind. One might say to the other, "I'll pay *the fare* if you pay *the tip*." To make sense of these uses of the definite article, the concept frame would be populated with entities from the taxi schema (including typical activities involved in using a taxi such as paying the fare and giving the driver a tip). *The fare*, just like *the tip*, is uniquely identifiable within the concept frame.

There are occasions of definite article use that are licensed by neither the immediate situation nor the previous conversation/text. These cases appear to be driven by the speaker's conceptualization of an entity and the speaker's expectation that her utterance of a definite NP will prove to be coherent for the hearer. For example, an individual may begin a late-evening conversation by talking about *the sun*. To interpret such uses of *the* through the concept frame, it is necessary to consider general knowledge and experience of the speaker and hearer. In this case, one possibility is to construct a concept frame based on a *sky* schema. This could include entities like the sun, the clouds, the moon, the stars, etc. Another possibility is a concept frame based on the earth's solar system, including entities like the sun, the earth, and the other planets. What is critical is that the representation for *sun* be uniquely identifiable within the frame.

The challenge when interpreting many first-mention uses of the definite article is to determine what might reasonably be in the concept frame evoked by the speaker. For instance, it is not uncommon for a speaker to mention *the store* even if she does not expect the hearer to know which exact store she has in mind. One way to account for the definite article here is to populate the concept frame with distinct institutions (e.g., store, bank, post office, train station, etc.). As such, the task of the hearer is to single out the store from among other institutions. Radden and Dirven (2007: 105) refer to this as functional uniqueness and state, "We are sometimes interested less in the identity of a referent but rather in its unique role or function within a certain socio-cultural frame".

The concept frame may similarly be utilized for what Radden and Dirven (2007) call qualified uniqueness. Here modification, often post-modification, within a NP headed by *the* is thought to enable unique identification of the appropriate entity. Consider the following brief description of an event on the Barbican Theatre's online schedule.

(2) Come celebrate the talent of a superstar hip-hop dance company as more than a hundred performers unite in a buoyant showcase matching synchronised moves with seriously thumping beats. ("A Night with Boy Blue", n.d.)

Upon reading *the talent of a superstar hip-hop dance company*, a reader is able to construct a concept frame populated by attributes of a dance company. These entities might include talent, style, fame, work ethic, etc. The key point here is that the author assumes that readers share the same general understanding of the attributes associated with a dance company and, so, will easily be able to retrieve them from memory.

A more conceptual understanding is also possible for the traditional rule to "use *the* with the superlative degree" (Cole 2000: 113). For instance, a description of Mt. Everest as *the tallest mountain in the world* may be interpreted through a concept frame of mountains of varying heights, as in the following figure.

**Figure 5:** Possible concept frame for the tallest mountain in the world

Within this image, both speaker and hearer can identify the relevant entity, the mountain that is the tallest.

The concept frame may further be employed to interpret the definite article in NPs of generic reference. Consider the sentence in (3).

(3) The tiger is a dangerous animal.

Under a generic interpretation of this sentence, *the tiger* refers not to one individual tiger, but to the individual class of tigers. Under my argument, the mental representation of this referent (tiger as a class) is uniquely identifiable in a frame filled with other classes of animals. Figure 6 provides an example of such a concept frame. "Animals" with the descending lines has been included in the figure to illustrate the taxonomical nature of this frame, while "etc…" reflects that there would be additional entities (animal classes) in the concept frame.

Such generic use can be contrasted with a non-generic use of *tiger*, as in the following example.

(4) The tiger at our zoo is a dangerous animal.

Here one single tiger is distinguished from other animals at the zoo, as well as from other tigers that might be roaming the jungle or housed at other zoos.

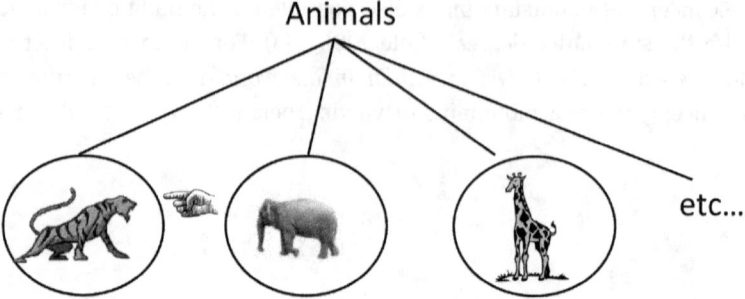

**Figure 6:** Possible concept frame for the tiger in (3)

Given that felicitous use of the definite article requires the referent be uniquely identifiable, the sentence in (4) implies that there is only one tiger at the zoo in question. A concept frame for this use of *the* might look like Figure 7.

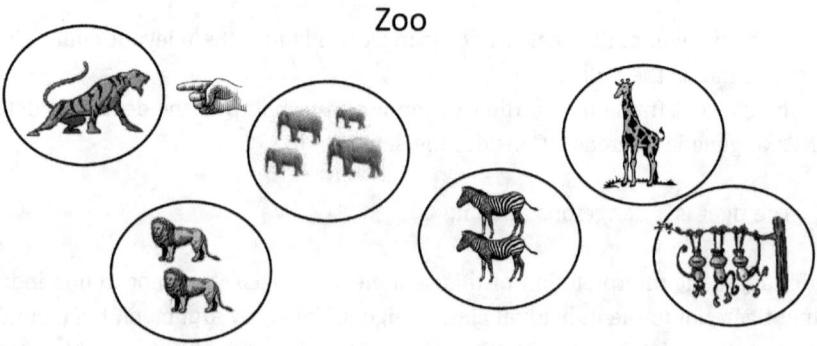

**Figure 7:** Possible concept frame for the tiger in (4)

### 2.1.3 Text frame

The text frame covers discourse reference, most often anaphoric reference. This sub-frame allows learners to apply the schematic to cases of definite article use that fall under the traditional textbook rule of subsequent mention. As with the other sub-frames, learners must populate the text frame with entities from which the definite NP is singled out. The entities in the text frame are those that have been introduced by prior discourse, what Prince (1992) would call discourse old entities.

To illustrate application of the text frame, consider the following start to a joke.

(5) A guy walks into a bar and asks for ten shots of the establishments [sic] finest single malt scotch. The bartender sets him up, and the guy takes... ("A Prairie Home Companion," n.d.).

By the time the joke teller utters *the establishment's*, three entities have been explicitly introduced into the discourse: *guy*, *bar*, and *ten shots*. Use of the definite article signals that one of these (*establishment = bar*) is being singled out from the others in the text frame. Similarly, utterance of *the guy* in the second sentence singles out *guy* from a slightly expanded text frame (expanded because more NPs have been uttered). Notice no explicit mention of any kind of bartender is made in the first sentence. Thus, *the bartender* at the start of the second sentence must be explained through the concept frame. Mention of *a bar* activates a bar schema in the mind of the hearer. From this schema, a concept frame may be populated with entities that include one bartender.

While the text frame serves mostly as a frame for interpreting anaphoric reference, it may occasionally be used for the introduction of a new referent. Epstein (2002, ex. 11) offers the following start to a dialog he (A) had with his mother (M).

(6) M: Did you hear about *the fight*?
    A: What fight?
    M: Between Bob and Grandpa...

Adopting the framework of mental space theory (e.g., Fauconnier 1994, 1997), Epstein (2002: 355) observes that this example "involves the introduction into the discourse of an entity that manifestly requires further elaboration, that is, the speaker intends it to be a new topic and assumes that the addressee is aware of this intention." In this sense, the speaker uses the definite article for cataphoric reference, as a cue alerting the hearer that a new topic is worthy of note. Under such an interpretation, one could say that the entity signaled by *the fight* is uniquely identifiable from other entities in the text frame. The difference, however, between this and anaphoric reference is that the entity is new to the text frame upon utterance of the NP. There is also the possibility that the speaker assumed the hearer might actually know about the fight, in which case the concept frame would be appropriate for interpreting the definite article here.

As may be observed in the examples of NPs headed by the definite article above, use of the pedagogical schematic requires the entity to which the NP refers to be located in the discourse frame. A further step is to identify an appropriate sub-frame and possible entities against which the entity is uniquely identified. Learners are able to map a NP to the schematic by physically drawing representations for the entities within the sub-frame and an arrow (or index finger) singling out the definite NP.

# 3 Study

The pedagogical schematic for the definite article was presented to a small group of international MA TESOL students. This was part of a larger study that investigated students' reactions to a more comprehensive article framework that included schematics for *the*, *a/an*, unstressed *some*, and the zero article (see White 2010). For this chapter, the following research question is considered:

How does exposure to the pedagogical schematic for the definite article influence international MA TESOL students' explanations for uses of *the* in authentic texts?

## 3.1 Participants

International graduate students at Michigan State University were solicited for participation in the project. The researcher sought students who (a) spoke a first language (L1) without articles, (b) were enrolled in the university's M.A. TESOL program, and (c) expressed both frustration with and an incomplete understanding of the English article system. A total of five students, all in their second year of the M.A. program, participated. Each of these participants had begun studying English in primary school in his/her home country. Basic background information for these individuals is presented in the table below.

**Table 1:** MA TESOL participants

| Participant | L1 | Home Country |
|---|---|---|
| P1 | Korean | Korea |
| P2 | Thai | Thailand |
| P3 | Chinese (Mandarin) | China |
| P4 | Korean | Korea |
| P5 | Korean | Korea |

These students were considered a particularly attractive group to work with for a number of reasons. Given that they were native speakers (NSs) of article-less languages and had learned English as a second language, they would be sensitive to the difficulties of mastering appropriate use of articles. By their own admission, the participants were frustrated by articles and had yet to master their use. Because they planned to teach English in the future and had expressed dissatisfaction with their own understanding of articles, they were expected to be motivated to take part in the study. Finally, these individuals possessed a high level of English proficiency enabling them to carry out explanation and reflection tasks in English.

## 3.2 Materials

The materials consisted of an explanation elicitation task and a comparative reflection task. The explanation elicitation required two steps. First, participants read four extracts from authentic texts. No articles were highlighted within these texts in order to encourage reading for content. It was considered important that participants build an overall understanding of the texts before they set out to make article explanations. Second, participants read the four extracts again – this time with 20 individual articles highlighted. The participants verbally explained to the researcher why they thought the authors had used each of the 20 highlighted articles. Through these explanations, the participants would be problematizing articles and seeking reasons for why particular choices were made, thus engaging in the practice of languaging (Swain 2006). This explanation task was repeated after the intervention.

The reflection task asked participants to compare their responses given on the first explanation elicitation task (Elicitation A) with those given on the second (Elicitation B). Immediately after completion of Elicitation B, participants read a transcript of what they had said in Elicitation A. They were asked to (a) identify any explanations that were different from what they had just said, (b) explain how the explanations were different, and (c) describe any changes in their thinking. The task combines elements of stimulated and immediate recall (Gass and Mackey 2005). That is, the transcripts prompt participants to think back to their original explanations and the timing of the task draws upon participants' immediate recollection of explanations given in their second completion of the explanation elicitation task.

The sources for the excerpts were chosen to (1) reflect expository types of writing that might appear in university courses and (2) cover topics that were thought to be of interest to the participants[1]. The excerpts consisted of text

---

[1] One book was on language pedagogy (Interaction in the Language Curriculum: Awareness, Autonomy and Authenticity by Leo van Lier), one on language learning (How Languages are Learned by Patsy Lightbown and Nina Spada), one on philosophy with attention to language (Philosophy in the Flesh: The Embodied Mind and its Challenge to Western Thought by George Lakoff and Mark Johnson), and a final book on leading American intellectuals (The Metaphysical Club by Louis Menand).

from the opening page of each book, either from the forward or the main text. This decision was made because article choice is discourse sensitive (e.g., the definite article may be chosen to refer to an entity which has previously been mentioned in the discourse). By including only the beginnings of books on the task, participants were required to offer explanations based exclusively on what they read and not on what they thought may have appeared in earlier elided text. Excerpts were kept under 350 words in length and complete paragraphs were included.

The highlighted articles, the target items to be explained on the task, were chosen to reflect a variety of article uses. Target items included eight instances of *the*, six instances of the zero article, four instances of *a* (or *an*), and two instances of *some*[2]. These articles appeared before a range of noun types – including common and proper nouns with singular, plural, and noncount forms. The intention was to challenge the participants. While some article uses could be interpreted to reflect traditional rules such as *use the indefinite article for first mention* and *use no article with the names of countries*, a greater number of items were less easily explained by such rules. [See Appendix for definite article target items.]

## 3.3 Procedure

Each participant undertook a series of one-on-one meetings with the researcher over the course of 7 weeks[3]. All sessions were audio-recorded with a Sony MP3 IC Recorder. Each meeting ranged from 60 to 100 minutes. The decision not to enforce a strict time limit on meetings was made in recognition that participants would differ in terms of time required to complete tasks. The researcher entered each meeting (1–6) with a protocol of basic instructions for tasks to be conducted. The same protocol was followed for each participant. Throughout the project, the researcher made field notes as tasks were carried out.

**Table 2:** Meeting outline

| | |
|---|---|
| Meeting 1 | Interview; Elicitation A |
| Meeting 2 | Presentation and Application of Framework Concepts |
| Meeting 3 | Application of Framework |
| Meeting 4 | Application of Framework |
| Meeting 5 | Application of Framework |
| Meeting 6 | Elicitation B; Comparative Reflection |

---

2 Only explanations for the definite article are considered in this chapter.
3 Due to illness, one participant took 8 weeks to complete the meetings.

Meeting (1) allowed the researcher to interview participants about their experiences learning, using, and teaching English articles. The purpose here was both to prompt participants to begin thinking about the topic of articles and to collect information on their backgrounds. Following the interview, participants were given the explanation elicitation task.

In Meetings (2) and (3), participants were presented the conceptual framework – including schematics for *the*, *a/an*, unstressed *some*, and the zero article – in the form of a handout and an application worksheet. In Part I of the worksheet, participants were asked to explain to the researcher how highlighted noun phrases could be mapped to the schematic. For initial explanations, participants were required to draw representations on the schematic handout. Participants continued to draw as they moved through items on the worksheet. The highlighted noun phrases contrasted different article choices for similar contexts. The contexts took the form of short dialogues created by the researcher. In Part II, participants explained how highlighted noun phrases in examples of traditional textbook article rules and exceptions to the rules could be mapped to the schematic. In Part III, participants considered how highlighted uses of the definite article in a brief narrative could be mapped to the framework's *discourse frame*. The narrative was created in order to spotlight a variety of uses for the definite article.

In preparation for Meetings (4) and (5), each participant was asked to email the researcher the name of a journal article the participant was currently reading for a graduate course and one academic paper that the participant had written in a previous semester at the university. In Meeting (4), after a brief review of the framework's basic concepts, participants considered NPs in the abstract of the journal article they had shared with the researcher. Participants read one sentence at a time and underlined uses of *the*, *a*, *some*, and Ø. If participants missed an article in their underlining, the researcher pointed it out. For each sentence, participants explained how the NPs of the identified articles could be mapped to the framework. In the remainder of the meeting, participants followed the same procedure for their academic papers. Article uses were identified and discussed in relation to the framework. The participant was specifically asked why each identified article had been chosen during the writing of the paper and how the framework could be applied to the corresponding noun phrase. Meeting (5) saw the continued consideration of article uses in participants' academic papers.

The decision to use authentic texts and the participants' own writing in Meetings (4) and (5) was made in an effort to respect the context in which the MA TESOL students found themselves. Namely, graduate school at an American university is replete with the reading of journal articles and the writing of formal research papers. It was assumed that by working with contextually relevant texts, participants would be engaging in a more meaningful endeavor as they examined article uses.

In Meeting (6), participants were again given the explanation elicitation task. As they completed the task, participants did not have access to any of their notes or to handouts from earlier sessions. At no prior point were participants told that they would be performing the explanation task a second time. In fact, the researcher asked participants at the end of final meetings not to divulge anything about this task to other participants who had yet to complete Meeting (6). Following the final meeting, participants were emailed a post-project questionnaire soliciting their opinions on the pedagogical schematics and their understanding of the English article system.

## 3.4 Data analysis

Audio files of each participant's Elicitation A, Elicitation B, and comparative reflection were transcribed. The first step in analysis was to code for article explanations that had changed from Elicitation A to B. The researcher went item by item for each participant, reading the explanation for an item on the A transcript and then immediately reading the explanation for the same item on the B transcript. Each pair of A and B explanations was coded as one of three possibilities. If the reasons given in the B explanation were the same or similar as those in the A explanation, the pair was coded *similar*, as in the following explanations for Item (6) by Participant (2).

> P2, Elicitation A, Item (6):
>
> Hmm, number 6, I don't know why he used *the reader*... maybe to like address, to the one who are reading this book or this general... Yeah, and if I were the student, I will ask that. Why, why do the author use readers? Because it's just like general, in general.
>
> P2, Elicitation B, Item (6):
>
> Here I feel like the writer, like, talk to us when we read. So he suggest *the reader*. Make me feel this way because I am the person who, like, who will read this book. So maybe *the reader* just emphasize that it's the person who will read this.

If the reasons given in the B explanation were novel from those given in the A explanation, the pair was coded *different*, as in the following explanations for Item (14) by Participant (5).

> P5, Elicitation A, Item (14):
>
> *The most*, OK, *a thorough rethinking of the most*, yeah. Superlative, *the*. Ah, it's the rule. It's the rule that I learned.

P5, Elicitation B, Item (14):

And, *the most popular current approaches,* namely, OK. *A thorough rethinking of the most....* Hmm, it's about philosophy, trend. So it's one of approaches, of philosophy... among other approaches or other things about philosophy.

Finally, if the B explanation both repeated any reasons in the A explanation and contained novel reasons, the pair was coded as *amended*. For instance, on Item (17), Participant (3) repeated the idea of specific reference to the United States and added the notion of unique identification.

P3, Elicitation A, Item (17):

*The war was fought to preserve the system of government that had been established by the nation's founding... at the nation's founding.* Because *the nation* is our nation, which is the United States of America. So this is, um... this is specifically referred to our country. So we want to use *the* here.

P3, Elicitation B, Item (17):

*The war was fought to preserve the government... at the nation's founding.* Um, here, when the author said *the nation*, um, it's very specific. Ah, it's very, ah, it's uniquely identified. This nation means, ah, the United States of America. So, um, it's uniquely identified. So he uses the definite article *the* here.

Next, the researcher read transcripts of the Comparative Reflection in search of any discrepancies between the above coding and what the participants expressed. Any reflection that either (1) stated the A and B explanations were similar where the coding was *different* or (2) stated the A and B explanations were different where the coding was *similar* were noted. The next step was to identify each and every reason given in each explanation across Elicitations A and B, which helped to confirm the original *similar*, *different*, or *amended* coding.

In order to identify patterns in Elicitation B explanations, the researcher examined reasons given by article type. The researcher flagged any reason given by the same participant in more than two explanations for items with the same article. Recurring reasons, along with the item numbers for which they were given, were noted.

In order to identify patterns in changes between Elicitation A and B explanations by participant, the researcher (1) compared reasons across the two elicitations, (2) examined patterns identified in Elicitation B explanations, and (3) considered comments made in the Comparative Reflection. Within items of the same article (e.g., all explanations for *the*), themes and trends were noted.

## 3.5 Results

As may be observed from the table below, the great majority of explanations for the definite article were changed in some way from Elicitation A to B. That the MA TESOL students changed the majority of their explanations is not surprising. Between the two elicitations, the participants had been introduced to a novel way of conceptualizing articles. They had each met with the researcher on four occasions, during which they had applied the conceptual framework to a range of article uses. Each participant spent somewhere between (285) and (335) minutes practicing application of the conceptual framework. Given such focused attention, it is reasonable to expect individuals to alter their performance on the explanation task. It is also possible that the participants may have felt obligated in Elicitation B to try to use the ideas they had been practicing throughout the meetings. Of more interest is the nature of the changes made in participants' article explanations.

**Table 3:** Changes in explanations from elicitation A to B

|         | Participant 1 | Participant 2 | Participant 3 | Participant 4 | Participant 5 |
|---------|---------------|---------------|---------------|---------------|---------------|
| Item 3  | D             | D             | A             | S             | D             |
| Item 5  | D             | D             | D             | D             | D             |
| Item 6  | D             | S             | S             | A             | D             |
| Item 7  | A             | D             | D             | D             | D             |
| Item 11 | D             | A             | D             | D             | A             |
| Item 14 | D             | A             | A             | A             | D             |
| Item 17 | D             | S             | A             | A             | D             |
| Item 18 | D             | A             | D             | D             | D             |

S = similar; A = amended; D = different

The clearest pattern to emerge after analysis of the Elicitation Tasks was more unity in participants' Elicitation B explanations. For example, Participant (1) gave a variety of reasons for uses of the definite article in Elicitation A: *specific referent* (Items 3, 6, 7), *modification* (Item 5), *superlative degree* (Item 14), *emphasis* (Item 17), *rule* (Item 18), and *phrase* (Item 18). For all eight of her explanations in Elicitation B, she mentioned that the target item referent was *one among others*. For instance, she said the referent for Item (5) (*the importance of encouraging "natural" communication between students as they engage co-operatively in tasks or projects while using the new language*) was one among other important points, and the referent for Item (6) (*the reader*) was one among other people associated with the book. This greater unity in explanations for the definite article would suggest that the participant is approaching a more systematic understanding of the meaning of the definite article across different uses. In fact, Participant (1) commented in her post-project questionnaire that prior to the treatment she had thought articles did not convey meaning.

Similarly, all of Participant (5)'s explanations for the author's choice of *the* in Elicitation B included the idea of reference to *one entity among others*. While this was explicitly stated in six of the eight explanations, the idea was implied in the remaining two explanations because in these, the participant talked about the referent being in a concept frame. This unity in explanations was lacking in Elicitation A, where the following reasons for the definite article were given: *assumed reader knowledge* (Item 3), *modification* (Items 5 and 7), *previous mention* (Items 6 and 17), *uniqueness* (Items 11 and 18), and *superlative degree* (Item 14).

Participant (2) used the expression *pick up* to describe use of the definite article in five of eight explanations in Elicitation B (Items 3, 5, 11, 14, 18). Not once did she use the term *pick up* in Elicitation A. Participant (4) suggested that the referent was *one of many* (e.g., "It means, the reader, means out of many readers, this reader is just for this book... um, the people who are reading this book." (Item 6)) in five explanations in Elicitation B (Items 5, 6, 7, 14, 18). Participant (3) used the term *uniquely identified* in six explanations in Elicitation B (Items 3, 5, 7, 14, 17, 18).

The explanations in Elicitation B exhibited some use of terminology from the pedagogical schematic, such as Participant (3)'s use of *uniquely identified* and Participant (5)'s utilization of the term *concept frame* in her explanation for Item (6).

> P5: *The reader should not see it*. OK, huh, maybe... ah, the, it is in the concept frame. So, if this is a book, maybe then reader must be, I mean, there's, there must be a reader. So, this is the reader, but I wonder why, why the readers, why the writer said, write readers, why not? And just the reader, the reader.

It should be noted, however, that at times the participants made changes to the terminology. For instance, instead of *text frame*, Participant (1) uttered "contextual frame" in her explanation for Item (6) and "context frame" for Item (14).

# 4 Discussion

It is not difficult to imagine learners being frustrated by the many different uses and textbook rules for the definite article. Learners and teachers may benefit from adopting a perspective that links these uses and rules to one overarching abstract concept. The pedagogical schematic proposed here may be one way to do this. The imagery of the schematic can be utilized by instructors to explain the abstract meanings of the definite article in a more concrete way than that typically found in textbooks. That the participants in this study provided more unified explanations across a range of definite article uses suggests the schematic may be an effective means toward establishing a systematic conceptual motivation for use of the definite article. The schematic may also serve as a motivational tool for learners. Three of the five participants expressed more confidence in their ability to continue to improve their understanding of English articles. For example, Participant (5) said that her confidence was at 60% prior to the treatment and was at 85% after the treatment.

Just as it may be used to concretize abstract explanations through imagery, the schematic may also be used as a tool to make intuitions explicit. That is, it can provide learners and teachers concepts with which to clarify and express their unarticulated insights regarding articles. For instance, while reflecting on her Elicitation A and B explanations for *the* in Item (5), Participant 4 made the following comments:

> P4: Yeah. But I think, I thought like that way before, as well, but I think I don't know how to explain it. But now I know how to explain it. I, I, um, I feel that I have kinda bridge between my concept, between my brain and my tongue.
>
> R: OK.
>
> P4: So, I think, I thought my, the way that I thought is the, is the same, before and now. But now, ah, now I know how to explain, how to express.

One challenge in implementing the schematic is helping learners identify possible contents of the discourse frame. This is especially so for the concept frame (as opposed to the text and situation frames). For it is this sub-frame that is most removed from the actual text. To identify the contents of the text frame, learners can look back across a conversation to see what referents have been mentioned. To identify the contents of the situation frame, learners can look around the immediate environs in which the conversation is taking place. But to identify the contents of the concept frame, learners must make reference to culturally appropriate schemata. This is a more challenging task. In her feedback on the project, Participant (2) wrote, "To me, it's difficult to explain and give the examples when we talked about each element which fits into the conceptual frame." Participant (5) commented on the challenge learners face in constructing the same concept frames as NSs:

> Article *the* is assumed to share a concept between speakers and hearers, but foreigners have different imaginary scenes in their mind. For example, I had a hard time to think of the other things of backgrounds in *the water in the basement*. I don't get used to the basement because we don't use a basement except for as parking lots under a big building. For a house I just thought of the floor with dust.

This comment underscores the influence of culture and experience on conceptualization and, in turn, on language.

Presenting the pedagogical schematic to international MA TESOL students has been a first step toward investigating its possibilities. The schematic should be tested in ESL/EFL classrooms. It may be found that it works better for learners at certain levels of proficiency or that materials need to be developed to provide more grounded examples of the application of the schematic for learners at lower levels. In their feedback on the project, three of the five participants expressed their belief that that the larger article framework would work better with learners at higher levels. They wondered if lower-proficiency students would possess enough English-language ability to make sense of the framework. They also believed advanced students' exposure to and frustration with article rules would make them more likely to appreciate the ability of the pedagogical schematics to offer a more systematic, unified account of English articles. This is an empirical question that remains to be tested.

# References

A Night with Boy Blue. (n.d.) http://www.barbican.org.uk/theatre/event-detail.asp?ID=18714 (accessed 15 December 2015).

A Prairie Home Companion with Garrison Keillor. (n.d.) http://www.publicradio.org/applications/formbuilder/projects/joke_machine/joke_page.php/?car_id=139970 (accessed 15 December 2015).

Bednarek, Monika A. 2005. Frames revisited – the coherence-inducing function of frames. *Journal of Pragmatics* 37. 685–705.

Bitchener, John, Stuart Young & Denise Cameron. 2005. The effect of different types of corrective feedback on ESL student writing. *Journal of Second Language Writing* 14. 191–205.

Brown, Gillian & George Yule. 1983. *Discourse analysis*. Cambridge: Cambridge University Press.

Christophersen, Paul. 1939. *The articles: A study of their theory and use in English*. Copenhagen: Munksgaard.

Cole, Tom. 2000. *The article book: Practice toward mastering a, an, and the*, revised edn. Ann Arbor, MI: University of Michigan Press.

Croft, William & D. Alan Cruse. 2004. *Cognitive linguistics*. Cambridge: Cambridge University Press.

Epstein, Richard. 2002. The definite article, accessibility, and the construction of discourse referents. *Cognitive Linguistics* 12. 333–378.

Fauconnier, Gilles. 1994. *Mental spaces: Aspects of meaning construction in natural language*. Cambridge: Cambridge University Press.

Fauconnier, Gilles. 1997. *Mappings in thought and language*. Cambridge: Cambridge University Press.

Fillmore, Charles J. 1982. Frame semantics. In Linguistics Society of Korea (ed.), *Linguistics in the morning calm. Selected papers from SICOL-1981*, 111–137. Seoul: Hanshin.
García Mayo, María del Pilar & Roger Hawkins (eds.). 2009. *Second language acquisition of articles: Empirical findings and theoretical implications*. Amsterdam: John Benjamins.
Gass, Susan M. & Alison Mackey. 2005. *Second language research: Methodology and design*. Mahwah, NJ: Lawrence Erlbaum.
Gass, Susan M. & Larry Selinker. 2008. *Second language acquisition: An introductory course*, 3rd edn. New York: Routledge.
Halliday, M. A. K. & Christian M. I. M. Matthiessen. 2004. *An introduction to functional grammar*, 3rd edn. London: Hodder Arnold.
Johnson, Mark. 1987. *The body in the mind: The bodily basis of meaning, imagination and reason*. Chicago: The University of Chicago Press.
Lakoff, George. 1987. *Women, fire and dangerous things*. Chicago: The University of Chicago Press.
Lakoff, George & Mark Johnson. 2008. *Philosophy in the flesh: The embodied mind and its challenge to Western thought*. New York: Basic Books.
Langacker, Ronald. 2002. *Concept, image, and symbol: The cognitive basis of grammar*, 2nd edn. Berlin: Mouton de Gruyter.
Langacker, Ronald W. 2008. *Cognitive grammar: A basic introduction*. Oxford: Oxford University Press.
Larsen-Freeman, Diane & Marianne Celce-Murcia. 2015. *The grammar book: Form, meaning, and use for English language teachers*. Boston: National Geographic Learning/Cengage.
Lightbown, Patsy M. & Nina Spada. 2006. *How languages are learned*, 3rd edn. Oxford: Oxford University Press.
Liu, Dilin & Johanna L. Gleason. 2002. Acquisition of the article *the* by nonnative speakers of English. *Studies in Second Language Acquisition* 24. 1–26.
Menand, Louis. 2002. *The metaphysical club: A story of ideas in America*. New York: Farrar, Straus and Giroux.
Prince, Ellen F. 1992. The ZPG letter: Subjects, definiteness, and information-status. In William C. Mann & Sandra A. Thompson (eds.), *Discourse description: Diverse analyses of a fundraising text*, 295–325. Philadelphia: John Benjamins Publishing.
Radden, Günter & René Dirven. 2007. *Cognitive English grammar*. Amsterdam: John Benjamins Publishing.
Russell, Bertrand. 1905. On denoting. *Mind* 14 (56). 479–493.
Swain, Merrill. 2006. Languaging, agency, and collaboration in advanced second language learning. In Heidi Byrnes (ed.), *Advanced language learning: The contribution of Halliday and Vygotsky*, 95–108. London: Continuum.
Tannen, Deborah. 1983. What's in a frame? Surface evidence for underlying expectations. In Deborah Tannen (ed.), *Framing in discourse*, 14–56. Oxford: Oxford University Press.
Taylor, John R. 2002. *Cognitive grammar*. Oxford: Oxford University Press.
Tyler, Andrea. 2012. *Cognitive linguistics and second language learning: Theoretical basics and experimental evidence*. New York: Routledge.
Van Lier, Leo. 1996. *Interaction in the language curriculum: Awareness, autonomy and authenticity*. New York: Routledge.
White, Benjamin J. 2010. *In search of systematicity: A conceptual framework for the English article system*. East Lansing, MI: Michigan State University dissertation.

# Appendix

## Definite Article Target Items

Sentences from Excerpt 1 (taken from Lightbown and Spada 2006):
- Teachers have seen many different approaches over **the**$_3$ past fifty years.
- Yet another stresses **the**$_5$ importance of encouraging "natural" communication between students as they engage co-operatively in tasks or projects while using the new language.

Sentences from Excerpt 2 (taken from van Lier 1996):
- **The**$_6$ reader should not see it as a finished product, therefore, but rather as a snapshot of work in progress, an illustration of an open-ended process that can and should have no closure.
- At the same time I have not taken any of **the**$_7$ common meanings of terms such as theory, practice, research, curriculum, and learning as given, but tried to find **Ø**$_8$ new meaning for them that fit new ways of thinking, and achieve terminological integrity throughout.

Sentences from Excerpt 3 (taken from Lakoff and Johnson 2008).
- **The**$_{11}$ mind is inherently embodied.
- They require a thorough rethinking of **the**$_{14}$ most popular current approaches, namely, Anglo-American analytic philosophy and postmodernist philosophy.

Sentences from Excerpt 4 (taken from Menand 2002):
- The war was fought to preserve the system of government that had been established at **the**$_{17}$ nation's founding – to prove, in fact, that the system was worth preserving, that the idea of democracy had not failed.
- But in almost every other respect, **the**$_{18}$ United States became **a**$_{19}$ different country.

# III Polysemy

Elizabeth M. Kissling, Andrea Tyler, Lisa Warren and Lauren Negrete

# Reexamining *por* and *para* in the Spanish foreign language intermediate classroom: A usage-based, cognitive linguistic approach

## 1 Introduction

Recently, many researchers in L2 learning have suggested that language learning is best understood as usage-based, i.e. gradual, emergent and grounded in meaning (e.g. Cadierno and Eskildsen 2016; Ellis and Cadierno 2009; Eskildsen and Wagner 2015; Ortega, Tyler, Park, and Uno 2016; Tyler 2012). Twenty plus years of empirical research in language learning has provided us with evidence that language emerges gradually: The learner, whether an infant or an adult, first gains understanding of individual instances of a language unit used in meaningful contexts. Full control of an item only comes after multiple exposures and multiple attempts by the learner to use it to express their own meaning. Moreover, learning proceeds more effectively when scaffolded, that is when presented in carefully supported increments with appropriate modeling of the fundamental concepts to be learned (e.g. Lantolf and Poehner 2013). Tyler (2012) argues that, in spite of many hopeful advances in researched language pedagogy, such as task-based language teaching, most L2 curriculum and instruction is driven by L2 textbooks which present the target language in terms of discrete rules and vocabulary items. Further, this treatment of language appears to assume that once grammar is introduced, the best path to learning is for students to memorize the rules and the many, seemingly arbitrary meanings associated with a single lexical unit. Such an approach is distinctly not usage-based and is generally disconnected from recent advances in linguistic theory, cognitive science and learning theory (Ellis and Wulff 2015).

Currently, the standard teaching format for the multiple meanings of the Spanish prepositions *por* and *para* is to present a list of distinct meanings for each preposition in a one- or two-day unit. The meanings are commonly represented as translations of English prepositions. Students are instructed to memorize

**Elizabeth M. Kissling**, University of Richmond
**Andrea Tyler**, Georgetown University
**Lisa Warren**, Beth Tfiloh Dahan Community School
**Lauren Negrete**, Arlington Public Schools

the different meanings and then test their understanding of the various meanings by way of fill-in-the-blank exercises. This basic lesson is recycled, and possibly expanded, approximately once every semester. There is ample evidence that this is not a particularly effective approach (e.g. Guntermann 1992; Lafford and Ryan 1995; Pinto and Rex 2006). Indeed, *por* and *para* are widely recognized as particularly difficult to master, often challenging even high proficiency L2 speakers (Guntermann 1992; Lafford and Ryan 1995; Pinto and Rex 2006; Sanz personal communication). Given their difficulty and the ineffectiveness of the standard approach to teaching them, it seems these prepositions represent particularly good targets for examining the efficacy of a more usage-based pedagogical approach. To this end, a large-scale, longitudinal investigation of the effectiveness of a more usage-based, Cognitive Linguistic-inspired presentation of *por* and *para* was undertaken.

The present chapter represents the first stage in the larger investigation; it examines two aspects of applying a usage-based, CL approach to teaching *por* and *para*. First, we presented the multiple meanings of the two forms gradually, building learners' knowledge in a series of scaffolded treatments, throughout the course of an entire semester rather than presenting them all in one concentrated lesson. Second, we presented the multiple meanings of *por* and *para* and structured their order of presentation according to a Cognitive Linguistic-inspired analysis, which emphasizes the systematic relationships among the multiple meanings. Such a systematic analysis is consistent with studies in cognitive psychology which have shown that it is easier to retrieve complexes of information if there is a systematic, organizing structure that specifies the relationship among the items, since this structure offers additional routes for accessing information (e.g. Bousfield 1953; Bower et al. 1969; Deese 1959; Lam 2009; Mandler 1967; Tulving 1962). A third area of interest was in examining the efficacy of providing explicit CL explanations of *por* and *para*, including discussion of CL concepts, such as the many meanings being represented by a systematically connected polysemy network whose central sense is a spatial relationship between a focus element and a background element, versus an approach which did not explicitly articulate CL concepts and did not explicitly present the multiple meanings as comprising a polysemy network.

## 1.1 Traditional methods of teaching *por* and *para*

It is widely recognized that prepositions are one of the most challenging areas for second language learners (Celce-Murcia and Larsen-Freeman 2015). For English-speaking learners of Spanish, *por* and *para* are two prepositions that are both particularly intractable and also figure prominently in the traditional grammatical syllabus. Both have multiple uses – *por* has up to 12 meanings, several of which are typically translated by a range of English prepositions such as 'through,' 'alongside', and 'by', and *para* has up to 8 meanings, including 'towards', 'by', and 'at'. Even more problematic, certain uses of both *por* and *para* are commonly translated as 'for', which itself has multiple meanings in English. These prepositions have proven difficult for learners until they reach very advanced proficiency levels, even with naturalistic exposure in an immersion environment (Guntermann 1992; Lafford and Ryan 1995). Pinto and Rex (2006) found that even after receiving repeated cycles of explicit grammar instruction over the course of a four-year university program, Spanish learners only reached an average of 61% accuracy on the two prepositions.

In order to determine how Spanish Foreign Language (FL) texts typically present *por* and *para*, nine popular intermediate textbooks were consulted. These textbooks' approaches to *por* and *para* were consistent with the researchers' experience as Spanish learners and teachers. Typically, in Spanish FL courses for L1 English speakers, *por* and *para* are presented in contrast during one self-contained grammar lesson, which is recycled through multiple curricular levels. We observed that the order varied widely from textbook to textbook, with no clear rationale offered for the ordering. In several of the texts, the first meaning of *por* is listed as "reason / motive / purpose / cause ('for')" or "means ('by')", and the first meaning of *para* is given as "purpose ('in order to'), goal / objective" (Spaine Long, et al. 2007; Nichols et al. 2009; Zayas-Bazan, Bacon, and García 2014). Note that both prepositions are confusingly glossed as "purpose", potentially giving the impression that they are interchangeable. In other texts, the first senses listed are "length of time" (*por*) and "deadline" (*para*) (Marinelli and Mujica Laughlin 2014; Pellettieri et al. 2011). Some intermediate textbooks provide explanations of *por* and *para* that incorporate diagrams of spatial scenes. For instance, *De paseo* presents a diagram of a spatial scene to illustrate the first sense presented for each preposition (e.g. destination or goal for *para*) but then lists several additional uses that are seemingly unrelated to this spatial scene (Long and Macián 2015). In sum, with few exceptions (e.g. Underwood et al. 2012), the typical presentation of *por* and *para* amounts to a laundry list of apparently unrelated uses for each preposition, the effect of which is to "bombard students with more than a dozen uses of *por* and *para*, often in one class session" (Pinto and Rex 2006: 620). Our review of several newly released intermediate Spanish textbooks (Blanco and Colbert 2012; Blanco and Tocaimaza-Hatch 2015; Spinelli, García and Galvin Flood 2013) and popular language learning websites (http://www.studyspanish.com/; http://www.spanishdict.com/) suggests that this traditional presentation is still being promoted.

The traditional presentation also often involves a contrastive emphasis. Contrastive sentences in which different uses of *por* and *para* can be translated by the same English preposition, most prominently the English preposition *for*, are presented side-by-side. For instance,

(1) a. *Este regalo es **para** Adela.*
'This gift is **for** Adela' where ***para*/for** indicates the recipient of an action.

b. *Pagaré $3 **por** este sándwich.*
'I will pay $3 **for** this sandwich' where ***por*/for** indicates an object in an exchange.

Students are given several examples of sentences involving these contrastive uses and instructed to memorize the different meanings or uses that go with each preposition. The literature shows that one common problem with *por* and *para* for FL learners involves substituting one for the other. This is not surprising, as psychologists have long established that presentation of two similar concepts in conjunction with each other often results in confusion and establishing the wrong associations. For instance, in the area of vocabulary Brown (2014) found that asking subjects to learn pairs of opposites led to substantially more errors than if the vocabulary items were presented in their own right.

There is ample evidence that the traditional approach is not very effective. Guntermann (1992) and Lafford and Ryan (1995) reported the errors that previously instructed learners in intensive, immersion situations made during oral proficiency interviews. Neither study reported intermediate learners producing above a 64% accuracy rate for the two prepositions. Indeed, Guntermann (1992) found that when participants' uses of *por* involving set phrases (e.g. *por ejemplo* 'for example', *por eso* 'for that reason', and temporal expressions) were eliminated, their accuracy rate fell to 32%. Guntermann (1992) also found that the 3 participants who reached the advanced proficiency level still only had a 70% accuracy rate. In addition, the advanced participants were accurately using just a limited number of the possible meanings of both *por* and *para*. Indeed, both Guntermann (1992) and Lafford and Ryan (1995) reported that their participants used a very limited range of meanings (2–3) for each preposition.

Employing a cross-sectional design, Pinto and Rex (2006) analyzed how accurate 80 university students enrolled in years 1–4 of Spanish FL instruction were with *por* and *para* on a discourse completion test. Throughout the four levels of instruction, the traditional pedagogical approach was used. Pinto and Rex (2006) found that the learners improved their accuracy in using *por* and *para* by only 8%, moving from 53% accuracy to 61% accuracy, after receiving repeated explicit grammar explanations over the course of a four-year university program. Additionally, the learners in their study showed relatively high levels of mastery of just two senses of *para* (beneficiary and purpose), which accounted for 94.6% of learners' accurate uses, and just three senses of *por* (duration of time, motive, and formulaic expressions), which accounted for 94% of learners' accurate uses.

In contrast, little empirical research has been done to test the effectiveness of alternative methods for teaching *por* and *para* in a more systematic, simplified, or motivated way. Mumin (2011) suggested presenting a simplified conceptual model for students to use as a semantic conceptual guide but did not empirically test its effectiveness. Mumin's model essentially posited that *para* is associated with precision, purpose, and specific limitations, whereas *por* is associated with imprecision, reason, and general lack of limitations. The model is not based on any apparent theoretical analysis and seems not to account for some common uses, such as *por* with a specific length of time, as in *Vivimos en San Juan por 2 meses* 'We lived in San Juan for two months'. Zyzik (2008) approached the multiple meanings of *por* and *para* in a somewhat more systematic way, presenting the meanings of the prepositions by first emphasizing the spatial meaning, then the temporal use, and finally several additional abstract uses; however, she offers no empirical data supporting the approach. Moreover, its semantic analysis relies on the traditional list approach. Mason (1992) suggested presenting rules for the semantically simpler preposition (*para*) with a mnemonic and instructing students to use *por* in situations that did not fit the mnemonic. Again, Mason did not provide empirical evidence of the effectiveness of this approach. A number of researchers (e.g. Guntermann 1992; Lafford and Ryan 1995) have criticized the assumptions underlying this approach, which asserts that *por* and *para* are pairs in an oppositional paradigm. They note that both *por* and *para* have a number of uses that do not fit this assumed "opposition". Furthermore, while this process of elimination technique might appear attractive in its simplicity, at best it only helps students decide between *por* and *para* in contexts where English is likely to use *for*, wrongly assuming that virtually all errors are *for*-based substitution errors. In fact, in Lafford and Ryan's (1995) study, the most common inaccurate uses of these forms were as substitutions for different prepositions (e.g. *en* 'in' or *a* 'at') or conjunctions or were uses of these prepositions where no preposition would normally appear in Spanish.

## 1.2 A Cognitive Linguistics approach

Recent advances in Cognitive Linguistics, which focus on understanding polysemy (multiple meanings for a single phonological form) and semantic extension (e.g. Tyler and Evans 2001, 2003), offer an alternative to the arbitrary list approach. Curry's (2010) Cognitive Linguistics-based (CL) analysis of *por* and *para* represents their many meanings as systematically motivated networks and offers an analysis that elucidates the complexities of *por* and *para*. According to the CL approach, the multiple meanings of *por*, *para* and other linguistic forms are not random historical accidents. Rather, they constitute a systematic polysemy network (a network of related meanings) that developed via a constrained set of principles governing semantic extension and are rooted in shared human experiences. The connections between the uses of a particular linguistic form are often based on our everyday experiences with the spatial-physical world we inhabit, as well as metaphor, which cognitive linguists define as understanding entities or events from one cognitive domain in terms of entities or events in another cognitive domain. For instance, from birth, humans experience intimacy and warmth as co-occurring, connected experiences in the comfort of their caregivers' embrace. This type of common experience provides a conceptual foundation for why we use language from the conceptual domain of temperature, i.e. describing people as warm, when we are referring to their emotional make up (Grady 1999). The CL approach recognizes that metaphor and polysemy are ubiquitous in human language and suggests that understanding them as rooted in human cognition and embodied experience can help us make sense of complex relationships between surface forms of language

Finally, CL offers analytical tools for more precisely representing the multiple meanings within a polysemy network. For instance, Curry's (2010) analysis helps tease apart the temporal extensions for *por* and *para*. Curry's analysis, with its spatially based central sense, allows the representation of both a "temporal containment" sense and an "elapsed time" sense for *por*. The textbooks we consulted failed to distinguish these two senses, coupling them together (e.g. as "amount of time or time of day" in *Conexiones*) or subsuming them under one broad heading (e.g. "time" as in *De paseo* or "length of time" as in *En comunidad* and *Interacciones*).

There is mounting evidence that a CL approach is effective for teaching complex systems in language such as prepositions (Littlemore 2009; Tyler 2012) and English modals (Tyler, Mueller, and Ho 2011), as well as vocabulary (Boers and Lindstromberg 2008; Verspoor and Lowie 2003). Lam (2009) empirically tested the effect of adding CL-based descriptions and visual aids to an otherwise traditional *por* and *para* lesson. Although overall there were no large effect-size differences between the control and CL groups in the study, Lam found some evidence in support of the CL approach in terms of students' increased confidence, accuracy in free writing, and accuracy on delayed posttests. Lam's experimental lesson was based in part on the textbook descriptions of the central spatial and temporal senses provided by Lunn and DeCesaris (2007) and presented a number of the different uses of *por* and *para* as embodying their central spatial meanings: "an object passing through another object" (*por*) and "an object aimed towards another object" (*para*). Lam's presentation was simplified for the intermediate students and omitted several important uses of the prepositions, as well as common idioms using *por* and *para*. Nevertheless, students in that study described the CL materials as less clear than the traditional materials; Lam suggested that the novel CL approach, which was presented in just two days, might take more time for students to process. We agree that a CL analysis involves learning many new concepts and new ways of thinking about language. Thus, it is likely to challenge L2 students in ways that the familiar, traditional approach does not. Most students are familiar with the strategy of memorizing meanings and, in the case of *por* and *para*, have already learned to try to contrast the two prepositions. Lam appeared to try to avoid the complex jargon and technical explanations found in Lunn and DeCesaris's (2007) advanced textbook and Delbecque's (1995) analysis of *por* and *para*, e.g. resultative, causative, global/local scope, and deictic. However, asking the students to reconceptualize the many meanings as a systematically-related network of senses organized around a central spatial relationship is a sharply different way of understanding prepositional meanings and calls for importantly different learning strategies. The CL approach is likely to present a substantially higher cognitive load that cannot be overcome in one or two days. Moreover, it would not be surprising for learners to find a novel approach to learning somewhat disruptive, and thus its positive effects might not emerge until much later. Lam's lesson spanned just two days and so still may have had the effect of bombarding students with too much at once. Moreover, we would suggest that such a short intervention is counter to a usage-based approach, which emphasizes gradual, scaffolded emergence of knowledge of language use. Even though Lam provided students with a CL analysis of the prepositions rather than rules, it may be that students experienced the lesson much like a traditional presentation of *por* and *para*, with too many meanings presented in one intense lesson.

## 1.3 The current study

In contrast to all previous studies, the multiple meanings for *por* and *para* based on Curry (2010) (see Appendices 1 and 2), were presented to our learners in semantically related mini-clusters over the entire semester. When new meanings were introduced, learners were reminded of previous meanings they had studied, and thus important scaffolding intended to support the learning of new meanings was a key component of the interventions. Curry's analysis involved a constrained set of principles of meaning extension that highlighted embodied experience and well-documented cognitive processes such as experiential correlation (as explained in Grady, 1999). The novel analysis identified a number of senses not covered by Lam (2009), e.g. "employment" and "use" for *para*, "inclination" and "proportion" for *por*; neither were all these meanings covered by the texts we examined. We tested learners' ability to use the prepositions accurately with fill-in-the-blank and multiple-choice tests before and after receiving instruction.

The research questions that motivated the present study were:

1. Is distributing the presentation of *por* and *para* across the semester in small, semantically related units more effective than the typical one-off, laundry list presentation?
2. Are intermediate-level students able to gain in accuracy with a wider range of meanings identified through a CL-inspired analysis that more closely matches the subtle, multiple uses by native speakers of Spanish?
3. Does adding an explicit explanation of CL concepts, including explicit presentation of the polysemy network, to teaching *por* and *para* provide added benefit?

## 2 Methods

### 2.1 Participants

Our learners were enrolled in third semester (intermediate) Spanish courses at a large, public US university in the Mid-Atlantic. One of the researchers was the instructor. She taught two sections of this course. One student chose not to participate, five students dropped the course, and one student's data were eliminated from the analysis because she was a native speaker of Portuguese, which uses *por* and *para* like Spanish. The resulting group included 21 learners who received explicit explanations (+EE) of key CL concepts, and 15 learners who received no explicit explanations (−EE). In pre-study questionnaires, all but two learners reported having received prior instruction on *por* and *para*, usually one lesson per course, but not understanding them well (average of 5.38 on a 1–10 scale of comprehensibility). While learners thought that being accurate in using *por* and *para* was important (average 8.58 on a scale of 1–10), they rated their own accuracy quite low (average 3.83 on a scale of 1–10). When asked to list the uses for each preposition, only a few learners could name more than two (average of 1.5 uses per preposition), and the vast majority (29) believed that there was no connection between these uses.

One class (+EE) received explicit CL-based explanations of the prepositions' uses while the other class (–EE) was presented with the same clusters of meanings, supported by the same visuals, but with no explicit explanations involving the notions that the spatial meaning was the central one or that each of the clusters of meanings were systematically related to the spatial meaning or any other meanings.

## 2.2 Instructional materials and procedures

In accord with a usage-based approach and following the suggestion of other researchers (Lam 2009; Lindstromberg 1996; Pinto and Rex 2006), we broke the traditional, single, intensive lesson into smaller learning units. Determination of how the small, semantically related units were configured was based on the CL assumption that the many meanings associated with *por* and *para* are systematically related. In our gradual, scaffolded approach, learners started with *por* and first learned the primary sense. The other senses were then introduced at multiple points throughout the semester and connected to the course's grammatical syllabus. In total, the instruction presented 11 senses of *por* and 8 senses of *para*, broken up into 11 total lesson units delivered over 14 weeks, as outlined in Tables 1 and 2. These lessons also included 7 idioms that use either *por* or *para* because the idioms appeared frequently in the course's textbook.

The instruction presented all the senses of one preposition before the other preposition so as to avoid a contrastive emphasis or presenting the prepositions in an oppositional paradigm; as mentioned above, psycholinguistic research (e.g. Brown 2014) has indicated that doing so can confuse learners and encourage them to establish the wrong associations. Furthermore, the contrastive approach tends to erroneously assume all learners' errors are *for*-based substitution errors, whereas our approach (in lesson units 1 and 10) specifically instructed learners on how to avoid another common error, which is overextending the prepositions to utterances where no preposition is needed (Lafford and Ryan 1995). The instruction first presented all the senses of *por*, because learners typically exhibit the lowest accuracy with *por*, with the exception of a few set phrases like *por ejemplo* 'for example' (Guntermann 1992), and they typically overuse *para* as a default preposition. Thus a main goal of the instruction was for leaners to learn to use *por* accurately and in a wider variety of target-like senses. An unavoidable consequence of this pedagogical choice was that learners were not instructed on *para* until the last month of the term.

**Table 1:** Instructional sequence for *por*

| Unit | +EE Instruction | −EE Instruction | Example Items (+EE and −EE) | Thematic Syllabus (Grammatical Syllabus) |
|---|---|---|---|---|
| 1 | No preposition used with *buscar* ('to look for'), *esperar* ('to hope for'), *pedir* ('to ask for') | | | Chapter 1: Personal Relationships (Present tense, *ser* and *estar* ('to be'), present progressive, object pronouns) |
| 2 | Path through a container | 'Through' | La futbolista corre por el campo hasta la portería. ('The soccer player runs through the field toward the goal.') | |
| | Alongside | 'Alongside' | Las personas caminan por la playa. ('The people walk along the beach.') | |
| | Time elapsed | 'For' with time elapsed | Estudiamos por dos horas. ('We studied for 2 hours.') | |
| 3 | Containment (spatial) | 'Around' | Vagaron por la casa y encontraron a sus amigos en la cocina. ('They wandered around the house and found their friends in the kitchen.') | Chapter 2: Diversions (*Gustar* ('to like') and indirect verbs, reflexive verbs) |
| | Temporal containment | 'During' | El gato duerme por el día. ('The cat sleeps during the day.') | |
| | *por ahora* (idiom, 'for now') | | Tenemos bastante comida por ahora. ('We have enough food for now.') | |
| | *por lo general* (idiom, 'in general') | | Por lo general, la familia come a las ocho. ('In general, the family eats at eight.') | |
| | Inclination | 'In, for, to' with inclination | Siempre voto por el mejor candidato. ('I always vote for the best candidate.') | |
| | *por supuesto* (idiom, 'of course') | | ¡Por supuesto puedes venir a la fiesta! ('Of course you can come to the party!') | |
| 4 | Proportion | Math | El 30 por ciento de los estudiantes habla inglés. ('30 percent of the students speak English.') | |
| | Multiplication and division | | Cinco por dos son diez. ('Five by two is ten.') | |
| | Units of measure | 'Per, a' for units of measure | ¡El límite de velocidad es 80 millas por hora! ('The speed limit is 80 miles per hour!') | |
| | Exchange | 'For' with exchange | La tomé por Carolina. ('I mistook her for Carolina.') | |

**Table 1:** Continued

| Unit | +EE Instruction | −EE Instruction | Example Items (+EE and −EE) | Thematic Syllabus (Grammatical Syllabus) |
|---|---|---|---|---|
| 5 | Means | 'By' | Las personas van a Madrid por tren. ('The people go to Madrid by train.') | Chapter 3: Daily Life (Preterite past tense, imperfect past tense) |
| | *por casualidad* (idiom, 'by chance') | | ¡Por casualidad encontré el vestido perfecto! ('By chance I found the perfect dress!') | |
| | Motivation | 'Because of' with motivation | El hombre lucha por la justicia. ('The man fights for (because of) justice.') | |
| | *por eso* (idiom, 'because of this') | | Tenía mucho que hacer. Por eso, me levanté temprano. ('I had a lot to do. Because of this, I got up early.') | |
| | Cause | 'Because' | Pablo estaba cansado por su tarea. ('Pablo was tired because of his homework.') | |
| | Passive | 'By' with passive | *War and Peace* fue escrito en 1869 (por Leo Tolstoy). ('*War and Peace* was written in 1869 (by Leo Tolstoy).') | |
| 6 | Review of *por* network | Review of list of *por* uses | | |

Table 2: Instructional sequence for *para*

| Unit | +EE Instruction | –EE Instruction | Example Items (+EE and –EE) | Thematic Syllabus (Grammatical Syllabus) |
|---|---|---|---|---|
| 7 | Destination | 'Towards' | El profesor salió para la universidad. ('The professor left for the university.') | Chapter 4: Health and Wellbeing (Subjunctive in nominal clauses, commands) |
| | *para colmo* (idiom, 'to top it all off') | | Me caí y me perdí y para colmo empezó a llover. ('I fell and got lost, and to top it all off it started to rain.') | |
| | Deadline | 'Due' | La tarea de matemáticas es para el viernes. ('The math homework is due Friday.') | |
| | *para entonces* (idiom, 'by then') | | ¡Mañana es el examen! Tengo que estar listo para entonces. ('The test is tomorrow! I have to be ready by then.') | |
| | Recipient | 'Giving' | Julio hizo el pastel para Juanito. ('Julio made the cake for Juanito.') | |
| | Review of exchange (*por*) and recipient (*para*) | Review of 'for' as exchange (*por*) and giving (*para*) | Julio hizo el pastel por/para Juanita. ('Julio made the cake for Juanita.') | |
| | Work | 'For' with work | Trabajo para una compañía muy grande. ('I work for a very large company.') | |
| 8 | Comparison | 'For' with comparison | Javier es muy alto para un niño de 10 años. ('Javier is very tall for a 10-year-old boy.') | Chapter 5: Travel (Comparisons, superlatives, subjunctive in adjectival clauses) |
| | Judgment | 'For' with opinion | Estudiar mucho es importante para los estudiantes. ('Studying a lot is important for students.') | |
| 9 | Desired outcome | 'In order to' with goal | Consuelo camina rápidamente para no llegar tarde a la clase. ('Consuelo is walking fast so as not to arrive late to class.') | |
| | Review of motivation (*por*) and desired outcome (*para*) | Review of 'because of' with motivation (*por*) and 'in order to' with goal (*para*) | Él salió por tabaco / para comprar tabaco. ('He left for / to buy tobacco.') | |
| | Use | 'For' with use | Uso tijeras para cortar el papel. ('I use scissors to cut / for cutting paper.') | |
| 10 | No preposition with impersonal expressions | | Es importante que hagas ejercicio. ('It's important for you to exercise.') | |
| 11 | Review of *para* network | Review of list of *para* uses | | |

**Table 3:** Differences between +EE and −EE instruction

| +EE | −EE |
|---|---|
| A spatial relation was specifically identified as the central sense for each preposition: path through a container (*por*) and an object aimed at another object (*para*). | This sense was simply termed 'the first use.' Rather than emphasizing the spatial components, the instruction simply provided English translations of the sample sentences and so relied more heavily on English prepositional equivalents (e.g. "this sense of *por* means 'through'"). |
| Each new sense was presented as systematically related to the polysemy network. | The instruction did not formally present a polysemy network. |
| Each distinct sense was presented as a unique spatial scene, depicted in an accessible diagram. | The instruction did not include these diagrams. |
| The instruction included explanations of concepts such as metaphor and terms of spatial relations such as the use of "path" and "container" in the definition of *por*. | The senses were not defined in these more elaborate spatial terms. |

Both the +EE and -EE lessons were delivered as 11 units lasting 10–15 minutes each. The total instructional time was thus roughly equivalent to two class sessions, which is similar to the instructional time traditionally allotted. The instructor delivered the lessons in English, supported with numerous examples and visual aids. The lessons prepared for the +EE instruction and −EE instruction groups were identical in terms of instructional time, sequencing, examples, number of photos/illustrative visuals, and amount of practice. There were four differences in the instruction, which are summarized in Table 3.

The prepositions' polysemy networks used for +EE instruction and which served as the underlying guide for −EE instruction are provided in Appendices 1 and 2. During the presentations learners filled out worksheets with their own example sentence in Spanish for each new sense of the preposition. The instructor checked these sentences for accuracy and reviewed errors during the following class period.

Although our intent was to provide +EE instruction to just one group of learners, we purposefully balanced the instructional conditions in other ways (i.e. order of presentation, time on task, example items, visual support) that may have resulted in learners in the −EE group being able to construct CL-informed knowledge of the prepositions on their own. First, though CL-based concepts were not explicitly articulated in the −EE instruction, many of the slides in the −EE presentations discussed the meanings of *por* and *para* using spatially motivated explanations. For instance, "towards a place, time or goal" was given as the first meaning for *para* in the –EE explanation. This meaning was illustrated by sentences such as:

(2) *El profesor salió para la universidad.*
 'The professor left for (headed towards) the university'.

*El profesor* was identified as the person heading in the direction of a place; *para* was identified as "towards" and *la universidad* was identified as where the professor was heading. Thus, the narrative accompanying the slide laid out a scenario of movement along a path in the direction of a destination or goal, even though the terms 'path' and 'goal' were not explicitly mentioned.

A spatial understanding was also evident in the explanation for *para* as it occurs in the so-called "give" use:

(3) *Este regalo es para ti.*
 'This gift is for you'.

In the narrative explaining this use, *este regalo* was identified as "the gift being given"; *para* was identified as "telling us where the gift is going" (Notice the choice of the verb "going" in the explanation emphasizes movement of the object, as does the use of *where* which identifies location as part of the scene), and *ti* was identified as "the person who is getting the gift" (the final destination for the moving gift). The illustrative visual depicted the meaning in such a way that the spatial underpinnings of both *para* and the "give" construction were present.

Second, some of the –EE slides also incorporated non-literal or metaphoric language into the explanation. The examples in (4) show the +EE narrative and the –EE narrative for the first sense for *para*:

(4) a. +EE: The primary meaning of *para* is "an object aimed towards another object" or the "destination" sense. That is, the focus of the sentence is on the destination. This destination can be **literal** (i.e. "school" or "Spain") or **it can be metaphorical** (i.e. "a time of day or a goal to be accomplished").

 b. –EE: The first use of *para* is 'towards.' You could be heading towards a place, a time, or even a goal.

Although the term "metaphorical" was not mentioned in the –EE narrative, by referencing "towards a time or a goal", a metaphorical definition of *para* was introduced. Moreover, the presentation closely tied the spatial meaning to the metaphorical meanings. In three of the illustrative −EE narratives, the word "destination" was used.

Finally, we noted above that one final way in which the +EE and −EE presentations differed was that in the +EE presentation, the different uses were explicitly represented as part of a network of senses, while the −EE senses were labeled as being part of a list. However, since the senses were presented in exactly the same order, the −EE group was exposed to a small cluster of related meanings in each presentation. Additionally, in the −EE presentations there was a strong tendency for a new meaning to refer back to previous meanings. For instance, the first use of *por* presented in the treatment was "through", which was exemplified by sentences such as *La futbolista corre por el campo hasta la portería* 'The soccer player runs through the field toward the goal', in which some sort of container (here the soccer field) was referenced. The second sense for *por* was presented in the −EE treatment as 'around', as in (5). The bolded language in (5) indicates references to the spatial relationship of containment, thus relating the "around" sense back to the "through" sense. The third sense of *por* was "alongside". The visual was a photo of people walking along a beach. The narrative, provided in (6), explicitly relates 'alongside' to 'through'. Thus, there were several elements of the −EE treatment which indicated that the senses were related in some sort of organized way.

(5) *Vagaron por la casa y encontraron a sus amigos en la cocina.*
 'They wandered around the house and found their friends in the kitchen'
 In this case, *por* means 'around,' **as the action is happening within a certain area**. In this use, the action occurs **around a certain area**. In (5), that area was a house. Where that action takes place might be more general, as **in a country or a neighborhood**".

(6) "The '*alongside*' sense of *por* is similar to '*through*'. However, this time the movement is along the side of something, as in this beach".

## 2.3 Testing materials and procedures

Two assessment measures were used for pretests and posttests: a fill-in-the blank test and a multiple-choice test. There were practical reasons to employ both tests. Fill-in-the blank tests are commonly used for assessment of *por* and *para* and so allow for some comparison between our findings and those of other language programs and researchers (e.g. Pinto and Rex 2006). However, Lam

(2009), the only previous study testing a CL approach to teaching *por* and *para*, employed a multiple-choice test. In order to make our results comparable to the broad range of previous studies, we decided to use the two types of tests. More importantly, however, the tests' qualitative differences were of interest here. The fill-in-the blank test presented learners with a subject, verb, and the object of the preposition, leaving a blank for just the preposition (Table 4). The fill-in-the blank test items in effect set up a complete spatial scene for learners, similar to what they experienced in the instruction. The fill-in-the blank test also mimicked the processing learners typically experience as they produce the target language (i.e. while speaking or writing) when they are planning an utterance and must choose between *por* or *para* (or some other word) to complete the utterance. In contrast, the multiple-choice test presented the subject, verb, and preposition, leaving four choices for how to finish the sentence with a logical object of the preposition (Table 4). The multiple-choice test items in effect required learners to mentally construct four different scenes and choose which was most appropriate or logical, arguably a more cognitively challenging task. The multiple-choice test also mimicked the processing learners experience as they interpret incoming information in the target language (i.e. while listening or reading), constructing possible spatial scenes as they hear or read a preposition and anticipate what comes next. Both types of knowledge are involved in real-world communicative tasks.

Each test included one item for each of the senses taught (11 senses and 4 idioms for *por*, 8 senses and 2 idioms for *para* – see Table 1), for a total of 25 items. The fill-in-the blank test had four options to fill in the blank: *por*, *para*, another word, or leave blank. The multiple-choice test presented learners with sentences that included either *por* or *para* and four options to complete the sentence. All the options were semantically related to the prompt, but only one would constitute native-like usage. Test items were designed to mirror the expressions that learners had been exposed to during instruction in terms of their verb and prepositional phrases, since in our usage-based approach we were interested in whether or not students learned the expressions to which they were exposed. However, the test item sentences' subjects were not identical to those used in the instruction. The subjects were varied in an effort to ensure that students could not identify the correct response merely from recognizing a familiar sentence subject. As an example, Table 4 provides the sentences used in instruction and both tests for the primary sense of *por*. Three versions of the test items were created and their order was scrambled among learners' tests so that no learner saw the same item more than once (to avoid practice effects) and so that the item versions were spread out among the testing times (to avoid results being skewed by differences in test items' relative difficulty).

**Table 4:** Items in instruction and tests. Example: Path through a container (primary sense of *por*)

**Instruction Items**

1. La futbolista corre por el campo hasta la portería. ('The soccer player runs through the field toward the goal.')
2. En caso de incendio debes salir por la ventana. ('In case of fire, you should exit through the window.')
3. El gato mira por la ventana. ('The cat looks through the window.')
4. Caminar por el parque ('walk through the park')
5. Pasar por la aduana ('pass though customs')
6. Pasear por el centro comercial ('stroll through the mall')
7. Volar por el aire ('fly through the air')

**Multiple-choice Test Items (\* indicates the correct choice)**

1. Los estudiantes corrieron por ____ durante el recreo. ('The students ran through ____ during recess.')
   a. las piernas ('their legs')                   c. la profesora ('the teacher')
   b. el fútbol ('the soccer ball')                * d. el campo ('the field')

2. Los niños caminaron por ____ porque querían ver las flores. ('The kids walked through ____ because they wanted to see flowers.')
   a. el árbol ('the tree')                        * c. el parque ('the park')
   b. sus amigos ('their friends')                 d. sus zapatos ('their shoes')

3. La familia caminó por ____ a sus asientos en el concierto. ('The family walked through ____ to their seats at the concert.')
   a. el boleto ('the ticket')                     c. el calor ('the heat')
   * b. el pasillo ('the aisle')                   d. la pelota ('the ball')

4. El pájaro entró en la casa por ____. ('The bird entered the house through ____.')
   * a. la ventana ('the window')                  c. el suelo ('the floor')
   b. el agua ('the water')                        d. el pan ('the bread')

**Fill-in-the-blank Test Items**

1. Los niños corrieron ____ el parque hasta la piscina. ('The kids ran ___ the park to the pool.')
2. El ratón salió ____ la ventana abierta. ('The mouse left ___ the open window.')
3. Ella camina ____ el túnel hacia el campus. ('She walks ___ the tunnel towards campus.')
4. La pareja camina ____ el parque al lago. ('The couple walks ___ the park to the lake.')
* a. por b. para c. another word d. leave blank

# 3 Results

Learners' scores on the fill-in-the-blank tests and multiple-choice tests were analyzed with repeated measures analyses of variance (RMANOVA). The within-group factor was Time of test (pretest and posttest) and the between-groups

**Table 5:** *Por* usage and accuracy (Aggregate of +EE and −EE)

| Senses of *por* | Accuracy on tests (%) (*n* = 37) | | | |
|---|---|---|---|---|
| | Fill-in-the-blank | | Multiple-choice | |
| | pre | post | pre | post |
| Aggregate of all senses | 50 | 74*** ($\eta_p^2$ = .63) | 53 | 70*** ($\eta_p^2$ = .45) |
| Path through a container | 33 | 86*** | 75 | 75 |
| Alongside | 50 | 89** | 64 | 83* |
| Time elapsed | 61 | 89** | 58 | 75 |
| Containment (Spatial & Temporal) | 44 | 69* | 39 | 56 |
| Inclination | 41 | 75** | 67 | 78 |
| Proportion | 56 | 92** | 33 | 81*** |
| Exchange | 53 | 50 | 64 | 69 |
| Means | 58 | 81 | 64 | 86* |
| Motivation | 39 | 47 | 72 | 75 |
| Cause | 36 | 53 | 67 | 75 |
| Passive | 50 | 53 | 58 | 58 |

Significant gain at *$p$ < .05, **$p$ < .01, ***$p$ < .001

factor was Instructional condition (+EE instruction and −EE instruction). This analysis was done for the overall test scores per preposition as well as each unique sense of the prepositions. There was no interaction effect of Instructional condition, suggesting that incorporating an explicit CL explanation into the instruction did not provide added benefit. This conclusion must be interpreted with caution, however, because observed power levels were low (5–30%) for the Time × Instructional condition interaction effect. Thus, it is possible that a relationship existed but could not be found in these data, perhaps due to low number of participants. Though learners in the +EE group believed that their accuracy had improved slightly more (average perceived gain score of 3, on a scale of 1–10) than the −EE group (2.4), as reported on the post-instructional questionnaires, their actual performance on the posttests was not significantly better. Since there was not a statistically significant difference between the +EE and −EE groups' scores, those scores are presented in aggregate form here. Tables 5 and 6 present the scores for various senses, in the order that they were presented to learners.

As noted in Tables 5 and 6, learners' aggregate gain scores (all senses) were statistically significant on all four tests. There was a significant main effect of Time for *por* fill-in-the-blank ($F(1,35)$ = 59.62, $p$ < .001, $\eta_p^2$ = .63), *por* multiple-choice ($F(1,35)$ = 28.59, $p$ < .001, $\eta_p^2$ = .45), *para* fill-in-the-blank ($F(1,35)$ = 6.62,

**Table 6:** *Para* usage and accuracy (Aggregate of +EE and –EE)

| | Accuracy on tests (%) ($n = 37$) | | | |
| --- | --- | --- | --- | --- |
| | Fill-in-the-blank | | Multiple-choice | |
| Senses of *para* | pre | post | pre | post |
| Aggregate of all senses | 56 | 65* ($\eta_p^2 = .16$) | 51 | 67*** ($\eta_p^2 = .36$) |
| Destination | 53 | 59 | 81 | 72 |
| Deadline | 63 | 76 | 22 | 81*** |
| Recipient | 53 | 70 | 67 | 67 |
| Work | 39 | 64* | 58 | 67 |
| Comparison | 47 | 72* | 41 | 78** |
| Judgment | 69 | 81 | 56 | 61 |
| Desired outcome | 67 | 61 | 89 | 97 |
| Use | 67 | 81 | 72 | 86 |

Significant gain at *$p < .05$, **$p < .01$, ***$p < .001$

$p < .05$, $\eta_p^2 = .16$), and *para* multiple-choice ($F(1,35) = 19.41$, $p < .001$, $\eta_p^2 = .36$) tests. The observed power levels for the main effect of time were in the 90–100% range. We interpreted the significant main effect of time as a reflection of learners having received instruction between pretest and posttest. Thus the results indicated that our approach – presenting *por* and *para* gradually in semantically related clusters, informed by an underlying CL analysis, and with many visuals aids and opportunities for spontaneous production practice – was effective in terms of learners increasing their accuracy on tests. Our learners agreed that our novel approach was effective. A questionnaire was distributed via e-mail after the semester ended, and although only a third of the learners returned it ($n = 10$), their responses were consistent and encouraging. These learners' self-reported estimated accuracy increased (on average from 4.60 pre-instruction to 7.30 post-instruction, on a scale of 1–10), and they reported comprehending our *por* and *para* lessons better (on average 8.50, on a scale of 1–10) than more traditional lessons they had in the past (average 5.78).

The partial eta square statistic indicated that 16–63% of the variation in learners' scores could be attributed to time of test. That wide range of effect sizes suggested that learners did not fare equally well on all tests. Learners generally improved more on *por* than on *para*, which was likely due to having presented *por* first, thus providing the learners a longer period of time in which the meanings could become entrenched. Moreover, since each new lesson included some recycling of prior lessons, learners had much more exposure to and practice with *por* than with *para* over the course of the semester. Again, this finding is consistent with a usage-based approach, which emphasizes the importance of frequency of the input. Learners' gain scores were greater on the fill-in-the-blank test compared to the multiple-choice test for *por*, which was likely due to the fill-in-the-blank test being more similar to the instructional intervention than the multiple-choice test. We also hypothesize that the fill-in-the-blank test was somewhat less cognitively challenging. For most individual senses of *para* learners also made greater gains on the fill-in-the-blank test than the multiple-choice test. Even though their *para* aggregate gain scores were higher for the multiple-choice test, this appeared to be an artifact of one very exceptional score ("deadline"), and with this outlier removed from the analysis, the effect size on the *para* multiple-choice test was much more similar ($\eta_p^2 = .20$) to the fill-in-the-blank test.

As far as the individual senses of the prepositions, learners made gains on almost every sense on all the tests, suggesting that their large aggregate gains could not be attributed to gains in just a few senses. There were aggregate gains on all senses of *por* except the "exchange" sense on the fill-in-the-blank test and the Passive sense on the multiple-choice test. There were aggregate gains on all senses of *para* except the "desired outcome" sense on the fill-in-the-blank test and the "destination" and "recipient" senses on the multiple-choice test. Even with the small number of items (one per sense per test) and participants, about half of the senses' gain scores reached statistical significance, and most of these were the first senses taught, thus the senses which learners got the most exposure to and practice with. Learners also demonstrated improvement on the seven idioms included in the instruction, with their scores increasing from pretest to posttest for all idioms and both test types (range of 6–25% increase in accuracy), and again with more improvement on *por* than *para*

For the five senses for which learners' test scores did not improve over time on both tests, even though learners had demonstrated improvement during in-class work, an item analysis revealed that the results were likely related to problematic test items. Recall that there was just one item relating to each sense on each test, but four versions for each item were created and were counterbalanced across learners and test times. Once scores were grouped by item version, it became clear that a few item versions challenged learners more than others and lead to the inconsistent results. For instance, one item for the "desired outcome" sense of *para* was *Eduardo guardó la mitad de su almuerzo ___ comerlo más tarde* 'Eduardo saved half of his lunch ___ to eat it later'. This item was the only one to involve an object pronoun attached to an infinitive, which may have inadvertently increased the difficulty of the item. Once a few such problematic item versions were removed from the analysis, the posttest scores were greater than pretest scores on every single sense and every single test. Thus, the results indicated that our approach was effective in terms of learners increasing their knowledge of a wider range of the prepositions' senses.

# 4 Discussion

Although Spanish FL learners in the US typically receive a traditional grammar lesson contrasting *por* and *para* several times during their high school and university language studies, their use of the prepositions usually remains highly inaccurate (Pinto and Rex 2006), which calls into question the effectiveness of the status quo for teaching *por* and *para*. Our study empirically tested an approach that was usage-based in nature and novel on two accounts: it presented *por* and *para* incrementally across a semester and presented the senses in semantically related, CL-inspired mini units. We found strong evidence in support of the gradual, scaffolded approach in learners' gain scores on accuracy on fill-in-the-blank and multiple-choice tests, which increased substantially both for several individual senses of the prepositions as well as the aggregate scores, with large effect sizes. The progress our learners made in one semester stands in dramatic contrast to the gains typically made by similar learners in instructed university-level Spanish FL programs, who have been shown to improve only 8% over the course of a four-year university program (Pinto and Rex 2006).

We suggest these results indicate that a cognitive linguistic analysis of the multiple meanings of prepositions, with its emphasis on systematically related senses and principled semantic extension (via metaphor and embodied experience, etc.) provides teachers with the tools to offer more precise representations of the many meanings associated with the prepositions, clarify the relationships among the different meanings, and explain patterns of meaning extension. This allows teachers to offer more coherent, meaningful, scaffolded instruction as opposed to telling the learners to simply memorize an arbitrary list of meanings. Learners stated on the post-instructional questionnaire that our lessons were "way more organized and understandable (than types of lessons I've received in the past). They were helpful and easy to remember" and reported appreciating the visual support, depth, and connections made between senses in our lessons, e.g. "We created a map of the different types of uses and in the past we were just given a couple of differences". Of course it is difficult to directly compare across studies because different researchers have organized the senses into different functional/meaning categories and used different assessment methods, but it appears to be the case that our presentation of *por* and *para* helped learners acquire substantially more new meanings for each of the prepositions than reported in previous literature. For instance, learners in an instructed, university-level context similar to ours have been reported as relying 94% of the time on just two distinct senses of *por* (Pinto and Rex 2006).

In addition to exploring a usage-based, CL-inspired approach, one group received an explicit Cognitive Linguistics (+EE) explanation while the other group (–EE) did not receive this explicit explanation. The instructional condition +/– explicit CL explanation did not make a statistically significant difference in learners' performance on tests. We were somewhat surprised by this as we thought that the CL-inspired diagrams and the explicit representation of the relationships among the senses illustrated in the diagrams for the semantic network would provide important learning supports.

After some reflection, we have come to the conclusion that the results are not all that surprising. First, our +EE and –EE presentations taught the *por* and *para* networks in exactly the same order. The sequence of presentation might have had the effect of making the –EE group aware of semantic connections between senses even though they were not explicitly taught about the connections. In fact, it is consistent with a usage-based approach to language learning that learners would be able to make these connections themselves. Moreover, as we saw earlier, careful examination of the –EE materials showed that the narratives often related a new sense back to other senses, thus providing scaffolding for both groups and potentially equalizing the +EE and –EE conditions that we initially believed to be rather different. This conclusion is supported by comments made by the learners, some of whom stated that they did not experience the –EE condition as unsystematic or like the traditional (list) approach. For example, on the post-instructional questionnaire we received comments such as, "I have never had such a methodical approach to teaching *por* and *para*", "the charts were a great touch", and "same grammar concepts but you taught them differently than past teachers". Of course, the real test is whether both groups continue to retain their increased accuracy. If these gains hold over time, the findings suggest that effective classroom materials and pedagogy, which does not require as much explanation, can be developed. This will undoubtedly be good news for many teachers.

## 4.1 Conclusion and future directions

There are several important limitations for this study. It lacked two important control treatments – a traditional list presentation concentrated in one intensive lesson and a traditional list presentation but presented incrementally across a full semester. Since the gradual treatment and organization of the CL-inspired semantic mini-clusters were conflated, we cannot say with confidence if one of these adjustments to the traditional approach would be sufficient to result in the large gains we saw with both our groups. Adding the two additional treatments would give us a much fuller picture.

Another limitation is the lack of a delayed posttest. Time constraints of the semester system kept us from being able to gather these data. We plan to expand the current study by collecting these additional data. We hypothesize that learners receiving CL-inspired instruction would show sustained improvement, as we are convinced that research in psychology supports the argument that systematically organized information is easier to access than arbitrarily related information. We are also convinced that the principles of semantic extension utilized in Curry's (2010) analysis, and which were central to our materials development, provide learners with valuable tools for further independent analysis as they encounter instances of *por* and *para*. Following the usage-based tenets of gradual, exemplar-based learning, we expect that additional encounters with the various uses of *por* and *para* would result in entrenchment of the polysemy networks and, thus, more efficient processing.

*Por* and *para* are not the only items in the Spanish FL syllabus which are likely to benefit from being presented using a usage-based, CL framework. We hypothesize that all Spanish prepositions are equally analyzable using a CL, polysemy approach. A growing body of research has demonstrated that prepositions and other spatial language across a wide range of languages can be effectively analyzed using the same CL principles that guided Curry's (2010) study: Russian (Shakhova and Tyler 2008), Vietnamese (Ho 2011), Chinese (Huang 2013), Korean (Kang 2012), Farsi (Mahpeykar and Tyler 2011), and Arabic (Jan 2014), among several others. Indeed, most lexical items, particularly nouns and verbs, are also polysemous; both Spanish FL teachers and students are likely to benefit from having access to informed polysemy analyses of high frequency, polysemous items.

# References

Blanco, José A. & María Colbert. 2012. *Enfoques*, 3rd edn. Boston, MA: Vista Higher Learning.
Blanco, José A. & C. Cecilia Tocaimaza-Hatch. 2015. *Imagina*, 3rd edn. Boston, MA: Vista Higher Learning.
Boers, Frank & Seth Lindstromberg (eds.). 2008. *Cognitive linguistic approaches to teaching vocabulary and phraseology*. Berlin & New York: Mouton de Gruyter.
Bousfield, Weston A. 1953. The occurrence of clustering in the recall of randomly arranged associates. *Journal of General Psychology* 49. 229–240.

Bower, Gordon H., Michael C. Clark, Alan M. Lesgold & David Winzenz. 1969. Hierarchical retrieval schemes in recall of categorized word lists. *Journal of Verbal Learning and Verbal Behavior* 8. 323–343.

Brown, H. Douglas. 2014. *Principles of language learning and teaching*, 6th edn. White Plains, NY: Pearson.

Cadierno, Teresa & Søren Wind Eskildsen. 2016. *Usage-based perspectives on second language learning*. Berlin & New York: Mouton de Gruyter.

Celce-Murcia, Marianna & Diane Larsen-Freeman. 2015. *The grammar book: An ESL/EFL teacher's course*, 3rd edn. Boston, MA: Heinle ELT.

Curry, Kaitlin. 2010. *¿Pero Para? ¿Por Qué? The application of the principled polysemy model to por and para*. Washington, DC: Georgetown University MA thesis.

Deese, James. 1959. Influence of inter-item associative strength upon immediate free recall. *Psychological Reports* 5. 305–312.

Delbecque, Nicole. 1995. Towards a cognitive account of the use of prepositions *por* and *para* in Spanish. In Eugene H. Casad (eds.), *Cognitive linguistics in the redwoods: The expansion of a new paradigm in Linguistics*, 249–318. Berlin & New York: Mouton de Gruyter.

Ellis, Nick C. & Teresa Cadierno. 2009. Special section. Constructing a second language. Introduction to the special section. *Annual Review of Cognitive Linguistics* 7(1). 111–139.

Ellis, Nick C. & Stefanie Wulff. 2015. Second language acquisition. In Dabrowska, Ewa & Dagmar Divjak (eds.), *Handbook of cognitive linguistics*, 409–431. Berlin & New York: Mouton de Gruyter.

Eskildsen, Søren Wind & Johannes Wagner. 2015. Embodied L2 construction learning. *Language Learning* 65. 419–448.

Grady, Joseph. 1999. A typology of motivation for conceptual metaphor: Correlation vs. resemblance. In Raymond W. Gibbs and Gerard J. Steen (eds.), *Metaphor in cognitive linguistics*, 79–100. Amsterdam: John Benjamins.

Guntermann, Gail. 1992. An analysis of interlanguage development over time: Part 1, *por* and *para*. *Hispania* 75. 177–187.

Ho, Vu. 2011. A principled polysemy account of the Vietnamese preposition *trên*. Paper presented at International Cognitive Linguistics Conference (ICLC) 2011, Bejing, China, 7–17 July.

Huang, Lihong. 2013. The principled polysemy of the Chinese particle *dao*. Paper presented at International Cognitive Linguistics Conference (ICLC) 2013. Edmonton, Canada, 20–25 July.

Jan, Hana. 2014. The Arabic preposition 'alaa (on): A motivated polysemy network. Paper presented at Georgetown University Round Table (GURT) 2017. Washington, DC, 14–16 March.

Kang, Yunkyoung. 2012. A cognitive linguistic approach to the semantics of spatial relations in Korean. Washington, DC: Georgetown University dissertation.

Lafford, Barbara & John Ryan. 1995. The acquisition of lexical meaning in a study abroad context: The Spanish prepositions *por* and *para*. *Hispania* 75. 528–547.

Lam, Yvonne. 2009. Applying Cognitive Linguistics to teaching Spanish prepositions *por* and *para*. *Language Awareness* 18(1). 2–18.

Lantolf, James & Matthew Poehner. 2013. *Sociocultural theory and the pedagogical imperative in L2 education: Vygotskian praxis and the theory/research divide*. London: Routledge.

Lindstromberg, Seth. 1996. Prepositions: Meaning and method. *ELT Journal* 50. 225–236.

Littlemore, Jeannette. 2009. *Applying cognitive linguistics to second language learning and teaching*. Basingstoke: Palgrave Macmillan.

Long, Donna R. & Janice L. Macián. 2015. *De Paseo*, 3rd edn. Boston, MA: Thomson Heinle.
Lunn, Patricia & Janet DeCesaris. 2007. *Investigación de gramática*, 2nd edn. Boston, MA: Thomson Heinle.
Mandler, George. 1967. Organization and memory. In Kenneth W. Spence & Janet Taylor Spence (eds.), *The psychology of learning and motivation: Advances in research and theory*, 328–372. New York, NY: Academic Press.
Marinelli, Patti J. & Lizette Mujica Laughlin. 2014. *Puentes*, 6th edn. Boston, MA: Heinle Cengage Learning.
Mason, Keith. 1992. Legal Spanish: The truth, the whole truth, and nothing but the truth. *Hispania* 75(2). 432–436.
Mahpeykar, Narges & Andrea Tyler. 2011. The Semantics of Farsi *be*: Applying the principled polysemy model. *Lecture notes in computer science* 689. 413–433.
Mumin, Zahir. 2011. Clearing up native English-speaking students' semantic and morphosyntactic confusion with Spanish *por* and *para*. *Journal of Linguistics and Language Teaching* 2(1). 195–214.
Nichols, Pennie, Jane Johnson, Lynne Lemley & Lucia Osa-Melero. 2009. *En comunidad*. New York, NY: McGraw-Hill.
Ortega, Lourdes, Andrea Tyler, Hae In Park and Mariko Uno (eds.). 2016. *The usage-based study of language learning and multilingualism*. Washington, DC: Georgetown University Press.
Pellettieri, Jill, Norma López-Burton, Rafael Gómez, Robert Hershberger & Susan Navey-Davis. 2011. *Rumbos*, 2nd edn. Boston, MA: Heinle Cengage Learning.
Pinto, Derrin & Scott Rex. 2006. The acquisition of the Spanish prepositions *por* and *para* in a classroom setting. *Hispania* 89(3). 611–622.
Sanz, Cristina. 2015. Personal communication. Professor of Spanish, Georgetown University.
Shakhova, Darya & Andrea Tyler. 2008. Extending the principled polysemy model beyond English: The case of Russian *za*. In Paul Chilton & Vyvyan Evans (eds.), *Language, cognition and space: The state of the art and new directions*, 267–291. London: Equinox Press.
SpanishDict. Basic por vs para (motion vs. destination. Curiosity media, Inc, n.d. http//www.spanishdict.com/topics/show 10 (accessed December 29, 2015).
Spaine Long, Sheri, Ana Martínez-Lage, Lourdes Sánchez-López & Lloreç Comajoan Colomé. 2007. *Pueblos*. Boston, MA: Houghton Mifflin.
Spinelli, Emily, Carmen García & Carol E. Galvin Flood. 2013. *Interacciones*, 7th edn. Boston, MA: Thomson Heinle.
Study Spanish. Ryan, Ken, Juan Gómez Rodríguez, Alfredo Duarte, Tony Federico, Mónica Zapico Falconer & Jeff Arndt. "Por" and "Para". Study Languages, LLC., n.d. http://studyspanish.com/lessons/porpara.htm (accessed December 29, 2015).
Tulving, Endel. 1962. Subjective organization in free recall of "unrelated" words. *Psychological Review* 69(4). 344–354.
Tyler, Andrea. 2012. *Applying cognitive linguistics to second language learning: Theoretical basics and empirical evidence*. London: Routledge.
Tyler, Andrea & Vyvyan Evans. 2001. Reconsidering prepositional polysemy networks: The case of over. *Language* 77(4). 724–765.
Tyler, Andrea & Vyvyan Evans. 2003. *The semantics of English prepositions: Spatial scenes, cognition, and the experiential basis of meaning*. Cambridge: Cambridge University Press.
Tyler, Andrea, Charles Mueller & Vu Ho. 2011. Applying cognitive linguistics to instructed L2 learning: The English modal verbs. *AILA Review* 23. 30–49.

Underwood, Jan, Charo Cuadrado, Pilar Melero & Enrique Sacristán. 2012. *Protagonistas*. Boston, MA: Vista Higher Learning.
Verspoor, Marjolin & Wander Lowie. 2003. Making sense of polysemous words. *Language Learning* 53. 547–586.
Zayas-Bazán, Eduardo J., Susan Bacon & Dulce M. García. 2014. *Conexiones*, 5th edn. Upper Saddle River, NJ: Pearson.
Zyzik, Eve. 2008. A novel format for teaching Spanish grammar: Lessons from the lecture hall. *Foreign Language Annals* 41(3). 434–453.

# Appendix 1

## Polysemy network of *por* (+EE group)

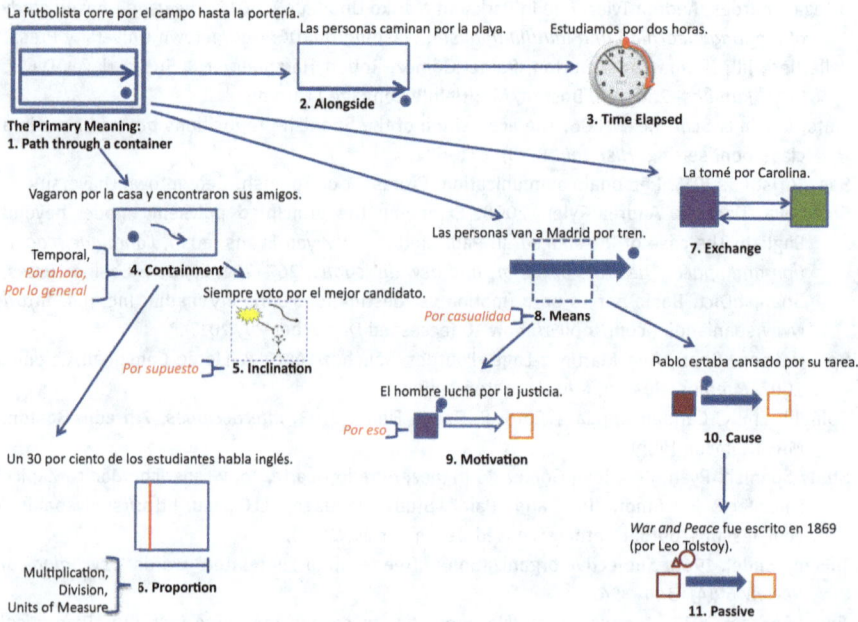

# Appendix 2

## Polysemy network of *para* (+EE group)

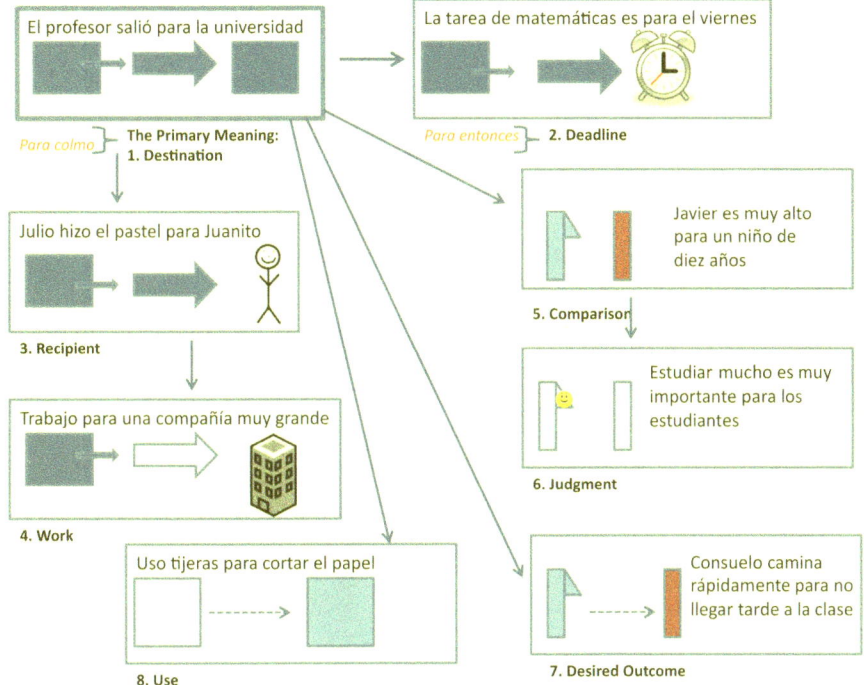

Helen Zhao, Thomas Siu-ho Yau, Keru Li, and
Noel Nga-yan Wong
# Polysemy and conceptual metaphors: A cognitive linguistics approach to vocabulary learning

## 1 Introduction

Vocabulary teaching has always received a great deal of attention in teaching English as a second language. Over the past decades, there has been a strong argument opposing the traditional teaching method of rote memorization in vocabulary instruction (Khoii and Sharififar 2013). Yet, there has been no agreement upon an effective alternative method. With the rise of applied cognitive linguistics (e.g., Boers and Lindstromberg 2008a; Littlemore 2009; Pütz, Niemeier, and Dirven 2001), CL researchers have been bringing in their theoretical perspectives to the issue of L2 vocabulary learning. CL argues for the position that there are common structuring principles that hold across different aspects of language including the lexical system (Evans and Green 2006) and that these might be usefully exploited in L2 instruction.

Polysemy and conceptual metaphors are proposed as two of the fundamental organizational factors of language and cognition (Evans and Green 2006; Tyler and Evans 2001, 2003). Both factors have achieved considerable success in generating a new perspective for analyzing the lexical system. Therefore, they have been adopted to guide CL-based vocabulary instruction in empirical studies (e.g., Beréndi, Csábi, and Kövecses 2008; Boer 2000, 2004). The assumption in such studies is that explicit teaching of metaphorical motivation behind the connection between polysemous senses of lexical items would facilitate comprehension and retention. This paper outlines a study that built on previous work on CL-based vocabulary instruction. We mainly relied on the principles of polysemy, embodiment, and conceptual metaphors as the meditational tools to guide vocabulary learning. In addition, we incorporated the concepts of image schemas and conceptual metonymy in our CL instruction. We compared the CL approach to the traditional approach to teaching vocabulary in an Asian ESL context which has been less studied in applied CL literature.

---

**Helen Zhao, Thomas Siu-ho Yau, Keru Li,** and
**Noel Nga-yan Wong,** The Chinese University of Hong Kong

https://doi.org/10.1515/9783110572186-010

## 2 Literature review

### 2.1 Polysemy and semantic networks

Polysemy gives rise to lexical ambiguity (two or more meanings associated with one word). A polysemous item is associated with two or more meanings which are related to one another in some way. For example, we can look at the uses of 'hold' in sentence (a) '*She held the bottle in her right hand*' and (b) '*She held more than 50% of the company's stocks*'. The *hold* in (a) carries a physical-spatial GRASP IN HAND sense; the meaning of *hold* in (b) is a non-physical-spatial POSSESSION sense. For formal linguists, who view polysemy as a surface phenomenon, these two senses are treated as distinct. Some argue that they may be derived from a single abstract underlying sense and interpreted on the basis of context, pragmatic principles, speaker intention, recognition of that intention by the hearer, and so on (Ruhl 1989; Putsejovytsky 1995).

Cognitive semantics, in contrast, views polysemy as a fundamentally conceptual phenomenon. In his work on cognitive lexical semantics, George Lakoff (1987) posits that polysemy reflects conceptual organization and exists at the level of mental representation rather than being a purely surface phenomenon. The meanings associated with each word are conceived as being stored in the form of a conceptual category termed a 'radial category' by Lakoff (1987), which is composed of a semantic network of distinct but related (polysemous) senses. The network is organized around a central sense, which is often more clearly physical or spatial in nature (e.g., the GRASP IN HAND sense). The extended senses are considered more peripheral (e.g., the POSSESSION sense) due to their more abstract meaning and conceptual remoteness from the physical-spatial configuration. Less central senses are derived from more central senses by multiple mechanisms; here we consider, conceptual metaphor. For example, the POSSESSION sense is derived metaphorically from the GRASP IN HAND sense; the meaning extension due to the conceptual metaphor is clearly based in our embodied experiences, POSSESSING (SOMETHING) IS HOLDING (IT IN THE HAND). As humans, we have innumerable physical experiences involving our hands grasping objects. Our embodied experiences inform us that if we grasp an object, we have possession and control of it. According to Lakoff (1987), meaning extension and radial categories are assumed to be psychologically real and are instantiated in long-term semantic memory (Evans and Green 2006).

Building on Lakoff's (1987) work, Tyler and Evans (2001, 2003) proposed a constrained methodology and set of principles to account for a principled semantic network. This newer approach introduced criteria for differentiating senses and also criteria for identifying central senses. It provided a more objective means of making semantic judgments concerning the polysemous senses.

Inspired by the above theories, the present study explored the use of semantic networks as represented by schematic diagrams as a tool for strengthening language learners' understanding of the metaphoric and metonymic relationships between various senses of polysemous lexical items and ultimately of the knowledge of the target words.

## 2.2 Image schema and vocabulary learning

Lakoff (1987) claimed that human knowledge is structured by our bodily experience in the real world. These patterns from our perceptual understanding of actions form experientially-based configurations known as image schemas. Different image schemas, with the annotation of Landmark and Figure, along with trajectories, appear regularly to reflect people's thinking and reasoning in everyday life and can be metaphorically elaborated to facilitate our understanding of the abstract domains of life experience. Clausner and Croft (1999) listed "SPACE", "SCALE", "CONTAINER", "FORCE", "UNITY/MULTIPLICITY", "IDENTITY" and "EXISTENCE" as major image schemas reflected in human cognition.

Rudzka-Ostyn (2003) believes that the meaning of vocabulary items can be visualized through diagram type representation of a schema, which illustrates the spatial relationships between objects which are moving or located with reference to other objects in the background. Ueda (2001) explored how ESL learners use schematic diagrams as a vocabulary learning strategy and discovered that participants re-categorized the different word senses in the process of vocabulary acquisition. These findings suggest that schematic diagrams can motivate L2 learners to develop their mental lexicon and facilitate their understanding of polysemous senses. Likewise, Khodadady and Khaghaninizhad (2011) showed that, compared with the translation-based instruction, schematic diagram instruction enabled learners to figure out how the intra-lexical structure of a polysemous word is organized and how senses are derived from the central sense. Such instruction promises to be beneficial to students' learning as they remember and use the polysemous words more easily (Csábi 2004). This is particularly useful to ESL learners in many Asian contexts where the translation approach has long been prevalent. Moreover, with the use of schematic diagrams, learners are given opportunities to process different senses of a polysemous word and potentially reflect on its core meaning through deep processing (Craik and Lockhart 1972). As a result, learners potentially invest more cognitive effort into word acquisition, leading to better knowledge retention.

## 2.3 Conceptual metaphor

Within cognitive linguistics, metaphor is a regular process by which people think of entities or events in one domain in terms of a second domain. According to Conceptual Metaphor Theory (CMT) by Lakoff (1993), metaphor is more than just a rhetorical tool, but importantly the manifestations of fundamental conceptual associations between various conceptual domains in cognition (Tay 2013). By this analysis, conceptual metaphors reflect a speaker's system of thought, and are grounded in our embodied experience with the external world. In every conceptual metaphor, there must be a conventional link at the conceptual level between a target domain and a source domain. The target domain, usually abstract, is the one being described and the source domain, often more concrete, provides the means for describing the more abstract idea. A classic example of conceptual metaphor is LOVE IS A JOURNEY by Lakoff and Johnson (1980), where the target domain LOVE is described by the source domain JOURNEY.

## 2.4 Conceptual metonymy

In contrast, Lakoff and Johnson (1980) pointed out that conceptual metonymy is motivated by a direct relationship between two entities in terms of contiguity or conceptual proximity (often this involves a part/whole relation). In a particular discourse situation, an entity (the vehicle) is activated by conceptualization and used to highlight another entity (the target) in the real world (Croft 1993). Kövecses and Radden (1998: 39) summarized various proposals and defined conceptual metonymy as "a cognitive process in which one conceptual entity, the vehicle, provides mental access to another conceptual entity, the target, within the same domain".

It should be noted that conceptual metonymy does not imply a substitution of one entity for another, but reveals the importance of our physical perceptions and experience of the world which interrelate them to form a new, complex meaning (Radden and Kövecses 1999). Conceptual metonymy is thus considered to be motivated by communicative and referential requirements, exemplified by the formula '*vehicle* for *target*'.

## 2.5 Teaching vocabulary with metaphors and metonymies

To stimulate L2 learners' *metaphoric competence* is regarded as a primary objective of vocabulary teaching by advocates of applied conceptual metaphor and metonymy (Boers 2013a; Littlemore and Low 2006; MacArthur 2010). Littlemore and Low (2006: 269) suggest metaphoric competence includes "both knowledge of, and ability to use, metaphors". Metaphoric competence foregrounds the capability to perform metaphoric pragmatics, i.e. ability to use their knowledge of conceptual metaphors to appropriately interpret polysemous uses of words (Low 1988).

In pedagogical practice, an important application of conceptual metaphor is presented in the teaching of idiomatic expressions (see Tyler 2012 for an extensive review). Teachers can instruct students to bridge source and target domains with the demonstration of lists of relevant idiomatic expressions classified into specific metaphorical themes (e.g. Beréndi, Csábi and Kövecses 2008; Skoufaki 2008). Another approach is to reveal the motivations that initiate the meaning extension of polysemous lexis at the conceptual level (e.g. Csábi 2004; Tyler and Evans 2001, 2003). Teacher-instructed semantic analysis of polysemous words can be provided by presenting the central meanings first, followed by presentation of metaphorically motivated extension to peripheral senses until a systematic polysemous network is established (Littlemore 2009). Reference to contextual clues have been found to be useful in facilitating the comprehension of metaphorical meanings (e.g. Boers 2000; Littlemore 2008). Visual aids in vocabulary instruction for certain "imageable" expressions or word senses can generate positive effects on mental image formation, thus stimulating meaning retention and extension (e.g. Boers et al. 2008; Lindstromberg 1997; Littlemore 2008). The other fundamental approach can be summarized as cross-linguistic metaphor comparison. Reflection on similarities and differences in "metaphorical encoding" across cultural contexts has been well-discussed in CM-based pedagogy (Lennon 1998: 21; see also Bailey 2003; Littlemore 2009; Mitchell 2014), in which translation plays a supplementary role in metaphorical awareness-raising (e.g., Sacristán 2005).

Conceptual metonymy, on the other hand, allows learners to conceptualize one thing through its relation with another, resulting in meaning extension of lexical items (Guan 2009). An example illustrating this aspect of meaning extension would be *lend me your ear*, in which *ear*, the physical organ that has a listening function, has an extended meaning that refers to the abstract quality of being attentive through listening. Besides, Guan (2009) conceived that lexical conversion occurs when conceptual metonymy operates at the morphological level. For example, in the sentence '*The librarian shelved the books*', the word *shelf* has been extended from a noun to a verb (*shelve*) to highlight the action of putting the books (undergoer or patient) onto the shelf (location/landmark). With regard to the two aspects mentioned above, Guan (2009) argues it is worth teaching vocabulary with the use of conceptual metonymy. Teachers are encouraged to introduce the cognitive nature of conceptual metonymy to students and assist them in understanding the relationship among different meanings of a polysemous word through appropriate cognitive interpretations, with an ultimate aim to expand their vocabulary bank. However, it should be noted that as metonymy, as well as metaphor, is associated with the way people conceptualize the world, its comprehension is deeply affected by the social norms and cultural backgrounds of learners.

There have been a number of empirical studies that tested the theorized benefits of conceptual metaphor- and metonymy-based vocabulary pedagogy. Among them, Csábi (2004) is one of the most cited and the one most relevant to the current study. Hungarian-speaking intermediate ESL learners were assigned to an experimental group, which received a 45-minute CL-based intervention with the aid of explicit knowledge of conceptual metaphors and metonymies, schematic diagrams and profile shifting explanations that link the polysemous senses of *hold* and *keep*, and a control group which were taught using L1 (Hungarian) equivalents. The participants took a 22-question gap-filling test twice: the first time immediately after treatment and the second time the day after as a delayed posttest. There was no pretest. Her results revealed that the CL-group outperformed the control group significantly in both the immediate posttest and the delayed posttest. Csábi (2004) concluded that the CL-based instruction could provide learners with an effective and systematic approach to learning vocabulary. Additionally, Csábi (2004) hypothesized that the cognitive exercise of understanding the conceptual metaphors and metonymies could enhance students' learning motivations when compared to being simply a receiver of ready-made L1 translations.

Beréndi, Csábi, and Kövecses (2008) replicated Csábi's study (2004) with secondary school students aged 14–15 years old in Budapest. Instead of explicitly being taught the actual conceptual metaphors and metonymies as in Csábi (2004), the CL-group was given the central sense of the two target items *hold* and *keep* and were encouraged to figure out the conceptual metaphors and metonymies by themselves with the aid of schematic pictorial guides. The control group was introduced to several English sentences with dictionary senses of *hold* and *keep* and asked to translate the sentences into Hungarian. Their results largely echoed the (2004) study. The CL-group outperformed the control group at the posttest and the delayed posttest (one or two days after the posttest).

In another highly relevant study to the current one, Morimoto and Loewen (2007) investigated the effect of schematic diagram-mediated conceptual metaphor teaching on two polysemous words: *break* and *over*. 58 Japanese-speaking high school EFL learners were assigned to two groups. The CL-group was trained to inductively figure out the core senses and the extended senses of the two words by themselves with the aid of schematic diagrams, exemplar sentences, and L1 translation. The metaphorical derivation between the core sense and the extended senses were explained as well. This was followed by a consolidation exercise asking participants to translate English sentences containing the target items into their L1 (Japanese). The control group also completed a sentence-translation exercise, but with a larger number of sentences. The senses were explained with dictionary-like definitions in their L1. Participants' vocabulary knowledge was assessed in a vocabulary acceptability judgement test and a production test. The tests were administered three times: a pretest, a posttest two days after the instruction and a delayed posttest 16 days after training.

The study obtained mixed results regarding the effectiveness of CL-based instruction. The acceptability judgement test revealed that the CL-group outperformed the control group on the learning of *over* but not of *break*. The production test showed no difference between the two groups for both *break* and *over*. The control group even performed slightly better on *over* than the CL-group in the delayed posttest. We should bear in mind that, instead of concluding that it is not effective to operationalize CL concepts in L2 learning in general, such weak results could have arisen from the inductive learning activity which required learners to figure out the polysemous senses on their own. Given a limited amount of training time (20 minutes), participants might not have been able to accurately figure out the semantic networks of the two words on their own. The control group, on the other hand, was trained with a familiar paradigm and was provided with more practice items.

Morimoto and Loewen's (2007) study generated two important implications related to the current study. First, given a relatively short duration of instruction time, explicit teacher-led CL-instruction may work more effectively than student-initiated inductive vocabulary learning. Second, CL-based instruction may turn out to be more effective in teaching certain words than others. '*Break*' and '*over*' showed different learning effects under the CL-instructional paradigm. Yet to some extent, they are not directly comparable since they belong to two word classes. Their semantic networks are very different from each other. Therefore, comparisons on words from the same part of speech with similarly structured semantic networks have the potential to provide a better answer to the exploration of any lexical effect of CL-instruction.

## 2.6 Current vocabulary pedagogy in Hong Kong

English learners in Hong Kong spend a large amount of time memorizing vocabulary items (Biggs 1992). McNeill (1996: 69) noted that many English learners in Hong Kong see vocabulary learning as "memorization of bilingual word lists". As not much research has been devoted to the examination of how English vocabulary is taught in Hong Kong ESL classrooms, a review of current English textbooks offers an alternative way to study the current vocabulary pedagogy in Hong Kong.

Yeung (2002) reviewed the English textbooks used in most secondary schools in Hong Kong. It was discovered that the textbooks are comprised of different theme-based chapters. New vocabulary items are mainly presented through reading comprehension passages, often accompanied by exercises including blank filling, matching and synonym finding. Yeung (2002) further explained that textbooks catering for students of lower abilities offer blank filling exercises in the form of choices from a few given words. Contrastively, textbooks designed for higher ability students require them to find the answers from the passages. Students were also instructed to match the target vocabulary items with their synonyms or definitions. Yeung's (2002) study clearly illustrates that current vocabulary pedagogy in Hong Kong cannot help students develop a 'deep' semantic knowledge of new items as it mainly focuses on developing learners' abilities to identify synonyms.

To deepen investigation on local vocabulary pedagogy, Yeung (2002) also reviewed teachers' textbooks. It was worth noticing that nearly all teachers' versions consist of bilingual vocabulary checklists. Together with semi-structured interviews with five English teachers about their vocabulary teaching approaches, Yeung (2002) observed that all the teachers in the interviews taught English vocabulary through reading comprehension passages, with instruction focusing on the bilingual checklists. This approach would easily allow students to produce equations on vocabulary items between their first and second languages. Nevertheless, as English is different from Chinese at the grammatical, syntactic and lexical level, a word cannot be accurately represented by a translation in another language without changing its meaning. Therefore, the use of bilingual vocabulary checklists may not facilitate Chinese learners' acquisition of the target vocabulary.

## 3 Objective and research questions

In light of the above problems with the existing pedagogy and potential advantages of a cognitive approach to vocabulary teaching, the present study aims to investigate the effectiveness of a CL-based teaching approach in the specific context of Hong Kong secondary ESL education. Most of the successful studies using applied CL were undertaken in European or North American settings. Cantonese, which is the first language of Hong Kong students, comes from a different language family from that of Indo-European languages. It is likely that collocations and conceptualizations of vocabulary items in an unrelated L2 might be very different.

Given that other L2 learners have been reported to achieve successful understanding of L2 conceptual metaphors and metonymies, Cantonese-speaking learners are predicted to be able to form an accurate conceptualization of L2 vocabulary usages through the CL instruction designed for the current study. Therefore, this study seeks to answer the following research questions:
1. Does CL-inspired instruction promote more effective vocabulary learning effects than the traditional instructional approach that relies on translation and memorization?
2. Are there any lexical specific effects regarding the effectiveness of CL-based instruction?

# 4 Methodology

## 4.1 Settings and participants

The current study took place in a former British colony where learners receive institutionalized English language education from as early as 3 years old. Hong Kong students are streamed into different secondary schools in 3 bandings according to their learning performance, with Band 1 as the top schools. The secondary schools in Hong Kong are either teaching with Chinese as the medium of instruction (CMI) or English as the medium of instruction (EMI).

The participants in the study were 33 secondary Form 1 students (12–13 years old) from a Band-1 EMI school. The participants had at least 10 years of English learning experiences. The English instructors of the participants described their general English proficiency as intermediate. None had prior exposure to CL-based English grammar.

## 4.2 Design

The current study was a quasi-experimental study that tested the effectiveness of CL-based vocabulary instruction. The participants were assigned to two groups: an experimental group (n = 16) and a control group (n = 17). A school test conducted three months before the experiment revealed that the two groups of students were of similar English proficiency, with an average score of 80/100 in the experimental group and 82/100 in the control group.

Data collection was composed of three sessions. The first session included a pretest and intervention. The second and third sessions were a posttest (two days after training) and a delayed posttest (two weeks after the posttest). Thus, the intervention component was only 45 minutes in length. Table 1 provided a detailed description of the experimental procedure.

**Table 1:** Procedure

| Sessions | The Experimental Group | The Control Group |
| --- | --- | --- |
| Pretest | Participants took the pretest under supervision (15 mins). | |
| Instruction (45 mins) | The teacher gave a PowerPoint presentation on *hold*. The teacher distributed copies of the semantic network and went through the schematic diagrams of the senses and related them to the conceptual metaphors and metonymies followed by example sentences. (15 minutes) | Teacher distributed reading comprehension materials to the students. Participants completed the exercise, followed by a discussion on the whole text. (15 minutes) |
| | Consolidation exercise (see Appendix I) on *hold* (5 mins) | The teacher highlighted the use of *hold* and *keep* in the text. (5 mins) |
| | Repeat the same process for *keep* (20 minutes) A Q&A session (5 mins) | Teacher continued to elaborate the different senses of the two target vocabulary items with dictionary definitions (10 mins on *hold* and 10 mins on *keep*) |
| Posttest | The posttest (15 mins) was conducted two days after the instruction. | |
| Delayed posttest | The delayed posttest (15 mins) was conducted two weeks after the posttest. | |

At the preparation stage, two English language teachers of similar backgrounds were selected and trained to conduct the instruction of the two groups. Both teachers had received postgraduate training in English language teaching for secondary students in Hong Kong and had at least five years of teaching experience in the participating school. Neither had received any training in cognitive linguistics or related pedagogy before the study. Each teacher was provided with a one-hour teacher training session separately. For the teacher in charge of the experimental group, essential theoretical constructs (including conceptual metaphor, metonymy, and semantic networks, as well as corresponding teaching methods) were explicitly explained. For the control group teacher, the mainstream teaching approach was re-addressed, with focus on the rationale of instruction for designed materials.

To facilitate the teaching, a script and PowerPoint slides were provided for the teacher in charge of the experimental group. The script served as a reference for the teacher, explaining the motivated senses with appropriate examples.

Also, PowerPoint slides with animations were shown to the students. Animation is extremely helpful, especially during the explanation of the underlying force dynamics for the semantic network of the word *keep*, since different force patterns can be well illustrated through the animated movement of the objects.

Before training started, the participants took a sentence-cloze test (pretest) using their existing knowledge of the two verbs. The pretest results provided a basis for analysing changes of test performance over time, and also evidence that the two groups were comparable in the initial proficiency. After taking the pretest, the experimental group was introduced to the semantic networks of *hold* and *keep*. The teacher then explained the relevant conceptual metaphors, metonymies and force dynamics that connected the different senses. Example sentences were provided to help participants understand the senses and the metaphors/metonymies in actual usage contexts. After the explanations of the senses, a consolidation exercise (see Appendix I) was given to participants, who were required to match the senses to a new set of example sentences. The teacher provided feedback to student answers in the exercise. A Q&A session occurred at the end of training when the teacher resolved students' questions on the lesson. Meanwhile, participants in the control group received conventional instruction on the two verbs with reading comprehension materials and a translation package (see Materials). The two groups of participants then took the same cloze test used in the pretest as a posttest two days after training. Two weeks later, a delayed posttest was given to the participants to measure if they could retain the knowledge gained from training. No further instruction on *hold* and *keep* was given between this period.

## 4.3 Materials

The major rationale for the design of the teaching materials for the CL-group was to present the links among polysemous meanings in the semantic networks systematically and explicitly to the students. Motivated by persistent problems her students experienced in accurately using *keep* and *hold*, Csábi (2004) developed a detailed analysis of the different senses of *hold* and *keep*. For *hold*, the root meaning (*hold -1*) is the grasping action involving human hands. This ubiquitous, human action can be extended through conceptual metaphor to another sense (*hold -2*) by the metaphor POSSESSING SOMETHING IS HOLDING (IT IN THE HAND). This variant suggests that the object being held is not necessarily in one's hand but can be in one's possession more generally (e.g. *The Fisher family holds 40% of the stock*). The third sense (*hold -3*) is the sense of controlling, which is motivated by the metonymy THE HAND STANDS FOR CONTROL and the metaphor CONTROL IS HOLDING SOMETHING IN THE HAND. The focus on possession is extended to the control of something as in *The terrorists held them hostage*.

The verb *keep* also has the sense of possession, but unlike *hold*, it does not denote the emphasis of grasping action by hand. Csábi (2004) relied on Talmy's (1988) *force dynamics* analysis, which described the interaction of entities with respect to force, in explaining the meanings of *keep*. *Force dynamics* included (but were not limited to) exertion of force and resistance to the exerted force. According to Talmy (1988), exertion of a force and resistance to it make up the key pair of interactions underpinning the force dynamics within the meanings of *keep*. The force tendency in the word *keep* is considered to be a conflicting one, with one force inclined to remain stationary or at rest while the other tends towards change or motion, thus achieving a state of equilibrium. The central meaning (*keep-1*) refers to the general concept of *possession* for an indefinite stretch of time, as in the example *You can keep the notebook*. With respect to the extended meanings of *keep*, Csábi (2004) considered that their minimal differences (Norvig and Lakoff 1987) are in the foregrounding and backgrounding of different aspects in each sense. In *keep-2*, since it is a commonplace in authentic language use that people assign a time constraint on the state of possession, the durative property (Tyler 2012) of *keep* is highlighted, thus leading to the meaning *possess for a period of a time*. For instance, *I've kept that suitcase for many years*. In *keep-3*, the force dynamic pattern and the notion of continuity are both foregrounded. Hence, *keep-3* contains the sense of *maintaining something* (at the conceptual level) *for a period of time*, as exemplified by the sentence *Paul did not keep secrets from his sister*, in which *secret* is conceptualized as an objective entity. Finally, *keep* is further extended to a more abstract 'state' meaning: maintaining the state of something possessed (against a force) (*keep-4*). For example, in the sentence *My aunt keeps a grocer's shop*, the state of ownership is maintained against forces which are potential factors, such as costs, customer satisfaction, etc., that may affect the maintenance of the state.

With reference to Csábi's (2004) analysis, two semantic networks for *hold* and *keep* (Figure 1) were designed as the teaching materials for the experimental group. Participants of the experimental group were presented with these two semantic networks as they served as visual input, and a clear explanation of how these extended meanings are coordinated was provided. After the introduction of two semantic networks, two consolidation exercises were put into practice. The students were required to match the sentences with the most appropriate senses associated with the two target vocabulary items by reflecting on what they had been taught.

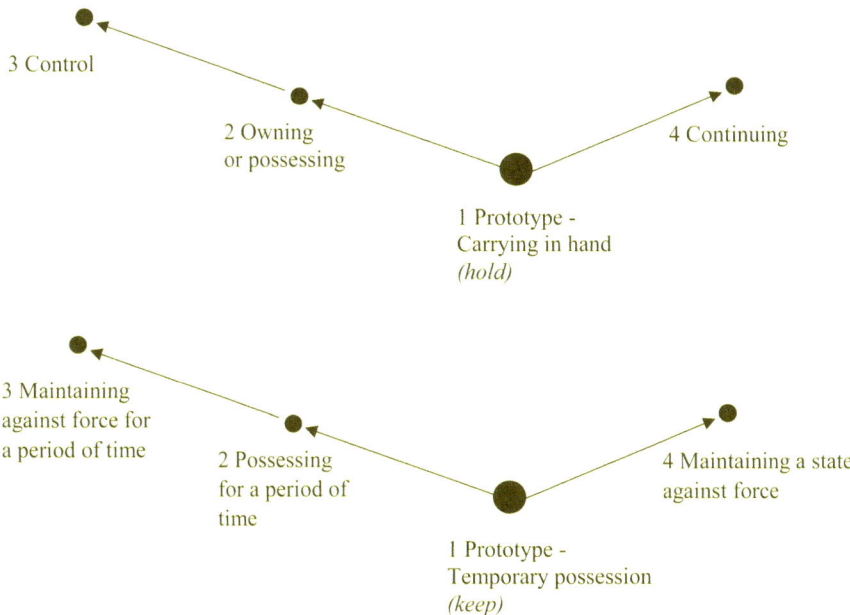

**Figure 1:** Semantic networks for *Hold* and *Keep* (Based on descriptions in Csábi, 2004)

In line with the current vocabulary teaching methodology in Hong Kong, the students in the control group learnt the different senses of the two polysemous words through a reading comprehension passage formatted as a diary (Appendix II). Four main senses of the word *hold* and four major senses of the word *keep* were incorporated in the reading passage. The teacher of the control group explained the passage, with a focus on introducing the students to the four different senses of the words respectively. After reading the comprehension passage, the control group was required to answer four questions which were not related to the different senses of the two target vocabulary items so that students could learn the target vocabulary items through a normal reading comprehension practice.

In the teaching of *hold* and *keep* after students had completed the questions for reading comprehension, the dictionary definitions listing the respective four major senses in English with the corresponding L1 (Chinese) translation, of the two target vocabulary items (Appendix III) were distributed to students. The selected senses in the notes were extracted from the *Oxford Advanced Learner's Dictionary* (2016). Example sentences were also provided for each sense to illustrate the word meanings.

## 4.4 Measurement and Data Analysis

In this study, both the experimental and the control group took a gap-filling test (Appendix IV) at the pretest, the posttest and the delayed posttest. It was a sentence-level cloze test that required participants to fill in the blank with the word *hold* or *keep*. For example, for the test sentence '*Kate is ___ a book in her right hand*', the participant was supposed to fill in the correct answer '*holding*' with the correct word choice and the *–ing* inflection. The test was composed of 10 items on *hold* and *keep* respectively. Each sense appeared in two items. None of the test sentences appeared in the example sentences given in either the experimental or control group teaching materials. The participants were given fifteen minutes to complete each test, and the two teachers were reminded that correct answers should not be given after the pretest and the posttest.

Following Csábi (2004), test data was coded for (a) "correct word choice" (CWC) (i.e., answers that are correct in word choice regardless of the correctness of inflection) and for (b) "correct word choice and inflection" (CWI) (i.e., answers that are correct in both word choice and inflection). The CMC marking was to examine the degree to which the participants could distinguish different senses of *hold* and *keep*. The CWI marking was to check whether entirely correct forms were provided.

Test scores were categorized by group (experimental group vs. control group) and lexical effect (*hold* vs. *keep*). The statistical analysis toolkit *SPSS version 22* was used to facilitate the measurement procedures. The following tests were performed accordingly: (a) a repeated-measures analysis of variance (ANOVA) to examine the time effect across the three time points on student performance; (b) an independent samples *t*-test to compare the performance between the two groups after respective teaching instruction; and (c) a repeated measures ANOVA to compare the instructional effects on *hold* and *keep* in both groups.

# 5 Results

## 5.1 Overall performance: Main effects and interaction

A repeated-measures ANOVA was used to check the effects of *time* (pretest, posttest & delayed posttest) and *treatment* (experimental & control group). The results from the repeated-measures ANOVA showed a significant main effect for time ($F(2, 62) = 4.270$, $p < 0.05$) and for treatment ($F(1, 31) = 19.476$, $p < 0.001$). Meanwhile, there was a significant interaction between time effect and treatment effect ($F(2, 62) = 7.086$, $p < 0.05$), i.e. the experimental and the control group had differentiating performance *across three time points* with obviously different change rates.

## 5.2 Instructional effectiveness

A summary of average performance across tests for both groups is exhibited in Table 2. In conjunction with the statistical presentation, Figure 2 graphically exhibits the performance trajectories of both groups. As indicated above, the results of the pretest, regardless of answer types, were not different between the two groups. An independent samples *t*-test does not yield $p$ values of significance for scores for either answer type (CWC: $p = 0.422$; CWI: $p = 0.420$). This finding justifies the selection of participants whose English proficiency and test performance was reported to be similar to each other before the experiment. In addition, CWC scores were generally higher than CWI scores, indicating that participants had difficulty with supplying the full correct form in addition to semantic differentiation.

Descriptive statistics showed a steady improvement on test performance for the experimental group, with increasing accuracy from pre- to post- and to the delayed posttest on both CWC and CWI measures. The result from the repeated

**Table 2:** Test performance across time (CWC and CWI)

| | Correct Word Choice (CWC) (Full score = 20) | | | | |
| --- | --- | --- | --- | --- | --- |
| | Pretest Mean (S.D.) | Posttest Mean (S.D.) | Delayed posttest Mean (S.D.) | $F$ value | $p$ value |
| Experimental Group (N = 16) | 12.81 (1.83) | 13.69 (1.62) | 14.07 (1.52) | $F(2, 30) = 2.026$ | 0.154 |
| Control Group (N = 17) | 12.06 (3.25) | 13.53 (2.00) | 9.82 (2.60) | $F(2, 328) = 7.489$ | 0.003* |
| | Correct Word Choice and Inflection (CWI) (Full score = 20) | | | | |
| | Pretest Mean (S.D.) | Posttest Mean (S.D.) | Delayed posttest Mean (S.D.) | $F$ value | $p$ value |
| Experimental Group (N = 16) | 7.19 (1.47) | 8.63 (1.93) | 8.94 (1.61) | $F(2, 30) = 5.050$ | 0.013* |
| Control Group (N = 17) | 7.82 (2.81) | 7.94 (2.44) | 5.41 (2.12) | $F(2, 32) = 7.955$ | 0.003* |

*$p < 0.05$ indicates that the test result is statistically significant.

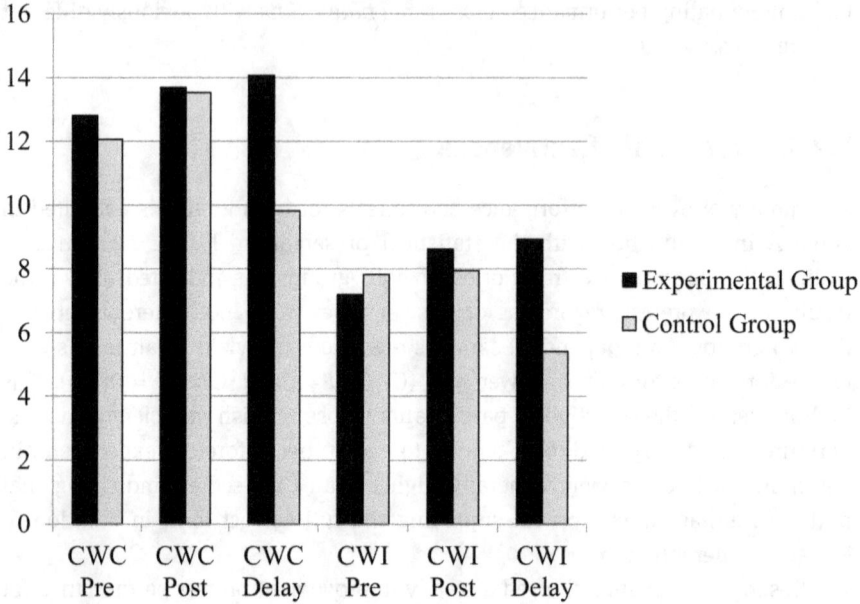

**Figure 2:** Test performance trajectory across time (CWC and CWI)

measures ANOVA demonstrates that the increase trend of the experimental group was not significant ($p = 0.154$) in CWC but was significant in CWI ($p = 0.013$). In contrast, the control group showed a different performance trajectory. They improved to some extent from pretest to posttest, mainly on the CWC measure, but showed a sharp drop in accuracy at the delayed posttest on both CWC and CWI measures. The repeated-measures ANOVA indicated that the accuracy drop was significant as indicated by CWC ($p = 0.003$) and CWI ($p = 0.003$). The following section will discuss the results in details.

The results on the posttest, in which the experimental group was expected to outperform the control group, did not meet the expectation. Although the experimental group showed some improvement, they only scored slightly higher than the control group, with a rather narrow gap between CWC and CWI scores.

Importantly, the performance diverged at the delayed posttest, with the experimental group continuing to improve and scoring significantly higher than the control group for both answer types (for CWC, $p < 0.001$; for CWI, $p < 0.001$) according to an independent samples $t$-test. The delayed test score for the experimental group hit the highest for all three tests. It is of particular interest that the rise between pretest and delayed posttest scores was of greatest significance on CWI scores ($p = .019$), whilst the increase on the CWC measure did not reach significance. In contrast, the control group showed a significantly lower score on the delayed posttest compared to the two previous tests, with a significant decrease between the posttest and the delayed posttest in both answer types (for CWC, $p = .003$; for CWI, $p = .006$) according to a pairwise comparison.

## 5.3 Lexical effects of instruction: A comparison between 'hold' and 'keep'

To obtain a closer examination of any lexical specific effects of instruction, we analyzed participants' performance on the two target words, *hold* and *keep*, respectively. In this case, only the CWC answer type was used, since we were mainly concerned with whether participants were able to discern the meanings of the two words. A repeated-measures ANOVA was used to examine lexical variations in the performance on the three tests. Table 3 and Figure 3 present these results.

For both groups, the scores on *keep* were higher than those on *hold* questions, except for the control group at the delayed posttest. Analyses indicate that in the experimental group, the scores on the two words were significantly different at the pretest ($p = 0.006$) and the posttest ($p < 0.0001$), whilst in the control group, the difference was only significant at the pretest ($p = 0.024$).

Overall, the experimental group showed an improving trajectory from the pretest to the delayed posttest, with a slight dip on *keep* between the posttest and the delayed posttest. In contrast, the control group exhibited improvement from the pretest to the posttest, followed by a sharp decline in performance at the delayed posttest. As shown in Table 3, the repeated-measures ANOVA indicates that participants' performance on *hold* in the experimental group and *keep* in control group differed significantly between the tests.

**Table 3:** Test performance across time for *Hold* and *Keep* (CWC)

| | Correct Word Choice (CWC) (Full mark = 10 for each targeted word) | | | | | |
|---|---|---|---|---|---|---|
| | Targeted word | Pretest Mean (S.D.) | Posttest Mean (S.D.) | Delayed posttest Mean (S.D.) | F value | p value |
| Experimental Group (N = 16) | hold | 5.88 (1.36) | 6.00 (0.97) | 6.88 (0.96) | $F(2, 30) = 3.834$ | 0.046* |
| | keep | 6.94 (0.85) | 7.69 (1.01) | 7.19 (1.28) | $F(2, 30) = 1.721$ | 0.203 |
| Control Group (N = 17) | hold | 5.53 (1.70) | 6.47 (1.28) | 5.00 (1.97) | $F(2, 32) = 2.965$ | 0.072 |
| | keep | 6.53 (1.94) | 7.06 (1.09) | 4.82 (1.63) | $F(2, 32) = 9.817$ | 0.001* |

*$p < 0.05$ indicates that the test result is statistically significant.

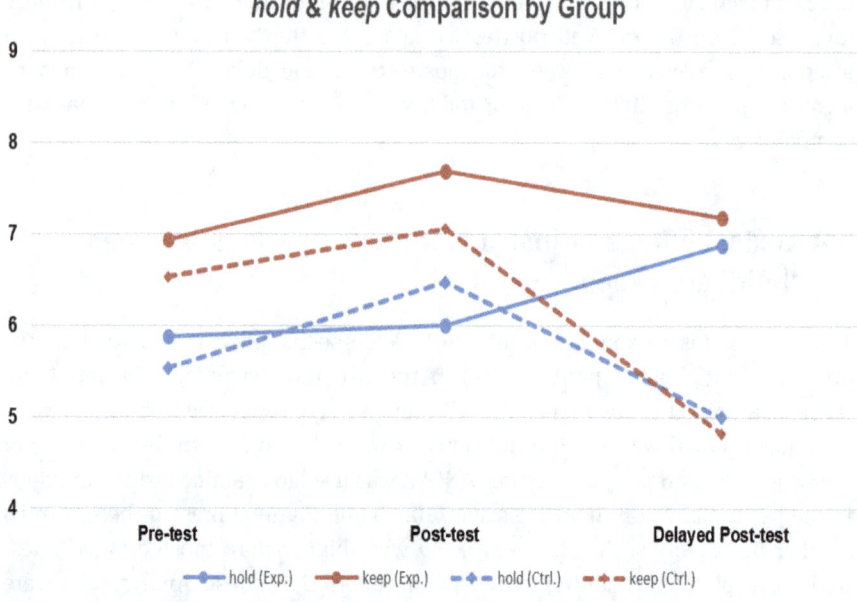

**Figure 3:** Test performance trajectories on *Hold* and *Keep* across time (CWC)

Pairwise comparison analyses of *hold* show that there was a significant gain in performance between the posttest and the delayed posttest for the experimental group ($p = 0.017$). In the case of *keep*, significant differences in performance were not found in the experimental group. For the control group, significant gains were found in the comparison between the pretest and the posttest ($p = 0.001$) but significant lowering of performance between the posttest and the delayed posttest ($p < 0.013$).

# 6 Discussion

## 6.1 CL-based vocabulary instruction and its long-term potential for retention

In general, our results suggest the CL approach to teaching polysemous vocabulary is superior, judged in terms of long time learning effects. In this study, the delayed posttest was conducted two weeks after the posttest, which was a considerably longer period of time than many previous studies (e.g. Beréndi, Csábi and Kövecses 2008; Condon 2008; Csábi 2004) in which the delayed posttest was administered one or two days after the immediate posttest. A longer time interval ensured instrument validity in measuring the long-term learning retention. Our results revealed that, regardless of the answer types (CWC or CWI), the experimental group demonstrated a progressive trajectory over the time span with a remarkable advantage in the delayed posttest. This indicates that the CL-based approach benefits long-term knowledge retention.

It is worth noting that the most significant improvement made by the experimental group was measured in terms of CWI performance. Though our CL-instruction was designed primarily to cultivate semantic understanding, we hypothesize that such an approach might also contribute to the development of grammatical knowledge, in this case, tense-aspect morphology. Several polysemous senses of '*keep*' and '*hold*' involve notions of continuity and duration with or without temporal boundaries. CL-instruction highlighted these senses and visualized their aspectual properties for the learner's attention. In other words, CL-instruction also helped learners on the lexical aspect of *hold* and *keep* and made the learners more aware of the temporal cues (e.g., adverbial phrases such as 'for 5 years') that suggested continuity with a temporal boundary in test sentences. We suspect that the enhanced aspectual awareness helped them make more accurate judgments on the grammatical morpheme required for the context.

The fact that the CL-group did not outperform the control group at the immediate posttest raises several issues. The first concerns immediate efficacy of the new approach. This is in distinction from a number of CL-inspired vocabulary instructional studies that reported encouraging immediate posttest results (see Tyler 2012; Boers 2013b for a comprehensive review). The ultimate goal of language learning is long-term gains, which was exactly what the current study found regarding the effectiveness of CL-based instruction. The nearly equal short-term gains for the two groups suggest that the control group used the strategies they were accustomed to and had already mastered. But in the long run, the control group actually got worse in their test performance. This suggests that, lacking any systematic rubric, the multiple meanings of the two lexical items may have become jumbled. This was in contrast to the CL group who were asked to think about vocabulary learning in very different ways which involved semantic networks organized around a central sense, conceptual metaphor and metonymy. As a result, the CL group was able to improve over the entire three weeks. Here the suggestion seems to be that presenting these learners with a systematic representation of the multiple meanings served as a useful rubric for learning and remembering.

Another issue concerned the duration of instruction. Despite the same instruction time for both groups, the control group was taught with an approach that was familiar, whilst the experimental group was confronted with a novel one. For the latter situation, learners may have experienced some challenges in terms of how to properly internalize the semantic motivation imparted to them within such a limited time. Yang and Hsieh's (2010) research in Taiwan lends some support to this hypothesis. In their experimental inquiry into the effect of metaphorical awareness on vocabulary teaching, some students reflected that extra time was needed to understand CMs before they moved to the linguistic level and that CM teaching "burden[ed] their process" (Yang and Hsieh 2010: 7). They suggested that more time be provided to raise sufficient CM awareness for students to foster the learning of figurative vocabulary.

In summary, the value of CL-based vocabulary instruction was justified in terms of both duration and degree. In pursuit of more satisfactory pedagogical benefits from the CL-based approach, continuous and steady efforts should be maintained. Long-term classroom support and reinforcement of various sorts are required, especially for an intensive stimulation of imagery learning strategy to fine-tune learners' habitual cognitive activities. Nevertheless, we are not necessarily denying the benefits of the conventional learning approach. Research has indicated that successful L2 vocabulary learners tend to employ an integration of learning strategies (e.g. Gu 2005; Moir and Nation 2008). As the popular learning approach in Hong Kong's L2 classroom could be more desirable in generating short-term efficacy, it is advisable that different teaching approaches be combined to suit specific learning purposes (Boers and Lindstromberg 2008b)

## 6.2 Learner age, cognitive maturity, and the efficacy of CL-based instruction

Most previous CL-oriented TESOL studies targeting metaphoric vocabulary learning involved participants of relatively older age (e.g. Boers 2000; Condon 2008; Gao and Meng 2010; Morimoto and Loewen 2007; Verspoor and Lowie 2003). The youngest L2 learners engaged in the abovementioned studies fall in the age range of 16–17, whose cognitive ability may be sufficiently mature to cope with the conceptualization and pedagogical presentation of conceptual metaphor and metonymy. The benefits of CL-based instruction among even younger teenagers as involved in the current research (12–13 years old) remain underexplored. This study reveals that younger learners can also yield significant, longer term retention improvement from CL intervention as compared with the conventional approach.

With reference to the long-term desirability of the CL-based approach, this finding suggests that the positive results may take longer to emerge.

## 6.3 Lexical effects of CL-based vocabulary teaching: Word imageability and embodied meaning

Csábi (2004) and Beréndi, Csábi and Kövecses (2008) provided detailed analyses of the semantic distinctions between *keep* and *hold*. But they did not address the question of whether learners might react differently to the two words introduced through CL-based instruction. The comparison between the learning of the two words produced is one of the most interesting findings of the current study. As with the instructional variation on *break* and *over* found in Morimoto and Loewen (2007), our results also demonstrated a lexical effect of CL-based vocabulary learning.

First of all, beginning with the pretest, both groups performed better on *keep* than on *hold*. The participants already had a more strongly entrenched understanding of '*keep*' than '*hold*' before instruction. Our account for this initial, deeper entrenchment of '*keep*' is due to its higher input frequency. The token frequency of '*keep*' is higher than that of '*hold*' according to both British National Corpus (The British National Corpus, 2007) and Corpus of Contemporary American English (Davies, 2008). It turns out that the *keep* phrases used in our gap-filling test (e.g., *keep a secret, keep talking to*) also have higher frequencies than most of the '*hold*' phrases (e.g., *hold the right degree, hold them prisoners, hold my attention*).

In fact, when we delved into each of the two words at the pretest, we found that the high-frequency phrases showed higher accuracy than the low-frequency phrases. This was true for both '*keep*' and '*hold*' and for both the experimental group and the control group. For example, several low-frequency *keep* items (i.e., *keep our luggage, keep a large house*) showed a pretest mean accuracy of 0.50, whereas several high-frequency *hold* items (i.e., *be held responsible, hold the line, hold more than 50000 people*) showed a pretest mean accuracy of 0.88. Consequently, based on arguments from the usage-based approach to language acquisition (Ellis and Ferreira-Junior 2009; MacWhinney 2008), we may conclude that the deeper entrenchment of the word *keep* than *hold* was due to a higher input frequency.

But why did performance on the word '*hold*' show significantly more gains than '*keep*' under the CL-based paradigm? We believe that it was due to the imageability of the central meanings of the two words, which also relates to embodied meaning and which was emphasized in the CL treatment. The central scene for *hold* is closely tied to the human experience of grasping and manipulating objects (Tyler 2012), and thus is easier to visualize in terms of mental imagery and potentially more easily retrieved from long-term memory. The central sense for *keep*, on the other hand, involves possession and somewhat abstract force dynamics more generally, without any focus on hands (Tyler 2012), and is therefore harder to visualize by resorting to embodied experience. For CL-based instruction, an essential element is for learners to accurately comprehend the central meaning of lexical items. A solid understanding of the central meaning is the foundation for instruction on the metaphorical extensions and other extended meanings. Our finding on word imageability and embodiment is consistent with Littlemore (2008: 215), who also found that for vocabulary learning, metaphoric extension strategies, which are intrinsically relevant to polysemous motivation, were more likely to be triggered by "highly imageable words". She demonstrated that L2 learners who preferred comprehending meanings by mental imagery were better at using metaphoric extension strategies. This finding was also supported by a study reported in Boers et al. (2008). These studies, including ours, imply that lexical items with higher imageability can be taught more effectively under the CL-based instruction supported by elucidation of images.

We find Talmy's (1988) force dynamic explanation for the meanings of *keep* compelling and would not advocate abandoning those insights. Our findings suggest the insights from Talmy (1988) allowed us to create teaching materials that allowed the participants receiving the CL treatment to make greater gains on the extended meanings of *keep* than the traditional group. However, much more work needs to be done on creating effective classroom materials that make these insights available and useful to L2 teachers and learners.

# 7 Conclusion

The current study assessed the effectiveness of cognitive linguistically oriented instruction in English vocabulary learning. Our findings suggest that raising learners' awareness of embodied semantics, conceptual metaphor and metonymy, aided by explanations with semantic networks and schematic diagrams, was effective for teaching polysemous words. Our study demonstrates that such an instructional approach, though unfamiliar and challenging to the learners as it is, could be accepted by teachers and learners of a younger age and led to desirable long-term effect of vocabulary knowledge retention. Talmy's (1988) force-dynamic insights are persuasive but required more challenge for the materials developer.

Despite the insightful findings, the current study was not without limitations. First of all, the instructional time was not sufficient for a wide implementation of a CL teaching strategy. As discussed, the information overload created by a new instructional paradigm in only one instructional session could potentially lead to incomplete understandings and even confusions among learners. Second, in the present study, we found that CL pedagogy tended to result in more favourable retention impact in the long term. More longitudinal research is needed to show whether the positive effect can be maintained for an even longer duration. Third, we need to further investigate whether learners can positively apply concepts such as a systematic polysemy network to cope with other similar polysemous encounters. As the test design in this study was particularly concerned with the retention of receptive knowledge, we may also examine the potential effectiveness of CL-pedagogy on learners' production of figurative language. Triangulated measurements will help to better address the question of potential effects of CL-based pedagogies on the grammatical aspect of vocabulary learning. Last but not least, individual differences regarding the usefulness of CL-based vocabulary teaching calls for more systematic enquiry. Very little research in CL pedagogies has addressed the age variable. In the Hong Kong context, similar research involving younger learners, at least below the age of 12, is expected to underpin the overall values of a CL-based teaching approach across age groups. Moreover, it is also necessary to base our findings on broader empirical evidence, which requires a larger experimental population.

Though not immune to such practical constraints as implementation time, this study also yields several practical implications. Firstly, polysemous words are teachable and teachers need not see them as a problematic topic in the classroom. Participating teachers agree that instructors should remind students that polysemous word senses are not unrelated and can be acquired as a coherent network. Secondly, instead of introducing the senses separately, teachers can try to explain and present the senses in a systematic manner to deepen the understanding of word usages. Such presentation of the links among senses may be the key to the success of understanding different meanings of polysemous words. We expect that in the long run, with more future research founded on learner factors (e.g. age) or learner language production, cognitive linguistics will provide more insights into language teaching and learning.

# References

Bailey, Richard. 2003. Conceptual metaphor, language, literature and pedagogy. *Journal of Language and Learning* 1(2). 59–72.

Beréndi, Márta, Szilvia Csábi & Zoltdn Kövecses. 2008. Using conceptual metaphors and metonymies in vocabulary teaching. In Frank Boers & Seth Lindstromberg (eds.), *Cognitive linguistics approaches to teaching vocabulary and phraseology*, 65–99. Berlin: Mouton de Gruyter.

Biggs, John Burville. 1992. *Why and how do Hong Kong students learn? Using the learning and study process questionnaire*. Hong Kong: Hong Kong University Press.
Boers, Frank. 2000. Metaphor awareness and vocabulary retention. *Applied Linguistics* 21(4). 553–571.
Boers, Frank. 2004. Expanding learners' vocabulary through metaphor awareness: What expansion, what learners, what vocabulary. In Michel Achard & Susanne Niemeier (eds.), *Cognitive linguistics, second language acquisition, and foreign language teaching*, 211–232. Berlin: Walter de Gruyter.
Boers, Frank. 2013a. Cognitive linguistic approaches to teaching vocabulary: Assessment and integration. *Language Teaching* 46(2). 208–224.
Boers, Frank. 2013b. Cognitive semantic ways of teaching figurative phrases: Assessment. In Francisco Gonzálvez-García, María Sandra Peña Cervel & Lorena Pérez Hernández (eds.), *Metaphor and metonymy revisited beyond the contemporary theory of metaphor: Recent developments and applications*, 227–261. Amsterdam: John Benjamins Publishing.
Boers, Frank & Seth Lindstromberg (eds.). 2008a. *Cognitive linguistic approaches to teaching vocabulary and phraseology*. Berlin/Boston, DE: De Gruyter Mouton.
Boers, Frank & Seth Lindstromberg. 2008b. How cognitive linguistics can foster effective vocabulary teaching. In Frank Boers & Seth Lindstromberg (eds.), *Cognitive linguistics approaches to teaching vocabulary and phraseology*, 1–61. Berlin/Boston, DE: De Gruyter Mouton.
Boers, Frank, Seth Lindstromberg, Jeanette Littlemore, Helene Stengers & June Eyckmans. 2008. Variables in the mnemonic effectiveness of pictorial elucidation. In Frank Boers & Seth Lindstromberg (eds.), *Cognitive linguistic approaches to teaching vocabulary and phraseology*, 189–216. Berlin/Boston, DE: De Gruyter Mouton.
Clausner, Timothy C. & William Croft. 1999. Domains and image schemas. *Cognitive Linguistics* 10(1). 1–31.
Condon, Nora. 2008. How cognitive linguistic motivations influence the learning of phrasal verbs. In Frank Boers & Seth Lindstromberg (eds.), *Cognitive linguistic approaches to teaching vocabulary and phraseology*, 133–158. Berlin/Boston, DE: De Gruyter Mouton.
Craik, Fergus IM & Robert S. Lockhart. 1972. Levels of processing: A framework for memory research. *Journal of Verbal Learning and Verbal Behavior* 11(6). 671–684.
Croft, William. 1993. The role of domains in the interpretation of metaphors and metonymies. *Cognitive Linguistics* 4(4). 335–370.
Csábi, Szilvia. 2004. A cognitive linguistic view of polysemy in English and its implications for teaching. Michel Achard & Susanne Niemeier (eds.), *Cognitive linguistics, second language acquisition, and foreign language teaching*, 233–256. Berlin/New York: Mouton de Gruyter.
Davies, Mark. 2008-. *The Corpus of Contemporary American English: 520 million words, 1990–present*. http://corpus.byu.edu/coca/ (accessed 25 August 2016)
Ellis, Nick C. & Fernando Ferreira–Junior. 2009. Construction learning as a function of frequency, frequency distribution, and function. *The Modern Language Journal* 93(3). 370–385.
Evans, Vyvyan & Melanie Green. 2006. *Cognitive linguistics: An introduction*. Edinburgh: Edinburgh University Press.
Gao, Li-qun & Guo-hua Meng. 2010. A Study on the Effect of Metaphor Awareness Raising on Chinese EFL Learners' Vocabulary Acquisition and Retention. *Canadian Social Science* 6 (2). 110–124.
Gu, Peter Yongqi. 2005. *Vocabulary learning strategies in the Chinese EFL context*. Singapore: Marshall Cavendish Academic.

Guan, Jialing. 2009. The cognitive nature of metonymy and its implications for English vocabulary teaching. *English Language Teaching* 2(4). 179–183.

Khodadady, Ebrahim & M. Saber Khaghaninizhad. 2011. Acquisition of French polysemous vocabularies: Schema-based instruction versus translation-based instruction. *Porta Linguarum* 17, 29–46.

Khoii, Roya & Samira Sharififar. 2013. Memorization versus semantic mapping in L2 vocabulary acquisition. *ELT Journal* 67(2). 199–209.

Kövecses, Zoltán & Günter Radden. 1998. Metonymy: developing a cognitive linguistic view. *Cognitive Linguistics* 9(1). 37–77.

Lakoff, George. 1987. *Women, fire, and dangerous things: What categories reveal about the mind*. Chicago: University of Chicago Press.

Lakoff, George. 1993. The contemporary theory of metaphor. In Andrew Ortony (ed.), *Metaphor and thought*, 202–251. Cambridge: Cambridge University Press.

Lakoff, George & Mark Johnson. 1980. *Metaphors we live by*. Chicago: Chicago University Press.

Lennon, Paul. 1998. Approaches to the teaching of idiomatic language. *IRAL, International Review of Applied Linguistics in Language Teaching* 36(1). 11–30.

Lindstromberg, Seth. 1997. *Vocabulary teaching in the light of an awareness of metaphor: a few ways of working*. Paper presented at the 31st IATEFL International Association of Teachers of English as a Foreign Language Conference, Brighton, 2–5 April.

Littlemore, Jeanette. 2008. The relationship between associative thinking, analogical reasoning, image formation and metaphoric extension strategies. In Mara Sophia Zanotto, Lynne Cameron & Marilda C. Cavalcanti (eds.), *Confronting metaphor in use: An applied linguistic approach*, 199–222. Amsterdam: John Benjamins Publishing.

Littlemore, Jeanette. 2009. *Applying cognitive linguistics to second language learning and teaching*. Basingstoke, UK: Palgrave MacMillan.

Littlemore, Jeanette & Graham Low. 2006. Metaphoric competence, second language learning, and communicative language ability. *Applied Linguistics* 27(2). 268–294.

Low, Graham. 1988. On teaching metaphor. *Applied Linguistics* 9(2). 125–147.

MacArthur, Fiona. 2010. Metaphorical competence in EFL: Where are we and where should we be going? A view from the language classroom. *AILA Review* 23(1). 155–173.

MacWhinney, Brian. 2008. A unified model. In Peter Robinson & Nick C. Ellis (eds.), *Handbook of cognitive linguistics and second language acquisition*, 341–371. New York: Routledge.

McNeill, Arthur. 1996. Hong Kong learners and English words: the formal-semantic gap. In Roger Berry, Vivien Berry & David Nunan (eds.), *Language awareness in language education*, 69–86. Hong Kong: Department of Curriculum Studies, The University of Hong Kong.

Mitchell, Chase. 2014. The potential of metaphor in ESL pedagogy: A pilot case study. *Connexions International Professional Communication Journal* 2(1). 75–87.

Moir, Jo & Paul Nation. 2008. Vocabulary and good language learners. In Carol Griffiths (ed.), *Lessons from good language learners*, 159–173. Cambridge: Cambridge University Press.

Morimoto, Shun & Shawn Loewen. 2007. A comparison of the effects of image-schema-based instruction and translation-based instruction on the acquisition of L2 polysemous words. *Language Teaching Research* 11(3). 347–372.

Norvig, Peter & George Lakoff. 1987. Taking: A study in lexical network theory. *Annual Meeting of the Berkeley Linguistics Society* 14. 195–206.

Oxford Advanced Learner's Dictionary. 2016. http://www.oxfordlearnersdictionaries.com/ (accessed 13 May 2016).

Pütz, Martin, Susanne Niemeier & René Dirven (eds.). 2001. *Applied cognitive linguistics: Theory and language acquisition* (vol. 1). Berlin: Mouton de Gruyter.

Radden, Günter & Zoltán Kövecses. 1999. Towards a theory of metonymy. In Klaus-Uwe Panther & Günter Radden (eds.), *Metonymy in language and thought*, 17–58. Amsterdam: John Benjamins Publishing.

Rudzka-Ostyn, Brygida. 2003. *Word power: Phrasal verbs and compounds: A cognitive approach*. New York: Mouton de Gruyter.

Ruhl, Charles. 1989. *On monosemy: A study in linguistic semantics*. Albany, NY: SUNY Press.

Putsejovytsky, James. 1995. *The generative lexicon*. Cambridge, MA: MIT Press.

Sacristán, Marisol Velasco. 2005. Metaphor and ESP: Metaphor as a useful device for teaching L2 Business English learners. *Ibérica: Revista de la Asociación Europea de Lenguas para Fines Específicos (AELFE)* 10. 115–131.

Skoufaki, Sophia. 2008. Conceptual metaphoric meaning clues in two idiom presentation methods. In Frank Boers & Seth Lindstromberg (eds.), *Cognitive linguistic approaches to teaching vocabulary and phraseology*, 101–132. Berlin/Boston, DE: De Gruyter Mouton.

Talmy, Leonard. 1988. Force Dynamics in language and cognition. *Cognitive Science* 12(1). 49–100.

Tay, Dennis. 2013. *Metaphor in psychotherapy: A descriptive and prescriptive analysis* (vol. 1). Amsterdam: John Benjamins Publishing.

*The British National Corpus*, version 3 (BNC XML Edition). 2007. Distributed by Oxford University Computing Services on behalf of the BNC Consortium. http://www.natcorp.ox.ac.uk/ (accessed 25 August 2016).

Tyler, Andrea. 2012. *Cognitive linguistics and second language learning: Theoretical basics and experimental evidence*. New York/London: Routledge.

Tyler, Andrea & Vyvyan Evans. 2001. Reconsidering prepositional polysemy networks: The case of over. *Language* 77(4), 724–765.

Tyler, Andrea & Vyvyan Evans. 2003. *The semantics of English prepositions: Spatial scenes, embodied meanings and cognition*. Cambridge: Cambridge University Press.

Ueda, Norifumi. 2001. Image schemas and second language learning: A case study. *The Bulletin of the Graduate School of Education of Waseda University* 9(1). 177–183.

Verspoor, Marjolijn & Wander Lowie. 2003. Making sense of polysemous words. *Language Learning* 53(3). 547–586.

Yang, Ada Ya-ying. & Shelley Ching-yu Hsieh. 2010. *Conceptual metaphor awareness on English phrasal verbs teaching and learning for adolescents in Taiwan*. National Cheng Kung University Institutional Repository. http://ir.lib.ncku.edu.tw/bitstream/987654321/108255/4/Conceptual+metaphor+awareness+on+English+phrasal+verbs+teaching+and+learning+for+adolescents+in+Taiwan.pdf (accessed 22 August 2016).

Yeung, S. F. 2002. *A comparison of the vocabulary self-collection strategy (VSS) and the current methodology of vocabulary teaching in Hong Kong EFL classrooms*. Hong Kong: The Chinese University of Hong Kong MPhil thesis.

# Appendix I

## Consolidation exercises

Part I: Match the following sentences with the most appropriate senses associated with **hold** by writing letters A to D in the table:

| A. possession | B. control | C. continuity | D. carry in hand |
|---|---|---|---|

| Sentences | Sense associated with *hold* |
|---|---|
| 1. The ship is holding a south-easterly course. | C |
| 2. Laura Trott, a British track rider, now holds seven world titles. | A |
| 3. He was held prisoner for two months. | B |
| 4. She was holding a brown leather suitcase. | D |

Part II: Match the following sentences with the most appropriate senses associated with **keep** by writing letters A to D in the table:

| A. temporary possession | B. maintain something against a force for a period of time | C. maintain the state of something against the force | D. possess for a period of time |
|---|---|---|---|

| Sentence | Sense associated with *keep* |
|---|---|
| 1. Sally was keeping an English notebook when she was studying at secondary school. | D |
| 2. Paul did not keep secrets from his sister. | B |
| 3. I just need one copy of the notes. You can keep others. | A |
| 4. My aunt keeps a grocer's shop. | C |

# Appendix II

## Reading comprehension exercise

Friday, 13th January

What a terrible day I've had today! First, my alarm clock didn't work so I was late for school. I had promised my class teacher Miss Chan to give her my homework today, but I couldn't **keep** my word as I left my homework home. I apologized to her for my carelessness, but Miss Chan was still very angry. She even told me that I couldn't be the class monitor anymore because I was so irresponsible. I have been **holding** the post of class monitor for two years, so I felt really sad after knowing the news. In mathematics lesson, Sam, the boy sitting next to me, shared with me about Spiderman, the movie he watched last week. Spiderman is his favorite movie character and he even **keeps** more than twenty posters of Spiderman at home. I guess his interest on Spiderman will **hold** throughout his life! He was talking so loudly and excitedly that my mathematics teacher Mr. Lee noticed that we did not pay attention in class. I think we upset him as we were told to stay in the detention class after school.

When I left school at 5 p.m., I planned to go to McDonald's to get an ice-cream. When I was walking with a purse **held** in my hand, all of a sudden, a tall man wearing a brown jacket and blue trousers ran towards me and grabbed my purse. I screamed so loudly that everyone was staring at me. Luckily, a policeman was nearby. He caught the thief and gave me back my purse! I guess the policeman will **hold** him for robbery. I did not go to McDonald's eventually as I was in a really bad mood.

Finally, I came back home at 6 p.m. Unluckily I found that Doggie, the pet I **keep**, was sick. He looked not so well, so my mother took him to the veterinarian. I hope that he will get well soon!

I am so glad that I have the habit of **keeping** a diary, so that I can write down my unlucky yet unforgettable experience today!

**Answer the following questions using the information from the reading comprehension.**
1. What couldn't Patrick, the writer of the diary, be the class monitor?
2. How did Patrick feel about his experience today? Why?
3. What is the most unforgettable experience you have ever had? Why is it so unforgettable?
4. Do you keep a diary? Why / why not?

# Appendix III

## Dictionary definitions of *hold* and *keep* (control group)

Hold
1. To physically carry something in hand, arms etc.; supporting the weight of an object
   - She held the bottle in her right hand.
   - Will this branch hold me?
2. To own or have something; to have a particular job/position/qualification; to have some particular achievement
   - Mr. Chan holds 30% of the shares.
   - She finally holds the title of world champion.
3. To have control of something; to keep somebody and not allow them to leave
   - The army has been holding the building since yesterday.
   - The terrorists are now holding a woman hostage.
4. To make something stay at the same place/level/rate/status
   - We will hold your reservation for two days.

Keep
1. To continue to have something and not give it back or throw it away; to put or store something in a particular place.
   - You should keep the money from mother.
   - Mrs. Wong keeps her wedding ring in the safe.
2. To know something and not telling it to anyone.
   - I have been keeping this secret since the day I knew it.
3. To continue doing something/actions; to do something repeatedly.
   - Keep walking along the road and then you will find the museum.
   - My heart keeps beating quickly.
4. To support somebody to live; to maintain the status of something.
   - He scarcely earns enough to keep himself and his family.
   - The high rent makes it hard for shop owners to keep their business.

# Appendix IV

## Gap-filling test

*Fill in the gaps with the correct form of "hold" or "keep".*

1. Kate is _____ a book in her right hand.
2. Ronald Reagan _____ the office of President for 8 years.
3. Jim hasn't got enough money to _____ his family.
4. The terrorists _____ them prisoners.
5. Jack _____ Joe's secret for 5 years.
6. You can _____ the book I lent you; I don't want it back.
7. Police are _____ two men because of the jewel robbery.
8. Jane _____ a diary for 15 years.
9. It is very expensive to _____ a large house.
10. Mr. Smith does not _____ the right degree for this job.
11. The hotel can _____ our luggage for few hours before we check in.
12. The prime minister will be _____ responsible for the scandal.
13. Please don't let me _____ you here, I will be fine.
14. My grandmother used to _____ chickens and ducks at her home.
15. The presentation by Mr. Green cannot really _____ my attention.
16. The square has been _____ by demonstrators since last Friday.
17. The new football stadium can _____ more than 50000 people.
18. Peter _____ talking to Mary just for some minor issues.
19. Jane is _____ the line for you, just pick up the phone when you are ready.
20. You should finish off the cake today, it won't _____.

Answer keys:

| | | | |
|---|---|---|---|
| 1. holding | 2. held/ had held | 3. keep | 4. hold/ are holding |
| 5. has kept | 6. keep | 7. holding | 8. has kept |
| 9. keep | 10. hold | 11. keep | 12. held |
| 13. keep | 14. keep | 15. hold | 16. held |
| 17. hold | 18. keeps | 19. holding | 20. keep |

Marlene Johansson Falck
# Embodied experience and the teaching and learning of L2 prepositions: A case study of abstract *in* and *on*

## 1 Introduction

When and why do L1 speakers of English say *in my opinion*, and when and why do they say *opinion on*? How does one know which preposition to use, and why is a given preposition used? How can we make the teaching and learning of grammatical constructions such as these more interesting?

Learning how to use the prepositions of a second language (L2) in a target-like manner is notably difficult (Morimoto and Loewen 2007). Despite the high frequency of prepositions as a class, questions regarding when and why prepositions are used are only partly answered in traditional "dictionary + grammar book" approaches to L2 teaching and learning. Learner dictionaries do not typically discuss why a preposition is used in a given context, and grammar books tend to merely state that a given preposition (e.g., *in*) is used in a given expression (e.g., *in my opinion*, see Murphy 2004: 254), or explain usage patterns by accounting for the contexts in which a given preposition should be used. Murphy (2004: 244), for instance, explains the usage of the prepositional phrase *on time* by saying that it is used in reference to something that happens at the time which was planned, and that *in time* is used in reference to something that happens soon enough for something to be done. Few grammar books, if any, focus on the ways in which people's embodied experiences of the world around them might have motivated the usage patterns, or on the ways in which L2 learners' body-world knowledge may be used to help them learn the patterns in a systematic and intuitive way.

A growing body of experimental studies shows that both literal and metaphorical language use and comprehension are guided by embodied simulation processes (i.e., the "reenactment of perceptual, motor, and introspective states acquired during experience with the world, body, and mind" (Barsalou 2008: 618;

---

**Acknowledgment:** The study was funded by the Royal Swedish Academy of Letters, History and Antiquities, supported by a grant from the Knut and Alice Wallenberg Foundation (KAW 2009.0295).

**Marlene Johansson Falck,** Umeå University

see e.g., Bergen and Wheeler 2010; Gibbs 2006b; Gibbs and Matlock 2008; Johansson, Holsanova, and Holmqvist 2006; Spivey and Geng 2001; Stanfield and Zwaan 2001; Zwaan, Stanfield, and Yaxley 2002)). Studies such as these are consistent with the cognitive linguistic premises that meaning is embodied (Johnson 1987; Gibbs 2006a) and that abstract concepts are largely understood by means of our embodied understandings of more concrete, or more delineated concepts (Grady 1997; Lakoff and Johnson 1980, 1999).

Cognitive linguistic scholars would thus argue that the abstract *in* and *on* instances discussed in this chapter go back to people's embodied understandings of abstract domains of experience by means of spatial ones. For instance, Tyler and Evans (2003/7), Lindstromberg (2010), and Navarro (1999, 2000) all suggest that abstract uses of *in* and *on* derive from the spatial relations associated with them. Tyler and Evans (2003/7) account for five abstract *in* senses in terms of two clusters of polysemous senses that ultimately go back to correlations in experience between the spatial and abstract domains involved. The extended uses of *in* are considered to ultimately derive from a spatial relation in which a *focus element* ([FE] i.e., located entity, [see Langacker 2002: 6]) is located within, and contained by, a *landmark* ([LM] i.e., the final position of a moving or locating entity [see Langacker 2002: 6] [Tyler and Evans 2007: 183]), and *on* refers to a spatial relation that involves "contact and support between a TR and a LM" (Tyler and Evans 2007: 179).

A related, but different, way to describe the usage patterns of prepositions is to focus, not on the relationship among the uses of the prepositions (i.e., their basic spatial and extended meanings), but on the terms that are used together with the prepositions and the types of concepts they refer to. My previous corpus linguistic analyses of temporal *in* and *on* instances from the *British National Corpus (BNC)* (Johansson Falck 2014) and of other non-spatial *in* and *on* instances from the same corpus (Johansson Falck 2017) show that the concepts referred to in abstract *in* and *on* instances fall into categories of concepts that are systematically related to specific types of body-world knowledge.

The present chapter discusses some of the categories of abstract concepts that emerge from this corpus data (Johansson Falck 2014, 2017), and the relationships between the concepts that are part of these categories and body-world knowledge. My analysis is based on the premises that abstract *in* uses go back to a spatial relation in which a FE is located within, and contained by a LM (Tyler and Evans 2007: 183), and that abstract *on* uses go back to a spatial relation that mediates contact and support between a TR and a LM (cf. Tyler and Evans 2007: 183). My main aim is to show that people's understandings of the underlying bodily experiences which sanction the abstract concepts expressed by *in* or *on* provide useful insights for the teaching and learning of the usage patterns of the prepositions involved. The tendencies for certain abstract concepts to be expressed by *in* constructions, and for others to be expressed by *on* constructions, shed additional light on the cognitive connections between the physical/spatial uses and abstract uses of *in* and *on* (i.e., of phrases such as *in/on time, in my opin*ion and *opinion on*).

Moreover, it is argued that discussions about the embodied motivations for the categories of abstract *in* and *on* instances are useful starting points for working with grammar in a playful, creative, and collaborative way. Explanations in terms of body-world knowledge were tested in two small-scale, qualitative studies involving Swedish L2 learners of English. Three twelve-year-old learners participated in the first study, and six thirteen-year-old learners in the second. After a short introduction to a few *in* and *on* categories, and an embodied way of thinking about the *in* and *on* instances in these categories, they all discussed, made drawings, and gestured their way through no less than 177 *in* and *on* phrases divided into 11 categories. The interventions show that the L2 learners, during an approximately one hour period, increased their proficiency in spotting similarities between the concepts in each category, and in finding embodied motivations for the uses. Their increased proficiency in these areas over the course of the intervention, and the learners' enthusiasm throughout the task, emphasizes the potential for instruction based on the premises that linguistic patterns are motivated by body-world knowledge. The first group of L2 learners, who had more time at their disposal, even said they did not want to quit when this was suggested by the experimenter (the present author).

The categories of abstract concepts expressed by *in* are discussed in Section 2, and the categories of abstract *on* concepts in Section 3. The study devoted to pedagogical applications of this data is dealt with in Section 4, and the findings summarized in Section 5.

## 2 Abstract *in* instances

Table (1) presents the categories from my previous analyses of abstract *in* instances (see Johansson Falck 2017) that were presented to the L2 learners in the present study. They fall into four categories of related concepts (column 2), which are explicable in terms of specific types of embodied experience (illustrated in column 1 and further discussed below). Phrases included in the abstract *in* instances are shown in column 3.

One category of abstract *in* instances that are particularly close to bodily experience includes phrases that refer to cognitive concepts such as thoughts, feelings, opinions, or human qualities (Table 1, row 1). These uses are construed

**Table 1:** Abstract *in* uses

| Embodied motivations: | Abstract *in* categories: | Phrases included in the *in* instances: |
|---|---|---|
| 1 | A IN B; thoughts, feelings, opinions, qualities in body/body part | bear sth. *in* mind, keep sth. *in* sb's memory, sth good *in* sb, a good quality *in* sb, *in* someone's heart |
| 2 | A IN B; content in opinions, views, segments of language | *in* sb's opinion, *in* sb's view, *in* these terms, *in* a single phrase, *in* sb's speeches, *in* verbal statements, *in* constitutional talks, *in* her soft Irish singsong, *in* a language, *in* English |
| 3 | A IN B; in an (abstract) area, field, subject, matter | have knowledge and expertise *in* the field of plastic surgery, a breakthrough *in* gastronomy, training *in* psychiatry, a revolution *in* the economy of Europe |
| 4 | A IN B; in a category, group, family, tribe, band, pair, marriage, partnership, league, committee etc. | the young adults *in* the family, the pupils *in* mixed ability groups, films *in* documentary and feature categories |

in line with the fact that our own bodies, minds, and heads may be perceived as containers for certain bodily processes and qualities (see Table 1, picture 1). Our particular languages indicate that our discourse community conceptualizes where in the body a given thought, feeling, opinion or quality is located. For instance, thoughts are in people's heads or in their minds as in (1), and feelings are in certain body parts or in the person as a whole as in (2).

(1) Everything the government did from this date onwards had privatisation *in mind*. (BNC, my emphasis)

(2) So do you feel better *in yourself* then? (BNC, my emphasis)

The close connection between the ways in which instances such as these are construed and specific bodily experiences provides useful information for L2 learners of English. No matter if the English L2 patterns are similar to those in their L1 or not, such embodied concepts would seem to have the potential to help L2 learners understand and remember the constructions. In part, this is because the semantic systems of all languages draw on embodied experience and so, even if the exact experiences map differently in their L1, the underlying conceptual structure is the same. Moreover, explanations in terms of embodied experiences may be used as starting points for discussions about the ways in which different languages construe the world. For instance, L1 speakers of Swedish might realize that their L1 does not focus on the containing function of opinions (i.e., that they contain their contents), but on the fact that opinions are sources for what we say or write. Instead of using a prepositional *in* phrase to refer to their opinions (e.g., say *in my opinion)*, they might use the (somewhat formal) expression *enligt min åsikt* (En. 'I think'. lit. 'according to my opinion') in reference to opinions.

Another category of abstract *in* instances (Table 1, row 2) is made up of *in* instances that represent the contents of cognitive concepts such as thoughts, views, terms, phrases, speeches, talks, languages, etc., in terms of containment. They all have what we refer to as their contents and are consistently cast as containers for these contents. In sentence (3), something is *in* someone's opinion, i.e., the opinion is the container, the contents of the opinions are the Focal Elements being contained.

(3) **In my opinion** Karenin acted in quite an unpredictable way but I think this was because he was so entirely shattered by Anna's actions. (BNC, my emphasis)

Instances such as these are consistent with Reddy's (1979/1993) observation that English construes communication like a conduit that transfers thoughts bodily from one person to another. When people speak or write they transform their thoughts and feelings into words, which then contain and convey the thoughts or feelings. When they listen or read, they extract the meanings contained by the words. However, not only words are construed as containers. The usage patterns of abstract *in* additionally show that the thoughts and feelings that are transformed into words are also cast this way.

Some abstract *in* instances include terms such as *area, field, market, environment, subject,* or *matter* (Table 1, row 3). They are structured in line with people's embodied experiences of real world spatial fields or physical areas which are construed as being bounded. The notion of containment and our experiences with containers (such as objects being held by containers or elements located within a bounded space) provide useful conceptual structure for communicating about more abstract topics. Instances that include terms such as *area, field, market, subject,* or *matter* as well as those that implicitly refer to concepts such as these (i.e., by means of the name of a given area, field, market, subject, matter, etc.) are construed this way. In (4), someone has a breakthrough *in gastronomy*. That is, the breakthrough is in this specific area of inquiry.

(4) Did that commingling of unrelated flavours remind me of another dish, or had it produced a breakthrough *in gastronomy*? [BNC, my emphasis]

Another category of abstract *in* instances includes terms that refer to categories such as groups, tribes, bands, families, marriages, partnerships, pairs, leagues, committees, societies, etc. (e.g., *young adults in the family*, and *pupils in mixed ability groups*, Table 1, row 4). Real-world referents of containing terms such as these do not have a physical boundary, an interior and an exterior, nor do the Focal Elements necessarily consist of objects or individuals that are located within the same physical space. Yet each of these categories may be conceptualized as an entity with a boundary and an interior space. Researchers (cf. Lakoff 1987: 428; Tyler and Evans 2007: 185) argue that this category may arise from our embodied experience of seeing similar entities at a distance and perceiving them as members of a group or category (for instance, a stand of daisies or a herd of cows) within a defined or visually bounded space (see Table 1, picture 4). Accordingly, language referring to these categories is structured in line with the metaphorical patterns A CATEGORY CONTAINS ITS MEMBERS, and A GROUP IS A WHOLE AND ITS MEMBERS ARE PARTS OF IT (Navarro 2000: 200; 208).

## 3 Abstract *on* instances

Table (2) presents the categories of abstract *on* instances (see Johansson Falck 2017) that were presented to the L2 learners. Some of these instances also refer to cognitive concepts such as thoughts, opinions, and segments of language (Table 2, row 1, a; b). Unlike abstract *in* instances that involve abstract concepts such as these, however, abstract *on* instances do not focus on the contents of people's thoughts, opinions, or segments of language, but rather on the relationship between people's thoughts and views and the topics on which they have opinions or on which they comment (Table 2, picture 1). *On* instances such as these are construed in line with what would be the spatial structure of people conceptualizing the trajectory of their thoughts, or of language, onto other abstract concepts, that is, with conceptualizations originating from a human vantage point (i.e., "the position from which a scene is viewed" [Langacker 1987: 123], [Table 2, picture 1], cf. the structure of the metaphor SEEING IS TOUCHING). The relationship between the abstract concepts involved is like that of a person putting an object on another object (as in *putting a on b*). Navarro's

**Table 2:** Abstract *on* uses

| | Embodied understanding: | Category: | Examples: |
|---|---|---|---|
| 1 | thoughts / feelings | A ON B; thoughts/feelings/ opinions/segments of language (from a person's head or body) on sth. | a) *perspective/outlook/viewpoint/opinion/ ideas, doubts, stance on, keep our eyes on,*<br>b) *state, statement, speech, a word, advice, give hints, expand, present proposals, comment, talk, cast a question mark, raise questions, insist, report, assurances, reports, warning on*<br>c) *have a crush/be keen on*<br>d) *work on assignments, tasks, data, computer programs*<br>e) *negotiations/agree/decide/vote/reach an agreement/have a referendum on*<br>f) *meetings/conferences/committees on* |
| 2 | | A ON B; have an effect/ influence/impact on (i.e. apply force on something as indicated by the large arrow emanating from the actor) | a) *have an effect/influence/a great impact/ impress/[be]etched on*<br>b) *reduce spending on, 20% limit on foreign investment, restraints on free expression, cutting down on*<br>c) *the crews' ban on overtime, they'll put a stop on me doing anything, a clampdown on inflation*<br>d) *an assault/ attacks/thrive/inflict/pour cold water/imposing a heavy cost/the shearing force on sth.* |
| 3 | | A ON B; focus/emphasis on | a) *focus, concentrate on*<br>b) *emphasis/place stress on* |
| 4 | | PUT A ON B; spend/waste sth. on | *spend money on, waste sth on,* |
| 5 | | ON B; on film, tape, cassette | *on tape/film/discs/camera/JVC's video-disc system/the Mega Drive* |

**Table 2:** Continued

| Embodied understanding: | Category: | Examples: |
|---|---|---|
| 6 | A ON B: on the basis, based on | a) *on social grounds/scholarships, on a base/ basis/foundation/ground, on (certain) grounds, based on, depend on, rely on and piggyback on*<br>b) *on a diet/low income/supplementary benefit/the dole*<br>c) *negotiate something on forecasts of something, being arrested on charges of something*<br>d) *on my own, on their own* |
| 7 | A ON B; burden on | *shame on* [sb.], *have sb. on one's conscience, imposing on someone, the burden of proof of causation remained on the plaintiff, obligations that fall on social services departments, take on sth.* |

analysis of the preposition *on* (1999: 151) accordingly suggests that TOPICS ARE PIECES OF GROUND. In (5), someone's or some people's perspectives are on how to get round a problem.

(5) There are a number of tortured *perspectives on* how to get round this problem, but they are themselves fraught with problems. (BNC, my emphasis)

Abstract *on* instances that refer to people's emotions towards something (e.g., we are *keen on* something [Table 2, row 1, c, cf. Lindstromberg 2010: 65]), people who work on problems or assignments (Table 2, row 1, d), and people who have *negotiations* on something, or *agree, decide, vote*, or *have a referendum on* something (Table 2, row 1, e) have the same structure. Moreover, *on* instances that refer to *committee[s]* and *conference[s]*, which are only indirectly related to people's thoughts, are construed this way (Table 2, row 1, f). Sentence (6), for instance, discusses a *Committee on Agriculture*, where the general topic (agriculture) is the ground upon which the committee is located.

(6) The *Select Committee on Agriculture*, of which I am a member, is about to launch a major inquiry into Britain's food trade gap, which is estimated to be about £6 billion. (BNC, my emphasis)

A related category of abstract *on* instances construed in line with a human vantage point includes instances that discuss abstract concepts that are somehow affected by people's interactions with them (Table 2, row 2). They include phrases such as *have an effect on*, and *have a great impact on* (Table 2, row 2, a), phrases that refer to reducing or limiting something for someone, or to decisions about maintaining something (Table 2, row 2, b), phrases that refer to restricting, banning, or stopping something (Table 2, row 2, c), and phrases that involve force or violence (Table 2, row 2, d). Instances such as these are coherent with the fact that people or things located above someone or something else are usually in a good position to affect those located further down. As argued by Navarro (1999: 159), they are structured in line with the spatial metaphors CONTROL IS UP and POWER IS UP.

One category of abstract *on* instances includes phrases that refer to visual and/or mental focus (Table 2, row 3). They too are connected with a human vantage point, but also involve narrowing in on a given aspect of something. That is, they discuss people who *focus* or *concentrate on* something (Table 2, row 3, a [cf. Lindstromberg 2010: 181]), or place emphasis or stress on something (Table 2, row 3, b).

Other *on* instances construed in line with our experiences of putting real world objects on other objects refer to spending or wasting money on things (Table 2, row 4), and to things recorded or installed ("things" e.g., *on tape, on film, on discs, on camera*, on *JVC's video-disc system*, and *on the Mega Drive* [Table 2, row 5]). Instances such as these do not refer to the direction of cognitive concepts such as thoughts, opinions, segments of language, and the like but to putting abstract entities on one another (Table 2, pictures 4 and 5). Spending or wasting money on something, and recording or installing something is like putting objects on other objects (Table 2, picture 4), and money spent or wasted, and "things" recorded or installed are like objects that have been put on other objects (Table 2, row 5). Sentence (7) discusses someone's record that could not be found on a computer, that is, something that should have been on a computer but does not seem to be so.

(7) So I rang United Airlines head office, at my own expense, and spoke to a woman who could find no record of me *on* the UA computer. (BNC, my emphasis)

Navarro (1999: 158) similarly suggests that English refers to the contents of books, tapes, and lists as if they were physically attached to the objects.

Not all *on* instances are related to manipulating objects. One category of abstract *on* instances refers to abstract bases or grounds (Table 2, row 6), and these are discussed as if they were real world physical supporting surfaces located underneath the things that they support (Table 2, row 6 [cf. Lindstromberg 2010: 65]). The category includes phrases that directly refer to this specific type of spatial relationship (e.g. nouns such as *base, basis, foundation* or *ground*, and verbal phrases such as *based on, depend on* and *rely on* [see Table 2, row 6, a]), but also ones that indirectly involve the notion of support (e.g. phrases that discuss someone's living from something [Table 2, row 6, b]), phrases that discuss on what grounds certain decisions were made (Table 2, row 6, c), and pronominal phrases discussing people or things that support themselves (Table 2, row 6, d). Instances such as these may all be summarized by the general principle that any concept that may be conceived of as a supporting entity is expressed by *on*.

Other abstract *on* instances are connected with the ways in which burdens weigh us down and cause trouble (Table 2, row 7 [cf. Lindstromberg 2010: 61; Navarro 1999: 153–154]). They reflect people's using their experiences of burdens to describe difficulties or negative impact on people or things (e.g. obligations that fall *on* social services departments, shame *on* [someone], have [someone] *on* [one's] conscience, or imposing *on* someone [Table 2, row 7]). Instances that include the phrasal verb *take on* are related to experiences such as these (Table 2, row 7), but do not necessarily imply a heavy weight on the person taking someone or something on.

To sum up, cognitive linguistics scholars tend to agree that abstract *in* and *on* uses derive from the original spatial scenes or relations associated with the prepositions (Tyler and Evans 2007; Lindstromberg 2010; Navarro 1999, 2000). Accordingly, corpus linguistic analyses (Johansson Falck 2014, 2017) show that abstract *in* and *on* instances fall into categories of related concepts that are construed in line with (a) the spatial relationships associated with the prepositions, and (b) people's embodied understandings of the concepts referred to in the *in* and *on* instances. The uses appear guided by general categorization processes (cf. Rosch 1978) in which certain types of abstract concepts (i.e. ones involving the contents of cognitive concepts such as thoughts, opinions, views, and segments of language, Table 1, picture 2) are construed one way (i.e. as *in* relationships), and other types of concepts (e.g. ones discussing the direction of cognitive concepts such as these, see Table 2, picture 1) construed another way (i.e. as *on* relationships). Given our embodied understandings of the world, *in* constructions appear more apt in talk about some abstract relationships, and *on* constructions in talk about others.

Importantly, the matches between our embodied experiences and the meaning communicated by the categories of abstract *in* and *on* instances provide useful didactic information for L2 teaching and learning of English of patterns involving abstract *in* and *on* instances. Section (4) reports on two studies testing an explanatory model based on this type of knowledge. Specifically, the use of explanations in terms of body-world knowledge as prompts for collaborative ways of figuring out the motivations for the usage patterns of abstract *in* and *on* instances was tested. My primary aim in this part of the study was to see whether working with grammar could be turned into an inspiring collaborative activity that made students aware of embodied motivations for abstract language patterns.

# 4 Embodied explanations as input for collaborative ways of working with grammar

To begin to ascertain the potential benefit of presenting an embodied analysis of the abstract uses of *in* and *on* to L2 learners, two small-scale, qualitative experiments were undertaken. All examples were taken from the BNC). Three twelve-year-old L1 speakers of Swedish (two girls and one boy) participated in the first intervention, and six thirteen-year-old L1 speakers of Swedish (four boys and two girls) in the second one. Prior to the interventions, the learners' parents were given the required information about their rights, and the purpose of the study (i.e. they learned that the purpose of the study was to test the usefulness of an explanatory model for working with words and phrases in English), and asked to sign a consent form.

As a first step in both interventions, the instances that were part of the study were presented to the participants in a randomized order to establish the learners' familiarity with the uses of *in* and *on*. Their answers (self-reports) suggest that they knew some of the phrases, but not all. The first group of learners did so by reporting on their overall impression of how familiar they were with the sentences. The second group of learners were shown 19 random *in* and *on* instances (see Appendix, Table 4) and asked to put a mark next to the uses that they were already familiar with. The learners reported knowing between 16% (one learner) and 74% (two learners) of the instances (see Appendix, Table 3). Three of them reported knowing between 32% and 63% of the instances. All learners in this group said that they knew that *on* should be used in the phrase *vote on* (see Appendix, Table 4), and five of them that they were familiar with the use *on camera*. None of them said that they knew which prepositions to use in the phrases *a clampdown on inflation, in a group of something,* and *be keen on*, and only one of them reported that s/he knew which preposition to use in *the shearing force on* something. Their answers do not suggest that the uses that they were familiar with fall into certain categories. However, the frequency of the terms included in the phrases likely played a role. Two of the uses that they did not know include terms (i.e. *clampdown*, and *shearing*) that, according to Rundell and Fox (2007), are not part of the core vocabulary of English. Prior to the intervention, the learners also reported that they had no mnemonic rules for remembering uses of the two prepositions, did not know why *in* or *on* was used in a particular context or the other, and had not worked with similar expressions at school. None of them indicated that s/he saw any similarities among the uses prior to the study.

During the interventions, the learners were seated around a table together with the experimenter. There were technical problems with the recording during the first intervention, but the second was audio-recorded and transcribed. The experimenter began by discussing the meanings of *in* and *on* (in Swedish to ease communication between the experimenter and all the participants) with the learners by showing them real world objects that were either *in* or *on* some other object. At this point, the learners were also made aware of the fact that bodily experiences and experiences of the external world are crucial for describing abstract concepts and relationships. This was done by briefly discussing some temporal relationships that are really hard to discuss unless spatial knowledge is used. Examples include 'the future', which in both English and Swedish is conceptualized as a location ahead of us, 'the past' which is conceptualized as a location behind us, and 'the present' which is conceptualized as our present location. As shown by Lakoff and Johnson (1999: 139–161) spatial relationships such as are essential for structuring our understanding of TIME.

After the short introduction, category (1), Table (1) (which refers to thoughts, feelings, opinions, or qualities in the body, or in a particular part of the body) was introduced. In the introduction, the leaners were shown slightly modified versions of all the *in* instances that are part of this category (i.e. phrases such as *something is going on in somebody's head* and *keep something in your memory*), and asked if they could find any common denominators between the instances, and if they could see patterns concerning where in the body the language seemed to locate thoughts and feelings. Together with the experimenter they then came to the conclusion that the language located feelings in the body, while the head and the mind are treated like containers for our thoughts and our memories. Next, this category of *in* instances was contrasted with those in category (7), Table (2) (e.g. *shame on* [sb.], *have sb. on one's conscience*, and *imposing on someone*), which the experimenter said had to do with things that are difficult for us. The discussions of things that are difficult for us was used as a starting point for talking about how our experiences of being burdened by something influence constructions such as these, and the picture intended to illustrate cognitive burdens on people (Table 2, picture 7) shown to the participants.

After comparing the first two categories, some of the participants started suggesting common denominators for the instances within each category and possible motivations for their uses. For instance, when we moved to the third category (i.e. instances including phrases such as *opinion on, ideas on, perspective on, viewpoint on* and *outlook on* [category 1, Table 2]) one learner in the first intervention suggested that the instances deal with "someone's perspective on something" (my translation). Another suggested that instances such as *in the field of plastic surgery, in an area, in a market* and *in a subject* (category 3, Table 1) seem to refer to something that is within an area with a border around it.

The rest of the participants soon joined in suggesting motivations for the uses, and they were all encouraged to make their own drawings of the motivations for the uses. One learner made a drawing of a comet coming towards the ground to illustrate *a great impact on*, and several of them made drawings of people's eyes, or pupils, directed towards some other object, or dashed lines from people's eyes onto some other object to illustrate *focus on*. One learner argued that boxes could be used to illustrate all the instances, and used them as containers for certain things (e.g. to illustrate that the head is a container for our thoughts) and as supporting surfaces for something else (e.g. to illustrate that people *waste money on* something else drawn as a box).

With each new category, the participants got better and better at finding common denominators for the categories of *in* and *on* instances, they had more and more comments to make, and they got more enthusiastic about drawing possible motivations for the uses. To avoid feelings of failure, individual interpretations were encouraged and differences between illustrations used as reasons for continued discussions of the usage patterns.

The first intervention lasted for about 70 minutes, and the second one for 60 minutes. The learners' enthusiasm throughout the interventions suggests that they enjoyed using their embodied experiences for thinking about abstract *in* and *on* uses. Accordingly, their written answers to post-test questionnaires (see Appendix, table 5, question 5) show that this way of working "made it easier [for them] to understand", was "a clever way to learn abstract words", "was funnier than just reading and stays in one's memory", was "great" and "interesting" (my translations). Their answers also suggested that they had learned from this way of working. After the interventions, 7 learners (out of 9 total participants in the two interventions) rated themselves as knowledgeable about when to use *in* and *on* in sentences such as these. To the question, "What would you call this way of working with *in* and *on* instances grammar?" one learner replied that s/he would rather call it "learn grammar because we learned, rather than worked" (my translation).

# 5 Conclusion

This chapter shows that abstract *in* and *on* instances fall into categories of related concepts that are explicable in terms of specific types of body-world knowledge. Two qualitative studies in which Swedish L2 learners of English worked with these categories show that the matches between our body-world knowledge and the categories of *in* and *on* instances are useful starting points for working with grammar in a playful, creative, and collaborative way. As an additional bonus, this way of presenting grammar can be used as a way of getting away from framing many L2 errors as failures or mistakes on the part of the L2 learner, and instead turn them into new insights into L1 transfer (i.e., "any type of semantic or pragmatic influence from the first language, or from a second language in L3 acquisition [Odlin 2008: 310]). In the interventions, the focus was on figuring out the motivation for the uses rather than on giving a correct answer to a task. Any plausible motivation that was suggested by the learners was accepted.

Last, but not least, the learners' self-reports suggest that this approach to grammar has positive effects on learning. Post-test questionnaires suggest that the majority of the participants considered themselves to be more knowledgeable about the uses after the interventions.

There are, of course, many limitations to this study. At the very least, the next step would be to develop an experiment which tested a larger number of participants and included a pre- and post-test which tested for the participants' gains in accuracy in using these two prepositions.

# References

Barsalou, Lawrence. 2008. Grounded cognition. *Annual Review of Psychology* 59. 617–645.
Bergen, Ben & Kathryn Wheeler. 2010. Grammatical aspect and mental simulation. *Brain and Language* 112. 150–158.
Gibbs, Raymond W., Jr. 2006a. *Embodiment and cognitive science*. Cambridge: Cambridge University Press.
Gibbs, Raymond W., Jr. 2006b. Metaphor interpretation as embodied simulation. *Mind and Language* 21. 434–458.
Gibbs, Raymond W., Jr. & Teenie Matlock. 2008. Metaphor, imagination and simulation: Psycholinguistic evidence. In Raymond W. Gibbs, Jr. (ed.), *The Cambridge handbook of metaphor and thought*, 247–261. Cambridge: Cambridge University Press.
Grady, Joseph. 1997. *Foundations of meaning: Primary metaphors and primary scenes*. Berkeley: CA: University of California dissertation.
Johansson Falck, Marlene. 2014. Temporal prepositions explained: Cross-linguistic analysis of English and Swedish unit of TIME landmarks. *Cognitive Linguistic Studies* 1(2). 271–288.
Johansson Falck, Marlene. 2017. Embodied motivations for abstract *in* and *on* constructions. In Francisco Ruiz de Mendoza, Paula Pérez & Alba Luzondo (eds.), *Constructing families of*

*constructions* (HCP). Amsterdam: John Benjamins.

Johansson, Roger, Jana Holsanova, & Kenneth Holmqvist. 2006. Pictures and spoken descriptions elicit similar eye movements during mental imagery, both in light and in complete darkness. *Cognitive Science* 30(6). 1053–1079.

Johnson, Mark. 1987. *The body in the mind: The bodily basis of meaning, imagination, and reason*. Chicago: University of Chicago Press.

Lakoff, George. 1987. *Women, fire, and dangerous things: What categories reveal about the mind*. Chicago: University of Chicago Press.

Lakoff, George & Mark Johnson. 1980. *Metaphors we live by*. Chicago & London: The University of Chicago Press.

Lakoff, George & Mark Johnson. 1999. *Philosophy in the flesh*. New York, NY: Basic Books.

Langacker, Ronald W. 1987. *Foundations of cognitive grammar: Volume I: Theoretical prerequisites*. Stanford: Stanford University Press.

Langacker, Ronald. W. 2002. *Concept, image, and symbol: The cognitive basis of grammar*, 2nd edn. Berlin & New York: Mouton de Gruyter.

Lindstromberg, Seth. 2010. *English prepositions explained*. Amsterdam: John Benjamins.

Morimoto, Shun & Shawn Loewen. 2007. A comparison of the effects of image-schema-based instruction and translation-based instruction on the acquisition of L2 polysemous words. *Language Teaching Research* 11(3). 347–372.

Murphy, Raymond. 2004. *English grammar in use: A self-study reference and practice book for intermediate students of English with answers*, 3rd edn. Cambridge: Cambridge University Press.

Navarro I Ferrando, Ignasi. 1999. The metaphorical use of *on*. *Journal of English Studies* 1. 145–164.

Navarro I Ferrando, Ignasi. 2000. A cognitive semantic analysis of the English lexical unit IN. *Cuadernos de Ivenstigación Filológica* XXVI. 189–220.

Odlin, Terence. 2008. Conceptual transfer and meaning extensions. In Peter Robinson & Nick. Ellis, (eds.), *Handbook of cognitive linguistics and second language acquisition*. New York & London: Routledge.

Reddy, Michael. 1993 [1979]. The conduit metaphor: A case of frame conflict in our language about language. In Andrew Ortony (ed.), *Metaphor and thought*, 164–201. Cambridge: Cambridge University Press.

Rosch, Eleanor H. 1978. Principles of categorization. In Eleanor. H. Rosch & Barbara. B. Lloyd (eds.), *Cognition and categorization*, 27–48. Hillsdale, NJ: Lawrence Erlbaum.

Rundell, Michael & Gwyneth Fox (eds.). 2007. *Macmillan English dictionary for advanced learners*, 2nd edn. Oxford, UK: Macmillan.

Spivey, Michael J. & Joy. J. Geng. 2001. Oculomotor mechanisms activated by imagery and memory: Eye movements to absent objects. *Psychological Research* 65. 235–241.

Stanfield, Robert A. & Rolf. A. Zwaan. 2001. The effect of implied orientation derived from verbal context on picture recognition. *Psychological Science* 12. 153–156.

Tyler, Andrea & Vyvyan Evans. 2007 [2003]. *The semantics of English prepositions: Spatial scenes, embodied meaning and cognition*. Cambridge: Cambridge University Press.

Zwaan, Rolf A., Robert A. Stanfield & Richard. H. Yaxley. 2002. Language comprehenders mentally represent the shapes of objects. *Psychological Science* 13. 168–171.

# Appendix

**Table 3:** Proportion of uses reported to be known by the L2 learners prior to study 2.

| Learner | Proportion of known uses |
|---|---|
| 1 | 0.16 |
| 2 | 0.74 |
| 3 | 0.47 |
| 4 | 0.63 |
| 5 | 0.32 |
| 6 | 0.74 |

**Table 4:** Self-reports on familiarity with (19 random) *in* and *on* instances prior to study 2.

| | *in/on* instances: | Number of learners (out of 6) marking the instances as known | Prop. of learners marking instances as known |
|---|---|---|---|
| 1. | a word on | 2 | 0.33 |
| 2. | have an effect on | 4 | 0.67 |
| 3. | a clampdown on inflation | 0 | 0.00 |
| 4. | advice on | 3 | 0.5 |
| 5. | being arrested on charges of something | 4 | 0.67 |
| 6. | depend on | 4 | 0.67 |
| 7. | in a group of something | 0 | 0.00 |
| 8. | in a matter | 3 | 0.5 |
| 9. | on camera | 5 | 0.83 |
| 10. | reach an agreement on | 2 | 0.33 |
| 11. | take on something. | 3 | 0.5 |
| 12. | the shearing force on something | 1 | 0.17 |
| 13. | training in science | 2 | 0.33 |
| 14. | vote on | 6 | 1.00 |
| 15. | on social grounds | 3 | 0.5 |
| 16. | spend money on something/somebody | 5 | 0.83 |
| 17. | a speech on | 3 | 0.5 |
| 18. | be keen on | 0 | 0.00 |
| 19. | comment on | 4 | 0.67 |

**Table 5:** Post-test questionnaires (questions and answers translated from Swedish into English, my translations).

| Questions to the participants: | Answers by the participants in intervention 1: | | Answers by the participants in intervention 2: | |
|---|---|---|---|---|
| | Yes/no | Comments: | Yes/no | Comments: |
| 1. Do you know when to use *in* and *on* in abstract instances such as these? | 3 learners replied "yes" | | 4 replied yes, 1 "sort of", and 1 "usually" | Mostly<br><br>Better now than before. I am pretty sure I will.<br><br>[I am] better at this now than I was before [the intervention]<br><br>I usually do. I just do. |
| 2. Would you be able to explain *in* and *on* instances such as these? | 1 yes. | Think literally (i.e. something is in your thoughts, Your thoughts are on something else).<br><br>Think literally!<br><br>I could try (by telling them to think literally) | 1 "I think so", 1 "yes" | Yes, by using examples and pictures the way we did today.<br><br>I would be somewhat insecure, but I would. I would say that thoughts and feelings are within you, and so you then know when to use *in*. You meet on something or focus on something, then it's on.<br><br>Yes, it's like Swedish, if you don't know, you guess.<br><br>I'm bad at explaining, and this is pretty hard to explain.<br><br>I just know. It's hard to explain, but I usually get it right.<br><br>I don't think so, I am lousy at explaining. |
| 3. Do you have any strategies for remembering which uses are correct? | 3 "yes" | Think literally! (2 replies)<br><br>Look at my nice drawings | 2 "yes", 2 "no" | Saying phrases out loud (and then decide which sounds better), and by using various scenarios the way we did today.<br><br>Yes, I will remember the pictures we made today.<br><br>I have just learned them.<br><br>Not, until today.<br><br>I have my "box theory" |
| 4. What ways are there to learn uses such as these? | | Think literally! (2 replies)<br><br>Come up with one's own ways of remembering. | | By reading, listening, writing and last but not least by talking a lot. This gives a feel for what is correct/incorrect.<br><br>By making drawings and reading expressions many times.<br><br>I don't know. I've learned from movies and computer games.<br><br>By practicing.<br><br>By doing like we did today.<br><br>Use my box theory. |

| | | | | | |
|---|---|---|---|---|---|
| 5. What did you think about using your body-world knowledge to learn *in* and *on* uses? | | It facilitates understanding It's good. It worked well, because now I understand much more. | | It was a great and clever way to learn abstract words and phrases. It's good because it makes it easier to remember. It's funnier than just reading and it stays in one's memory. It's great. It was interesting. I hate learning things, and rather learn in a funnier way (i.e. by drawing). |
| 6. Were some instances easier than others? If so, Why? | 2 "yes" | some phrases are more familiar. | 2 "yes", 2 "no" | some of the *in*-instances. *Focus on*, *spend money on*, and [thoughts] *in the head*. Maybe some of them because one has heard them more often. No specific categories, but some words. When it was possible to use the "box theory" |
| 7. Were some instances more difficult than others? If so, why? | 2 "yes" | some phrases are less familiar. | 2 "no" | The *on* instances seemed easier. Those that included terms I did not know. Not any that come to my mind right now. See above. |
| 8. Do you think that you will remember when to use in and on in instances such as these? | 2 "yes" | Now I know that I can think literally about them. Perhaps not always, but I will know them better after having worked with in and on instances this way. | 2 "yes", 1 "no" | I think so. Better, but not perfect. I still have a lot to learn. Yes, I've known these expressions for a while and so they won't disappear. For instance, when you use *in an area*. I've always remembered them after 1–2 times. No, but I might if we did this again. |
| 9. Do you collaborate when working with grammar at school? | 3 "yes" | Sometimes, in the form of lectures. sometimes | 3 "yes", 1 "no" | We collaborate and discuss a lot while working with grammar. Sometimes. It is pretty boring. The teacher usually lectures and then we get it as homework. We work with grammar, but not together. |

# Index

abstract concepts 26–27, 288–289, 292, 295–296
aspect 16–17, 23–25, 157–159, 165, 167–168, 170, 172–173, 177, 184, 275, 279

blend 2, 14–15, 181, 184, 186–188, 191–192, 197
body-world knowledge 287–289, 297, 300

Chinese (L1) 24, 29, 214
– Cantonese L1 students 264–265
cognitive semantics 258
– cognitive lexical semantics 258
conceptual blending 2, 181, 197
conceptual metaphor 3, 21, 24–25, 29, 158, 257–258, 260–262, 265–267, 275–276
conditionals 2–3, 15–16, 18–19, 157, 160–161, 181, 184, 186, 188, 190–193, 195, 197–198
construal 3, 14, 16–21, 53, 55, 151, 158–159, 175, 181–182, 188, 205
– L1 construal 17, 19, 182, 198
construction 3–4, 6–9, 11, 13, 15–17, 39–41, 43–44, 49–50, 57–59, 63, 65, 68–73, 75–79, 81–85, 88–91, 100–101, 105–106, 108, 114, 117–118, 127–129, 131, 134–138, 140, 142, 146–147, 157–158, 163–168, 171–172, 175, 187, 189–190, 193
– construction learning (learning of) 11, 68, 70, 73, 165
– constructional perspective 11
– sub-construction 47
context 2–5, 7–10, 14, 16, 18–19, 25, 28, 38–39, 48, 56–57, 85, 87, 118, 123, 133, 153–158, 164, 166, 171–173, 181–186, 188, 193–198, 204–205, 229, 233, 261, 287, 298
conversation analysis (CA) 63
coordination 10–11, 63, 65–66, 70, 72, 85, 88–91
corpus/corpora 7, 10–12, 16, 24, 26–28, 63, 104–108, 123, 126, 143–144, 166–167, 193, 197, 277, 288

diagram 3, 20–21, 24–27, 187, 203, 205–206, 231, 241, 250, 259, 262, 266, 278
discourse frame, *see* frame 20, 206–207, 214, 217, 222
discussion 266, 289, 291, 296
distance 125, 158, 160, 168, 173–174, 188, 192, 195, 292
Dutch 13–14, 28–29, 121–126, 128–130, 132–148
– L1, speakers of Dutch 14, 123–124, 126, 134–135, 137
– L2, learners of Dutch 122–126, 134, 137–138, 141, 147

EFL 24, 104, 184
– EFL classroom 223
– EFL learners 203, 262
embodied 7, 10, 26–27, 84, 155, 288–290, 296–297
– embodied experience 2, 4, 7, 9, 18, 22, 24, 26, 28, 183, 234, 236, 249, 258, 260, 278, 287, 289, 291–292, 296, 299
– embodied meaning 3, 7, 18, 21, 277
– embodied motivations 26, 289, 297
– embodied semantics 23, 25, 28, 278
English
– English L1 speakers, speakers of English, English L1 learners, English speakers, English speaking 17–18, 79, 191, 265
– L2 English learners, English learners, learners of English, ESL learner (English as a Second Language) 16–17, 68, 99, 103, 109, 191, 203, 214, 257, 263, 265, 289–290, 300
– English L2 classroom 10, 63
– English article 203–204, 214, 217–218, 222–223
epistemic 16–17, 158, 160–161, 164–165, 168–171, 174
– epistemic access 83–84
– epistemic stance 155, 160–162, 189
– epistemic viewpoint 16, 160, 163, 171–172
– epistemic verb 100, 109, 117, 173

frame
- sub-frame 20, 207, 212, 214, 222
- discourse frame 20, 206–207, 217, 222
- situation frame 20, 207–208, 222
- concept frame 20, 208–213, 221–222
- text frame 20, 212–213, 221–222
French 8–10, 13–14, 28–29, 38–40, 42, 49, 51, 55–56, 58, 121–128, 133–135, 137, 141–145
- L1 French 13, 143–144
- French speaking learners 122–126, 134, 137–138, 147

genitive 157–158, 173
German 11–12, 28–29, 101–102, 104–105, 114, 116–118
- L1 German speaker 11–12
- German L2 learner, German learner 99, 103, 105, 115–118

hypotheticals 15, 18, 57, 87, 184–185, 188–193

if 86–87, 153–155, 161–163, 171–173, 186
- if-clause 18, 71, 162, 184–189
- if-construction 19
impersonals 9, 38, 40–42, 44, 47, 55–58
in 287–292, 296–300
instructed SLA (or instructed L2) 181
- instructed university-level 23, 249–250
- teacher-instructed 261
interactional competence 63, 67–68, 70, 72, 77, 79, 81–83, 86, 90
intervention 10, 19–20, 24, 26, 190, 215, 235–236, 248, 262, 266, 276, 289, 297–300, 303

L1
- L1 transfer 11–12, 29, 300
- L1 construal 17, 19, 182
L2
- L2 instruction, L2 teaching 3, 15, 17, 28, 181, 183–184, 198, 257, 287, 296
- L2 learner, L2 learning 1–3, 5–7, 11–17, 23, 25–26, 29, 37, 54, 63, 65–66, 68, 91, 99, 103, 118, 141, 182–184, 189, 197, 229, 259–260, 265, 276, 278, 287, 289, 290, 300, 302
- L2 speaker 11–13, 17, 63, 87, 90, 182, 230
linguistic inventory 64, 67
locative construction 13, 128, 130–131, 134–135, 139, 141–142, 147
- Basic Locative Construction 13, 128, 131, 134–135, 138–140, 142, 144

mental spaces 15–16, 18, 153, 156–157, 162, 186
metaphor 3, 21–22, 24–25, 38, 158, 160, 234, 249, 257–258, 260–262, 267, 276, 292, 295
- metaphoric competence 260–261
- metaphorical encoding 261
metaphorical/metaphoric extension 123, 242–243, 278, 287, 292
metonymy 260
- conceptual metonymy 260–262, 265–267, 275–276, 278
mixed effects models 104, 109
modals 157, 168, 173, 204, 234
MuPDar 100, 109, 117

on 44–45, 47, 56

pedagogical schematic 203, 206, 213–214, 218, 221, 223
polysemy 6–7, 16, 25, 28, 53, 164, 234, 257–258
polysemy network 21–23, 230, 236, 241, 251, 279
posture verbs 13, 122–123, 126–127, 130, 133–134, 138–142, 147
prepositions 21–24, 27–28, 183, 229–238, 241, 248–251, 287–289, 296–298
present perfect 16, 164–167, 170–172
presentational constructions 13, 128, 131, 137–140, 142, 147
proximity 57, 260
- proximity and distance 173–174

S-language 13–14, 121–122
SLA 1, 5, 28–29, 65, 67, 107, 155, 164, 172, 175, 181, 198

schematic 9, 15, 20–21, 65, 67, 186, 203–207, 212–214, 217–218, 221–223, 262
– schematic diagram 20–21, 25, 206, 259, 262, 266, 278
semantic network 25, 122, 250, 258–259, 263, 266–268, 275, 278
*since* 15–17, 153–155, 162–173, 177–179
Spanish 6, 11, 22, 28–29, 52, 101–106, 114, 229–233, 236, 249, 251
– Spanish speaker, L1 Spanish speaker, Spanish speaking 10–12, 63, 65, 68, 116
– Spanish learner, Spanish L2, learner of Spanish 12, 22, 99, 103, 105, 109, 115–119, 122, 231
spatial relations 21, 27, 131, 230, 235, 241, 243, 259, 288, 296, 298
subordination 10, 63, 65–66, 70, 72, 85–86, 88–91, 145, 184
Swedish 26, 29, 289, 291, 297–298

task-supported, task-supported language teaching 18–19, 181, 190, 195–197

tense 3, 15–16, 18–19, 21, 154, 159–161, 164, 167–168, 175, 177–178, 185, 187–189, 192–195, 197
– tense/aspect 16–17, 160, 165, 167–170, 172–173, 275
*that*-variation 99–100, 103–104, 107, 118–119
transfer 11–12, 17, 29, 114–115, 118, 123, 141

uniquely identifiable 41, 205, 209–213, 219
usage-based 48–50, 63–65, 68, 70, 90, 118, 154, 163, 165, 172, 181, 190–191, 229–230, 235, 237, 244, 249, 251, 277

V-language 13–14, 121–122
viewpoint 3, 14–17, 151, 153–165, 168, 170–175, 189–190, 193
visual 3, 18, 21, 25, 155, 183, 190, 193, 197–198, 234, 237, 241–243, 247, 249, 268, 277–278, 292, 295
– visual representations 3, 196
vocabulary instruction 257, 261, 265, 275–276

www.ingramcontent.com/pod-product-compliance
Lightning Source LLC
Chambersburg PA
CBHW070301240426
43661CB00057B/2607